D0500230

ALSO BY NEIL MACGREGOR

Shakespeare's Restless World

A History of the World in 100 Objects

Germany

Germany

Memories of a Nation

Neil MacGregor

ALFRED A. KNOPF
New York
2015

The British Museum

THIS IS A BORZOI BOOK
PUBLISHED BY ALFRED A. KNOPF

www.aaknopf.com

Library of Congress Cataloging-in-Publication Data
MacGregor, Neil, [date]
Germany: memories of a nation / Neil MacGregor.
pages cm
Includes bibliographical references and index.
ISBN 978-1-101-87566-7 (hardback)
1. Germany—History. 2. Germany—Civilization. I. Title.
DD17.M33 2015
943—dc23 2014048396

Jacket design by Peter Mendelsund

Printed in Germany
First United States Edition

For Barrie Cook

curator at the British Museum

polymath, colleague and counsellor

sine quo non

Contents

KINGDOM OF DENMARK
NORTH SEA
SCHLESWIG
Barth
DITHMARSCHEN
HOLSTEIN
Rostock
Ritzebüttel
Lübeck
Wismar
Neukloster
Ratzeburg
SCHWERIN
MECKLENBURG
EAST FRIESLAND
Jever
Hamburg
Lauenburg
BREMEN
Leeuwarden
Groningen
Bremen
Weser
VERDEN
Elbe
RUPPIN
Havelberg
ALTMARK
Stendal
Wildeshausen
Verden
BRUNSWICK-LÜNEBURG
HOLLAND
UTRECHT
MÜNSTER
HOYA
MITTELMARK
Lingen
OSNABRÜCK
Hanover
Amsterdam
Bentheim
MINDEN
BRUNSWICK-KALENBERG
Brunswick
MAGDEBURG
Tecklenburg
Utrecht
GELDERLAND
RAVENSBERG
Wolfenbüttel
Magdeburg
Münster
LIPPE
HALBERSTADT
Ravenstein
CLEVES
Wesel
Lippstadt
Paderborn
BRUNSWICK
Caslor
Dessau
ANHALT
Wittenbe
ELECTORAT OF SAXONY
Dortmund
Nordhausen
Eisleben
RABANT
MARK
WESTPHALIA
Halle
Antwerp
COLOGNE
Merseburg
Kassel
Leipzig
BERG
Waldeck
Meuse
JÜLICH
Cologne
HESSE
Mühlhausen
Altenburg
Aachen
Eisenach
Erfurt
Jena
DUCH
Brussels
Liège
NASSAU
Wetzlar
Zwickau
FULDA
HENNEBERG
Koblenz
TRIER
LIÈGE
Frankfurt
WÜRZBURG
Mainz
MAINZ
Schweinfurt
BAYREUTH
Eger
LUXEMBOURG
Bouillon
Trier
Darmstadt
Würzburg
Bamberg
Sedan
Worms
UPPER PALATINATE
Luxembourg
ZWEI-BRÜCKEN
PALATINATE
Heidelberg
Mosel
Speyer
Nuremberg
Rothenburg
Saarbrücken
VERDUN
Verdun
Rhine
Heilbronn
Metz
METZ
ANSBACH
Hall
Regensburg
BAR
Weissenburg
WÜRTTEMBERG
Eichstätt
Nördlingen
BARROIS MOUVANT
Hagenau
BADEN
Stuttgart
Esslingen
Toul
Nancy
Wefl
Danube
TOUL
Strassburg
Freising
Reutlingen
Passa
Ulm
BAVARIA
Augsburg
LORRAINE
STRASSBURG
Schlettstadt
Zollern
KINGDOM
F FRANCE
Rottweil
Münster
Colmar
Biberach
Munich
Kaufbeuren
Mühlhausen
FÜRSTENBERG
AUGSBURG
Salzburg
SUNDGAU
Wangen
1507 to Tyrol
Basel
Kempten
Constance
Isny
Montbéliard
Lindau
SALZBUR
Inn
BASEL
Zurich
Innsbruck
Besançon
VORARLBERG
TYROL
COUNTY OF BURGUNDY
Lienz
Berne
Pontarlier
Brixen
SWISS CONFEDERATION
Meran
Bozen
TRENT
REPUBLIC OF VENICE
Geneva
Trent
SAVOY
Riva
MILAN
Milan
Venice

BALTIC SEA
ÜGEN
KAMMIN
Kolberg
POMERANIA
Kammin
Stettin
NEUMARK
PRUSSIA (ROYAL)
Königsberg
Danzig
Elbing
Marienburg
TEUTONIC ORDER
Marienwerder
KINGDOM OF POLAND
Toruń
Vistula
BRANDENBURG
Lebus
Berlin
Frankfurt
Storkow
to Lebus
Schwiebus
Poznań
Warsaw
Oder
LOWER LUSATIA
Kottbus
SAGAN
Sagan
Glogau
Wohlau
UPPER LUSATIA
Görlitz
Meissen
Dresden
F SAXONY
Liegnitz
Breslau
SILESIA
1478 to Hungary
Brieg
Oppeln
Beuthen
Leitmeritz
Glatz
KINGDOM OF BOHEMIA
Prague
Elbe
Jägerndorf
Troppau
Ratibor
Oderberg
Krakow
Pilsen
Vltava
Olmütz
MORAVIA
1478 to Hungary
Iglau
Brünn
Budweis
ASSAU
AUSTRIA
Linz
Vienna
Pressburg
Waidhofen
KINGDOM OF HUNGARY
Gröbming
STYRIA
Graz
Landsberg
Lake Balaton
Villach
CARINTHIA
Mur
to Brixen
to Freising
Laibach
Sava
Drava
Görz
CARNIOLA
Trieste
Danube
The Holy Roman Empire c. 1500
Archbishopric
Boundary of the Holy Roman Empire
Church lands
House of Hohenzollern
House of Wittelsbach (Palatine branch)
House of Wittelsbach (Bavarian branch)
House of Saxony (Albertine branch)
House of Saxony (Ernestine branch)
House of Hapsburg (Austrian branch)
House of Hapsburg (lands formerly held by Burgundy)
Free Cantons of Swiss Confederation
Allied Cantons of Swiss Confederation
Imperial Free Cities
Minor states

KINGDOM OF DENMARK
NORTH SEA
SCHLESWIG
HOLSTEIN
POMERANI
MECKLENBURG
Hamburg
BREMEN
Bremen
Weser
Elbe
BRUNSWICK-LÜNEBURG
SPANISH NETHERLANDS
Amsterdam
MINDEN
Hanover
Brunswick
Magdeburg
MÜNSTER
Münster
LIPPE
BRUNSWICK
Wittenberg
CLEVES
Halle
BRABANT
MARK
WESTPHALIA
Kassel
Leipzig
Antwerp
BERG
Meuse
Cologne
HESSE
ELECTORATE OF SAXONY
Brussels
Aachen
JÜLICH
Liège
NASSAU
FULDA
TRIER
Frankfurt
WÜRZBURG
BAYREUTH
Mainz
MAINZ
Eger
LUXEMBOURG
Bamberg
Trier
Luxembourg
Worms
PALATINATE
Mosel
Speyer
Nuremberg
Verdun
Metz
Rhine
ANSBACH
WÜRTTEMBERG
Eichstätt
Regensburg
BADEN
Stuttgart
Toul
Strassburg
Danube
Passau
BAVARIA
Augsburg
KINGDOM OF FRANCE
LORRAINE
Munich
FÜRSTENBERG
AUGSBURG
Salzburg
Basel
Constance
Montbéliard
Zurich
SALZBURG
Innsbruck
Inn
TYROL
FRANCHE-COMTÉ
Berne
SWISS CONFEDERATION
Geneva
SAVOY
REPUBLIC OF VENICE
MILAN
Milan
Venice

KINGDOM OF SWEDEN
BALTIC SEA
Königsberg
PRUSSIA
Danzig
POMERANIA-STETTIN
WOLGAST
Stettin
KINGDOM OF POLAND
BRANDENBURG
Berlin
Vistula
Poznań
Warsaw
Oder
Kottbus
Görlitz
Liegnitz
Breslau
Dresden
Brieg
Glatz
SILESIA
Prague
Elbe
Krakow
BOHEMIA
Vltava
MORAVIA
Brünn
AUSTRIA
Vienna
IMPERIAL HUNGARY
STYRIA
Lake Balaton
Mur
CARINTHIA
Drava
Sava
CARNIOLA
Trieste
Danube
Central Europe by religious affiliation c. 1560
Boundary of the Holy Roman Empire
Lutherans
Calvinists and Zwinglians
Waldensians and Moravians
Anabaptists and Socinians
Roman Catholics

KINGDOM OF DENMARK
NORTH SEA
SCHLESWIG-HOLSTEIN-GOTTORP
HELIGOLAND
(to Holstein)
-HOLSTEIN
Rostock
Lübeck
Wismar
Ritzebüttel
-GLÜCKSTADT
Neukloster
Ratzeburg
MECKLENBURG-
Hamburg
EAST FRIESLAND
Jever
Lauenburg
-SCHWERIN
-GÜSTROW
BREMEN
Groningen
Leeuwarden
OLDENBURG
UNITED PROVINCES
Bremen
Weser
VERDEN
Havelberg
Verden
Wildeshausen
BRUNSWICK-LÜNEBURG
Stendal
MÜNSTER
HOYA
Spandau
Lingen
OSNABRÜCK
Hanover
Brandenburg
Potsdam
MINDEN
Amsterdam
Bentheim
BRUNSWICK-KALENBERG
Brunswick
MAGDEBURG
Tecklenburg
RAVENSBERG
Magdeburg
Wolfenbüttel
Utrecht
Münster
LIPPE
BRUNSWICK
Dessau
Wittenbe
Ravenstein
Lippstadt
Paderborn
Caslor
Halberstadt
ANHALT
Meuse
Wesel
CLEVES
PADERBORN
Eisleben
Dortmund
Nordhausen
Halle
MARK
WESTPHALIA
to Mainz
Merseburg
Leipzig
Antwerp
Kassel
Naumburg
SAXONY
COLOGNE
BERG
Waldeck
Mühlhausen
Cologne
HESSE-CASSEL
Altenburg
Erfurt
Brussels
Aachen
JÜLICH
Eisenach
Jena
LIÈGE
NASSAU
HESSE-DARMSTADT
Liège
SAXONY
Wetzlar
Zwickau
FULDA
SPANISH NETHERLANDS
Koblenz
TRIER
WÜRZBURG
BAMBERG
Frankfurt
Schweinfurt
BAYREUTH
Mainz
MAINZ
Eger
Darmstadt
Bamberg
Trier
Würzburg
Sedan
Bouillon
PFALZ-SULZBACH
Worms
to Mainz
Luxembourg
LOWER PALATINATE
Heidelberg
Mosel
Nuremberg
ZWEI-BRÜCKEN
Speyer
Rothenburg
UPPER PALATINATE
Saarbrücken
Verdun
Rhine
Heilbronn
ANSBACH
Metz
METZ
Weissenburg
Hall
Regensburg
BAR
Eichstätt
PFALZ-NEUBURG
WÜRTTEMBERG
Nördlingen
BARROIS MOUVANT
Hagenau
BADEN
Stuttgart
Esslingen
Toul
Nancy
Danube
Strassburg
Wefl
TOUL
STRASSBURG
Freising
Passau
HOHENZOLLERN
Reutlingen
Ulm
BAVARIA
to Barrois mouvant
Schlettstadt
Augsburg
LORRAINE
Rottweil
Biberach
Munich
Münster
Colmar
Kaufbeuren
Mühlhausen
FÜRSTENBERG
AUGSBURG
Salzburg
SUNDGAU
Wangen
Kempten
Basel
Constance
Isny
Montbéliard
Lindau
SALZBURG
Inn
Zürich
Innsbruck
Besançon
VORARLBERG
TYROL
FRANCHE-COMTÉ
Lienz
Berne
Brixen
SWISS CONFEDERATION
date of independence: 1648
Meran
Bozen
Geneva
TRENT
REPUBLIC OF VENICE
Trent
SAVOY
Riva
MILAN
Lyons
Rhone
PIEDMONT
Milan
Venice

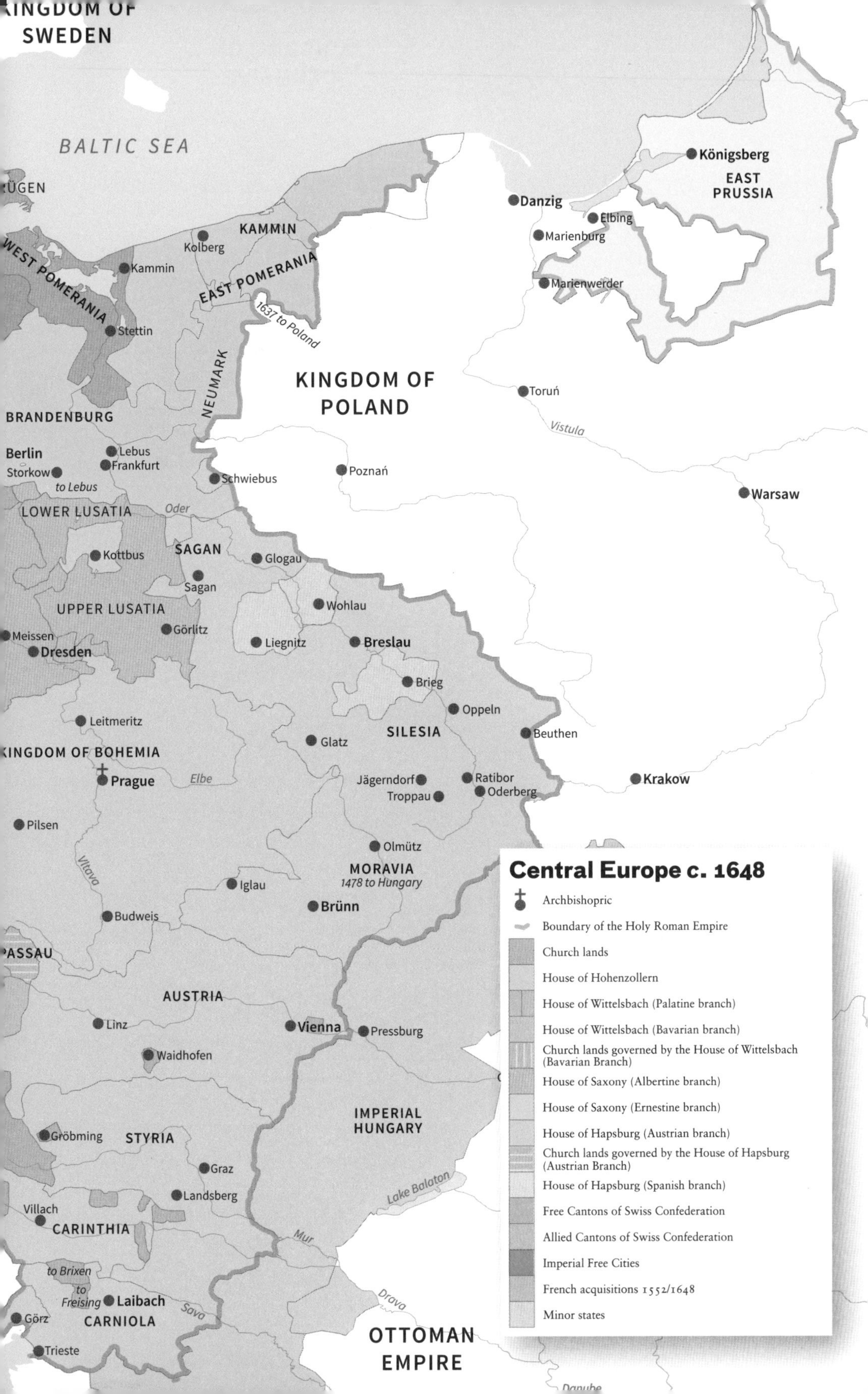
KINGDOM OF SWEDEN
BALTIC SEA
RÜGEN
WEST POMERANIA
KAMMIN
Kolberg
Kammin
EAST POMERANIA
1637 to Poland
Stettin
NEUMARK
BRANDENBURG
Berlin
Lebus
Frankfurt
Storkow
to Lebus
Schwiebus
LOWER LUSATIA
Oder
SAGAN
Kottbus
Sagan
Glogau
UPPER LUSATIA
Wohlau
Meissen
Görlitz
Liegnitz
Breslau
Dresden
Brieg
Oppeln
Leitmeritz
Glatz
SILESIA
Beuthen
KINGDOM OF BOHEMIA
Prague
Elbe
Jägerndorf
Ratibor
Oderberg
Troppau
Pilsen
Vltava
Olmütz
MORAVIA
1478 to Hungary
Iglau
Brünn
Budweis
PASSAU
AUSTRIA
Linz
Vienna
Pressburg
Waidhofen
IMPERIAL HUNGARY
Gröbming
STYRIA
Graz
Landsberg
Lake Balaton
Villach
CARINTHIA
Mur
to Brixen
to Freising
Laibach
Sava
Drava
Görz
CARNIOLA
Trieste
OTTOMAN EMPIRE
Danube
KINGDOM OF POLAND
Danzig
Elbing
Marienburg
Marienwerder
Königsberg
EAST PRUSSIA
Toruń
Vistula
Poznań
Warsaw
Krakow
Central Europe c. 1648
Archbishopric
Boundary of the Holy Roman Empire
Church lands
House of Hohenzollern
House of Wittelsbach (Palatine branch)
House of Wittelsbach (Bavarian branch)
Church lands governed by the House of Wittelsbach (Bavarian Branch)
House of Saxony (Albertine branch)
House of Saxony (Ernestine branch)
House of Hapsburg (Austrian branch)
Church lands governed by the House of Hapsburg (Austrian Branch)
House of Hapsburg (Spanish branch)
Free Cantons of Swiss Confederation
Allied Cantons of Swiss Confederation
Imperial Free Cities
French acquisitions 1552/1648
Minor states

KINGDOM OF DENMARK
NORTH SEA
SCHLESWIG
SWEDISH POMERANI
HOLSTEIN
Lübeck
MECKLENBURG-SCHWERIN
Hamburg
MECKLENBUR
UNITED PROVINCES
OLDENBURG
Bremen
Weser
HANOVER
Stendal
Amsterdam
Potsdam
Hanover
Osnabrück
MÜNSTER
Magdeburg
Münster
Meuse
Dortmund
Halle
Antwerp
Kassel
Leipzig
SAXONY
BERG
COLOGNE
LIÈGE
Cologne
JÜLICH
Erfurt
Jena
Brussels
Liège
HESSE-DARMSTADT
FULDA
AUSTRIAN NETHERLANDS
TRIER
WÜRZBURG
BAMBERG
Frankfurt
Mainz
MAINZ
Eger
Bamberg
Trier
Würzburg
Luxembourg
Mosel
Speyer
Heilbronn
Rhine
SAARWERDEN
BADEN
Regensburg
LORRAINE
Stuttgart
WÜRTTEMBERG
Danube
Strassburg
SALM
Passau
KINGDOM OF FRANCE
BAVARIA
ALSACE
Augsburg
Munich
Mühlhausen
AUGSBURG
Salzburg
Montbéliard
Basel
SALZBURG
Inn
Zurich
Besançon
Innsbruck
LIECHTENSTEIN
TYROL
Berne
SWISS CONFEDERATION
Lienz
Brixen
Geneva
TRENT
REPUBLIC OF VENICE
Trent
SAVOY
Lyons
Rhone
KINGDOM OF SARDINIA
PIEDMONT
Milan
Venice

INGDOM OF SWEDEN
BALTIC SEA
ÜGEN
Königsberg
EAST PRUSSIA
Danzig
Elbing
Marienburg
Kolberg
WEST PRUSSIA
ERMLAND
POMERANIA
Marienwerder
KINGDOM OF PRUSSIA
TRELITZ
Stettin
Toruń
BRANDENBURG
Vistula
MAZOVIA
Berlin
Frankfurt
Kunersdorf
Poznań
Warsaw
GREAT POLAND
KINGDOM OF POLAND
Oder
Kottbus
Dresden
Liegnitz
Breslau
SILESIA
Landshut
LITTLE POLAND
KINGDOM OF BOHEMIA
Prague
Elbe
Krakow
AUSTRIAN SILESIA
Teschen
Pilsen
GALICIA AND LODOMERIA
Olmütz
Vltava
MORAVIA
Brünn
Budweis
AUSTRIA
Vienna
Pressburg
KINGDOM OF HUNGARY
STYRIA
St Gotthard
Lake Balaton
CARINTHIA
Mur
Laibach
Drava
Sava
Görz
CARNIOLA
Trieste
CROATIA
Central Europe c. 1786
Boundary of the Holy Roman Empire
Church lands
Hohenzollern lands of Brandenburg-Prussia
House of Wettin (Electorate of Saxony)
Church lands governed by the House of Wettin
House of Wittelsbach (Bavarian branch) united from 1777
Church lands governed by the House of Wittelsbach (Bavarian branch)
House of Hapsburg (Austrian Hapsburgs extinct 1740: continued by Hapsburg-Lorraine)
Church lands governed by the House of Hapsburg
Great Britain and Hanover, united from 1714
Minor states

KINGDOM OF DENMARK
NORTH SEA
SWEDISH POMERANI
Lübeck
DUCHY OF MECKLENBURG-SCHWERIN
Jever
Hamburg
DUCHY OF MECKLENBURG STRELITZ
Bremen
Weser
HANOVER
Stendal
BRANDENBUR
KINGDOM OF WESTPHALIA
Hanover
Potsdam
Amsterdam
Osnabrück
Brunswick
KINGDOM OF HOLLAND
Magdeburg
Münster
Meuse
Halle
GRAND DUCHY OF HESSE
Leipzig
Antwerp
Cassel
GRAND DUCHY OF BERG
Cologne
Erfurt
Brussels
Aix-la-Chapelle
Liège
THURINGIAN STATES
FRENCH EMPIRE
GRAND DUCHY OF FRANKFURT
Frankfurt
GRAND DUCHY OF WÜRZBURG
Eger
Mayence
PR. OF BAYREUTH
Trèves
Würzburg
Luxembourg
Moselle
Nuremberg
KINGDOM OF BAVARIA
Rhine
KINGDOM OF WÜRTTEMBERG
Regensburg
Stuttgart
Danube
Strasbourg
Ulm
Augsburg
GRAND DUCHY OF BADEN
Munich
Salzburg
Basel
SALZBUR
Zürich
Innsbruck
Inn
LIECHTENSTEIN
Neuchâtel
HELVETIA
Berne
TYROL
Lienz
Brixen
Geneva
REPUBLIC OF VALAIS
KINGDOM OF ITALY
Trent
VENETIA
Lyons
Rhone
Milan
Verona
Venice

INGDOM OF
SWEDEN
BORNHOLM
BALTIC SEA
GEN
Kolberg
Danzig
REPUBLIC
OF DANZIG
Königsberg
Graudenz
Stettin
INGDOM OF PRUSSIA
Thorn
Vistula
GRAND DUCHY
OF WARSAW
erlin
Frankfurt
Posen
Warsaw
Oder
Kottbus
NGDOM OF
SAXONY
Dresden
Breslau
SILESIA
Ratibor
Krakow
Prague
Elbe
BOHEMIA
AUSTRIAN SILESIA
Pilsen
Olmütz
MORAVIA
Vltava
Iglau
Brünn
Budweis
assau
AUSTRIAN EMPIRE
Danube
Wagram
Vienna
Aspern
Pressburg
AUSTRIA
Buda
(Ofen)
STYRIA
KINGDOM OF
HUNGARY
Lake Balaton
CARINTHIA
Drava
Mures
Drava
Laibach
Sava
ILLYRIAN PROVINCES
Trieste
(KINGDOM OF)
SLAVONIA
Napoleonic Germany 1810
Boundary of the Confederation of the Rhine
Minor states

KINGDOM OF DENMARK
Copenhagen
NORTH SEA
SCHLESWIG
Kiel
Stralsund
HOLSTEIN
Lübeck
DUCHY OF MECKLENBURG-SCHWERIN-STRELITZ
Hamburg
Bremen
Weser
GRAND DUCHY OF OLDENBURG
HANOVER
Elbe
BRANDENBUR
KINGDOM OF NETHERLANDS
PR. OF SCHAUMBURG-LIPPE
Hanover
Berlin
KINGDOM
Münster
PR. OF LIPPE-DETMOLD
DUCHY OF BRUNSWICK
Paderborn
DUCHY OF ANHALT
Rhine
WESTPHALIA
PR. OF WALDECK
Antwerp
SAXONY
Leipzig
Langensalza
Erfurt
KINGDOM OF SAXONY
Brussels
Cologne
HESSE-NASSAU
RHINE-PROVINCE
KINGDOM OF BELGIUM
THURINGIAN STATES
GRAND DUCHY OF HESSE
Koblenz
Frankfurt
Main
GRAND DUCHY OF LUXEMBOURG
1867 neutral
Sedan
PR. OF LICHTENBERG
PALATINATE
Metz
KINGDOM OF BAVARIA
ALSACE-LORRAINE
KINGDOM OF WÜRTTEMBERG
Strasbourg
Danube
FRENCH EMPIRE
PR. OF HOHENZOLLERN
Munich
Rhine
GRAND DUCHY OF BADEN
Basel
Inn
LIECHTENSTEIN
Bad Gastein
SWITZERLAND
Geneva
Rhone
Milan
Venice

INGDOM OF SWEDEN
BALTIC SEA
ÜGEN
Memel
Königsberg
Danzig
WEST PRUSSIA EAST
united 1824–1878
POMERANIA
Stettin
RUSSIAN EMPIRE
Vistula
Bug
POSEN
Posen
Warsaw
OF PRUSSIA
Oder
POLAND
SILESIA
Breslau
Königgrätz
Prague
Elbe
Krakow
AUSTRO-HUNGARIAN EMPIRE
Vltava
Nikolsburg
Danube
AUSTRIA
Vienna
Lake Balaton
Drava
Mures
Drava
Laibach
Sava
Trieste
The German empire, 1864–71
Boundary of the North German Confederation 1867
Boundary of the German Empire 1871
Prussia 1864
Acquisitions of Prussia 1865/66
Imperial Territory of Alsace-Lorraine 1871
Free Cities

SWEDEN
THE REICHSKOMMISSARIAT OF NORWAY
SHETLAND ISLANDS
Bergen
Olso
Uppsala
ORKNEY ISLANDS
Scapa Flow
Stavanger
Gothenburg
Kalmar
DENMARK
Glasgow
Edinburgh
NORTH SEA
Copenhagen
Malmö
BORNHOLM
Belfast
UNITED KINGDOM
Leeds
Lübeck
Dublin
Liverpool
Manchester
Hamburg
Szczecin
EIRE
REICHSKOMMISARRIAT OF THE NETHERLANDS
Bremen
Norwich
Birmingham
Amsterdam
Potsdam
Berlin
Poznań
The Hague
Cardiff
Bristol
London
Dortmund
Leipzig
Dunkirk
BELGIUM
Dresden
Wroclaw
Lille
Brussels
Cologne
GERMANY
English Channel
Frankfurt
Main
Prague
CHANNEL ISLANDS
Le Havre
Rouen
Rhine
Nuremberg
PROTECTORATE OF BOHEMIA-MORAVIA
Paris
Seine
ALSACE-LORRAINE
Stuttgart
Brest
Rennes
Orleans
Munich
Vienna
Salzburg
Loire
Basel
Nantes
FRANCE
LIECHTENSTEIN
Innsbruck
AUSTRIA
Berne
SWITZERLAND
Trent
Vichy
Limoges
Lyons
Milan
Trieste
Zagreb
Venice
Sava
Grenoble
Turin
Bordeaux
Garonne
Genoa
SAN MARINO
Nice
Florence
Toulouse
La Coruña
Marseilles
Adriatic Sea
ITALY
Pamplona
ELBA
Burgos
Ebro
ANDORRA
CORSICA
Bragança
Valladolid
Saragossa
VATICAN CITY
Rome
Barcelona
PORTUGAL
SPAIN
Madrid
Naples
Tajo
Toledo
SARDINIA
Valencia
BALEARIC ISLANDS
Guadiana
MEDITERRANEAN
Palermo
Cartagena
Seville
Granada
SICILY
Algiers
Tunis
Gibraltar to UK
Tangier
Ceuta
Oran
TUNISIA
MALTA
SPANISH MOROCCO
Melilla to Spain
ALGERIA
MOROCCO
LIBYA

Europe at the height of German domination, November 1942
Furthest extent of German control
Boundary of Germany in 1937
Hitler's Germany with Austria and Protectorate of Bohemia-Moravia
Subject territories under German administration
Territories under German occupation
Powers co-operating with Axis
Territories occupied by Axis
France, Vichy-governed
Italy with annexed territories
Unconquered territory of USSR
Territory of the Allied Powers
Neutral countries
FINLAND
UNION OF SOVIET SOCIALIST REPUBLICS
RSFSR
1941 REICHSKOMMISSARIAT OF OSTLAND
GENERAL GOVERNMENT OF POLAND
1941 REICHSKOMMISSARIAT OF UKRAINE
SLOVAKIA
UNGARY
RUMANIA
TRANSNISTRIA
BESSARABIA
SERBIA
BULGARIA
ALBANIA
GREECE
TURKEY
GEORGIA
CRIMEA
CYPRUS
CRETE
BALTIC SEA
BLACK SEA
Lake Onega
Lake Lagoda
Gulf of Finland
Lake Pskov
Volga
Pripyat
Don
Donets
Dnieper
Sea of Azov
Bosporus
Marmara
Aegean Sea
Vaasa
Turku
Aland
Helsinki
Hanko
Vyborg (Viipuri)
Leningrad
Tallinn
Narva
Tartu
Novgorod
Pskov
Vologda
Kalinin
Riga
Moscow
Gorki
Kaunas
Vilnius
Konigsberg
Danzig
Smolensk
Minsk
Bialystok
Gomel
Warsaw
Voronezh
Kiev
Krakow
Lvov
Kharkov
Poltava
Stalingrad
Dnepropetrovsk
Budapest
Debrecen
Iași
Rostov
Odessa
Kherson
Szeged
Timișoara
Kerch
Belgrade
Krasnodar
Stavropol
Sevastopol
Yalta
Bucharest
Constanța
Nis
Varna
Sofia
Plovdiv
Skopje
Edirne
Tirana
Istanbul
İzmit
Salonika
Bursa
Ankara
Ioannina
CORFU
Smyrna
Konya
IONIAN ISLANDS
Patras
Athens
PELOPONNESE ISLANDS
KYTHIRA
Antalya
Rhodes
Nicosia
JORDAN

DENMARK
Copenhagen
Flensburg
Stralsund
SCHLESWIG-HOLSTEIN
Lübeck
HAMBURG
Hamburg
MECKLENBURG-VORPOMMER
Oldenburg
BREMEN
Bremen
BRANDENBUR
NIEDERSACHSEN
NETHERLANDS
BERLI
Potsdam
Amsterdam
Hanover
Osnabrück
Braunschweig
Magdeburg
Münster
Bielefeld
SACHSEN-ANHALT
Meuse
NORDRHEIN-WESTFALEN
Dortmund
Gottingen
Kassel
Leipzig
Antwerp
Düsseldorf
THÜRINGEN
SACHSE
Jena
Cologne
Brussels
HESSEN
Bonn
BELGIUM
Koblenz
Coburg
Moselle
Frankfurt
Wiesbaden
Mainz
RHEINLAND-PFALZ
LUXEMBOURG
Würzburg
BAYERN
Mannheim
SAARLAND
Nuremberg
Heidelberg
Saarbrücken
Regensburg
Stuttgart
Ingolstadt
Strasbourg
BADEN-WÜRTTEMBERG
FRANCE
Ulm
Augsburg
Munich
Freiburg
Salzburg
Basel
Dijon
Zurich
LIECHTENSTEIN
Innsbruck
Berne
SWITZERLAND
Geneva
Lyons
ITALY
Milan
Verona
Venice

Modern Germany, showing Länder

Introduction: Monuments and Memories

Monuments in Germany are different from monuments in other countries.

Since the middle of the nineteenth century, the visitor to Paris, London and Munich has been greeted in each city by a triumphal arch in the grand Roman style commemorating national triumphs in the convulsive European wars of 1792–1815. At Hyde Park Corner, the British erected the Wellington Memorial Arch, capping it nearly a century later with the huge bronze quadriga. It stands not just at what was then the western edge of London, but in front of the house of the victor of Waterloo himself. The Arc de Triomphe, colossal and over-scaled, carrying scenes of soldiers setting off to battle, is set at the centre of a star of broad avenues, three of them named after great Napoleonic victories over the Prussians and Austrians.

In Munich, the Siegestor, or Victory Gate, was built in the 1840s to celebrate the valour of Bavaria in the Revolutionary and Napoleonic Wars. Like its Roman model the Arch of Constantine, the Siegestor is richly decorated, its two upper registers on the north side adorned with relief sculpture. On top stands the bronze figure of Bavaria in her chariot drawn by lions, proudly facing north, the direction from which most visitors enter the city. Below her is the inscription "Dem Bayrischen Heere"—"To the Bavarian Army"—to honour whose feats the arch had been erected.

Opposite: The Siegestor in Munich, north side

DEM SIEG GEWEIHT VOM KRIEG ZERSTÖRT ZVM FRIEDEN MAHNEND

The Arc de Triomphe, Paris

The Wellington Arch, Hyde Park Corner, London

So far, so completely conventional. At first sight you might think that the Wellington Arch, the Arc de Triomphe and the Siegestor are all doing exactly the same thing in exactly the same way. But what makes the Munich arch so interesting is its other side, which tells quite a different story. It was badly damaged in the Second World War, but its restoration makes no attempt to reconstruct the sculpted classical details that were destroyed by bombs. The top register on this side of the arch is merely a blank expanse of stone. Underneath this uncompromisingly empty space are the words "Dem Sieg geweiht, vom Krieg zerstört, zum Frieden mahnend"—"Dedicated to victory, destroyed by war, urging peace."

Where the London and Paris arches look back only to moments of high success, presenting a comfortable, if selective, narrative of national triumph, the Munich arch speaks both of the glorious cause of its making and the circumstances of its later destruction. Unlike the other two, its original celebratory purpose is undercut by a very uncomfortable reminder of failure and guilt. It proclaims a moral message: that the past offers lessons which must be used to shape the future. Perhaps the most distinctive feature of the role of history in

---

Opposite: The Siegestor, south side

Germany today is that, like this arch, it not only articulates a view of the past, but directs the past resolutely and admonishingly forward.

If German monuments are different from those in other countries, it is because German history is different. Both Britain and France, shaped by centuries of strong central power, can (more or less) credibly present their history as single national narratives. The long political fragmentation of Germany into autonomous states makes that kind of history impossible: for most of German history there can be no one national story. Although the Holy Roman Empire, which encompassed most of German-speaking Europe (Map 1), offered a framework for a sense of German belonging, it was rarely in a position to coordinate, let alone command, the many political units that made up the Empire. In consequence, much of German history is a composite of different, sometimes conflicting, local narratives.

Perhaps the clearest example of this conflict is the figure of Frederick the Great, King of Prussia in the middle of the eighteenth century, whose military successes would in other countries have ensured his status as a national hero. But Frederick's victories—certainly most of his territorial gains—were in large measure won at the expense of other German states. A hero in Berlin, he is a villain in Dresden. In the course of the Seven Years' War (1756–63) Prussia roundly defeated Saxony and in 1760 Frederick's troops caused huge damage in the Saxon capital. Bernardo Bellotto, whose paintings of baroque Dresden captured one of Europe's most beautiful cities (see Chapter 18), also recorded the Kreuzkirche reduced to ruins by Frederick's bombardment. As a key ally in the Seven Years' War against France, Frederick the Great was both celebrated and revered in Britain: the Worcester factory produced a whole series of tributes in porcelain and as late as 1914 there were still pubs across England proudly called The King of Prussia. But there can be no pan-German view of Frederick the Great: Dresden porcelain unsurprisingly failed to celebrate Frederick and no Saxon hostelry bears his name. A similar ambivalence lies behind the Munich Siegestor. It is dedicated carefully "To the Bavarian Army," leaving unstated the uncomfortable fact that that army, for most of the Napoleonic Wars, fought with the French against other German states. So the Siegestor is a doubly ambiguous monument: not simply an untriumphal triumphal arch, recording defeat as much as victory, but also the troublesome fact that the enemy could be German as easily as foreign.

The history of Germany is thus inevitably, enrichingly and confusingly fragmented. There is a strong awareness of belonging to the same family, but until the unification of Germany in 1871, there was only a flickering sense of common purpose. There are, however, a large number of widely shared memories of what Germans have done and experienced: evoking and engaging with some of them is the purpose of this book. It does not attempt to be—it cannot be—in any sense a history of Germany, but it tries to explore through objects and buildings, people and places, some formative strands in Germany's modern national identity. The earliest object is Gutenberg's bible of the 1450s, perhaps the first moment at which Germany decisively affected the course of world history—indeed laid one of the foundations of all modern European culture. The latest is the very recently restored and refurbished Reichstag, seat of the German Parliament. Of the making of memories there is no end: I have tried to select those that seem to me particularly potent, likely to be shared by most Germans, and especially those that may be less familiar to non-Germans.

Many of those memories are of course also shared by the Swiss and the Austrians, but this book is about the Germany that came into being twenty-five years ago and the memories of those who now live there. Switzerland began to separate politically from the rest of Germany at an early date; its neutrality in the two great wars of the last century has left it with a radically different past. Austria, whose story has been far more closely intertwined with its neighbour's, is dissimilar in many defining respects. It was not permanently split by the Reformation; its response to the Napoleonic invasions was not

---

Overleaf: The ruins of the Kreuzkirche, Dresden, destroyed in 1760 by Prussian bombardment. Bernardo Bellotto, 1765.

to articulate national particularism so much as to consolidate the ancestral Hapsburg lands; and it did not experience the long Cold War division of the state, with all that has since flowed from that for Germany. Above all, Austria has not carried out the public, painful examination of memories and responsibilities in the time of the Nazi Reich with anything like the rigour and integrity of modern Germany. A book which included Austrian memories would be very different.

All major countries try to construct a reading of their history that leads them, reassured and confident, to their current place in the world. The United States, strong in its view of itself as a "city on a hill," was long able to affirm its manifest destiny. Britain and France in different ways saw their political evolution as a model for the world, which they generously shared through imperial expansion. After Bismarck had welded the different constituent states into the German Empire in 1871 and then into the leading industrial and economic power of the continent, Germany might have been able to devise some similar national myth. But defeat in the First World War, the collapse of the Weimar Republic and the murderous criminality of the Third Reich have made any such coherent narrative impossible. German scholars have struggled in vain to piece the different parts of the jigsaw together, but none has been able, convincingly, to fit the great intellectual and cultural achievements of eighteenth- and nineteenth-century Germany and the moral abyss of the Nazis into a comprehensible pattern. This is in a profound sense a history so damaged that it cannot be repaired but, rather, must be constantly revisited—an idea powerfully visualized by Georg Baselitz's tattered and confusedly inverted national flag.

However diverse the experiences of the different regions and states of Germany, all have been marked by four great traumas that live in the national memory.

The first, the Thirty Years' War (1618–1648), saw every German

Inverted Eagle with the Colours of the German Flag, by Georg Baselitz, 1977

state, and troops from all the major European powers, fighting in Germany. It was devastating for the civilian population and for the economy. As armies criss-crossed the country they spread terror and plague. Jacques Callot recorded the brutal impact on villagers in Lorraine (then part of the Holy Roman Empire) of the arrival of a pillaging army. Similar horrors were experienced across all Germany, and were never forgotten. It is generally conceded that the economic consequences of the war were still discernible well into the nineteenth century. In early May 1945, Hitler's successor, Admiral Dönitz, ordered the German armed forces to stop fighting. Albert Speer, Hitler's architect and Armaments Minister, rationalized the capitulation by explaining:

> The destruction that has been inflicted on Germany can only be compared to that of the Thirty Years' War. The decimation of our people through hunger and deprivation must not be allowed to reach the scale of that epoch.

The outbreak of European war in 1792 saw French Revolutionary armies invade the Rhineland and occupy large parts of western Germany. Many historic cities, including Mainz, Aachen and Cologne,

The Hanging, from *The Miseries and Misfortunes of War*, by Jacques Callot, 1633

Germania, by Adolph Menzel, 1846–57

were incorporated into France and were to remain French cities for nearly twenty years. In 1806, after routing the Prussian army at the battles of Jena and Auerstädt, Napoleon entered Berlin in triumph. By 1812 the French had effectively occupied all Germany from the Rhineland to Russia. There was no effective military resistance left on German soil. Every major German ruler was compelled to send troops to fight with the French in the Russian campaign. It was a humiliation deeply felt, but one that eventually stirred the nation to define itself in a new way and to unite in resistance against the invader. The memory of the great humiliation of 1806 was burnt into the consciousness of all Germans, enduring to the end of the nineteenth century and beyond.

The most devastating and intractable of the four traumas was the

Third Reich. This child's cut-out paper model of Hitler reviewing the Nazi Brownshirts exemplifies the extent to which the Nazi regime infiltrated and contaminated every aspect of German life. The crimes committed by the Third Reich, both in Germany and across Europe, and the part played in those crimes by members of almost every German family, are a widely shared memory—in many cases a shared silence—still highly charged today and still far from being exorcised. The terrible price paid by the German population, flight and expulsion from the east, and the destruction of cities like Hamburg and Dresden (Chapter 27), are a second memory which the Third Reich has bequeathed to almost all Germans.

The ultimate consequence of Nazi aggression was the invasion and occupation of all Germany by the four Allied powers, and its

Children's cut-outs, *c.* 1935

Hamburg after the Allied bombing raids of 1943

long division between the Federal Republic in the west and the German Democratic Republic in the east. It condemned East Germany to a further forty years of dictatorship and oppression. The human cost of that division, epitomized by those who lost their lives desperately trying to cross the Berlin Wall, is still being assessed.

It is now twenty-five years since the Wall came down and nearly twenty-five years since a new Germany was born. In that time Germans have made enormous efforts to think clearly and courageously about their national history. The re-unification of Germany coincided with a more clear-eyed historical investigation into the complicity of much of the German population in crimes long simply ascribed to "the Nazis." As Berlin has been rebuilt there has been a conscious attempt

to make public the most painful memories, the supreme example being the Holocaust Memorial to the murdered Jews of Europe. In this also it can be said that German monuments are not like those in other lands. I know of no other country in the world that at the heart of its national capital erects monuments to its own shame. Like the Siegestor in Munich, they are there not only to remember the past but—and perhaps even more importantly—to ensure that the future be different. As Michael Stürmer, a distinguished political commentator, observes: "In Germany, for a long time, the purpose of history was to ensure it could never happen again."

The photograph on the following pages shows three great monuments at the centre of modern Berlin. To the right in the middle distance is the Brandenburg Gate, subject of my first chapter. Behind it is the Reichstag, the subject of my last chapter. In the foreground is the Holocaust Memorial, which commemorates events discussed in the later sections of the book. These three monuments and their meanings together convey much of modern Germany's unique attempt to wrestle with its historical inheritance and its complex and changing memories.

Opposite: Peter Fechter, aged eighteen, the first person to be shot dead climbing over the Berlin Wall, August 1962

Part One

Where Is Germany?

"Germany? Where is it? / I do not know where to find such a country," wrote Goethe and Schiller in 1796. In Germany both geography and history have always been unstable. Borders move. The past keeps changing. Cities and regions which were for centuries German are now firmly parts of other countries. What does that mean for them, and for the Germans? For most of the 500 years covered by this book Germany has been composed of many separate political units, each with a distinct history. Enfeebling division, or enriching complexity?

Overleaf: The Brandenburg Gate by C. G. Langhans, built between 1788 and 1791, badly damaged 1945, restored after 1990

1

The View from the Gate

If the modern state of Germany can be said to have a village green on which communal events are marked and celebrated, then it is the area around the Brandenburg Gate. It has long been Berlin's preferred setting for the city's meetings and rallies, but since the reunification of the two Germanys, the severe neo-classical gateway has become the natural backdrop to all great national events.

Professor Monika Grütters, the German Federal Minister of Culture, says:

> "It is *the* national monument. There is no other that can compete with it. It is of course the symbol of the Berlin Wall, of a world divided into East and West. And it is at the same time the symbol of the fall of that Wall and of liberty regained. It stands for the division of Germany, and the division of the world, into two blocs: two ideas of society. It reminds us of the loss of freedom; but it is in itself also the great symbol of freedom regained. It is the national and the international monument of freedom and unity."

Monika Grütters is talking about the meanings that all across the world have attached to the Brandenburg Gate since the Wall fell twenty-five years ago, but the history of the Gate, its own experiences and its far-reaching associations, go back ten times longer than that.

Originally the site of one of a number of gates around Berlin, at which customs dues were collected from goods wagons entering the city, it was rebuilt in the 1780s on the orders of the Prussian king, Frederick William II, to a grand neo-classical design by C. G. Langhans. Based on the gateway to the Acropolis, it was conceived as a monument to peace, and it was one of the first architectural signals that Berlin—which under Frederick the Great had acquired a magnificent library, opera house and other similar institutions (see Chapter 30)—now felt entitled to proclaim itself a cultural and intellectual city in the Athenian tradition.

The Brandenburg Gate stands at the western end of the long avenue Unter den Linden (Under the Lime Trees), which, rather like the

The Hohenzollern Stadtschloss, 1700–1950

Napoleon's triumphant entry into Berlin, at the Brandenburg Gate, 1806

Champs-Elysées in Paris, runs from the edge of the city down to its very heart. At the end of the avenue, closing the vista, was the Stadtschloss, the palace of the Hohenzollern kings. Some time after the Gate was built, a bronze figure of Victory, her chariot drawn by four horses, was placed on top, giving it the appearance of a triumphal arch.

The first person actually to use it for a triumphal entry was not, however, the King of Prussia, but Napoleon Bonaparte. After the defeat of Austria at the Battle of Austerlitz in December 1805, the only German state still offering serious resistance to the invader was Prussia. But on 14 October of the following year, Napoleon humiliatingly routed the Prussian army at the battles of Jena and Auerstädt. Two weeks later, on 27 October 1806, the French emperor entered Berlin in triumph, leading his troops through the Brandenburg Gate, marching them down Unter den Linden towards the palace of the king. The royal family fled to the eastern city of Königsberg (now

Kaliningrad), where they began to plan Prussia's survival and recovery. Berlin was abandoned to French occupation. Napoleon, eager to demonstrate that his authority was now absolute and the Prussian king powerless in his own capital, removed the bronze quadriga from the top of the Gate and carried it away as a trophy, to be exhibited as war booty in Paris. For eight years the Brandenburg Gate was without its crowning sculpture.

In Königsberg the king and his advisers effected a complete reordering of the Prussian state, enabling it ultimately to take the leading part in resisting and expelling the French. In 1813, Prussian and Russian troops together forced Napoleon out of Berlin, and pursued him and his army all the way to Paris. In 1814, to scenes of public jubilation, the quadriga returned to the Brandenburg Gate. It was, however, modified before being reinstated. In the bronze chariot you see today, the statue of Victory is accompanied by the Prussian eagle, and her lance proudly bears the Iron Cross (see Chapter 14), the decoration awarded by the King of Prussia to those who had fought with valour against the French invader. The chariot makes clear that Napoleon had been defeated by a Germany which his invasion had largely created. The Gate had become a Prussian triumphal arch.

The Brandenburg Gate is not just a monument to which history has added layers of meaning. It is also a remarkable standpoint from which to view some of the key moments in German history. In fact, from this place alone, you can see evidence not just of the Napoleonic Wars, but of many other great events that have shaped the German national memory.

If you turn west and look along the broad avenue that leads to the royal palace at Charlottenburg, you see another figure of Victory, this time gilded and alone, standing on top of the 200-foot-high Siegessäule (Victory Column), designed in 1864 to celebrate the Prussian victory over Denmark, which began the process of German unification. By the time it was finished, Prussia had also trounced the Austrians in 1866 and defeated the French in 1870 and the base was

---

Opposite: The Siegessäule, by Heinrich Strack, 1864–73

Albert Speer's model for the Third Reich's giant Hall of the People, with the Brandenburg Gate in the foreground

decorated accordingly to mark the triple triumph. Under Bismarck's guidance, the King of Prussia had become the German emperor, head of a united Germany which was the leading industrial and military power on the continent. The Victory Column's inauguration in 1873 signalled Berlin's new role in Europe and the world. In 1945 the French insisted on the removal of the sculpted plaques showing their defeat, but the column is otherwise broadly as intended, and still speaks today of the confident optimism of Berlin in the 1870s.

You could say that the westward view from the Brandenburg Gate is a view of Germany's place in the world as it actually was between 1870 and 1914. If things had gone as Hitler and Albert Speer had planned, the view north in the late 1940s would have shown their idea of what that place ought to be. Speer, Hitler's cherished architect, designed a colossal Volkshalle, a Hall of the People. An enormous dome, over 1,000 feet high, crowned the assembly room in which 180,000 people could gather to listen to the Führer. It would have dwarfed completely the nearby Reichstag, and been an uncomfortable, megalomaniac neighbour to the Brandenburg Gate, itself a favourite site for Nazi marches and rallies. It is a strange experience, to stand on the spot from which you would have seen Speer's dome, had history turned out differently, and from which if you turn south, you can today see the approaches to the Holocaust Memorial.

But the views west, north or south from the Brandenburg Gate were always intended to be secondary. In a virtuoso piece of urban scenography it was the view east that mattered, down Unter den Linden, past Frederick the Great's library and opera house, and on to the end of the vista and the Stadtschloss. The Schloss, a huge baroque city-palace, was completed around 1700 and effectively designed to make one great statement: after seventy years of turmoil, in spite of the Thirty Years' War (1618–48), in spite of Swedish invasion (in the 1670s), Brandenburg—the modest state of which Berlin was the capital—had not only survived, but had emerged as a serious European power.

Its survival was remarkable. It is reckoned that in the 1630s the urban population of Brandenburg declined from 113,500 to 34,000, while its rural inhabitants fell from 300,000 to 75,000. Something like three quarters of the population had died or fled. After the war, the position in both town and country was stabilized and prosperity slowly began to return. In the 1670s the Swedes, the great military power of northern Europe, had invaded again, in alliance with the French. The then Elector of Brandenburg, known to history as the Great Elector, had brilliantly outmanoeuvred and defeated them. In a pleasing twist of political and economic revenge, when Louis XIV revoked the Edict of Nantes and expelled the Protestants from France in 1685, many of the most educated and most skilled of the Huguenots came to work in, and to enrich, Berlin. Among them were some of the craftsmen who shaped and embellished the palace. The Stadtschloss told the world that you did not mess with Brandenburg.

But as you look down Unter den Linden today, you can't see it. Badly damaged by bombing, it survived the Second World War, and could well have been rebuilt. The Soviet authorities decided instead to bulldoze the Hohenzollern Schloss, which they regarded as the physical symbol of a Prussian militarism that they now had the opportunity to annihilate. Only one small part of it was preserved—the balcony from which, on 9 November 1918, the Communist Karl Liebknecht had proclaimed the Free Socialist Republic of Germany, an attempt to create a Communist state which was rapidly crushed (see Chapter 22).

On the site of the old royal palace, the government of the German

The Palast der Republik of the GDR, 1973/6–2008, on the site of the former Schloss

Democratic Republic built the new, modernist Palast der Republik, a steel structure clad in bronzed mirror-glass that was the seat of the People's Chamber and a centre for cultural and leisure activities until the GDR ended in 1990. But today you can't see that either. In the years after reunification there was intense debate about the proper future of the Palast der Republik in a new reunited Berlin, now that the people's representatives sat once again in the pan-German Reichstag. By 2008 the Palast der Republik had been demolished, allegedly because asbestos made it unfit for future use. With it disappeared many of the happier memories of old East Berlin. Its steel skeleton was sold and used to build the Burj Khalifa in Dubai.

Thus from the Brandenburg Gate today you can admire neither the triumph of the Great Elector nor the Socialist achievement of the German Democratic Republic. The historic vista now ends on a building site, where a reconstruction of the old Stadtschloss is rapidly taking shape (see Chapter 30). Behind it, though, still stands the other great monument of East Berlin, the thousand-foot-high Alexanderturm, a hi-tech telecommunications tower of the late 1960s designed to be unmissably visible in West Berlin and to broadcast, in every sense, the virtues of the Socialist state. Still one of the tallest buildings in Germany, it dominates the skyline across the city. Just

Reunification medal by Erich Ott, 1989. The prison bars on one side turn into the Brandenburg Gate on the other. The prison side carries the title of the German national anthem: "Einigkeit und Recht und Freiheit" ("Unity and Justice and Freedom").

World Cup celebrations at the Brandenburg Gate, June 2014

below its summit is a spherical operations centre with the inevitable revolving restaurant. But that is not the reason why the Alexanderturm has become part of Berlin's world of memories. By a quirk of geometry and reflection, whenever the sun shone, there appeared on the sphere a large incandescent cross—it still appears today and draws ironic smiles from the spectators at the Brandenburg Gate who remember the frustration and embarrassment the cross caused the atheist authorities in the GDR—it was quickly dubbed "the Pope's revenge."

Knocked about in the war, the Brandenburg Gate was patched up and repaired by the occupying authorities. Situated right on the boundary between the Western and Eastern zones (and later between the two states), it was one of the authorized crossing points. As in the eighteenth century, it again became an entrance to Berlin, taking on a particular, charged, significance as a place for demonstrations. In

Opposite: The Alexanderturm, by Hermann Henselmann and Gerhard Kosel, operational 1969

1953 it was the scene of the first major rebellion against Soviet rule in Eastern Europe, as tens of thousands of striking workers called for free elections and tore down the red flag flying over it. The unrest was put down by Soviet tanks. On 14 August 1961, one day after the building of the Wall began, West Berliners gathered on the other side of the Gate to protest against the erection of the Wall and the division of their city. Using these demonstrations as a pretext, the East German authorities closed the checkpoint there "until further notice." For twenty-eight years the Gate became a barrier. It did not reopen until 22 December 1989, when the West German Chancellor, Helmut Kohl, walked through it to be greeted by the East German Prime Minister, Hans Modrow. There is no building or site that speaks so powerfully to Germans everywhere of the division and the reunification of their country.

Since reunification, the Brandenburg Gate has once again been renovated and is now at the centre of a pedestrianized zone, the gathering point of choice for celebrations of all sorts. And in the summer of 2014 it was once again used for a triumphal entry into the city—not by a French invader, but by the German football team, returning victorious from the World Cup in Brazil.

In the next chapter I shall be going down Unter den Linden towards the east, to explore some of the memories of the Cold War division of Germany. It was so effective and profound that those who lived in East and West have few memories in common. What all do remember is the difficulty of travelling from one Germany to the other and the price paid by those who tried to do so without authorization.

2

Divided Heaven

The restored Reichstag, where the German Parliament meets, stands in the heart of Berlin. Because of its position near the former border dividing East and West Berlin, there are now few buildings near it and it is set between a meadow on one side, and the banks of the River Spree on the other. On most days, the riverside is busy with sightseers and strollers, such as you might find by the Seine or the Thames. But it quickly becomes obvious that this could not be either London or Paris; it could only be in Berlin. In various places beside the river are rows of white crosses.

GÜNTER LITFEN 24 AUGUST 1961
UDO DÜLLICK 5 OCTOBER 1961
HANS RÄWEL 1 JANUARY 1963
KLAUS SCHRÖTER 4 NOVEMBER 1963
HEINZ SOKOLOWSKI 25 NOVEMBER 1965
MARINETTA JIRKOWSKY 22 NOVEMBER 1980

It seems like a war cemetery, because all the dead were young. But it is not—the names are of some of those who were killed trying to escape from East to West Berlin after the building in August 1961 of the most

Overleaf: White crosses by the River Spree, with the Bundeskanzleramt behind

Spree-Blick II
www.reederei-riedel.de

Christa Wolf, *Der geteilte Himmel* (*Divided Heaven*, or *They Divided the Sky*), 1963

potent symbol of the Cold War: the Berlin Wall. The deaths range in date from ten days after the building of the Wall to ten months before its removal. Twenty-five years after its fall in 1989, the most vivid, painful and problematic of all Germany's many memories of division remains the brutal splitting of the country. Every German over the age of thirty-five, whether from East or West, knows of families split, the human cost of an arbitrary, callous bureaucracy that regulated what movement there was between the two states—and of those who paid with their lives.

Der geteilte Himmel (*Divided Heaven*), written by the East German novelist Christa Wolf, was published in 1963, two years after the Berlin Wall went up. It made Christa Wolf's reputation, and has long been seen as the most thoughtful, poignant account of the divergence of the two Germanys as seen from the East. It tells the story of Rita and Manfred, young lovers living in the East before the Wall was built, when travel from East to West Berlin was still easy. Manfred becomes disillusioned with the East and does not return from a conference in West Berlin, where he feels the opportunities for his career are greater. Rita visits him but does not warm to the crowded consumerism of West Berlin. She decides to end her relationship with

Manfred and to continue with her life in the East. She knows it is flawed, but she feels more at ease in a society where people at least aspire to work together. The couple, ideally matched in every other respect, founder as the two Germanys diverge.

"At least they can't divide the sky," says Manfred at the climax of the novel, when Rita chooses the communal ideals of East Germany, over a life with him in the individualist West. "The sky?" thinks Rita, "This vault of hope and desire, love and sadness?" "Oh yes, the sky is what gets split first." Throughout the novel, the sky—in German "Himmel" means both "sky" and "heaven"—stands for aspirations, and ideals, for what a society strives to be. The divided heaven: two separate and separated political structures, two irreconcilable ways of organizing hopes and desires. A couple that should be together, growing apart.

Christa Wolf, like her heroine Rita, decided to stay in the East. As a famous writer she was comparatively well treated and allowed to travel. And although she did criticize the regime, and her works were censored, she retained an abiding loyalty to the state's ideals, or at least to what she hoped it might achieve. Her faith in the regime was stretched, but she remained, and she remained committed.

On 23 May 1949 the Western sectors of Germany, occupied by the U.S., the UK and France, were merged to form the Federal Republic of Germany; and a few months later, on 7 October 1949, the Soviet zone became the German Democratic Republic, or GDR (see map, p. 501). At first, movement between the two Germanys was relatively easy. But the relative poverty of East Germany, partly the result of war reparations, led more and more citizens towards *Republikflucht* (flight from the Republic) to West Germany, where economic opportunities and political freedoms seemed—and were—much greater. After 1952, the GDR monitored the border severely but in spite of the growing risks of arrest and capture, somewhere around 200,000 people still managed to escape every year. By 1961 around 3.5 million East Germans had left, approximately 20 per cent of the entire

---

Overleaf: The Berlin Wall in 1980, separating the disused Reichstag in West Berlin from the Brandenburg Gate in East Berlin

GDR population, with serious economic consequences. In response to that mass emigration, the GDR sealed the Inner German Border, and then, on the night of 12–13 August 1961, East German soldiers began erecting the Berlin Wall, which prevented anyone from escaping. From the beginning, the policy was brutal: during its construction, soldiers stood in front of it with orders to shoot anyone who attempted to defect.

GDR authorities officially referred to the Wall as the "Anti-Fascist Protection Rampart" (*Antifaschistischer Schutzwall*), implying, quite justifiably, that neighbouring West Germany had not been fully de-Nazified. Whatever it was called, the Wall did its job. Between 1961 and 1989, it prevented almost all emigration from East to West. The haemorrhage of skilled workers stopped, and the GDR economy stabilized, for a time. But although most accepted the Wall as impenetrable and insurmountable, during its existence around 5,000 people managed to escape over, under or around it, with an estimated death toll of around 100 in the Berlin area alone.

A hundred or so miles north of Berlin was another favoured route for attempted escapes to the West: the Baltic. Made of bright blue synthetic fibre, armless, trimmed with white zips on the front and legs, the wetsuit pictured opposite would fit a man around six feet tall. Although it is now over twenty-five years old and housed in the German Historical Museum in Berlin, it looks as though it has never been worn. Dr. Regine Falkenberg, a curator at the museum, takes up the story:

> "After 1961, 5,609 citizens of the GDR attempted to escape via the Baltic Sea. Only 913 reached West Germany, Denmark or Sweden. 174 died from exhaustion or hypothermia, or drowned at sea. 4,522 would-be escapers served prison sentences of many months. Among them was the owner of this wetsuit. The suit, and another just like it, belonged to two young men, two friends from Leipzig. In November 1987 they planned to paddle an

---

Opposite: The wetsuit used in an escape attempt from East to West Germany, November 1987

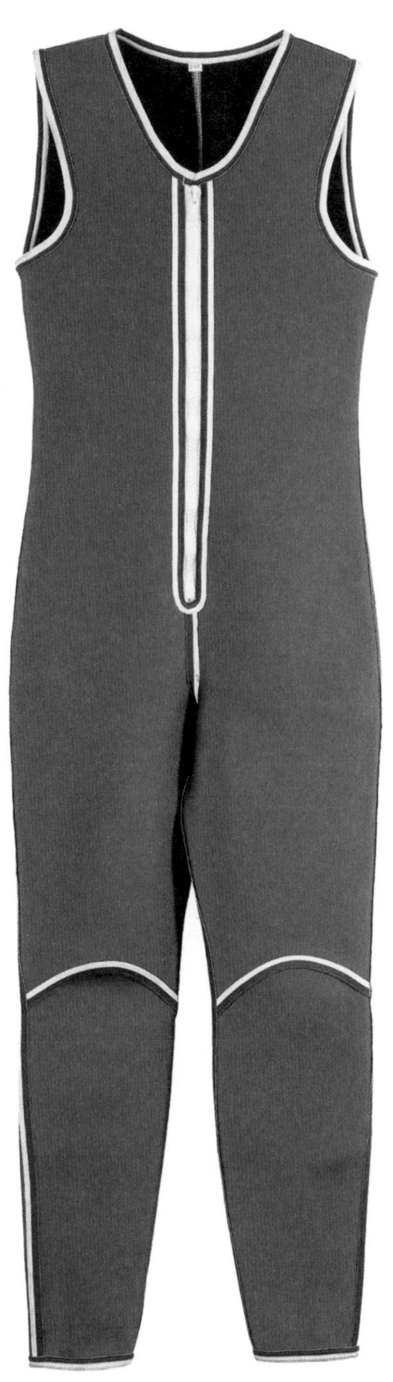

> inflatable rubber dinghy—painted black, to make it invisible—from Boltenhagen, a seaside resort about thirty kilometres east of Lübeck, to the West. They hoped that their tightly fitting wetsuits would protect them from hypothermia. Both of them were arrested before they even got into the boat. In March 1988 they were convicted by the District Court in Leipzig of 'an aggravated case' of attempted illegal crossing of the frontier, and sentenced to eighteen months in prison. The older man, thirty-five, was recently divorced and eager for a new life in the West."

For Dr. Falkenberg, one of the most challenging tasks in establishing the history behind objects like this is deciphering the official records of the GDR:

> "The difficulty in presenting or explaining a totalitarian state like the GDR is that the written records are there, but they are deliberately devious, concealing and banal. The great difficulty for the historian now is to go behind the seemingly inoffensive words, to discover the cruelty and oppression of a totalitarian state, and that is what is so difficult. The surface looks very calm, very clear, very positive. But the words are designed to mislead. So how, using the things and the words of the time, do we recover the reality of an oppressive totalitarian state?"

Yet the wetsuit itself is unambiguous evidence that two men in 1987 concluded that living in the GDR was so unfulfilling it was worth risking death to leave it. There is something unbearably poignant about it. It is not just that it was never used, or that it speaks of high hopes dashed. It is made of such poor, cheap fabric, absurdly inadequate for a November Baltic night. Had they not been so amateur in their planning as to get themselves arrested while still on shore, they might well have died of cold, or drowned—or been shot—once they put to sea. They could easily have wound up as two more names on small white crosses. And, of course, most poignant of all, had they waited just another two years, they could peacefully and legally have strolled to the West through the Brandenburg Gate.

Between 1961 and 1989 some citizens of the GDR were officially permitted to travel to the West—above all the politically sound, or those whose family ties would ensure their return, and the old (who were regarded as a burden on the economy: it did not matter whether they came back or not). From the 1970s an agreement between the four occupying powers in Berlin made it slightly easier for West Germans to visit the East. But the process was never simple, and for East Berliners the West remained as remote as ever. The building of the Berlin Wall had made it physically impossible for most people to move from one half of their city to another, but some contact did necessarily continue, not least because since the late nineteenth century the transport system of the city had been devised on the basis

Friedrichstrasse Station, 1956

of one integrated space, not two divided halves. The underground systems and the overground rail systems intersected, above all at the Friedrichstrasse Station, and it was this station that most German people had to use, to cross from one side to the other. The process was meticulously controlled and governed, particularly on the Eastern side, by a determination to prevent escape and an equal determination to keep a very close eye on those who were allowed to come in. The experience of leaving or entering East Berlin through the Friedrichstrasse Station was for a whole generation of Germans an unforgettable and distressing emotional experience. The Friedrichstrasse Station was known throughout Germany as the *Tränenpalast*, the Palace of Tears.

The best way to understand how that process of crossing the border was devised and controlled is by looking at a model of the station which is now in the German Historical Museum. Dr. Sabine Beneke, a curator at the museum, explains how the station worked.

> "I made the journey from West to East Berlin several times. You always had to change twenty Deutschmark into Ostmark, the so-called *Zwangsumtausch*—the compulsory exchange—which every person who went from West to East had to do. Normally I took the way by the Friedrichstrasse. You can see clearly on the model that the station was constructed in a deliberately complex way. The spaces are divided up by very tall walls to give the effect of a labyrinth. There was no clear orientation. You can see the different train tracks were completely separated, so tracks which operated within the East German side were kept separate from those which ran through to the West German side or beyond. As you moved from the train to the exit, you kept having to change direction and change level. You went into small doors and then large spaces, then small spaces, and everywhere in the model you can see the high windows in which observation agents or cameras were placed. Inside the interview cabin you can see the mirrors at ceiling level, so that the person looking at your documents could see your back. You were always being watched by people whom you could not see. You were being monitored at every stage. It

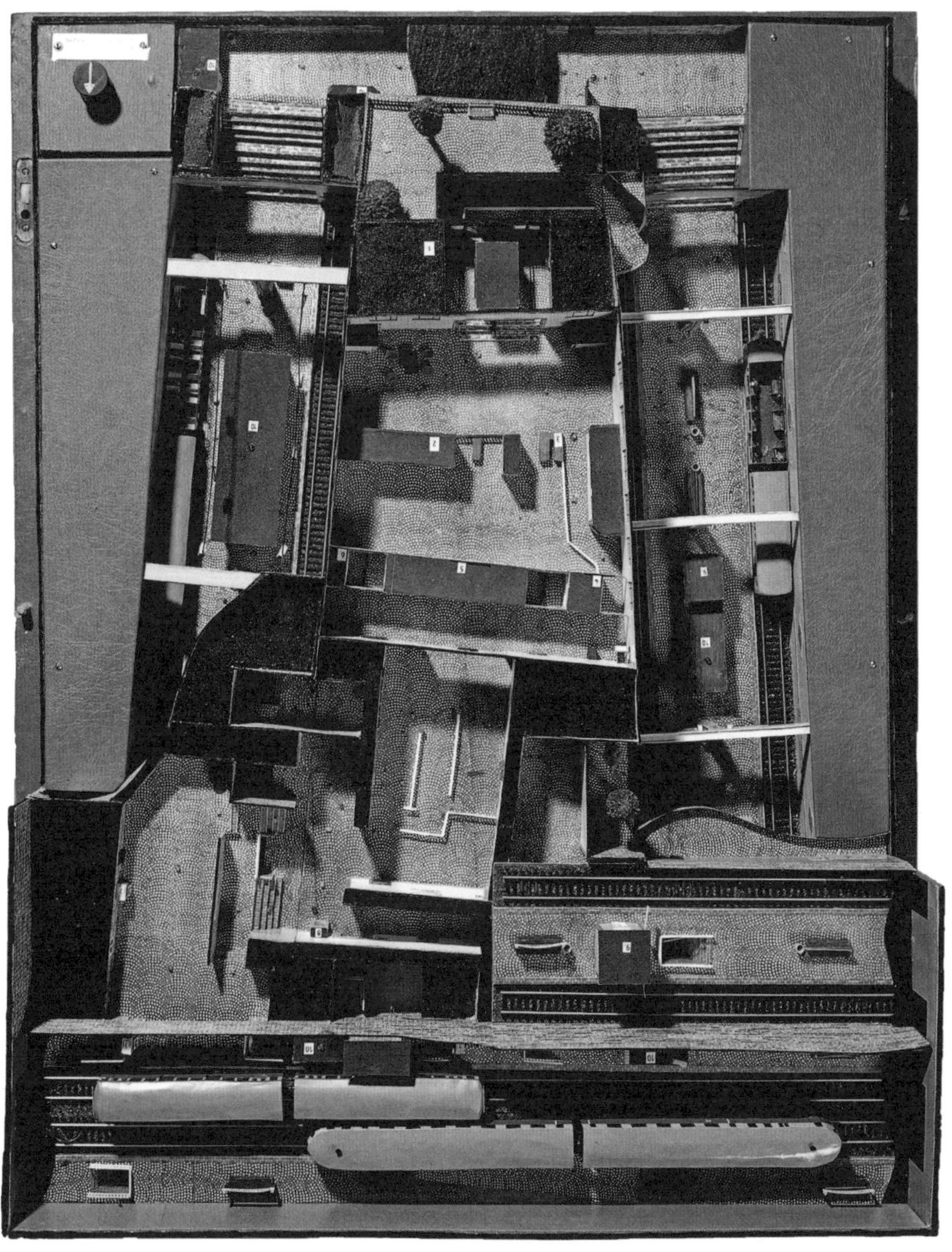

Model of the transit area between West and East Berlin, Friedrichstrasse Station, 1970

was really threatening. This model was made, we think, for the training of Stasi staff, which had a training headquarters here. If you turn it around, at the back of the model you can see there is a key and some buttons. One set of buttons, for example, illuminate lamps, which simulate an alarm. So the Stasi could instruct its trainees on what to do should somebody try to leave the GDR illegally."

This intriguing cross between a model railway and a doll's house is doubly disturbing because it looks at first sight like a plaything. It takes some time to realize that it has a very grown-up purpose: to train border guards in their duties. Particularly striking are the wires suspended between beams, holding video cameras, so that everything that happens on the platforms can be watched. There is a complex warren of dividers, walls, changing directions, changing spaces, with cabins for individual interrogation, and with mirrors at high levels, so that the traveller is observed at every stage; confused about where they are going, uncertain about what the next space will be, or how far they have got in the process. As an exercise in disorientation, this would be hard to beat. As a way of watching people move under stress and with fear, it has probably never been bettered. This is a surveillance state at the top of its game. Nobody who came through this station forgot the experience.

To police the frontiers, it was not enough to observe people as they left, or prepared to escape. *Republikflucht* was ideally to be anticipated and prevented long before it could come to an attempted crossing. In the 1980s, as the economic gap between East and West widened, the number of attempted illegal emigrations rose steadily. Dr. Regine Falkenberg explains how the Stasi responded:

"As the number of attempts rose—from 2,200 in 1985 to 3,700 in 1986—a separate section of the Stasi was set up to deal with spectacular escape attempts, like trying to penetrate the border barriers by force, trying to fly with improvised aircraft, and all sorts of boats. Between 1987 and 1988 the number of people trying to emigrate continued to rise, and the Stasi increased its

> supervision of 'suspect' categories, especially people between eighteen and thirty-five who were unmarried, divorced men, or people who had unsuccessfully applied for emigration. One part of the Stasi focused on collecting flying machines of various sorts, and then from the beginning of 1989 there was a permanent exhibition, used for training purposes, of objects and materials used to prepare illegal frontier crossings. That is why we now have the wetsuits. They and the rubber dinghy used in the escape attempt were transferred to the Volkspolizei—the GDR police in Leipzig—and then transferred to the Ministry for State Security [Stasi] in Berlin.
>
> "The Stasi collected these objects firstly to understand how they had been made, what kind of materials had been acquired, and what kind of skills were needed to put them together. The aim was to make sure that their informants and their colleagues understood what was going on, what kinds of attempts to escape were being made, with what kinds of objects, so that they could watch who was buying what kind of material, what quantities of rubber, what kind of books about aeronautics, and so on. Objects like this wetsuit served a didactic purpose: they let the Stasi informants know what they needed to look out for, as other citizens prepared criminally to escape."

Both wetsuit and model tell not only of the distress and danger attendant on any attempt, legal or illegal, to leave the GDR; both became training devices to develop the Stasi's capacity to spy on the citizen, and to sharpen the observations of its network of hundreds of thousands of informants. It has been reckoned that one in three GDR citizens was involved in giving information to the Stasi about their colleagues and neighbours, and sometimes their families.

The experience of that stifling nexus of spying is the subject of Christa Wolf's 1979 novella, *Was Bleibt* (*What Remains*). It is an account of a day in the life of a writer who knows she is under surveillance: men sit in cars parked outside the house; she is followed and watched; the phone is tapped. The stress and distress that this causes are carefully catalogued, along with the moments of despair

Christa Wolf at her writing desk in the 1980s

and paranoia, above all the frustration of not knowing who is doing this, having no person with whom to hold even a hostile dialogue. The removal of this apparatus of oppression was one of the first gains of reunification. But the memory of it has profoundly shaped key aspects of modern Germany.

The memory of all-pervasive Stasi observation, combined with earlier memories of Nazi spying, has made Germans from both East and West uniquely vigilant—and vigorous—in their refusal to authorize their state to observe their movements without specific parliamentary authority and oversight. Visiting the Friedrichstrasse Station today, there is no sense of the labyrinth of disorientation and constant observation that made it for nearly thirty years so intimidating. Nothing in the shopping malls and coffee bars would now give any clue as to why this complex was long known as the Palace of Tears. As the commuters bustle and push, carrying their drinks and snacks, one could, again, be in London or Paris. But whereas on the banks of the Spree it is the presence of the white crosses which declares that this must be Berlin, here it is an absence. Nowhere—not on the platforms, nor hanging from the roof, nor on kiosks or pylons—can a surveillance camera be seen. This station is definitely not in Britain.

The power of the memory of surveillance was also strikingly demonstrated in the different responses of the UK and German governments to Edward Snowden's revelations from June 2013 of U.S. engagement in surveillance and information-gathering, even from its closest allies. Whereas in Britain the official reaction was generally hostile or dismissive, in Germany Snowden's claim that he wanted merely "to inform the public as to that which is done in their name and that which is done against them" was taken seriously and attracted much public support. In the Rhineland city of Mainz, for example, a model of Snowden was the heroic figure on a float pulled through

The Snowden carnival wagon "Der Aufdecker" ("The Uncoverer"), Mainz, March 2014

the streets on *Rosenmontag*, the carnival held just before Lent, where political themes are often addressed or satirized. The admiration for Snowden was clear and vociferous. And in the Bundestag, speaking on 29 January 2014, Chancellor Merkel articulated to the assembled Members of the Bundestag the seriousness with which such questions must be considered:

> "The possibility of total digital surveillance touches the essence of our life. It is thus an ethical task that goes far beyond the politics of security. Millions of people who live in undemocratic states are watching very closely how the world's democracies react to threats to their security: whether they act circumspectly, in sovereign self-assurance, or undermine precisely what in the eyes of these millions of people makes them so attractive—freedom and the dignity of the individual."

Perhaps only a German political leader, and one brought up in the GDR, could have put that argument with such conviction.

The debate about Stasi surveillance, and the huge numbers of those complicit in it, is still very much alive. And it brings us back to Christa Wolf, with whose *Divided Heaven* this chapter began. That book, published in 1963, is remarkably open about the shortcomings of the GDR, the gap between high ideals and daily compromises and evasions. Wolf's later memoir about the destabilizing experience of being under surveillance, *Was Bleibt* (*What Remains*), was written in 1979. She did not, however, publish it until 1990, after the Wall had fallen. Its appearance then caused a literary storm. Critics, mostly from West Germany, accused her of cowardice or worse for not publishing it while the GDR and the Stasi were still in power, when its appearance might have done something to limit the abuses of the state. Instead, they alleged, she had chosen to remain silent—complicit—while enjoying the privileges granted to her as an internationally celebrated author, licensed to make mild criticisms of the regime.

There was worse to come. Having spoken, and indeed written, about her dislike and disapproval of the GDR state surveillance system, in the early 1990s Wolf began studying the forty-two volumes

Angela Merkel speaking in the Bundestag about digital surveillance, 29 January 2014

that the Stasi had compiled about her and which were now open to inspection in the state archives. There, to her great surprise and even greater dismay, she discovered a number of reports that she herself had delivered to the Stasi between 1959 and 1961. She had been an informant, part of that great network of citizens reporting on each other to the authorities. She had had meetings with Stasi agents. And she had forgotten about it completely.

Again attacked for hypocrisy and complicity with the GDR regime, Wolf explored the incident at length in her *City of the Angels*, a book she wrote while on a fellowship at the Getty Research Institute in Los Angeles. She concluded that her contacts with the Stasi agents were short and insignificant. And she could see that her few reports to them were so banal that they must have lost interest in her. After 1961, and the building of the Wall, there was no more contact.

Yet she does not let herself off the hook. The real question, she argued, was not about her actions. It was about her forgetting. How could she have suppressed that memory so totally as to have forgotten

Joachim Gauck in the Stasi archives, August 1992

it? How could she have been so gullible, so willing to defer to authority? She concluded that deference, the desire to support the state in whatever way was asked, was a legacy of her childhood under the Nazis. She, like so many of her generation, had been conditioned to conform. Her mind's ability to suppress the shameful memory she could only acknowledge, not excuse.

It is easy to judge Wolf's prose: she writes with a rare lucidity and integrity, and there is no reason to doubt the sincerity of her recollections. It is much harder to come to any decided view on the other issues. The story of Christa Wolf shows, in acute and disconcerting relief, one of the key problems of modern history in Germany. It is a commonplace for all of us that some memories are so painful, so shameful, that we will suppress them, and the act of recovering them will disorient and distress. The case of this one writer exemplifies why so many of the huge questions surrounding the Holocaust, and the role in it of so many Germans as perpetrators, went until the 1990s not just unanswered, but unasked. And it gives a very sharp edge to the decision by the German government over the last decades to force remembering by researching archives, by introducing vigorous programmes of public education, and by the building of monuments like the Holocaust Memorial. It is no coincidence that Joachim Gauck, who, after reunification, led the commission inquiring into the Stasi records, is now the head of state, President of the Federal Republic. The debate about memory in Germany is as much about what is not remembered as what is. Many countries, reviewing their wars, failures and losses, invoke the rubric "Lest we forget." It is a phrase that today has perhaps a deeper resonance in Germany than anywhere else.

Tankard made of amber, Königsberg, 1640–60

3

Lost Capitals

In thinking about the intellectual history of any country, a good place to start is its oldest university, the place where that society first organized the public teaching of ideas. For France it is unsurprisingly the capital, Paris; for Scotland, the seat of the archbishop, St. Andrews; for England, nobody really knows why, insignificant Oxford. For the Germanophone world, it is Prague, where in 1348 the emperor Charles IV founded the first German-speaking university. For centuries Prague, capital of Bohemia and occasional residence of the Holy Roman Emperors, was at the heart of German cultural and intellectual life. The Karls Universität, the Charles University, stands at the head of the great German university tradition. It still exists today, but as a Czech university in a city where German is no longer spoken. Hundreds of miles to the north is another great university city, equally central to the intellectual history of Germany, and there too German is no longer heard. This chapter is about Prague and Königsberg—now Praha and Kaliningrad—the home of Kafka and the home of Kant, two cities no longer in any sense German but in every sense still part of German cultural and intellectual consciousness.

Deutschland? Aber, wo liegt es?	Germany? But where is it?
Ich weiss das Land nicht zu finden.	I don't know how to find the country.

That question was asked not by a bewildered foreigner, puzzling over the patchwork map of eighteenth-century Germany, but by the giants of German literature, Goethe and Schiller, together in a collection of poems published in 1796, the *Xenien*. It is a question to which there has only relatively recently been a clear answer. It is not just that the political frontiers of the German lands have always been many and moveable, but that from the early Middle Ages onwards German-speaking communities settled all over Central and Eastern Europe as a result of conquest, partnership or invitation. The German-speaking world, unlike the French, English or Italian, had given birth to numerous outstations and satellites within Europe, running all the way to the Volga. Most of these were extinguished brutally in 1945, but in the German cultural memory they remain, like phantom limbs: once constituent parts of the body, greatly valued, now definitively amputated and lost. The only comparable phenomena are perhaps the long-established Greek elites in Constantinople and Alexandria,

Prague University

Kaliningrad Cathedral, *c.* 1998. Until its destruction in the Second World War it was closely surrounded by other buildings.

equally integral to the national cultural self-image, and similarly dissolved by the politics of the twentieth century.

Evidence that modern Russian Kaliningrad was once a great German city can be found in its Gothic cathedral, a typical example of German Baltic brick architecture, destroyed by the RAF in the Second World War and carefully rebuilt in the 1990s. And at its north-east corner lies the tomb of the city's most famous son, Immanuel Kant. Born in Königsberg in 1724, the great philosopher never travelled more than ten miles from it, and never set foot in what is now Germany. On the plaque near his tomb are the famous words from his *Critique of Practical Reason* about the two things that inspired genuine and deepening awe in him, the more he considered them: "Der bestirnte Himmel über mir, und das moralische Gesetz in mir"—"the starry heaven above me and the moral law within me." German philosophy—European philosophy—is unthinkable without him.

Critik
der
practischen Vernunft
von
Immanuel Kant.

Riga,
bey Johann Friedrich Hartknoch
1788.

Left: Title-page of the first edition of Kant's *Critique of Practical Reason*, published in Riga, 1788

Right: Plaque near Kant's tomb, outside Kaliningrad Cathedral. The inscription, in German and Russian, reads: "Two things fill the mind with ever new and increasing admiration and awe, the more often and perseveringly my thinking engages itself with them: the starry heaven above me and the moral law within me."

Kant's Königsberg was on the edge of the world—at least of the German-speaking world, of which it was the easternmost outpost. It had been founded in violence in 1254 by the Teutonic Knights, fierce German crusaders who set out to conquer and convert the pagan Balts. Under their rule the "Borussia" of the Latin chronicles became Preussen, or Prussia, a deeply Germanized province. It grew rich thanks to trade in wheat and timber, but most famously in one special commodity: amber. Clear, golden, mysterious, this fossilized resin from forests long drowned could be harvested in great quantities on the Baltic shore and was traded as far as the Caspian, the Black Sea, the Mediterranean and the Atlantic. For centuries the Hohenzollern

Königsberg castle, *c.* 1905, incorporating the tower built by the Teutonic Knights in the fourteenth century. The castle was badly damaged during the Second World War and its remnants bulldozed in the 1960s. In the foreground is a monument to Bismarck.

KONIGSBERG

View of Königsberg, *c.* 1740

Fishing for amber on the Baltic coast, 1761. The right to collect amber was held by the local ruler: the gallows were intended as a grim warning to potential thieves.

dukes of Prussia, rulers of Königsberg from 1527, exploited their near monopoly of the material, far more precious than silver, to give sumptuous diplomatic gifts which nobody could match, and nobody would refuse.

The amber tankard in the British Museum, made in Königsberg around 1650, is a typical and splendid example. The whole idea of an amber tankard, elaborately carved, is absurd: it must have been difficult and disagreeable to drink out of, holding back the lid awkwardly as you drained the expensively imported wine or the ceremonial local beer. It is not of course principally designed for drinking, but for show. To have this on or at your table placed you very high: indeed the white amber (rarer even than the golden) used for the disc in the centre of the lid bears the arms of the Swedish crown. This tankard almost certainly belonged to Queen Christina of Sweden, a gift from the Elector of Brandenburg, who by 1650 was also Duke of Prussia, ruler of Königsberg and in search of powerful allies.

Gifts like these allowed the Hohenzollern House of Brandenburg, so ostentatiously frugal in its own court, to show off extravagantly in its gifts to others. For this was a house on the rise, with vaulting, royal, ambitions to which the peripheral Königsberg was paradoxically central; the city's very remoteness was its greatest advantage. Professor Christopher Clark, historian of Prussia, explains:

> "Königsberg was a city outside the Holy Roman Empire [see Maps 1–3], so it became very important in the claim of the electors of Brandenburg to a royal title. They could not get a royal title inside the Empire because to get one they would have had to ask the Austrian Holy Roman Emperor for his permission, something they did not want to do. So they sought their royal title from Königsberg, which as a result became the seat of the Prussian claim to royalty. The Brandenburg elector, Frederick III, who became King Frederick I, decided to make himself king in the Duchy of Prussia. He could not be King of Prussia for complex reasons to do with the fact that the name Prussia also applied to part of what was then Poland; he could only be called

The interior base of the tankard depicting the sun

The lid of the tankard with the Swedish royal arms

Krönung des
Königes wie Er selbsten
die Kron sich aufsetzet

Frederick as Elector of Brandenburg

Frederick as "King in Prussia"

> King in Prussia. But he made do with that rather odd title, and simply invented a new kingly status. But Prussia—Königsberg—was also where the Brandenburg polity got its name from. Until the seventeenth century the state was simply called Brandenburg. It was through the acquisition of East Prussia that it came to be first known as Brandenburg-Prussia, and later as Prussia. So in a sense the state we think of as Prussia actually stole its name as a kind of logo from its easternmost possession."

Frederick I's self-coronation in Königsberg in 1701 was a pivotal moment in the history of Germany, and of Europe. The electors of Saxony were, for the time being, kings of Poland, but that crown was itself elective, and would pass in due course to other families. The Elector of Hanover was about to become King of Great Britain, which would direct his interests elsewhere. But the King in Prussia was now, like the kings of Denmark and Sweden, an enduring royal presence

Opposite: Frederick I crowns himself "King in Prussia" in Königsberg Cathedral, 1701

with large territories in north Germany. In one respect, however, this new king did not pretend to be like the others. The coronation that took place in the brick Gothic cathedral of Königsberg on 18 January 1701 was a ceremony designed to show that this monarchy was different. Christopher Clark:

> "It was the most expensive single event in Brandenburg-Prussian history until that point. It was put together as a gigantic advertising spectacular, but—very unusually—it made no attempt to seek the authority of continuity with the past. The title was not granted by the Hapsburg monarch; it was seized and taken by the king himself. An interesting feature of the coronation was that Frederick crowned himself and then his wife. Nobody else was allowed to intervene in the process. This was a completely self-made monarchy."

From 1701 to 1914, as the new state of Prussia grew in strength and importance, marginal, liminal Königsberg retained its special, almost mythical place as the seat of monarchy. The royal residence may have been in the palace in Berlin, but the city in the east had a status of its own. So in 1806, when Napoleon routed the Prussian army at Jena and occupied Berlin, the royal family quite naturally took refuge in the furthest part of East Prussia, Königsberg. And it was there that the king and his counsellors refashioned the realm, drafting the reforms which enabled the Prussian army and the Prussian state to lead their German allies to victory over Napoleon, alongside the armies of Austria, Britain and Russia; and, then in 1871, to unite the whole of Germany north of Austria under their leadership. It was in and around Königsberg that Prussia was both made in 1701 and then remade in 1806.

And all the way through, it remained the city of amber. Perhaps the clearest demonstration of the ambitions of the new monarchy was the gift given by King Frederick William I in 1716 to his crucial ally, the Tsar of Russia, Peter the Great—not an amber tankard or casket, as his modest grandparents might have done, but a whole amber room. Weighing several tons, and dubbed the eighth wonder of the

The Amber Room at Tsarskoye Selo with a statue of Frederick the Great, *c.* 1930

world, the Amber Room gleamed in imperial splendour at Tsarskoye Selo, the Romanoff palace outside St. Petersburg, for around 200 years. During the Siege of Leningrad in 1941, German soldiers looted it and brought it back to Königsberg. It was there when the bombing began in 1944, and it has not been seen since.

Nor, in large measure, has Königsberg. In the latter stages of the war, the city was devastated first by British air raids and then by Soviet artillery. In 1945 the German population that had not already fled was killed or forcibly deported. A new population, from the Soviet Union, was brought in. The territory around Königsberg was given to Poland and Lithuania, and the city itself, renamed Kaliningrad, became Soviet territory, an enclave housing a militarized naval base. Between 1945 and 1989 the Soviet authorities, in what must be a classic case of Stalinist eradication of memory, demolished most of what had not already been destroyed. Every place name and street name was changed and the cradle of the Prussian monarchy was transformed into a modern Soviet city. Kant's Königsberg vanished.

A manhole cover in present-day Kaliningrad, still bearing the legend "1937 Königsberg"

Only one unchanged, continuing sign of the long German presence remains: the manhole covers. You can still see them today. Where, all around, you see Soviet buildings and statues, and the name of Kaliningrad in Cyrillic, beneath your feet, in stout cast iron, you can still read "L.STEINFURT.A-G-1937-KÖNIGSBERG."

The physical elimination of most of the city was matched by the legal abolition of the state of Prussia. Christopher Clark:

> "There is something extraordinary about the decision of the Allied control council, in February 1947, to abolish the state of Prussia by an act of law. Unlike most laws issued by the council, this one has a miniature history lesson in the preamble. It says Prussia, which had since times of yore been the seat of reaction and militarism, is hereby abolished. The explanation for the law is in its wording. This state is seen as the source of militarism and reaction in German history and for that reason it has to be

> exorcized from the European map. It is an unquiet spirit that must be dispelled. There is no precedent I can think of for the abolition of a state in peacetime by an act of the pen in this way. It is astonishing when you look at the map of Europe today—Prussia simply does not appear."

In fact, for most Germans today, the name of Prussia occurs only intermittently, in a historical or cultural context. But in one sphere it is very widely used in its original Latin form, though probably rarely recognized for what it is. The hugely successful Dortmund football team, founded in 1909, still proudly carries the memory that the city was once part of the Prussian Rhineland: it calls itself Borussia Dortmund.

In 1787, while Kant in Königsberg was working on his *Critique of Practical Reason* with its memorable phrase about "the starry heaven above me and the moral law within me," Mozart was on his way to Prague, where he was hoping for a warm reception from the public for the première of *Don Giovanni*; and where he was confident of finding a city that was, for most purposes, as German as Königsberg. R. J. W. Evans, a historian of the Holy Roman Empire, explains:

> "If you went to Prague in the eighteenth century, you would have a strong sense that the whole of the business of the Bohemian kingdom was something familiar to you in German terms. The outward appearance of it would have been typically German, not very different from the sort of places you would have travelled through from Saxony or Austria to reach it, and the language of a great deal of standard social intercourse was German."

But Prague was of course never an entirely German city. Capital of the old Kingdom of Bohemia, centre of Czech consciousness, it had a long and complex relationship with the German world. Where East Prussia and Königsberg had been taken by force of arms, the Germans had come to Prague—almost at the same time, in the later thirteenth century—by invitation. The Mongol invasions of Central Europe had resulted in serious depopulation, and the kings of Bohemia, eager to rebuild their towns and cities, encouraged German immigration and settlement. By 1300 there was a distinct German quarter in Prague.

From the beginning, the German community played a leading role in the intellectual and cultural life of the city. When the university was founded in 1348, most of the teachers and students were German-speaking. And when, in the years around 1600, Rudolf II, Holy Roman Emperor of the German Nation, established his main residence in Prague, it again became the intellectual capital of the German world, drawing artists and scholars, scientists and astronomers, from the whole of Europe.

For the next 200 years German ascendancy in Prague remained essentially unchallenged—as Mozart would have witnessed—until, like the rest of Europe, Bohemia was stirred by nationalist yearnings

The Emperor Rudolf II Introducing the Liberal Arts to Bohemia, by Adriaen de Vries, 1609

The old town square in Prague, 1922. Just behind the Hus Memorial (centre) was the Kafka family's photographic shop.

in the years of the Napoleonic Wars. Then, with the collapse of the Holy Roman Empire, things changed very fast indeed. Czech nationalist feeling grew steadily. The orientation of the inhabitants of Prague and Bohemia, after 500 years of cohabitation and inter-marriage, shifted firmly away from the German world. Between 1848 and 1880, Prague went from being a majority German-speaking city to a Czech-speaking one. In 1882 the last Germans resigned from the city council in protest at the new mayor's inaugural address, in which he talked of "our hundred-towered, beloved, golden, *Slavonic* Prague." The next year, Franz Kafka was born.

Karen Leeder, Professor of Modern German Literature at Oxford:

> "Kafka is one of the most important writers in German. His very name even brought a word into the language in English,

Kafka by Hans Fronius, 1937

> Kafka-esque: he pinpoints in many senses the unease, the spiritual desolation and the outsiderdom of modern man and has become a byword for alienation and a kind of modern loss of self in the twentieth century and beyond. The twentieth century is unthinkable without Kafka, not simply in German but in world literature. People will say he was a Czech writer, an Austrian writer, a Jewish writer. To try to define him this way is to enter the very problems that surround his unique voice. He wrote in German. He was living in Prague. He spoke German and Czech, but he wrote in German and in that sense many of his focal points were in German. At one level Prague defines Kafka."

Or, more specifically, the particular circumstances of German Prague do. The city that Kafka was born into in 1883, the city that moulded him, was one in which German was not just in retreat but in terminal decline. Officially Prague had become a one-language city and, as he grew up, the street signs were in Czech only. When he went to the

Charles University to read law in 1901, it had already been divided into two—a Czech-speaking and a German-speaking part—with the different students using separate entrances. So Kafka, as a German speaker, grew up almost as an outsider in a city that had within living memory decided to abandon its long German identity. The portrait of him by Hans Fronius, who illustrated some of his stories, shows a man clearly ill at ease, watchful and uncertain.

But Kafka, like most young Prague German speakers of the 1890s, was also an outsider in a second sense. At the Gymnasium, the German-language secondary school he attended, most of the students were, like him, Jewish. As a Jew in a land that had for 300 years been devoutly Catholic, and as a German speaker in a city which had recently decided to abandon its German inheritance, Kafka was by birth well placed to experience and understand the oppressions and alienations of modern political structures.

Kafka's novels *The Castle* and *The Trial*, and his short story *Metamorphosis*, whose hero wakes up to find himself transformed into a huge beetle, have become part of the canon of world literature. They are the last, enduring flowering of German Prague. Karen Leeder:

> "You can trace the paths of some of the characters in the real Prague, you can follow the streets they walk along. For example, the apartment where Kafka lived with his family is the location of his famous story *Metamorphosis*; it has exactly the same ground plan. Prague was an extraordinary melting pot of Czech, German, Jewish and Yiddish influences, and Kafka consorted in the café culture where all these different people came together."

It was the kind of cosmopolitanism that had blossomed under the Austro-Hungarian Empire, but was unlikely to survive in the post-1919 nation states. By the time Kafka died in 1924, only 5 per cent of the population of Prague were native German speakers. Most of them, like Kafka, were Jewish. And nearly twenty years later most of those, like his three sisters, were murdered in the Holocaust during the Nazi occupation of Czechoslovakia: it was, ironically, the Germans themselves who finally eliminated the German language and tradition in Prague. In 1945 the new government of Czechoslovakia expelled the entire remaining German-speaking population of the country, most of them in the Sudetenland, numbering in all about three million people. The government was, in the official words, "correcting the mistakes of our Czech kings, who invited the German colonists here." The expellees took refuge in a Germany most of them had never visited. After 700 years, the story of German Prague had ended, living on in the pages of Kafka's fiction.

At the beginning of this chapter these two cities, Russian-speaking Kaliningrad and Czech-speaking Prague, were described as no longer being in any sense German. The atrocities of the Third Reich, which killed so many Russians and Czechs, also killed that long chapter of German history. But the wounds inflicted by the Second World War, if by no means forgotten, are receding. The Russian University in Kaliningrad is now renamed the Immanuel Kant University and Kant's links with Russia are much discussed. Prague's links with Saxony (Dresden is only eighty miles away) are again as close as they were in the eighteenth century. Kaliningrad and Prague both now actively seek German visitors and German investment. Modern Germany and its eastern neighbours are now comfortable and secure within their shared borders. But Prague, Imperial capital and home of Kafka, and Königsberg, the city of Kant and the Prussian monarchy, remain in the German consciousness as crucial, quickening memories. The political boundaries of Germany are now fixed. But for the cultural historian, the frontiers still float far to the east.

4

Floating City

No river, not even the Danube, runs so deep in the German imagination, is freighted with more cultural, historical or musical associations, than the Rhine. It is the Rhine that flows peacefully in the evening sunshine as Heine's Lorelei combs her golden locks and lures sailors to destruction. It is on the Rhine that Wagner's Siegfried embarks on his epic journey. And in the 1840s, as a belligerent France sabre-rattles and talks once again of invading German territory,

> "They are not going to take it,
> The free, the German Rhine."

is the patriotic song that Schumann sets to rousing music.

But is the Rhine a German *river*, or a German *frontier*? The historic lands of German language and culture reach far beyond the boundaries of modern Germany, overlapping for hundreds of years, with more or less friendly neighbouring states. On the western side, the most problematic overlapping was always with France, and focused above all on one historic German city: Strasbourg. Over the centuries, many visitors have admired its great Gothic cathedral but

---

Overleaf: *Rhine Landscape with Landing Stage*, by Hermann Saftleven, 1666

Goethe in 1765, shortly before he visited Strasbourg

none with such rhapsodic poetic power as the young Johann Wolfgang von Goethe.

In 1770, at the age of twenty-one, Goethe came to study in Strasbourg and, standing in front of this cathedral façade, discovered two things: the transporting, transforming force of Gothic architecture and one aspect of what it meant to him to be German. The tourists of Goethe's day, just like those of ours, came to Strasbourg Cathedral not only to shiver in exaltation in front of its Gothic architecture, but to admire one of the most celebrated achievements of German Renaissance technology. Inside the cathedral is a great astronomical clock, housed in a three-storey stone structure where, on the hour, bells ring, figures move and the drama of salvation is briefly, mechanically, re-enacted.

The clock in Strasbourg Cathedral, completed in 1574, was the

Opposite: The astronomical clock in Strasbourg Cathedral

work of Isaac Habrecht, one of the greatest masters of mechanical precision instruments to flourish in Renaissance Germany, and Goethe certainly visited it as well as the cathedral. Its workings unfortunately broke down in the late eighteenth century and were removed—so they can no longer be admired. What's in Strasbourg Cathedral today is a nineteenth-century copy.

But, fortunately, in 1589 Habrecht made a smaller domestic version of his Strasbourg masterpiece, and that we can admire; for it is in the British Museum. It is a portable clock-tower. About three feet tall, its three square storeys of engraved brass are elegantly supported at the corners by free-standing columns. This is the House of Time, and its different dials and discs measure the minutes and hours of our lives from now to Judgement Day. The days of the week pass regularly by in a carousel, the changing phases of the moon are indicated, the position of the sun in the zodiac is charted. Every hour the universal tyranny of time is rehearsed. Individual lives—the Four Ages of Man, who strike the quarter-hours—are shown to be fleeting and transient, as are even the great empires of Greece and Rome, Assyria and Persia, engraved around the calendar. Like them, everything human will keep rising and dying until, at the end of time, and in the highest register, the figure of Christ returns to put Death, who strikes the hour, to flight. And on the hour, as Christ the Judge appears, and we mortals need to plead for divine mercy, this astonishing clock plays the music Luther wrote to accompany his version of the Lord's Prayer, "Vater Unser"—"Our Father."

Habrecht's clock combines astronomy with theology, mathematics with history, precision engineering with Luther's translation of the Bible (see Chapter 6), and exquisite silver sculpture with Luther's flair for matching scripture with music. It is a small, three-foot-high monument to German Renaissance humanism, and it could have been produced in only a very few German cities. One of them was Strasbourg, or, as it was then, Strassburg.

Joachim Whaley, the historian of the Holy Roman Empire, explains:

Opposite: The portable Strasbourg clock

COIFFURE
GEOX

> "Strassburg was simply a German city. It was an Imperial city of the Holy Roman Empire. It was a bishopric, whose bishop was a prince-bishop of the Empire. It was in a German-speaking—Alemannic-speaking [the form of German found in the Upper Rhine and Switzerland]—area and its elite were fully integrated into the German educational and political system. There were very few contacts with the west, largely because of this essentially Alemannic German identity. The University of Strassburg remained a German university through the eighteenth century, and a popular destination: the young Goethe studied there for example, and the Austrian statesman Metternich."

The Strassburg of the German Lutheran University, the city where Habrecht's clock proclaimed the prowess of German precision engineering and where Goethe discovered the German-ness of Gothic architecture had one surprising characteristic: a hundred years earlier, it had been forcibly made part of France. In 1681 Louis XIV, flushed by his successful wars of aggression in Alsace, attacked Strassburg without pretext. The French army could not be resisted and the Imperial Free City of the Holy Roman Empire was annexed to France.

A broadside print of around 1678, three years before the attack on Strassburg, shows how the French occupation of territory which was German-speaking and had always been part of the Holy Roman Empire appeared to the Germans: an angry eagle, carrying the Imperial orb, surrounded by smaller allies and brandishing a sword, swoops down to attack and repel the French cock, which is strutting on a map of the Empire, its shadow blotting out Strassburg. The allegory is clear: the Emperor and his supporters will soon expel the French. But hopes of swiftly recovering the region proved vain, and in 1697 de facto French possession was grudgingly acknowledged by the Emperor. Strassburg had become Strasbourg by force of arms.

For a hundred years, the French administered with a light touch. German remained the language of most of the population, and the

---

Opposite: Strasbourg Cathedral towering over the city. Between the fifteenth and nineteenth centuries it was the tallest building in the world.

German broadside print of Louis XIV's occupation of Alsace, 1678

German university continued. So, in 1770, the city that Goethe discovered was in fact a hybrid—German in character, but politically administered by the French.

But the cathedral, Goethe decided, was most certainly not hybrid: it was *German*, built by a supreme, German, architectural genius, Erwin von Steinbach. And it overwhelmed him. He wrote:

> An impression of oneness, wholeness and greatness filled my soul—an impression which, because it consisted of a thousand harmonizing details, I could savour and enjoy, but by no means

> understand or explain. They say that it is like this with the joys of heaven, and how often did I return to enjoy this heavenly-earthly bliss, to embrace the titanic spirit of our elder brethren [i.e., our fellow Germans] in their works. How often did I return to contemplate its dignity and glory from every side, from far and near, in every light of the day.

Goethe's little pamphlet on Strasbourg Cathedral, "Von Deutscher Baukunst," "On German Architecture"—his first separately published work—was inspirational, influential and in one key respect wrong. Unusually for his time, he could see that the myriad, appar-

Goethe in Strasbourg in 1770, from a print of 1870

ently confused details of the Gothic façade were in fact animated by a coherent aesthetic dynamic. But he convinced himself (he was not alone) that this Gothic architecture, which we now know to be in origin French, was quintessentially, triumphantly, German. Striking the twin romantic chords of genius and national distinctiveness, he declaimed:

> And now have I not reason to be indignant, holy Erwin, when the German art critic, on the word of envious neighbours, fails to recognize his advantage and belittles thy work with the meaningless word "Gothic"; when he ought to thank God to be able to proclaim aloud: that is German architecture, our architecture, since the Italian can boast none of his own, still less the Frenchman.

Strasbourg Cathedral, in a city which had by then for nearly a hundred years been French, became for Goethe a rallying cry to the Germans to reclaim their national traditions and take their rightful place among the cultures of Europe. Fittingly, it was in Strasbourg that Goethe met the twenty-six-year old philosopher Johann Gottfried Herder—the creative mentor of the *Sturm und Drang* (Storm and Stress) movement, one of the forerunners of Romanticism. In his writing on literature, Herder, who had studied with Kant in Königsberg, argued powerfully for the unique passion and expressiveness of the German language:

> Nature obliges us to learn only our native tongue, which is the most appropriate to our character, and which is most commensurate with our thought . . . We cannot be educated otherwise than in the language of our people and our country; so-called French education in Germany must by definition deform and misguide German minds.

Since the Renaissance, German culture had been dominated by the models of Ancient Rome and modern Italy and France. In Strasbourg in the 1770s it became clear to these two gifted young men that that would have to change.

Johann Gottfried Herder, by Angelika Kauffmann, 1791

Many cities could be chosen to support the argument that over the centuries, in a way inconceivable to the British, German intellectual, spiritual and cultural boundaries have not corresponded to political frontiers: but Strasbourg probably makes that point better than any other. It is impossible to write a cultural history of Germany without including this city, today linguistically, politically and administratively French. It was home to Gottfried von Strassburg, author of *Tristan*, a masterpiece of medieval German literature. As a great Renaissance German city, Strassburg provided the economic and intellectual context for Habrecht's mechanical achievements and its printers and preachers helped spread Luther's Reformation to the whole of Europe. Here Herder articulated the particular, vivifying attributes of the German language. And in Goethe's rhapsodic outpouring to the cathedral, Strasbourg stimulated the first great hymn to German cultural nationalism.

The light, tolerant, touch of the early French administration could not survive the steadily centralizing nation state of the nineteenth century. In an increasingly nationalist world, Strasbourg could no

Print of soldiers from the German principalities saluting the new German Emperor, 1870

longer be both German and French, and the several switches in control from one country to the other over the last 200 years have been increasingly oppressive, violent, and complete.

Another German print in the British Museum—this one celebrating the 1871 victory in the Franco-Prussian war and the recovery of Strassburg—shows the cathedral twinned with that of Cologne, which had only recently—finally—been completed by the Prussians as an emblem of national pride and unity. The two great German cathedrals are linked by the *freie deutsche Rhein* as Germany's great river is described on the print, in the words of the 1840 "Rheinlied" by Nikolaus Becker, set to music by Robert Schumann. The Holy

Roman Empire of the German Nation has been restored. Strasbourg, the print proclaims, is once again Strassburg, a German Imperial city.

In Paris, on the other hand, where politicians had never stopped dreaming of a return to Napoleon's Rhine frontier, abandoned after 1815, the loss of Strasbourg in 1871 became the symbol of a monstrous wrong. The statue of the city in the Place de la Concorde was draped in black and famously became the object of the de Gaulle family outings where the young Charles was instructed in his duty to help recover the lost city and France's lost honour. Strasbourg had been transformed into *the* totemic object of Franco-German enmity. The city itself became French again in 1919, German again in 1940, and French once more on 23 November 1944. Each time it changed hands, it was to a rising pitch of cultural nationalism and strident assimilation. Today this city, so important in the cultural history of Germany, is now definitively French.

For Joachim Whaley, the question is now unequivocally settled:

> "The final chapter in this long Franco-German history in the nineteenth and twentieth century is the German occupation from 1940. It was as brutal here as it was in almost every occupied territory and it finally resolved that question of identity in the minds of the majority of the population.
>
> "It is often said that the Germans achieved in four and a half years what the French had failed to achieve in the previous twenty years, which was to turn the population of Alsace into Frenchmen."

But in 1945 many of those "Frenchmen" still had one German characteristic—their language. It was the last evidence of nearly 2,000 years of German-ness. Tomi Ungerer is a veteran campaigner for the linguistic rights of Alsatians, but he acknowledges that the battle is lost.

> "I've spent a good thirty years fighting for the Alsatian identity and for our language because the language is part of our identity,

---

Overleaf: Strasbourg in 1871 after the German bombardment. The Prussian flag flies over the cathedral.

> and I think actually the way things are now in a way we lost our battle. We are practically left without a language, of our own, but only with an accent, an Alsatian accent. Alsace is now so French, I don't think that the young people now have any of the kind of identity problems that I have, because they are French now. The Jacobins have won the battle. But we don't have to worry any more, are we French, are we German? We are European. Alsatians are true Europeans because we have discovered a new identity."

Since 1945, the long Franco-German struggles over the Rhine have been resolved by a process in which de Gaulle—the child who stood in front of the statue of Strasbourg in the Place de la Concorde—played a key role. Tomi Ungerer's hopeful conclusions suggest that the floating frontiers of Germany, and the complexities and conflicts surrounding them, have now been subsumed in the new political order, the confederation of autonomous states known as the European Union. But this is a future with a very long past—one which has striking affinities to an earlier one: the Holy Roman Empire.

Strasbourg today as seat of the European parliament is a pivotal part of a new vision of Europe and it may be that the European Union will in time provide an organizing structure within which local particularisms like the Alsatian language can survive. If that happens it will in essence be merely a return to a structure that flourished for centuries and of which Strasbourg was also a significant part. Goethe saw in the cathedral façade a coherent structure with a thousand details which "I could savour and enjoy, but by no means understand or explain." It was a structure that left him, in spite of its detail and its diversity, with an impression of oneness, wholeness and greatness. He might have also been describing the Holy Roman Empire, that vast federation of different kinds of states and different kinds of Germanness which lasted for a thousand years, and which is the subject of the next chapter.

Statue in Paris personifying Strasbourg, draped in crepe and wreaths, 1905

Silver *Sterbethaler* (death-coin) of the Electress Sophia of Hanover, 1714

Gold five guineas, George I, King of Great Britain, 1716

5

Fragments of Power

Few people can ever have been more irritated about the timing of their death than Sophia, Electress of Hanover, nominated by Parliament in London as Protestant heir to the British crown. Having waited over a decade for her notoriously unhealthy and extremely remote relative, Anne, to die, Sophia herself was struck down, apparently hale and hearty and walking in her shrubbery, just weeks before Queen Anne at last died on 1 August 1714. So in the British Museum we have no coin celebrating the coronation of Sophia, Queen of Great Britain, but rather one struck in Hanover to mark her death, describing her still merely as heir to the throne of Great Britain.

Beside this modest silver coin on which Sophia appears in death is the coin she longed to adorn in life, the gold five-guinea piece of Great Britain. The example opposite shows her son, George I, proudly wreathed with laurel and surrounded by the titles of King of Great Britain, France (a title claimed by British sovereigns until 1802), Ireland and Defender of the Faith. But on the other side the same George is identified as Georg Ludwig, Elector and Archtreasurer of the Holy Roman Empire, Duke of Brunswick and Lüneburg. George's currency in Britain was the only one in the land. George's currency in Hanover was one of around 200 struck in the different territories of Germany that made up the Empire. The coin tells of one ruler living in two worlds.

A simple comparison of the coinage in George's new, British, realm with that in the Germany he left behind instantly demonstrates the profound differences between the political histories of the two countries in the eighteenth century, and explains something of their divergent address to the political questions of today.

For England—and later Britain—unity, if necessary enforced unity, was for centuries the aim and purpose of the state, the essential precondition of order and prosperity. The Holy Roman Empire of the German Nation, on the other hand, was a polity of many parts, elements of an elusive whole, held together not by military coercion but by a network of shared assumptions and customary frameworks.

Joachim Whaley elucidates a structure which frequently baffled foreigners:

> "From the outside it does look chaotic, particularly if you look at an historical atlas, where you see a blaze of colour, and little bits of territory here there and everywhere, everything looking very confused, but I think on the whole it worked as well as many other early modern states. One has to remember that the patchwork of territories that you see is not a patchwork of sovereign states. The princes and the Imperial cities were not independent and sovereign. They were subordinate to the Empire and they all worked within the common framework of law, which was agreed jointly between the Emperor and the princes at the Imperial Parliament—the Diet—on a regular basis. It was held together, I think, by a sense of belonging to the premier realm of Christendom, with a particular, universal mission."

If the institutional framework of the empire was complex, its coins offer a very physical way of grasping the range and limits of its diversity. At the summit of this whole political and monetary system was of course the Emperor himself, who around 1700 was Leopold I, shown here on a silver coin known as a thaler. He has an advanced case of Hapsburg jaw, with a strongly protruding lower lip—not surprisingly,

Silver thaler, Emperor Leopold I, 1700

Silver gulden, Lippe Detmold, 1714

as he was the fruit of a great deal of inter-marriage—and he was one of the greatest rulers of continental Europe, controlling what is now Austria, the Czech Republic, Slovakia, most of Hungary, Slovenia and parts of Romania. But, unlike the British ruler, the Emperor had no monopoly of coinage: essentially, everybody who had a seat in the Imperial Diet was allowed to strike their own coins—the princes, the electors, the bishops, the cities, the abbeys, and so on. Together, these were called the Estates of the Empire, part of the ruling ensemble that made the Empire what it was—a sort of strange aristocratic republic, with many authorities working together under the more or less genial presiding guidance of the Emperor.

Under that Imperial guidance, getting on for a hundred secular princes, fifty or sixty free cities and a similar number of bishops and archbishops *all* issued coinage for their territories. So, beside the Emperor's thaler, we find the Count of Lippe Detmold, who ruled over perhaps only 10,000 to 20,000 people in a tiny part of Westphalia, but who on his coin looks just as grand as the Emperor. He had his own assembly, he could muster his own army, he had his own courts of law and he struck his own money. In short he enjoyed what, in most of the rest of Europe, would be the attributes of sovereignty.

After the secular princes came the Imperial free cities, about fifty or so at this point, which made some very beautiful coins. Cities often take the opportunity to show off their sights, so Cologne presents its cathedral, with its tower, famously unfinished for centuries, topped by a crane to suggest that work would resume one day soon. Among the cities' coins the grandest are surely from Hamburg, the great financial capital of the north, which produced an enormous gold coin, 10 ducats—about 35 grams of gold—showing a panorama of the city, its harbour bristling with sailing ships. Above the masts and behind the spires is the word *Yahweh*, written in Hebrew, to remind you that this prosperous trading city is defended and blessed by God. The whole ideology of wealthy Hamburg, devoutly Protestant and with a strong Jewish community, is expressed in this one coin.

As well as the secular princes and the cities, there are also ecclesiastical coinages. The great prince-bishops and archbishops are of course princes of the highest level, but even quite small units—ecclesiastical abbeys and priories—also had the right to coin. They were not really functioning economic units, so they often made a coin just to show they *could* make a coin, as a sign of their jurisdictional or political authority, rather than as a real economic necessity. The Prior of St. Alban in the Rhineland, for example, who probably only ruled the estates of his abbey, controlling no more than a few thousand subjects, produced splendid golden ducats.

Perhaps counter-intuitively, it was only in the church territories that there was a long tradition of women striking coins. A handful of Imperial abbesses had longstanding coinage rights. So in places like Quedlinburg, in Saxony, you have the rare phenomenon—almost

Silver thaler, Cologne, 1705–11

Gold ten ducats, Hamburg, 1689

Gold ducat, St. Alban, 1744

Silver thaler, Quedlinburg, 1704

unique in Europe—of a succession of female rulers issuing coins. The Abbess of Quedlinburg shown on the coin above illustrates another key element in the functioning of the Holy Roman Empire. She was the daughter of the Duke of Saxe-Weimar, and she and her male relatives, rulers nearby, would usually work together to protect dynastic interests. If German coins demonstrate the extraordinary dispersal of power and authority across many centres, they also reveal the family connections between those centres, which made that dispersal often more apparent than real. There were quite likely to be cousins on different coins. Indeed the same person could appear on multiple coins, because the same person could be bishop in multiple places—for example, we have a silver thaler of Lothar Franz von Schönborn as Archbishop of Mainz and another thaler showing him as Bishop of Bamberg.

When you look at a map of the Holy Roman Empire it is so fragmented and broken up that it is almost impossible to grasp how it might fit together. The coins help us develop some sense of that. But the other thing that is difficult to understand is how it could have got like that, and here again the coins can help. The coin showing Friedrich, Duke of Saxe-Gotha-Altenburg has on the back seven family portraits, because the Duke had seven sons. He split his territories between the seven, who all took the coinage rights with them. So this coin encapsulates the complex disintegrations of territory into

Silver thaler, Bamberg, 1697, showing Schönborn as bishop

Silver thaler, Mainz, 1696, showing Schönborn as archbishop

Gold twelve ducats, Saxe-Gotha-Altenburg, 1723

multiple units, depending on local inheritance laws. Each line would marry, die out or inter-marry with another, so some units would come back together again, but in a new configuration.

You might expect that a currency system so decentralized would cause hopeless confusion. Foreign travellers did complain, but in fact the difficulties were fairly superficial. The gold and silver coins, wherever issued, were struck to fairly standardized systems of weight and subdivided into relatively consistent smaller units. So the silver thaler of the Emperor Leopold, the greatest ruler in Europe, would be worth the same as the silver thaler issued by the Prince of Hanau-Lichtenberg, one of the smaller principalities. And as well as being broadly similar in value and weight, the larger coins would often have on one side a common symbol—the Imperial eagle, showing they were part of an integrated, if not uniform, system. It is quite like the Euro today: in France most Euros look French but you might find an Italian or a German one. Similarly, if you were in Hanover, most of your coins would be the Elector of Hanover's, but you might have one from the Bishop of Paderborn next door, or one from Prussia, but both essentially of similar weight and worth. There was a fundamental consistency across the whole network, all firmly rooted in standards governed by Imperial law. It may have been complex, it may have seemed cumbersome, but, like the Holy Roman Empire itself, somehow it worked.

The story of the Empire's coins is not just a German one. We began with a British monarch, George I, who, beside his British coinage, on which he of course appears by divine grace as sovereign, also has a German coinage in which he appears as Elector of Hanover, a prince of the Holy Roman Empire. From 1714, until the end of the Empire in 1806, the King of Great Britain had a seat in the Imperial Diet. And the Elector of Hanover was not—as the coins show us—alone. The Elector of Brandenburg was King of Prussia, and two successive electors of Saxony, Augustus II and Augustus III, were kings of Poland. Other, totally external, monarchs also held territories in Germany under the Emperor, as Professor R. J. W. Evans describes:

Silver gulden, Wismar, 1673

> "Around the early eighteenth century, pretty much the whole of Europe was being tied into the Empire in this kind of way—Britain, Denmark, Prussia, Sweden, Poland, Bohemia, Hungary, all rulers with crowns outside the Empire, but intimately, functionally, connected to it. Even the Russian ruling house is a German house. So it's a form of much wider political constellation. The security of the Empire is inextricably linked with the security of Europe as a whole. This is a very important way in which, on the one hand, problems of the Empire can be exported, but also the rest of Europe can find it necessary to sustain some kind of order in Germany."

Germany as the pivot of a Europe-wide system of security—it seems a strikingly modern view. As does a Germany with strong regional differences and hesitant central power. For Joachim Whaley, the political practice of the Empire is still a potent force:

> "The system of devolved power, a framework within which localities and provinces are able to flourish without intervention of any kind of central controlling government: that, I think, is a deep legacy. It gives one a sense of the German willingness to compromise, their endless patience with negotiations within the

> European system today. That was very much characteristic of the Holy Roman Empire in the early modern period—for example, the principles of decision-making at the Imperial Diet, the Reichstag, where Emperor and princes and cities would deliberate. What could not be agreed upon by all simply was not enacted at all. In other words, it was a political system which operated by means of compromise."

To look at the coinage of the Holy Roman Empire is to realize how particular the histories of every part of the German-speaking lands are. What becomes clear is how difficult it is to talk about *a* German history. There can in fact only be German histories. Every coin-producing place, even one of these small units of administrative autonomy, has its own history, and many are still very much alive. The autonomy of Bavaria and Saxony, of Hamburg and Bremen, proclaimed in the coins, explains why each of them today is still a separate autonomous *Land* in the Federal Republic of Germany.

Adapting the celebrated paradox used to describe the workings of capitalism—creative destruction—one might describe the Holy Roman Empire as the triumph of creative fragmentation. The fragments know they belong together, are parts of a unit. The only questions are how tightly they should fit together and who is in charge of the process. These are not questions the British or French have been good at either asking or answering. Thanks to the Holy Roman Empire, the Germans have had a thousand years of practice.

Part Two

Imagining Germany

The stories we tell each other and the foods we eat bind our nations. A country as deeply diverse as Germany is held together as much by its poets, painters, prophets and storytellers as by its governments and frontiers. Goethe, Friedrich, Luther and the Brothers Grimm all contribute to Germany's national store of tales sacred and secular, mixtures of history and myth often seasoned with fantasy and humour. Together they have been key elements in building a national identity—along with beer and sausages.

6

A Language for All Germans

On 29 May 1945, three weeks after the end of the war in Europe, the writer Thomas Mann, who had left Germany after Hitler came to power, gave a speech to the Library of Congress in Washington to celebrate his seventieth birthday. In his opening remarks he said:

> Although I am an American citizen, I have remained a German writer, faithful to the German language, which, for me, is my true homeland . . . *meine wahre Heimat.*

What Mann was saying—very movingly—was that even at that moment of Germany's total disintegration, although his physical homeland was lying in ruins, his spiritual homeland remained intact: the German language. That was what indissolubly united Thomas Mann with "Germany and the Germans"—the title of his 1945 speech.

The same thought had, a century and a half earlier, inspired the future Bavarian king, Ludwig I, when in 1807 he first conceived the idea of building a monument to the great figures of history who had spoken German—the Walhalla (see Chapter 9). Ludwig commissioned his Walhalla after the destruction of the Holy Roman Empire and the humiliation of Germany by Napoleon. Both he and Thomas Mann, in times of utter national catastrophe, turned to language as

IN SILENCIO ET SPE ER FORTITVDO VESTRA

Martin Luther and his wife, Katharina von Bora, School of Cranach, 1529

the defining element of their *Heimat*, their homeland, solid ground on which a new and better idea of what it meant to be German could be built.

From the Baltic to the Alps, from the Rhineland to Poland, there are still today many widely differing varieties of spoken German. The fact that all these different dialects of German, some of them barely mutually comprehensible, all share one written form is a remarkable, and politically very significant, fact. Behind that fact stands the achievement of one man: Martin Luther.

In the German Historical Museum in Berlin are two portraits, a husband and a wife. The wife has sharp features. Hair drawn tightly back, she is wearing a crisp, smart, black and white bodice with a black shoelace tie and what must be a very expensive fur-lined jacket. The man is dressed all in black and is much plumper. Several chins jostle above the high collar of the obviously heavy cloth of his jacket. These are Dr. Martin Luther, theologian, and his young wife, Katharina von Bora, painted by their friend Lucas Cranach and his assistants. She had been a nun, he had been a monk. Now happily married, they look comfortable in themselves, at ease with the world. But this man, Martin Luther, in the years after 1517, had turned not just Germany but the whole of Europe upside-down. And in his translation of the Bible into German, he, more than any other single person, created the modern German language. This chapter is about that book—Luther's bible.

By long tradition, saints and holy men have been shown as thin, ascetic, other-worldly. Luther is different. He is clearly a man *in* the world and *of* the people. It was at least partly in defence of the people that, from his position as a theologian at the University of Wittenberg, he wrote his famous Ninety-Five Theses in 1517. The Theses were a protest against corrupt practices in the Church, above all against the sale of Indulgences by the Pope in order to raise money to rebuild St. Peter's in Rome. Luther believed this was a fraud practised on the poor: Indulgence—the forgiveness of sin—was, he held, a free gift that only God could bestow, not something that could be bought and sold. The Ninety-Five Theses began as a parochial scholarly dispute,

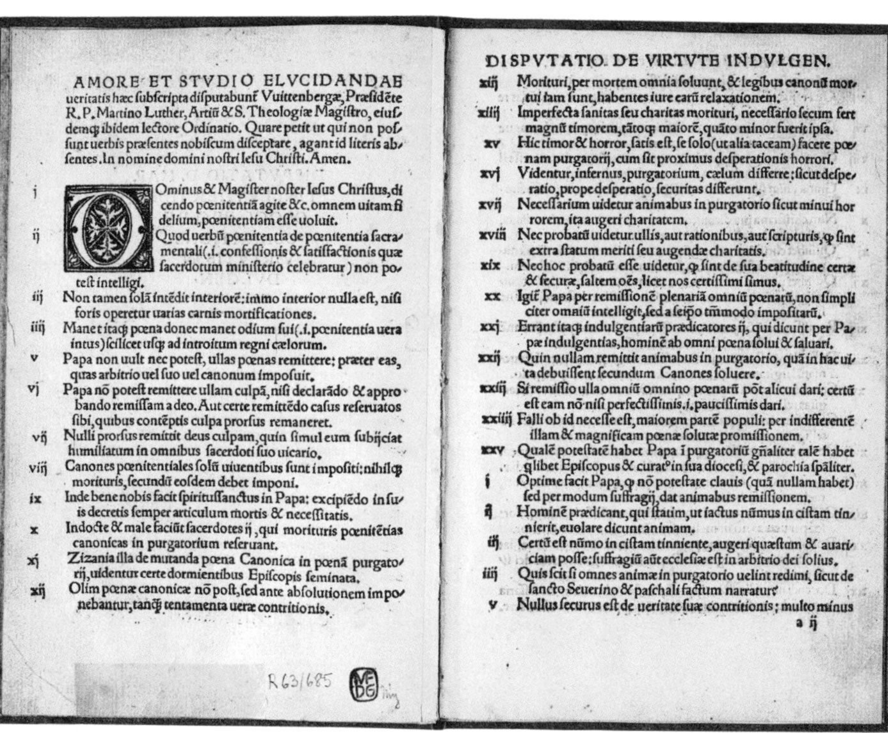

AMORE ET STVDIO ELVCIDANDAE ueritatis hæc ſubſcripta diſputabunt Vuittenbergæ, Præſidēte R. P. Martino Luther, Artiū & S. Theologiæ Magiſtro, eiuſdemqꝫ ibidem lectore Ordinario. Quare petit ut qui non poſſunt uerbis præſentes nobiſcum diſceptare, agant id literis abſentes. In nomine domini noſtri Ieſu Chriſti. Amen.

j Dominus & Magiſter noſter Ieſus Chriſtus, dicendo pœnitentiā agite &c. omnem uitam fidelium, pœnitentiam eſſe uoluit.

ij Quod uerbū pœnitentia de pœnitentia ſacramentali (.i. confeſſionis & ſatiſfactionis quæ ſacerdotum miniſterio celebratur) non poteſt intelligi.

iij Non tamen ſolā intēdit interiorē; immo interior nulla eſt, niſi foris operetur uarias carnis mortificationes.

iiij Manet itaqꝫ pœna donec manet odium ſui (.i. pœnitentia uera intus) ſcilicet uſqꝫ ad introitum regni cælorum.

v Papa non uult nec poteſt, ullas pœnas remittere; præter eas, quas arbitrio uel ſuo uel canonum impoſuit.

vj Papa nō poteſt remittere ullam culpā, niſi declarādo & approbando remiſſam a deo. Aut certe remittēdo caſus reſeruatos ſibi, quibus contēptis culpa prorſus remaneret.

vij Nulli prorſus remittit deus culpam, quin ſimul eum ſubijciat humiliatum in omnibus ſacerdoti ſuo uicario.

viij Canones pœnitentiales ſolū uiuentibus ſunt impoſiti; nihilqꝫ morituris, ſecundū eoſdem debet imponi.

ix Inde bene nobis facit ſpirituſſanctus in Papa: excipiēdo in ſuis decretis ſemper articulum mortis & neceſſitatis.

x Indocte & male faciūt ſacerdotes ij, qui morituris pœnitētias canonicas in purgatorium reſeruant.

xj Zizania illa de mutanda pœna Canonica in pœnā purgatorij, uidentur certe dormientibus Epiſcopis ſeminata.

xij Olim pœnæ canonicæ nō poſt, ſed ante abſolutionem imponebantur, tanꝗ tentamenta ueræ contritionis.

R63/685

DISPVTATIO DE VIRTVTE INDVLGEN.

xiij Morituri, per mortem omnia ſoluunt, & legibus canonū mortui iam ſunt, habentes iure earū relaxationem.

xiiij Imperfecta ſanitas ſeu charitas morituri, neceſſario ſecum fert magnū timorem, tātoqꝫ maiorē, quāto minor fuerit ipſa.

xv Hic timor & horror, ſatis eſt, ſe ſolo (ut alia taceam) facere pœnam purgatorij, cum ſit proximus deſperationis horrori.

xvj Videntur, infernus, purgatorium, cælum differre; ſicut deſperatio, prope deſperatio, ſecuritas differunt.

xvij Neceſſarium uidetur animabus in purgatorio ſicut minui horrorem, ita augeri charitatem.

xviij Nec probatū uidetur ullis, aut rationibus, aut ſcripturis, ꝙ ſint extra ſtatum meriti ſeu augendæ charitatis.

xix Nec hoc probatū eſſe uidetur, ꝙ ſint de ſua beatitudine certæ & ſecuræ, ſaltem oēs, licet nos certiſſimi ſimus.

xx Igit͛ Papa per remiſſionē plenariā omniū pœnarū, non ſimpliciter omniū intelligit, ſed a ſeipo tm̄modo impoſitarū.

xxj Errant itaqꝫ indulgentiarū prædicatores ij, qui dicunt per Papæ indulgentias, hominē ab omni pœna ſolui & ſaluari.

xxij Quin nullam remittit animabus in purgatorio, quā in hac uita debuiſſent ſecundum Canones ſoluere.

xxiij Si remiſſio ulla omniū omnino pœnarū pōt alicui dari; certū eſt eam nō niſi perfectiſſimis .i. pauciſſimis dari.

xxiiij Falli ob id neceſſe eſt, maiorem partē populi: per indifferentē illam & magnificam pœnæ ſolutæ promiſſionem.

xxv Qualē poteſtatē habet Papa ī purgatoriū gn̄aliter talē habet ꝗlibet Epiſcopus & curat⁹ in ſua dioceſi, & parochia ſpāliter.

j Optime facit Papa, ꝙ nō poteſtate clauis (quā nullam habet) ſed per modum ſuffragij, dat animabus remiſſionem.

ij Hominē prædicant, qui ſtatim, ut iactus nūmus in ciſtam tinnierit, euolare dicunt animam.

iij Certū eſt nūmo in ciſtam tinniente, augeri quæſtum & auariciam poſſe; ſuffragiū aūt eccleſiæ eſt in arbitrio dei ſolius.

iiij Quis ſcit ſi omnes animæ in purgatorio uelint redimi, ſicut de ſancto Seuerino & paſchali factum narratur?

v Nullus ſecurus eſt de ueritate ſuæ contritionis; multo minus

a ij

Luther's Ninety-Five Theses, published in 1517

but they launched a process that inspired—and then split—Western Christendom.

Sixteenth-century Germany was, as we have seen in the last three chapters, a mosaic of hundreds of states and statelets, governed by kings, electors, dukes, prince-bishops and a host of minor nobles, all holding their territories under the Emperor, divided by rivalries and intermittently united by changing alliances. The Reformation soon forced every ruler to choose: Catholic or Protestant. It created political crises, constitutional conflicts and religious and cultural divides that have in some cases lasted until today.

Compromise did not come easily to Luther, who is often in German history seen as the Great Divider (see Chapter 9). His attacks on his opponents were pitiless, often violent and shockingly brutal in tone, not least his virulent writings against the Jews. For some he bears responsibility for the long and bitter religious struggles that

followed the Reformation, and—even a century after his death—for the Thirty Years' War. For some, too, his anti-Semitism made a dire contribution to events in the twentieth century. But he is also, unquestionably, the Great Uniter. The language he forged, a powerful weapon in the disputes and disagreements of the sixteenth century, is a bond that holds all Germans together.

Luther's Ninety-Five Theses were condemned as heretical, but it is unlikely that he intended a public confrontation over them. He originally wrote them in Latin, and the controversy might never have happened if some of his friends had not translated them into German and had them printed. Although the printing press had been invented only in the 1450s, it is estimated that by this date there were over 3,000 printing shops in about 300 centres in Germany and central

Luther (at the bar centre right) appearing before the Emperor and electors at the Diet of Worms, April 1521

Europe. As a result, within a couple of weeks, Luther's Ninety-Five Theses were being read all over Germany.

The word of God was priceless, but printing it was cheap. Luther's ideas spread much more quickly than the Catholic Church could react. In 1521 Luther was summoned to appear before the young Holy Roman Emperor, Charles V, at the Diet of Worms and instructed to recant. In words which he probably never used, but which became part of the Luther myth which every German knows, he refused: "Here I stand. I can do no other. So help me God." He was declared a heretic by the Church and an outlaw by the Emperor. If such a thing had happened in England or France, that might well have been the end of him. In centralized kingdoms like these, there were few places to hide, and Luther could easily have been burnt at

The Elector Frederick III of Saxony, 1532

the stake, as many English heretics were. But in the political patchwork quilt of Germany, it was much more complicated. The writ of the Church, even if officially endorsed by the Emperor, ran only when local rulers chose to enforce it. In 1521, Saxony, where Luther lived and worked, decided not to follow the Emperor's lead. The Elector of Saxony spirited Luther away from Worms to safety in the Wartburg Castle in Eisenach.

It was in his solitary cell in the Wartburg that Martin Luther, forcibly removed from public debate but more than ever convinced of his calling, embarked on his translation of the New Testament. There had been German bibles before Luther, quite a few of them in fact—Albrecht Dürer's godfather, Anton Koberger, had published one in Nuremberg, others had appeared in Strasbourg and Augsburg, each in the local German. In Cologne two separate translations were published, in the two different dialects spoken in the region round the city.

None of these had much resonance beyond their locality. All of them had been banned by the Catholic Church. The Archbishop of Mainz (who received a percentage on all the Indulgences sold in his

Opposite: The Wartburg Castle, high above Eisenach

territories) claimed that the German language was simply too poor, too coarse, to convey the scriptures. Luther determined he would find a German that was both fit for the word of God and fit to be read by ordinary Germans.

Working with characteristic boundless energy, Luther completed his task in just eleven weeks. With matching dynamism, the Wittenberg printer Melchior Lotter organized double shifts on his presses. By the end of September 1522, Luther's German New Testament was being offered at the Leipzig Book Fair and distributed across Germany. It sold out almost at once. A second edition was needed within three months. Within a year there were twelve more authorized editions and over fifty pirated versions. No German text had sold in numbers like these since Gutenberg had invented the printing press seventy years earlier (see Chapter 16). Luther then turned his attention to the—much larger—task of translating the Old Testament. In 1534 the whole Bible was published in Luther's German.

Susan Reed, Lead Curator of Germanic Studies at the British Library, discusses one of the Luther bibles in her care:

> "He translated the New Testament very quickly. Then throughout the next decade he worked on the Old Testament. That took him a lot longer. He was working with Hebrew rather than with Greek, rather less familiar territory, and, of course, the Old Testament is longer. This one dates from 1541. It is known as the 'Medianbibel' (Medium Bible), because it is a slightly deluxe edition, larger than some of the earlier versions. It is one of ten editions of the complete Bible, printed between 1534 and Luther's death in 1546. This one was the first really to reflect a very thorough revision that Luther and his associates, particularly Aurogallos and Melanchthon, undertook between 1539 and 1541."

Inside the front cover is a handwritten text which is signed by Martin Luther himself. Susan Reed:

> "He is quoting the first line of the 23rd Psalm: 'Der Herr ist mein Hirt, mir wird nichts mangeln'—'The Lord is my shepherd, I

shall not want.' And he signs and dates it 1542. Beside that are signed inscriptions by the other translators. There are a few other copies that exist with similar inscriptions. This is a deluxe edition, so they may have done some signed copies to circulate or give to particular people—like this other copy here, which has only got an inscription by Luther with another quotation from the 23rd Psalm: 'Und ob ich wandern müßte im finstern Tal, fürcht ich mich doch nicht denn du bist bei mir'—'Though I walk in the valley of the shadow of death, yet shall I fear nothing.' Interestingly, that is not actually the translation as it appears in the printed bible. He has done it from memory, and has misremembered it."

The two British Library bibles, each with its inscription in Luther's hand, show how keen he was that copies should reach influential readers.

Alexander Weber is a philologist at Birkbeck College in London who has studied the language Luther used in his translation:

"He was a man of incredible learning, but he was also someone who could connect with ordinary people and who could pick up their use of language and that is exceptional. He was the son of a miner and he had very good knowledge of the use of colloquial language—you can imagine that the result of making the characters within the Bible speak like German peasants could have ended up being quite farcical. But quite the opposite was the case—it brought the Bible to life. This was because the formula was different from previous translations, which were very learned, very stilted, very educated and only understood properly by the people who knew the Latin Bible, the Vulgate, by heart anyway. The new format was Luther's success. He had this ability to handle the onslaught of the Catholic Church on his theology but at the same time speak to the general public. He modelled his written German on the spoken word: that is key. If you want to start writing, then one of the first guidelines to follow is: write the way you speak, and if you write a sentence, think about

Ps 23

Der HERR ist mein hirte · Mir wird nichts mangeln ·

Wers gleuben kündte · der were ein selig · fett · sicher Schaf
dieses trewen hirten · der auch sein Leben hat fur solche
schafe gesetzt   Wehe dem schendlichen unglauben
der solchem hirten nicht folget · Und lieber wil vom
wolffe gefressen sein zum ewigen Tode

Martinus Luther D

1542

The front endpaper of Luther's 1541 bible with portraits of Luther and Johannes Bugenhagen and Luther's transcription from the 23rd Psalm and signature

> whether a living human being would actually say such a thing, and if they would not, rewrite it. The genius of Luther was that the more he edited it, the more spontaneous and true to life it sounded. Luther's translation is immensely readable, it is vivid, credible, authentic."

How did Luther do it? He tells us, quite straightforwardly, in his *Open Letter on Translation*, which he published in 1530. He was not trying to translate word for word from the Latin or the Greek. He was trying to write in living German:

> You don't ask Latin literature how to speak German, you ask the mother at home, the children in the street, the common man in the market—look at how *they* speak, and translate accordingly. Then they will understand it, and they will see you are speaking German to them.

It is hard to know which is more revolutionary, a scholar refusing academic diction in favour of the language of the street or the order in which the intended audience is listed: women, children and—lastly—men. This language has a new purpose: to speak to everybody. The Gospel will be translated not as theology, but as conversations you might overhear in the streets or on the quaysides—Jesus speaking as a German carpenter to German fishermen.

It was not what the ecclesiastical hierarchy were used to. It gave the Gospel, if not yet power, to the people. The Luther bible ran to an astonishing half a million copies in his lifetime, truly a best-seller of its day. But how was it that it could sell all over Germany, in that collection of heterogeneous states, with their motley of regional dialects? German is split into what are called *High* and *Low,* or Upper and Lower, German. As an aide-memoire, it is sometimes stated that the mountains are high, the seas are low: so English, Dutch and the dialects of north Germany are *Low* German; the dialects of south Germany and Switzerland belong to *High* German.

An inhabitant of Salzburg in Luther's time spoke a form of High German that would be almost incomprehensible to someone from

Frankfurt, who spoke Franconian, and totally incomprehensible to someone from Hamburg, a speaker of Low German, and vice versa. That is still more or less the case today except that there is now a common language, the *Hochsprache*—standard German—the language that Luther created, as Alexander Weber explains:

> "We know from Luther's letters and conversations that he modelled his language on the language of the Chancery of Saxony, which is in the middle of Germany, to the east, where the dialects are not that extreme to begin with. There is a main dividing line, it is like a linguistic border, which divides High German from Low German and Luther moved across these borders as a child, with his parents, and he was totally bilingual. He spoke both Low German and High German as a native speaker. It is a stroke of luck in terms of the development of the German language that the key figure who had a major historical impact on the Reformation would actually be able to address an audience in Low German and High German and therefore find a balance between the two."

Luther's carefully crafted compromise language could more or less be understood everywhere. The vocabulary was often aggressively simple—he deliberately avoided high-flown words and used local idioms and folk sayings from everyday life (although a 1523 Basel edition of his New Testament, for example, contains a glossary, in case some of the words are strange). The syntax and word order were devised for clarity when the text was read aloud. Much of this work of finding a more widely graspable form of the language had already been done by the Saxon Chancery, whose model of spelling, grammar and sentence construction Luther adopted. But while Luther used this bureaucratic form of High German as a base, he rejected convoluted syntax or Latinate flourishes. In the process he made the language pithy, vigorous and expressive, with a catchy verve and rhythm.

The 1534 bible was a triumph of translation but no less a masterpiece of marketing. To present a complex theological view, Luther was able to find a language which the widest public could understand,

a tone that spoke directly and without condescension, and a style that was serious and at times poetic. And on top of all this, his old friend the artist Lucas Cranach, who had painted him and his wife, provided illustrations. No wonder this bible was a best-seller.

The success of the Luther bible was evident early on—at least two Catholic translations were rushed out to compete with it. These were full of notes on Luther's supposed errors and "false interpretations," of language and theology, but they were themselves largely based on Luther's translation and used Luther's new form of the German language to challenge his ideas and criticize his writings. The Reformation produced great controversies all over Germany, controversies which filled pamphlets that were printed in their thousands—and were printed in *Luther*'s German. So, as his ideas spread, his particular form of the language did also. The remarkable thing is that in the south, where his staunchest Catholic opponents were, and where German dialects are most obviously different, those opponents found that they had to use *his* language to counter *his* arguments. Thus, perversely, because of the depth and duration of the religious disagreements, the language of Luther became the language of all Germany, Catholic and Protestant. By the end of the sixteenth century, written German throughout the Holy Roman Empire was the German of the Luther bible. Alexander Weber says Luther's German influenced in equal measure the language of the street and of the literary salon:

> "The revolution of the Reformation was to say that Jesus was a figure from the ordinary people, and that you have to reconnect the understanding of the Bible and the biblical story with ordinary life. There are very many phrases and words that are used in German which you can trace back to Luther. The whole of German literary history is based on Luther's language and there are a lot of phrases which he coined or made popular. If you make a wordlist of the Luther bible, and then look at the great poems of the seventeenth century and the literature of the eighteenth

---

Opposite: One of Cranach's illustrations for the first complete edition of Luther's bible

> century, you can trace back a very large proportion of the language that was used to the Bible. That was the benchmark they used, the only model they had. There was nothing else in German that you could refer to."

For 500 years, all great German writers—Goethe, Nietzsche, Brecht, Mann—have honed their language on, and against, Luther's.

Thanks to the printing press, Luther's ideas also spread internationally: within two months of their appearance in Wittenberg, they were being read across all Europe. The sixteenth-century Church could no more control this new technology than a twenty-first-century government can control social media. Combined with social and political changes it ensured that Luther's local religious project convulsed the continent. Alexander Weber:

> "It's the combination of factors: the printing press as a new medium, the historical stage of development in the history of the German language, the theological and social political revolution of the Reformation—all these things happened at the same time and Luther was the great genius and catalyst that combined all these forces and spread them across the whole of Germany. Take one of these factors out—take out the printing press, the explosive situation of the Reformation, or the particular stage of development that the German language was at—and this revolution would not have happened. There is real individuality to the style and the language in which Luther writes. It shows for once that the individual in history matters. For Luther what mattered most was faith, and he saw the loss of faith around him. Everything else—the impact on the German language—is a by-product of his concern for the Christian faith."

There were other factors at work as well. The political protection given to Luther in the soon-to-be Protestant states of the Empire meant that both he and the printing presses there were safe. The fragmentation of power prevented an effective campaign of suppression. By contrast, in 1526 Lutheran books were burnt in England.

And ten years later, William Tyndale, one of Luther's great admirers, was executed by strangulation for producing an English translation of the Bible that drew heavily on Luther's.

The final crucial factor was literacy. Germans were generally more literate than many other Europeans. Each small state had its own literate bureaucracy. The complex network of markets and fairs had led to the development of hundreds of trading centres with a literate merchant class, people who could afford to pay one gulden for a Luther bible—that is, two months' salary for a schoolmaster or the cost of a calf at market. It has been estimated that one in five homes bought a copy of Luther's bible. It would often be the only book in the house. As one of his most effective and eloquent adversaries, Johannes Cochlaeus, gloomily observed:

> Even tailors and shoemakers, even women and other simple folk who have learned to read a bit of German, read it with great eagerness, as though it were a font of truth. Some touched it to their breast and learnt it by heart.

Today even Germans who have never seen, let alone touched, a Luther bible unknowingly use its words and phrases every day. *Sündenbock* (scapegoat) and *Herzenslust* (heart's content) are just two of the many new words he created and which are now standard German. *Der Geist ist willig, aber das Fleisch ist schwach* (The spirit is willing but the flesh is weak), *Richtet nicht, damit ihr nicht gerichtet werdet* (Judge not, lest ye be judged) and *Ein Land, wo Milch und Honig fliessen* (A land flowing with milk and honey)—just a few of the phrases so familiar they have become proverbial. Luther didn't just catch the way ordinary German people spoke, he also shaped the way they would speak. In the hands of storytellers over the following centuries, and in the pages of Goethe, Luther's German became one of the great literary languages of the world.

It also took on a quite different global existence, because Luther not only provided a German to be read, but also a German to be sung. He began the great tradition of the chorale, music suited for congregational singing that did not require a specialist choir. This,

J. N. J.

nach S. Herrn D. MARTINI LUTHERI
Deutscher Dolmetschung/ und Erklärung/
vermöge des Heil. Geistes/
im Grund-Text/
Richtiger Anleitung der Cohærentz,
Und der gantzen Handlung eines jeglichen Texts/
Auch Vergleichung der gleichlautenden Sprüche/ enthaltenen
eigenen Sinn und Meinung/
Nechst ordentlicher Eintheilung eines jeden Buches und Capitels/
und Erwegung der nachdrücklichen Wort/ und Redens-Art
in der Heil. Sprache/
sonderlich aber
Der Evangelischen allein seligmachenden Warheit/
gründ- und deutlich erörtert/
und mit Anführung
Herrn LUTHERI deutschen/ und verdeutschten Schrifften/
also abgefasset/
daß der eigentliche Buchstäbliche Verstand/
und gutes Theils auch
der heilsame Gebrauch der Heil. Schrifft
fürgestellet ist/
Mit grossem Fleiß/ und Kosten ausgearbeitet/
und verfasset/
von
D. ABRAHAM CALOVIO,
Im Jahr Christi cIↃ IↃc XXCI.
welches ist das 1681
5 6 8 1ste Jahr/ von Erschaffung der Welt.
Zu Wittenberg/
Nicht uns HERR/ nicht uns/ sondern deinem Namen gib Ehre/
umb deiner Gnade und Warheit!

Gedruckt in Wittenberg/ bey Christian Schrödtern/ der Univ. Buchdr.

JSBach 1733

like the Bible translation, was to be music for the people, not the privileged. He was himself a gifted creator of both words and music and many of Luther's chorales remain in use today, perhaps above all "Ein' feste Burg ist unser Gott" ("A Mighty Fortress Is Our God"), based on Psalm 46. In Eisenach, where Luther translated the New Testament in the solitude of the Wartburg, stands the Gothic Georgenkirche. Separated by two centuries, two boy choristers sang there, both products of the same Latin school: Martin Luther and Johann Sebastian Bach, perhaps the two greatest Saxons ever. In that church, week after week, the young Bach absorbed the words and rhythms of Luther's bible, until they became entirely his own. Later, he would own two complete sets of Luther's writings. Along with the many great works of literature which could not have come into being without Luther's bible, we must also count many of the cantatas and oratorios, and above all the Passions of Johann Sebastian Bach.

Opposite: The title-page of J. S. Bach's copy of the Luther bible, signed by Bach and dated 1733 (bottom right)

Snow White in the Forest, engraved by Ludwig Emil Grimm, 1825

7

Snow White vs. Napoleon

Rapunzel was the most beautiful child in the world. When she was twelve years old the witch shut her up in a tower in the midst of a wood.

When Little Red Riding Hood entered the woods a wolf came up to her. She did not know what a wicked animal he was, and was not afraid of him.

Near a great forest there lived a poor woodcutter and his wife, and his two children; the boy's name was Hansel and the girl's Gretel.

At last the Queen sent for a huntsman, and said, "Take Snow White out into the woods, so that I may set eyes on her no more. You must put her to death, and bring me her heart for a token."

Most of us know these stories. The words have the lyrical ring of the nursery rhyme: "Rapunzel, Rapunzel, let down your hair," "Mirror, mirror, on the wall, who is the fairest of them all?" Rapunzel, Snow White, Hansel and Gretel—the characters in the *Fairy Tales of the Brothers Grimm* are part of our childhood. What befalls them—the events, the adventures—we remember with fondness, and a shiver.

But they all share one characteristic: the action is firmly set in the woods, dark and forbidding. That is where character is demonstrated and evil is overcome. These fairy tales tell the fate of imaginary figures, but they are also about the destiny of Germany. The Grimms' fairy tales reflect national politics and indeed fears and hopes about the fate of the Germans. And one of the great traditions, or myths, of Germany is that its origins and destiny were forged—like Hansel and Gretel's—in the forest.

Archetypally Germanic is the Teutoburger Wald, the Teutoburg Forest, about sixty miles north-east of Cologne. There are conifers, beech and oak. It is immense—green and dense, frightening and dark, with cosy log cabins and alarming wild animals. If you lose your way, you might never be seen again. It is a place of enormous national significance, for in A.D. 9 the Teutoburg Forest was the site of the great German victory over Rome, grimly reported by the Latin historian Tacitus. A massive Roman army had invaded, intent on conquering and colonizing Germany east of the Rhine. The warrior Hermann, leading an alliance of German tribes, wiped the Romans out. The forest remained in German hands; the Rhine became the frontier of the Roman Empire; the rest of Germany remained unconquered. Here, in the Teutoburg Forest, so the patriotic legend runs, a nation was born out of resistance to Roman aggression and occupation.

Jumping forward to the early 1800s, both literature and painting set out to create a sense of German-ness, as a response to foreign aggression, and both of them are also often linked to the forest. In the first decade of the nineteenth century, the aggressors were not the Romans, but their Gaulish successors, the French. And this time the French had not only attacked the Germans: they had conquered them, dismantled the Holy Roman Empire of the German nation, and occupied their homeland, from the Rhine to the Russian border.

One book still found in almost every German home is the *Kinder- und Hausmärchen—Children's and Household Tales*—as told by

---

Opposite: *The Chasseur in the Forest,* by Caspar David Friedrich, 1814

Early editions of *Children's and Household Tales*, by the Brothers Grimm

Jakob and Wilhelm Grimm. The Grimm brothers collected these folk tales all their lives and they produced many editions of the book. They first appeared in 1812, just as the military resistance to Napoleon was gathering strength. But the Grimms were not interested in them merely as children's stories: their real obsession was the one thing all Germans share—their language.

Words were in their DNA. They were pioneers of the study of language and its origins. Jakob Grimm formulated what became known as Grimm's Law, the first rule about sound change discovered in linguistics, tracing the shifting of consonants between languages—why English-speakers say *fish* and *father,* Germans *Fisch, Vater,* while the Romans said *pisces, pater.* It was a new way of thinking about language. But, above all, the Grimm brothers immersed themselves in the history of German. The creation of a German dictionary, their *Deutsches Wörterbuch*, dominated their lives.

Professor Steffen Martus from Berlin's Humboldt University has published extensively on the Grimm brothers, and explains that they saw a close connection between how the German language worked and how German society functioned best:

> "What is interesting about the Grimms' research into language as well as into literary history is that they were trying to discover what could be described as 'German,' but always in an international context. If we look at their work on German grammar, for example, it is interesting how much time Jakob Grimm spent getting to understand that a language operates according to its own internal laws, that those laws are not shaped by outside forces, and that a language is an autonomous, living organism.
>
> "This concept had political significance: the Grimms were saying that, just as a language has its own internal form and logic, so do societies and communities. Laws cannot successfully be imposed from outside. Political, social and linguistic history are in that sense interchangeable. Changes in German society, then, will be effective only if they come from within, in keeping with the German way of doing things, not from foreign imposition."

In other words, the Grimms' fairy tales were part of a German political and social renaissance, evidence that in their language and their folk tales the Germans had an identity which no foreign invader could eradicate. By 1812, France had conquered and occupied all of Germany and had annexed great stretches of the Rhineland, and Cologne was a city in France. But the Brothers Grimm saw that Germany had something of immense value which the French could not claim—an antiquity of language reaching back to the mists of prehistory. This, according to Will Vaughan, Emeritus Professor of Art History at Birkbeck College in London, is what lay behind their fascination with philology, the study of language:

> "The idea that Germans had kept their original language was very important—that somehow the German language was expressive of the whole German character and psyche, because it had been

---

Overleaf: *The Solitary Tree*, by Caspar David Friedrich, 1822

> the language that Germans had always spoken. One of the things that the Grimms said in their famous dictionary was: what do we have in common but our language? In the Napoleonic period there was a lot of comparing between French and German. It was claimed that the French had not kept their original language—they were now speaking a version of Latin and the original language that the Celts had spoken had been lost. So there was not this visceral connection between the French and their language that there was between the Germans and theirs."

Hansel and Gretel, Snow White and the other tales collected by the Grimms are not just spine-tingling yarns. In the very words, phrases and syntax is the enduring story of the German self.

The forest is as powerful a force in the painting of the period as in the literature, as we can see in a work by the great romantic painter Caspar David Friedrich, *Der Einsame Baum*, or *The Solitary Tree*, painted in 1822. In the middle distance, set in a gentle green plain, is a village; in the background, a mountain range. And in the centre, in the foreground, dominating the composition, is a lone oak, its upper part battered and damaged, its lower branches in full leaf, giving shelter to a shepherd and his flock. Will Vaughan has studied the significance of this painting for German national consciousness. It brings us back to the Grimms and the forest:

> "Oak is at the root of the imagery for Germans as a people who had survived all sorts of hardship. The oak tree was part of the primitive landscape. It had always been there and Germans felt that it was part of them, that it defined them in a certain way. When Hermann defeated the Romans in the Teutoburg Forest it was almost as though the forest was on the side of the Germans—they had set an ambush up for the Romans, hiding behind the trees. It is very striking that the freedom fighters of the Wars of Liberation, against Napoleon, also used the forest, and there is a wonderful picture by G. F. Kersting, a friend of Friedrich's, called *At the Sentry Post*, that shows three of them leaning against oak trees, waiting for the French to come. Anyone in those days

At the Sentry Post, by Georg Friedrich Kersting, 1815

> would have immediately been able to feel a national identity with the oak. Friedrich had used the oak earlier, during the Napoleonic period, for other kinds of images, but as one of a group of oaks, surrounding old graves of the ancient Germanic type—a kind of heroic monument. What is interesting in this painting is that now it is an oak standing on its own, so it has a much greater sense of loneliness than before. Maybe the painter was expressing a personal feeling here—he is the lonely old oak; or maybe he was appealing to people who shared his radical sympathies and were hoping the oak would endure."

The oak tree was an image taken up by Germany's rulers on more than one occasion as an emblem of survival and rebirth: oak leaves on the Iron Cross in 1813, for instance (see Chapter 14), and on the country's first post-1945 coins. Friedrich's lonely oak, battered but still standing, offers shelter and nourishment in the early-morning light. It has come through the night. It has weathered the storm. Like Germany after the Napoleonic wars, it has survived.

The Grimms were studying the German language: the inner German-ness present in the folk tales they collected. Friedrich used landscape as an external vision of being German. Constable was doing something similar at the same date with his pictures of England—the *Hay Wain*, *Flatford Mill* and so on—and in each case there is an element of invention, which merely heightens the impact of these powerful national images, where landscape fuses with fantasy. Friedrich

One-Pfennig coin with oak leaves, West Germany, 1949

spent his life painting wild, sublime landscapes in which the individual discovers his potential and the nation does the same. Will Vaughan:

> "Friedrich still remains a very important artist in Germany today, because he represented the German soul in the landscape. He is a painter of the inner world as well as the outer world: it is not just the literal terrain that is being shown you, but the landscape perceived through a German soul, so it has an emotive charge to it."

In Friedrich's paintings the trees are sublime, in the Grimms' fairy tales the forest is threatening. Both are editing the German landscape for their own purposes. But, as Steffen Martus tells us, they are doing more than that: they are *inventing* the German landscape:

> "The German forests that we know today—huge woods with fir trees, and the other typical German broad-leaved trees—these were just as much an invention of Romanticism as were the fairy tales. Today's German forests largely originated through reforestation later in the nineteenth century, and this romantic woodland project became the backdrop for literature, for fairy tales and the like. The Grimms use the forest as a kind of double-edged sword. What happens in the forest in their fairy tales is often quite dreadful, quite cruel, and this is intended to frighten children, so that, at the end of the tale, they can be calmed and comforted by their mother's voice."

This was a particular kind of social engineering with strong political overtones. Good and evil faced each other off in the fairy tales—the children against the evil witch, the wicked stepmother, pretending to be kind. But always, waiting at the end of the storytelling, the *bürgerliche Mutti*, the bourgeois German mother, with her comforting words. Solid German virtues, encoded in the language, in the stories and ultimately in the people themselves. Steffen Martus says there was a strong, and in the later editions increasingly moralistic, element in Grimms' fairy tales, driven by the growing middle class in Germany:

> "These fairy tales were not just transcribed to make for good literature with a strong poetic element, they are also morality tales. They were edited and re-edited to fit the readers' tastes, a readership that knew romantic literature and wanted to bring up their children in the *bürgerliche Kleinfamilie*, the bourgeois nuclear family. This led to certain changes to the stories over time. In the early editions, the evil women were often mothers, as in the case of Snow White, for example, but later editions turned them into stepmothers: you could not have a real mother being evil in a proper bourgeois family. Take another famous story—Rapunzel. In the first edition of the tales, the evil fairy works out that Rapunzel must be having visits from men. How does she know? Rapunzel's clothes get too tight—she is pregnant. In later editions Wilhelm Grimm deletes this whole section from the story and makes Rapunzel contradict herself to the fairy, which is how she realizes men must have been visiting. Rapunzel has been desexualized and made respectable. These are Victorian values, German style, which is one reason the stories so appealed to the British as well."

Friedrich and the Grimms were re-establishing an identity for German-speaking people who had been dislocated when Napoleon destroyed the old Holy Roman Empire and the political structures that depended on it. They were providing an answer to the question: who are we now? Painters, historians and writers started to look back to Hermann, as a founding national figure. In 1808, Heinrich von Kleist wrote *Die Hermannsschlacht*, a play about that great battle in the Teutoburg Forest in which the Romans were defeated. It is a pretty terrible piece, mostly leaden anti-Napoleonic propaganda, which has gone virtually unperformed, although Friedrich was much moved by it. But Hermann, the romantic hero resurrected from the pages of Tacitus, has never lost his hold on the German imagination.

Today, over 100,000 visitors a year come to admire the colossal statue of Hermann that stands in the Teutoburg Forest, just outside the town of Detmold. Nearly ninety feet high, the bronze figure brandishes his sword—needless to say in the direction of France. Begun

RAPUNZEL

nach Grimm von Otto Speckter 1857

Es war einmal ein Mann und eine Frau, die wünschten sich lange vergeblich ein Kind, endlich machte sich die Frau Hoffnung, der liebe Gott werde ihren Wunsch erfüllen. Die Leute hatten in ihrem Hinterhaus ein Fenster, daraus konnte man in einen Garten sehen, der voll schöner Blumen und Kräuter stand, er war aber von einer Mauer umgeben, und niemand wagte hineinzugehen, weil er einer bösen Zauberin gehörte, die von aller Welt gefürchtet wurde. Eines Tages stand die Frau am Fenster und sah in den Garten hinab, da erblickte sie ein Beet mit den schönsten Rapunzeln bepflanzt, die sahen so frisch und grün aus, daß sie lüstern wurde und das größte Verlangen empfand, von den Rapunzeln zu essen. Das Verlangen nahm jeden Tag zu, und da sie wußte, daß sie keine davon bekommen konnte, so fiel sie ganz ab und sah blaß und elend aus; da erschrak der Mann und fragte: „Was fehlt Dir, liebe Frau?" „Ach," antwortete sie, „wenn ich keine Rapunzel aus dem Garten zu essen bekomme, so sterbe ich!" Der Mann, der sie gar lieb hatte, dachte, ehe du deine Frau sterben lässest, holst du ihr von den Rapunzeln, es mag kosten, was es will! In der Abenddämmerung stieg er über die Mauer in den Garten der Zauberin, stach in aller Eile einen Korb voll Rapunzel; er wollte eben damit fort, da erschrak er gewaltig, denn er sah die Zauberin hinter sich stehen. „Wie kannst Du es wagen," sagte sie zornig, „in meinen Garten wie ein Dieb zu kommen und mir meine Rapunzeln zu stehlen?" „Ach," antwortete er, „ungern hab' ich mich dazu entschlossen; meine Frau hat Eure Rapunzeln erblickt und hat ein so großes Gelüste darnach, daß sie sterben würde, wenn sie nicht davon zu essen bekäme." Da ließ die Zauberin in ihrem Zorne nach und sprach: „Verhält es sich so, so will ich Dir gestatten, Rapunzeln mitzunehmen so viel Du willst, allein ich mache eine Bedingung, Du mußt mir das Kind geben, das Ihr bekommen werdet." Der Mann sagte in der Angst alles zu, und als die Frau in die Wochen kam, so erschien gleich die Zauberin, gab dem Kinde den Namen Rapunzel und nahm es mit sich.

Rapunzel wurde das schönste Kind unter der Sonne. Als es zwölf Jahre alt war, schloß es die Zauberin in einen verlassenen Turm der Stadtmauer, der weder Treppen noch Tür hatte. Wenn die Zauberin hinauf wollte, so stellte sie sich unten hin und rief: „Rapunzel, Rapunzel, laß Dein Haar herunter!" Rapunzel hatte lange prächtige Haare, fein wie Gold. Wenn sie die Stimme der Zauberin vernahm, so band sie ihre Zöpfe los, schlug sie oben um einen Haken, dann fielen die Haare zwanzig Ellen tief herunter, und die Zauberin stieg daran hinauf. Nach ein paar Jahren trug es sich zu, daß der Sohn des Königs an dem Turme vorüber kam. Da hörte er einen Gesang, der war so lieblich, daß er stille hielt und horchte. Das war Rapunzel, die in ihrer Einsamkeit sich die Zeit damit vertrieb, ihre süße Stimme erschallen zu lassen. Der Königssohn suchte vergeblich nach einer Tür des Turmes, der Gesang hatte ihm aber so sehr das Herz gerührt, daß er jeden Tag hinausging und darauf horchte. Als er einmal im Gesträuch lauerte, sah er die Zauberin herankommen und hörte wie sie rief: „Rapunzel, laß Dein Haar herunter!" Alsbald fielen die Haare herab und die Zauberin stieg zu ihr hinauf. „Ist das die Leiter, auf welcher man hinauf kommt," sprach der Königssohn, „so will ich mein Glück auch versuchen." Und den folgenden Tag ging er zu dem Turme hinaus und rief: „Rapunzel, laß Dein Haar herunter!" Alsbald fielen die Haare herab und der Königssohn stieg hinauf. Anfangs erschrak Rapunzel gewaltig, als ein Mann zu ihr herauf kam, wie ihre Augen noch nie einen erblickt hatten. Doch der Königssohn fing an ganz freundlich mit ihr zu reden und erzählte ihr, daß von ihrem Gesang sein Herz so sehr sei bewegt worden, daß es ihm keine Ruhe gelassen und er sie selbst habe sehen müssen. Da verlor Rapunzel ihre Angst, und als er sie fragte, ob sie ihn zum Manne nehmen wolle, und sie sah, daß er jung und schön war, dachte sie, der wird mich lieber haben als die alte Frau Gothel, und sagte ja, und reichte ihm ihre Hand.

Sie verabredeten, daß er alle Abend zu ihr kommen sollte, aber die Zauberin, die nur bei Tage kam, merkte nichts davon, bis einmal Rapunzel anfing und zu ihr sagte: „Frau Gothel, wie kommt es nur, sie wird mir immer schwerer heraufzuziehn, ist doch der junge Königssohn in einem Augenblick bei mir." „Ach," rief die Zauberin, „so hast Du mich doch betrogen!" Und in ihrem Zorn packte sie die schönen Haare der Rapunzel, ergriff eine Schere und ritsch, ritsch, waren sie abgeschnitten. Und sie war so unbarmherzig, daß sie die arme Rapunzel in die Berge brachte, wo sie in großem Jammer und Elend leben mußte.

Denselben Tag aber, wo sie Rapunzel verstoßen hatte, machte die Zauberin abends die abgeschnittenen Haare oben am Haken fest, und als der Königssohn kam und rief: „Rapunzel, laß Dein Haar herunter!" so ließ sie die Haare hinab. Aber der arme Königssohn fand oben nicht seine Rapunzel, sondern die Zauberin schaute mit bösen, giftigen Blicken hinaus, indem sie ihm zurief: „Für Dich ist Rapunzel verloren, Du wirst sie nie wieder erblicken." Der Königssohn geriet außer sich vor Schmerz, und vor Schreck und Verzweiflung stürzte er von der Haarleiter herab.

Das Leben brachte er davon, aber die beiden Augen waren verletzt. Blind irrte er im Wald umher, aß nichts als Wurzeln und Beeren und tat nichts als jammern und weinen über den Verlust seiner liebsten Frau.

So irrte er umher und geriet endlich an den Platz, wo Rapunzel mit den Zwillingen, die sie bekommen hatte, einem Knaben und einem Mädchen, kümmerlich lebte; er vernahm eine Stimme und sie däuchte ihm so bekannt, da ging er darauf zu, und wie er heran kam, erkannte ihn Rapunzel und fiel ihm um den Hals und weinte.

Zwei von ihren Tränen aber benetzten seine Augen, da wurden sie wieder klar und er konnte damit sehen wie sonst.

Bald darauf führte er seine Frau und Kinder aus den Bergen heraus. Wie die Leute in der Stadt die frohe Kunde vernahmen, zogen sie ihm entgegen und führten sie mit großer Pracht und Ehren in die Stadt zurück.

Von da ging es auf das Schloß des Königssohnes hinauf, wo er mit seiner geliebten Frau und Kindern noch lange glücklich lebte.

Die böse Hexe aber wurde verbrannt.

1857 engraving of the Grimms' "Rapunzel"

Graves of Fallen Freedom Fighters (Hermann's Grave), by Caspar David Friedrich, 1812

after the Napoleonic Wars to mark the liberation of Germany, it was completed in 1875, a grandiloquent celebration of Prussian victory over France in 1871. The Hermann monument is the perfect physical demonstration of how the patriotic stirrings of the Wars of Liberation—the impulses that moved Friedrich and the Grimms—were appropriated and coarsened by later nationalisms from the 1860s.

Most Germans are now embarrassed by the shrill aggression of the Hermann statue, and are nervous or ashamed of the later misappropriations of the Battle of the Teutoburg Forest, not least by the Nazis. In 2009 there were no ceremonies here to mark the 2,000th anniversary of an event long seen as the founding moment of German national identity. But it did not go entirely uncelebrated. In Hermann, Missouri, a town founded by German settlers in the 1830s when the Hermann cult was at its height, the bimillennial was commemorated in 2009 by the erection, in Market Street, of a statue showing Hermann, conqueror of the Roman legions.

Both Friedrich and the Grimms had complicated histories in the

---

Opposite: The Hermann Memorial in the Teutoburg Forest, Detmold

twentieth century. Disney carried the stories—"Snow White" above all—to a worldwide audience which the brothers could never have imagined. But they had less welcome supporters too. For obvious reasons of intensifying feelings of national identity, the Nazis also loved the Grimms. They recommended that every home in Germany should have a copy of the *Children's and Household Tales*. In consequence, the stories were for a later generation stained not just by this official endorsement, but by a concern that the violence and cruelty in the tales might also be an enduring trait in the national character, and one not always redeemed by traditional German virtues. That moment seems to have passed. *Kinder- und Hausmärchen* is now again the country's most popular book after the Bible, says Steffen Martus:

> "After 1945 there was a long tradition of steering clear of the Grimms; their stories were too gruesome after the horrors of the Nazi period. But now there is a return to the older concept of the German family, pre-Nazi, and this is an interesting development. It is really interesting that in Berlin, for example, we now see a new, young middle class (we call them the Prenzlauer Berg set—successful yuppies) who have taken to reading *Grimms' Fairy Tales* to their children, almost as if they want to preserve and protect the old ideal of the bourgeois family."

Friedrich also suffered from the admiration of the Nazis and others who hailed him as a properly German national artist. But, as Will Vaughan explains, he has now come to mean something very far removed from strident patriotism:

> "It is very interesting to see that Friedrich has from the 1960s onwards been reclaimed by Germans with very different views. Friedrich is seen as almost a proto-eco warrior, defending the countryside."

The Germans' attachment to the forest is still there, as old as the hills, or at least as the oaks, and a central part of the national character.

Opposite: Poster for Walt Disney's *Snow White*, 1937

HIS FIRST FULL LENGTH FEATURE PRODUCTION!
Walt DISNEY'S
Snow White
and the
Seven Dwarfs
©W.D.P.
in the marvelous new
MULTIPLANE TECHNICOLOR
Distributed by RKO RADIO PICTURES, Inc.

Friedrich and the Grimms would be delighted. The forest now covers a third of the country and it is protected—the Greens have become more firmly established as a political party in Germany than anywhere else in Europe. The new nation's future, like its past, will be lived in part in the forest. In the next chapter we will be looking at a great admirer of both Friedrich and the Grimms—a writer who himself became a symbol of a new kind of German-ness and remains the most identifiable figure in the national pantheon.

8

One Nation Under Goethe

There is a portrait, painted in 1787 by the artist Johann Tischbein, that is to most German people instantly recognizable. In fact, it would probably be fair to say that this picture is by far the most famous portrait in the whole of Germany. It hangs in the Städel Museum in Frankfurt and shows us the writer Johann Wolfgang von Goethe in Italy, dashingly wrapped in a white traveller's cloak and wearing a broad-brimmed black hat, sitting on some Roman remains and looking purposefully into the middle distance. And if Germans know this image of their great national poet above all others, they also know him above all as the author of one supreme drama, which is not just a great poetic tragedy, but has long been a defining element in the German national myth: *Faust*.

Among the elements that hold together Germans of all regions and dialects—along with the written language forged by Luther and shared memories of fairy stories and wild landscapes—must be reckoned this greatest of all German poets, and *Faust*, the rambling, unperformable cosmic drama which he wrote and rewrote all through his life. There is a case for arguing that if Americans are one nation under God, the Germans are one nation under Goethe. And there is no doubt that it was Goethe, more than anyone else, who

---

Overleaf: *Goethe in the Roman Campagna*, by Johann Tischbein, 1786–87

The Goethe house in Frankfurt, 1832

made German a language read—and spoken—by educated Europe. All round the world today the German government promotes its language and culture through the Goethe Institute.

The house in which Goethe was born still stands (albeit in a reconstructed state after being badly bombed in the war): located in the centre of Frankfurt, four storeys tall and with five good rooms on every floor, it is a building that speaks of prosperous eighteenth-century comfort. And inside the house you can still see the splendid puppet theatre that Goethe was given on his fourth birthday, in 1753. It is a large, painted, wooden box that looks a bit like a doll's house, with the proscenium arch cut away at the front and lots of space behind in which you can hang coloured scenery flats, depending on which drama your puppets are engaged in.

Goethe's father could have had no idea what he was unleashing when he gave his son this present, but the puppet theatre, Goethe

Goethe's puppet theatre

would later write, changed his life, propelling him at the age of four into a world where the real and the imaginary lived side by side, the two of them often in conflict, always enriching and transforming each other. And so Goethe began to write. This was not what his father had intended: Goethe in his view was destined to be a lawyer, a secure profession that would guarantee wealth and social position. Predictable father/son tensions followed. The young Goethe was sent off to university, several universities in fact (see Chapter 4), to study law. He hated it, he messed around, he mixed with unsuitable people and he fell in love with the wrong women.

Goethe spent three years at Leipzig University, in theory studying law but actually attending poetry classes and writing verses to the first of his many loves, Käthchen Schönkopf. But he took little pleasure from what he was writing: he could not find the words to say what he felt. The literary German of the 1760s was modelled on the French style—refined and restrained by classical conventions—and to an ardent young man it seemed stilted and suffocating. Goethe wanted something stronger, more direct, more sincere. And rather as one year earlier he had discovered a German visual tradition in the cathedral at Strasbourg, he found an authentic literary model for living German in an unexpected place: Shakespeare.

Shakespeare introduced Goethe to the idea that language could be used to express deep thoughts and raw emotions. It was the answer to the question that had haunted him: how to articulate *being German* in a way that spoke to other young Germans.

> The first page of Shakespeare that I read made me his for life. I jumped high in the air, and for the first time, I felt that I had hands and feet.

These words come from the celebration of William Shakespeare that the twenty-two-year-old Goethe organized in his father's house on 14 October (in the German religious calendar, that is the name-day for Williams) 1771. The manuscript text of his address survives: a

---

Opposite: Goethe's manuscript of his "Shakespeare speech" delivered on 14 October 1771

Zum Schäkespears Tag.

Mir kommt vor, das sey die edelste von unsern Empfindungen, die Hoffnung, auch dann zu bleiben, wenn das Schicksaal uns zur allgemeinen Nonexistenz zurückgeführt zu haben scheint. Dieses Leben, meine Herren, ist für unsre Seele viel zu kurz, Zeuge, dass ieder Mensch, der geringste wie der höchste, der unfähigste wie der würdigste, eher alles müd wird, als zu leben; und dass keiner sein Ziel erreicht, wornach er so sehnlich ausging – denn wenn es einem auf seinem Gange auch noch so lang glückt, fällt er doch endlich, und offt im Angesicht des gehofften Zwecks, in eine Grube, die ihm, Gott weis wer, gegraben hat, und wird für nichts gerechnet.

Für nichts gerechnet! Ich! der ich mir alles bin, da ich alles nur durch mich kenne! So ruft ieder, der sich fühlt, und macht große Schritte durch dieses Leben, eine Bereitung für den unendlichen Weeg drüben. Freylich ieder nach seinem Maas. Macht der eine mit dem stärcksten Wandrerstab sich auf,

young man's carefully drafted and scripted account of being entirely overwhelmed. Goethe's speech on Shakespeare Day is a love song: "Nature, nature, nothing so like nature as Shakespeare's people!" "Shakespeare, my friend, if you were still among us, I could live nowhere but with you," and warming to his rhapsody, he compares them both to the heroes of Euripides' *Iphigenia*: "How happy I would be if I could play Pylades to your Orestes."

Anne Bohnenkamp-Renken, a great scholar of German romantic literature, says of Goethe and Shakespeare:

> "This was the first Shakespeare celebration in Germany. For Goethe, Shakespeare is a kind of symbol of a new, free way to write, to think—to live—and the catch phrase 'nature, nature' shows what he is finding there. It is a kind of religious awakening which takes place when Goethe meets this way of thinking and writing."

Something in Shakespeare also allowed Goethe to come face-to-face with his own ideas and ideals. When you read Goethe's thoughts on Shakespeare, you realize he is expressing more about his own feelings about encountering Shakespeare than about Shakespeare himself. Under the English writer's influence, Goethe wrote his first major work, which would begin his ascent to becoming the greatest of German authors: *The Sorrows of Young Werther*, published in 1774. What Goethe did in *Werther* was revolutionary; the novel was to become a watershed in the development of German literature. A story of youthful emotion and passion, it reflects Goethe's own disastrous love affair with a friend's fiancée, and it ends in tragedy: tormented by unrequited love, Werther shoots himself. *Werther* was the 1770s equivalent of *A Clockwork Orange* in the 1960s—a book that put violence in a new, shocking context, forcing people to face an aspect of human behaviour they would rather avoid. Goethe described the world through the eyes of one tortured young man and his tangled emotions of love and hope, disappointment and death. It was a best-seller across all of Europe. Everywhere young men dressed

---

Opposite: Title-page of Goethe's *The Sorrows of Young Werther*, 1774

Die Leiden des jungen Werthers.

Erster Theil.

Leipzig,
in der Weygandschen Buchhandlung.
1774.

C. W. M. Bergmann:

Meissen cup depicting Werther, *c.* 1790

like Werther—in blue coats and yellow waistcoats—and not infrequently, like Werther, shot themselves. But the book did something else: *Werther* established German for the first time as a European literary language. Goethe joined his hero, Shakespeare, as an author the world wanted to read.

Werther was a cult book for a generation, a passionate argument for the importance of the heart in the human condition; it is our emotional depth and power, Goethe is telling us, that really defines what it is to be human. The book is a sympathetic account of a young man following his feelings and disregarding the stifling conventions imposed by society. The flip side of Werther's stellar status was that it was considered a highly dangerous book which, in the hero's suicide, championed self-indulgence and immorality over duty and obligation. But the young read it and loved it—Napoleon famously took a copy with him when he sailed to conquer Egypt.

Werther brought Goethe fame. It also brought him to the attention of Karl-August, teenaged ruler of the small Duchy of Saxe-Weimar. The duke was a liberal and enlightened intellectual. He read Goethe's novel and became Goethe's patron: in 1775 he invited Goethe to Weimar and made him a member of his Privy Council, in charge, among other roles, of his silver and copper mines. For the newly famous author, this was a turning point: working closely with the ruler of a small state, Goethe had access to a range of opportunities that would never have been available to a writer in Paris or London. He was sent on diplomatic missions where he could meet other writers; he had a secure income and a job for life, and even better a job which allowed him to take time off when he pleased, giving him the freedom to write when and what he wanted.

Even so, Goethe's first decade in Weimar led to what we might today call a mid-life crisis. In Strasbourg, he had seen the full power of Gothic architecture. With his Shakespeare Day and then *Werther,* Goethe had explored and exploited the freedom and emotion of north European literature, but, like Shakespeare, his appetite for every kind of experience was growing, and his thoughts turned to the art and literature of the South. At the age of thirty-seven, he decided he must visit Rome and see it for himself. And it was here that he met the artist Tischbein, who painted that famous, instantly recognized portrait.

If *Werther* and the Shakespeare Day celebrations show us a Goethe soaked in the traditions of northern Europe, Tischbein's portrait shows him confronting the surviving fragments of Mediterranean civilization. Reclining languidly as though on a chaise longue, Goethe reposes on some fallen blocks from a grand Roman building. In the background there is a ruined aqueduct, beside Goethe there is the head of an Ionic column and a sculptured relief. After the buildings and literature of the North, here we have the visual arts of the South. But this picture is not simply about decay and the ancients. Although ivy crawls over some of the broken stones, at Goethe's shoulder a small tree has taken root—a very German oak. Out of these survivors of a dead culture, Goethe will make something living. The sculptured relief on the right shows the Greek princess Iphigenia, along with her brother, Orestes, and his friend, Pylades, the role Goethe himself had dreamed of playing to his hero, Shakespeare, in the Shakespeare Day speech of 1771. When this portrait was being painted Goethe was writing his own play on Iphigenia, a work which would draw not on

Weimar from the North-West, after a drawing by Georg Melchior Kraus, 1798

Shakespeare, but on Euripides, and which would transform the classical Greek myth into high German drama. Out of these fragments of Rome and Greece, Tischbein seems to suggest, Goethe is forging a new structure, in which the achievements of the Mediterranean can join the inheritance of the North.

When he returned to Weimar, Goethe addressed that great task with renewed energy. He looked back on his Italian journey as the happiest time of his life, and his writings about Italy became the words with which all Germans learn to sigh for the South, his blossoming lemon trees as familiar to them as Wordsworth's daffodils are to us: "Kennst du das Land, wo die Zitronen blühn." Tischbein's picture is not just the portrait of a poet: it is the supreme image of Germany's long love affair with Italy. In his house in Weimar, Goethe surrounded himself with plaster casts of Greek and Roman sculpture. Rome—albeit on a domestic scale—was to be reconstituted north of the Alps. But the Goethe-Haus is much more than that. In the small capital town of a tiny duchy, Goethe sought to collect and to understand the whole world. Visiting today you can see his collection of plants (one—*Goethea cauliflora*—is named in his honour) and minerals (a specimen of Goethite is on show). He collected, compared, studied and wrote about them all, as well as about the poetry of Persia and the optics of Newton. He was fascinated by the idea of genius and bought van Dyck's skull (or what he believed to be van Dyck's skull) to see if the shape of the head might explain the scale of the talent. Mechanical inventions also intrigued him: right at the end of his life, he acquired a tiny model of a great innovation: Stephenson's "Rocket." Weimar's first railway sat in miniature on Goethe's desk. He was interested in everything, artistic and scientific, ancient and modern, from all over the globe. The Goethe-Haus is a monument to the Enlightenment, a one-man British Museum—the world under one roof, to be studied and apprehended: Goethe the *Weltbürger*, the citizen of the world, more—far more—than just an author.

The Weimar of Goethe, which is also the Weimar of the writers and philosophers Schiller, Wieland and Herder, became the emblem of a new Germany: profoundly cosmopolitan, serenely humane. And when Germany, after the catastrophe of the Great War and the

Goethe's model of George Stephenson's "Rocket"

collapse of 1918, wanted to reimagine itself, it was in Weimar that it proclaimed the new republic, and its humane, enlightened principles. Even in his own lifetime Goethe himself became a symbol, a sight which tourists from all over Europe travelled to see—among them that early admirer of *Werther*, Napoleon, now the conquering emperor. The military might of France and the intellectual achievement of Germany met in Erfurt on 2 October 1808. Frustratingly, there is no satisfactory record of what they discussed, although we know that Napoleon wanted to talk about *Werther*. The puppet theatre of childhood now housed a very grown-up cast.

All this time—throughout his life—Goethe was writing *Faust*, the drama of the man who makes a pact with the Devil to enable him to explore and possess the world, who strives ceaselessly to understand and to enjoy, who does some good and much evil, and who at the end is saved—if indeed he is saved—by his inextinguishable desire to continue the quest. Ever since its publication from 1808 onwards, *Faust* has been tangled up with the question of what it means to be German, in many different ways, as Anne Bohnenkamp-Renken describes:

Plate from Goethe's *On the Theory of Colours*, 1810

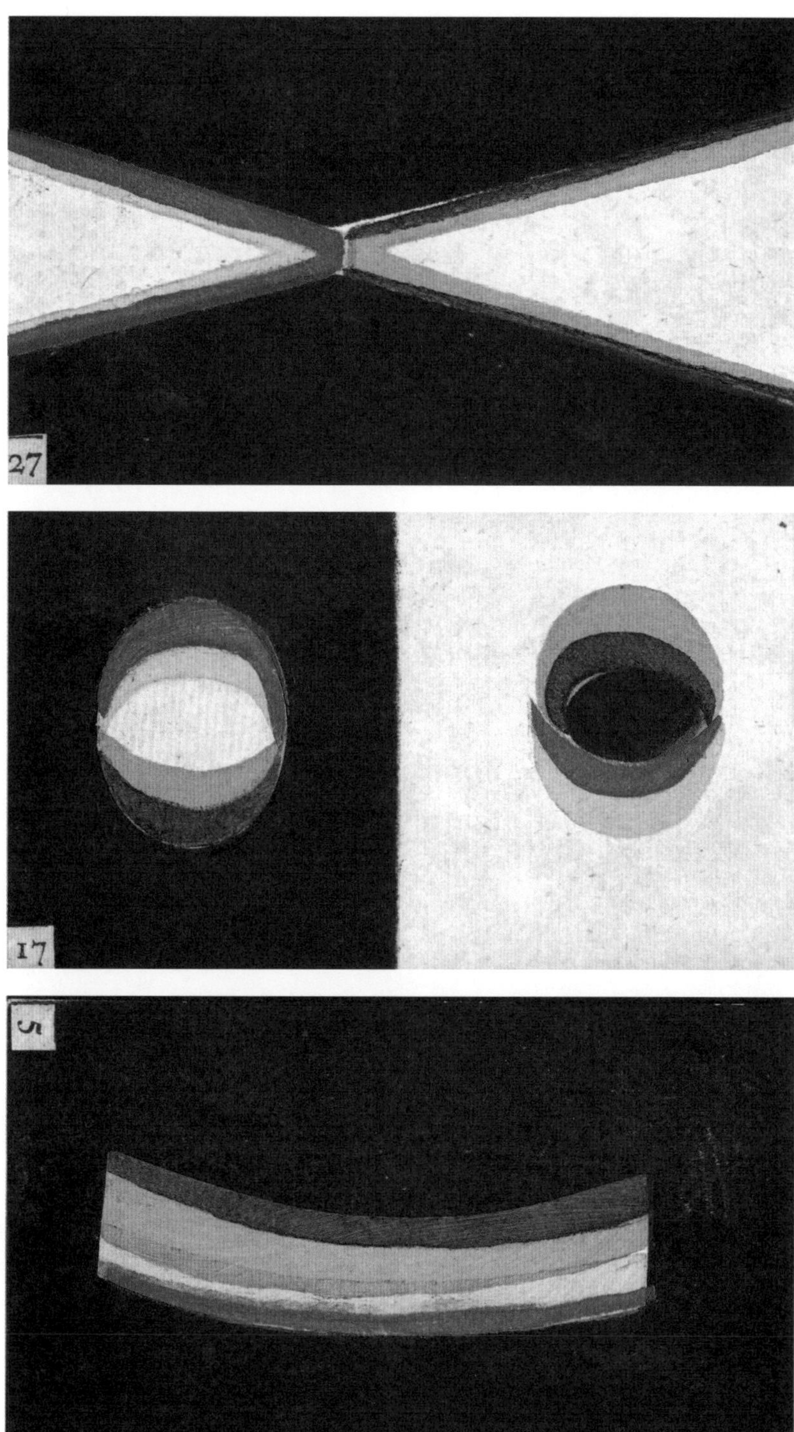

Goethe's colour theory cards, 1791

> "The late nineteenth century interpreted *Faust* as a kind of a symbol of the energy of the growing nation. Then during the Nazi regime, *Faust* was associated with the idea of the German who always strives and ultimately succeeds. The Communists took him as a symbol for their vision of society and nowadays, interpretation of *Faust* tends to accentuate the failure of his achievements—he is guilty, and can only be saved by divine love. My generation has been brought up with a very broken relationship with our nation. It is typical now to read the *Faust* as a very broken figure but one who is always striving, with both the failures and the guilt. Now there is no unified or simple image of German history, but of course there is an awareness of some intellectual dangers in the German tradition and this goes to the Faustian element of irresponsibility, of thinking without reflecting about the political and social consequences of certain ideas."

Perhaps in a reflection of how the nature of Goethe's German-ness can be read in many ways, Gustav Seibt, a leading critic and commentator on Goethe, takes a slightly different view from Anne Bohnenkamp-Renken. For Seibt, Goethe is no longer principally the author of the *Faust*—he now means something quite other. He is the emblem of a multicultural Germany:

> "The few who still love him and adore him, as I do, do so because they adore him as a person of highly civilized culture, who read books of all times and all languages, was interested in China and Islam and Serbia and much more besides. For our Muslims of course, he is extremely important because there is a poem in the *West-Eastern Divan*, a collection of Goethe's poems inspired by the Persian poet Hafiz, where he confesses that Allah is God and Mohammed is his prophet, which is enough to become a Muslim. We have a wonderful German Muslim writer, Navid Kermani, who is a theologian and a poet. He says Goethe is a Muslim, he is one of us."

Opposite: *Faust Conjuring Spirits*, by Carl Christian Vogel von Vogelstein, *c.* 1840

Statue of Goethe, based on Tischbein's portrait, in the café at Frankfurt airport

And, according to Seibt, it is not only German Muslims who look to Goethe with fellow-feeling:

> "I think if you ask people today they would answer he's an interesting model of how to manage your life. He had great depressions and fears and neuroses, fear of death, of insanity, of marriage—so great existential fears, and yet he succeeded in living so long, and completing everything—in the end."

Listening to Bohnenkamp-Renken and Seibt, it is clear that Germans today—like those young readers of *Werther* in the 1770s—can still explore their central preoccupations in the writings and the life of Goethe. If *Werther* has receded into literary history and *Faust* seems less of a national self-portrait than a generation ago, there is a continuing fascination with Goethe the man. And in him they discern an emblem of today's Germany, humanely negotiating the diverse challenges of modernity. Which is perhaps why the picture in the Städel is still so familiar and so cherished.

The Goethe in Tischbein's portrait is a handsome man in his late thirties. He is already a European celebrity, but Tischbein paints him as something more and it is strangely prophetic. Tischbein's Goethe is already larger than life size. He is a man embracing the culture of the whole world. He is literally on a plinth. Tischbein shows us Goethe as a monument, which now, at last, he is. When you arrive at Frankfurt airport, where people from all over the world now first encounter Germany, there to greet you is a statue based on Tischbein's Goethe, a painting transformed into sculpture, the symbol of Germany past and present.

9

Hall of Heroes

In 1808 virtually all German-speaking territory, from the Netherlands to the Russian frontier, was under French control. Every serious attempt at military resistance had failed. At the Battle of Austerlitz in December 1805, Napoleon had resoundingly defeated the Austrians and entered Vienna as conqueror. In the summer of 1806, after a thousand years of existence, the Holy Roman Empire of the German Nation had been dissolved. A few months later Napoleon crushed the Prussian army at Jena and Auerstädt, forcing a humiliating surrender. On 27 October 1806 he marched triumphantly through the Brandenburg Gate and entered Berlin (see Chapter 1). And in September 1808, in the central German city of Erfurt, now the principality of Erfurt, and designated part of the French Empire, Napoleon summoned the rulers of Germany to pay him homage in the presence of the Tsar of Russia. Many of those German rulers were now Napoleon's active allies (see Introduction). The others had been reduced to grudging acquiescence. No effective autonomous German political unit was left.

In circumstances like this, what did it—what could it—mean to be German? And in the face of enduring and effective French military aggression, what opposition was possible?

Opposite: The Walhalla monument by Leo von Klenze, 1842

> It was in the days of Germany's deepest degradation (the humiliation of Jena had taken place, and Germany had already begun to tear itself in pieces) that there arose in the beginning of the year 1807, in the mind of the Crown Prince Ludwig of Bavaria, the idea of having fifty likenesses of the most illustrious Germans executed in marble. And he commanded the undertaking to be commenced immediately.

The words came from Ludwig of Bavaria's own manifesto of his defiant dream of re-creating an enduring Germany by honouring its outstanding historical figures. It led over the next few decades to one of the most idiosyncratic expressions of national identity in nineteenth-century Europe—a temple to German-ness built high above the Danube: the Walhalla.

As Crown Prince, Ludwig could not, in 1807, embark on a major building, but he could, as he described in his memoir quoted above, commission portrait busts. In the years between 1807 and 1812, as the German states were, one after the other, humiliatingly forced into alliance with Napoleon in preparation for the attack on Russia, Ludwig charged the foremost sculptors of the day to produce likenesses of Frederick the Great and Maria Theresa, Gluck and Haydn, Leibniz and Kant, Schiller and Goethe. The great spirits of the past—only Goethe was still alive—would give dignity and hope to a defeated Germany. This was history as the highest form of passive resistance, a National Portrait Gallery as a step to national liberation. The Holy Roman Empire no longer existed, but the German empire of the spirit endured. With all the means he could command after he had become King of Bavaria in 1825, Ludwig resolved to build its temple.

In Norse mythology, Walhalla is the majestic hall to which the heroic dead are carried by the Valkyries, to join their predecessors and comrades. In the early 1800s, the legends of the north were in fashion. As the Brothers Grimm rediscovered German folk tales (see Chapter 7) medieval German epics like the *Nibelungenlied* (the Song of the Nibelungs) were expelled and extracted as part of the national

---

Opposite: *Crown Prince Ludwig of Bavaria*, by Angelika Kauffmann, 1807

inheritance. Richard Wagner would ultimately transform the sagas of the Vikings and the poetry of the German Middle Ages into his magisterial *Ring Cycle*, making the Valkyries and Valhalla familiar to every opera-goer, creating perhaps the supreme achievement of German music.

Ludwig's first idea for *his* Walhalla was that it should be sited in the English Garden in Munich. Later, he decided it should be near the former Imperial city of Regensburg (which had recently been incorporated into the Kingdom of Bavaria), where the Holy Roman Empire had held its parliaments, convening notables from the whole of Germany and beyond. Walhalla was to be a different kind of German Parliament. The Holy Roman Emperor had summoned delegates: King Ludwig now summoned the spirits of great Germans from the past in one stupendous assembly of achievement.

The site chosen by Ludwig and his architect, Leo von Klenze, is spectacular. J. M. W. Turner, England's great landscape painter, was present at the opening in 1842. Then nearly seventy years old, he was bowled over by it, painting one of his most complex late landscapes, now in the Tate Gallery, and composing some of his worst verse:

> But peace returns—the morning ray
> Beams on the Walhalla, reared to science and the arts,
> For men renowned, of German fatherland.

On a hill rising 300 feet above a secluded stretch of the Danube, facing south, the king and Klenze constructed not a Gothic evocation of the gods of the ancient north, but a version of the Parthenon. Approached from the river, the entrance is reached by a huge monumental staircase, a homage to the Propylaeum in Athens, which leads to the Acropolis and the Parthenon itself. It is impossible not to have the sense of being a humble pilgrim approaching a great shrine. As the building comes into view and the portico with its double row of fluted Doric columns looms above, the message is clear: here

---

Previous pages: *The Gods Entering Valhalla*, the final scene of Richard Wagner's *Das Rheingold*, print, *c.* 1876

Bust of Frederick the Great, by Schadow, 1807

Bust of Empress Maria Theresa, 1811

the greatest Germans are being inducted into a fellowship with the Ancient Greeks.

As on the Parthenon, the pediments of the temple start by telling the tribal creation myths. On the north pediment is a colossal statue of the heroic Germanic chieftain, Hermann, shown with his soldiers from different German tribes, all fighting together to defeat the Romans at the Battle of the Teutoburg Forest in A.D. 9—the first recorded moment of successful German resistance to the invader (see Chapter 7). On the south pediment, 1,800 years on, is the figure of Germania, the embodiment of the nation, surrounded by those who fought Napoleon to free Germany once again from foreign aggression and invasion. The whole history of what the German peoples had achieved, as shown in Ludwig's building, lies between these two defining moments, of national resistance against the Romans and national liberation from the French.

Inside is a noble, lofty space, about fifty yards long and twenty yards wide, and intensely, joyously colourful. The floor is paved with white and golden slabs, the walls are clad in pink marble, and the wooden ceiling, gold and blue, is held up by pairs of female figures. In Athens, these would be caryatids, but here they are Valkyries, the

Top: South pediment showing the 1813 Wars of Liberation

maidens who in ancient Germanic myth carried dead heroes from the battlefield to their heavenly abode—Walhalla. These particular Valkyries are wearing blue and white, the colours of Bavaria.

The centre of this magnificent building has been left entirely empty, because the purpose of this rich display of colour is merely to serve as backdrop to the 130-odd white marble busts who are the inhabitants of Walhalla—busts with whom we can engage one by one in a dialogue that will lead to an understanding of what it means to be German. The selection criteria were set out by Ludwig himself in his preface to the first guidebook:

> To become an inhabitant of Walhalla, it is necessary to be of German origin and to speak the German language. But as the Greek

Above: North pediment showing Hermann at the Battle of the Teutoburg Forest

> remained a Greek, whether from Ionia or Sicilia, so the German remains a German whether from the Baltic or Alsace, from Switzerland or the Netherlands. Yes—the Netherlands. For Flemish and Dutch are but dialects of Low German. What decides the continued existence of a people is not the place of residence but the language.

Ludwig had found a solution to the perpetual conundrum of Germany's lack of fixed frontiers: Germany was quite simply all the places where people spoke German. Like the Greek diaspora in the Mediterranean the Germans settled across Europe formed one coherent cultural world.

It was a view widely held after the Wars of Liberation. In 1813,

Ernst Moritz Arndt, the first bard of German nationalism, had composed a song that became hugely popular: "Wo ist des Deutschen Vaterland?"—"Where Is a German's Fatherland?" Verse after verse considers the different candidates—Pomerania and Bavaria, Saxony, Switzerland and the Tyrol—to conclude that wherever the German tongue is spoken, *there* is a German's fatherland. The link between language, national identity and shared aspirations, which Ludwig, Arndt and many others articulated for Germany, was mirrored in Britain: Wordsworth, in a sonnet of 1803, considering how the British should respond to French attack, had come to a similar conclusion: "We must be free or die, who speak the tongue that Shakespeare spake." It was an idea with a long life: in 1937, as war again threatened Britain, Churchill began to compile his *History of the English-Speaking Peoples*—based on the same assumption as Ludwig's in Walhalla, that a shared language implies enduring affinities.

Having established the key criterion for admission, Ludwig went on to explain the house rules of Walhalla:

> Beginning with the first Great German known, Hermann the conqueror of the Romans, there are in Walhalla the busts only of illustrious Germans, executed by German artists; or, if there are no contemporary likenesses, their names in bronze on plaques. No condition, not even the female sex, is excluded. Equality exists in Walhalla.

In this insistence on equality, there is a striking similarity between Ludwig's Walhalla and another royal initiative to rally the people against the invader—Frederick William of Prussia's institution of the Iron Cross and Order of Luise (Chapter 14). In Bavaria and in Prussia, the highest honours were now to be equally available to men and women, and rank was to play no part. It was a notion of equality that in both kingdoms was to remain eloquently symbolic, but emphatically not political.

The plaques above the entrance door immediately demonstrate the quirky, inclusive idiosyncrasy of Ludwig's choice. They start of course with the Roman-defeating Hermann. Beside him is Einhard,

Interior of the Walhalla monument, 1842

Bust of Catherine the Great, 1831

Bust of William of Orange (William III of Great Britain), 1815

the scholar-historian of Charlemagne's court: Germany is both valiant and scholarly. Alfred the Great (the English Alfred the Great), Saxon-speaking and so part of this great German family, is also here as the liberator of his country from the Danes. But Walhalla is not a place just for the grand. Beside Charlemagne, first German Emperor, is the plaque of Peter Henlein, of Nuremberg, who, it was believed, had around 1510 invented the first pocket watch (see Chapter 19). This is a very personal pantheon, and one of the great pleasures of wandering around Walhalla is to see who has been invited to this ultimately exclusive party—and who, definitively, has not.

Ludwig was understandably generous to his own Wittelsbach ancestors, and to monarchs in general. There might be a hint of snobbery in the inclusion of Empresses Maria Theresa and Catherine the Great, originally a German princess, whose incorporation into Walhalla irked the Russians (the French similarly bristled over the presence of Charlemagne). Walhalla in fact was the only pantheon of its time to include a significant number of women, as well as having a strong supporting cast, including Germania, the Valkyries and the Victories as decorative figures. All this was fitting, perhaps, for a monarch notorious for his fondness for women—it was the scandal of

Bust of Gutenberg, 1835

Bust of Luther, 1831, not installed until 1848

his liaison with the beautiful courtesan Lola Montez that contributed to Ludwig's downfall in 1848. As King of Catholic Bavaria, Ludwig naturally added saints and missionaries of both sexes, but in general those first two plaques, to Hermann and Einhard, set the tone, and military and cultural heroes account for most of the guests.

Intriguingly, the busts are not organized in any coherent chronological order, so the visitor keeps moving backwards and forwards through time and across space, adding to the almost dreamlike sense of encountering characters refracted through the erratic prism of Ludwig's historical imagination.

In spite of being both Prussian and Protestant, Frederick the Great was among the first selected for this Bavarian celebration. He had fought against, and defeated, many of his fellow Germans, but he had rescued his country in the Seven Years' War and made it into a European power. Near Frederick sits Blücher, a fellow Prussian, who fought with Wellington at Waterloo. And as the notion of Germanness here is a very wide one, we find a Russian general of Scottish descent who also fought against Napoleon—Barclay de Tolly—who slips in as a native German speaker. William of Orange, William III, King of Great Britain, is—unsurprisingly—here, Dutch being for

Ludwig a version of German, and William himself a German prince of the House of Nassau, who had, a hundred years before, led the European coalition to fight Louis XIV. Again and again the point is made: from Charles Martel defeating the Arabs at the Battle of Tours in 732 to the Battle of Waterloo, Ludwig chooses to celebrate individuals who spoke German and who had, through the centuries, fought bravely for their country.

On the cultural side, the great musicians are represented in force—Beethoven and Mozart, Haydn and Handel; the great writers and philosophers—Goethe and Schiller, Erasmus and Kant; and the great inventors and scientists—Gutenberg and Copernicus, as well as Henlein, and Otto von Guericke, inventor of the vacuum pump and the famous Magdeburg Hemispheres. The painters once again make clear just how wide Ludwig's idea of German-ness was: beside Dürer and Holbein are Rubens and van Dyck, both of German (in this case Flemish) tongue, and so perfectly proper residents of Walhalla.

But the real debate about who got to be in Walhalla did not concern literature or philosophy, science, music or the arts. It was about religion. When Walhalla opened in 1842, the most striking absence from among the 160 figures originally chosen to represent 1,800 years of German history—and widely commented upon at the time—was Martin Luther. Nobody of course would have disputed that he was a great religious figure, but for the Catholic Ludwig, king of the intensely Catholic Bavaria, Luther was a profoundly divisive figure in the history of Germany, responsible for a national schism that precipitated the cataclysm of the Thirty Years' War and the destruction of German religious unity. The Oxford historian Abigail Green, who has studied the use of history in the forging of national identities in German states after 1815, explains:

> "The religious balance in Germany shifted when the Holy Roman Empire died. It was not the case that the number of Catholics and Protestants changed, but in the Holy Roman Empire there had been many more Catholic polities, mostly small. After the Holy Roman Empire dissolved, there were more Protestant monarchs

> and a lot of states became religiously mixed. As the debate developed over what kind of Germany would come to be, the religious element was very important. For Protestants, Luther was clearly the most significant German—Germany's great contribution to world culture. But if you were a Catholic, Luther and Protestantism appear as a very divisive force. They divided the Christian community and they divided the German nation. And the legacy of the wars of religion, the Thirty Years' War, in particular, was terribly bitter."

A bust of Luther was in fact originally commissioned and sculpted, but then excluded at the last moment. Luther did not enter Walhalla until the year of liberal revolutions, 1848—the first to be added to Walhalla after it had opened, conceded by an increasingly unpopular Ludwig shortly before his forced abdication. Today, in reparation, Luther sits in a prime position beside Goethe. But, as Abigail Green points out, the religious debate went wider than Catholic and Protestant:

> "Only Christian Germans were, at the beginning, introduced into Walhalla by Ludwig. It is not realistic to expect that Ludwig would have put Moses Mendelssohn in, for example: but, at the same time, Mendelssohn was a giant of the German Enlightenment, one of the most significant figures in modern Jewish history, and a great friend of the writer and philosopher Gotthold Ephraim Lessing, who did make it in. His absence is noteworthy, and there are still now other notable Jewish absences, like Freud and Marx."

Most of the later arrivals at Walhalla are fairly unsurprising. There is nothing controversial about the arrival of Max Joseph von Pettenkofer, the pioneer of public health, or Wilhelm Röntgen, the inventor of x-rays. Any house of German memories must give a special place to music. The anonymous author of the *Nibelungenlied* is honoured in a plaque high on the wall, and among the busts you find, as you would expect, Wagner, whose later musical Valhalla has far outstripped Ludwig's building in worldwide fame. His bust was installed in 1913, followed three years later by Johann Sebastian Bach, a surprisingly tardy arrival. But one of the later musician guests is perhaps worth pondering: Anton Bruckner. His was the only bust to enter Walhalla during the Nazi period, and he is here not just as a great composer, but because he was born in Linz in Austria—near to where Hitler spent his childhood. The incorporation of Bruckner into Walhalla, at a ceremony attended by the Führer himself, was one way in which the cultural aspirations of Ludwig were taken over by the Third Reich. But interestingly—surprisingly—it was the only one. It might have

Installation of the bust of Anton Bruckner, 1937. Hitler is standing forward, bottom left.

Unveiling of the bust of Heinrich Heine by the Bavarian Prime Minister, Horst Seehofer, 28 July 2010

been expected that Hitler would exploit to the full Ludwig's idea of a temple to great Germans who had changed the world but in fact he left it relatively untouched.

The lower range of busts, almost at eye level, are now arranged in the order in which they arrived in Walhalla. There is nothing especially startling, after Luther, until the addition made in 1990: Albert Einstein, the first Jew in Walhalla. This was perhaps the moment at which it became clear that who is in Walhalla is still a matter of real importance and public debate. In this building, Germany—at least part of Germany (Bavaria)—is still deciding what kind of history it wants to write, which memories matter. Few countries offer a similar forum for the shaping of a national story.

The installation of Einstein, a Jew who left Nazi Germany to live in exile, was followed by Konrad Adenauer, the great architect of post-war democratic Germany. But it is perhaps the last three busts in Walhalla that raise the most interesting questions. The nineteenth-century poet Heinrich Heine, acerbic, lyrical and ironic, had long been absent—partly of course because of his Jewish descent, but also because he was a severe critic of the very idea of such a shrine to the great. He thought Walhalla absurd, publishing a satirical poem mocking Ludwig for building this "field of skulls." On 28 July 2010 the mocker joined the elect. But his bust is like no other. Running through the marble from the cheekbone to the middle of the chest is a split: the sculptor has tried to find a way of showing the irresoluble ambiguity implicit in having Heine, the critic of Walhalla, present in this space.

Surely the most difficult of recent decisions, perhaps the most difficult of any decisions about inclusion in Walhalla, concerns Germans who lived and died under the Third Reich. Included is the bust of the Jewish-born philosopher Edith Stein, who converted to Christianity, was murdered in Auschwitz and was later canonized by the Roman Catholic Church. Abigail Green:

> "It is important to realize that the people now deciding who goes into the Walhalla are the Bavarian State Parliament. The choice seems, to me, to be quite conservative. The absence of Marx, clearly such a globally significant figure, is striking. These decisions reflect the particular make-up of Bavaria, which has always been very strongly Catholic. Edith Stein is a curious choice in a lot of ways. You can see why she is there: she is of Jewish birth, a Holocaust victim, and also an important philosopher. But what about Hannah Arendt, who clearly had much more global significance? It does speak very much to the fact that there are still competing narratives about what Germany is and what Germany was, and what the German past consists of—and these vary locally, and also in religious ways."

As you move round Walhalla, the final interlocutor in this monumental chronicle of the achievements of the German-speaking world is Sophie Scholl—a non-violent resister to Hitler who was sentenced to death by the Nazis. Her bust stands above the last plaque, the final plaque at this level, engraved with these words:

Opposite: Bust of Sophie Scholl with plaque to the Resistance, 2003

SOPHIE SCHOLL

IM GEDENKEN AN ALLE, DIE
GEGEN UNRECHT, GEWALT UND
TERROR DES „DRITTEN REICHS"
MUTIG WIDERSTAND LEISTETEN.

> Im Gedenken an alle, die gegen Unrecht, Gewalt und Terror des Dritten Reichs mutig Widerstand leisteten.
>
> In memory of all those who courageously offered resistance to the injustice, the violence and the terror of the Third Reich.

In this building, as in so many others in Germany, the visitor can read a nation's struggle to make a history that has coherence and integrity.

There are many things about Walhalla that seem perverse or puzzling, but particularly striking is the choice of architectural style. High on the wall is a plaque to the unknown architect of Cologne Cathedral, while there is a bust of Erwin von Steinbach, architect of Strasbourg Cathedral, whom Goethe hailed as the great master of German Gothic architecture (Chapter 4). While Ludwig was building Walhalla on the Danube, the Prussians, by the Rhine, were completing the medieval gothic Cologne Cathedral as a symbol of the ancient Germany which must be restored. And yet Walhalla, which is all about German-ness, is not in a German gothic style at all, but in a Greek style, with eclectic flourishes that speak to ancient Egypt, Babylonia and India. Abigail Green again:

> "Classical architecture gave status. The French always identified with the Romans, either the Roman Republic or the Roman Empire. But the Germans always identified with the Greeks. They thought they were, like the Greeks, culturally superior, if militarily perhaps less hard-hitting than the Romans or the French. They also identified with Greek plurality: there were lots of different Greek city-states, in the same way as there were lots of German states. They thought the Greeks had a particular attachment to liberty, which they also saw as being particularly German. So I think the choice of a Greek architectural style for Walhalla is obvious, but significant."

For the Bavarians, this identification of Greece with Germany had one very particular resonance. While Ludwig I was building Walhalla, his second son, Otto, was chosen by Britain, France and Russia

Bust of Erwin von Steinbach, 1811

to be the first king of independent Greece, recently liberated from Ottoman rule. Bavarian Otto in many ways shaped the Greece we know today. He moved the capital to Athens, then embarked on the restoration of the Acropolis. The public buildings of modern Athens are strikingly similar to those of modern Munich, as both father and son set out to build two ideal Greek/German cities for the nineteenth century. In the late 1830s both the Parthenon in Athens and the Parthenon on the Danube were building projects of the Bavarian House of Wittelsbach. In this, as in many other respects, nineteenth-century Germans thought of themselves as embodying the virtues of ancient Greece. To this day a grammar-school in Germany is called, in open homage to Greek education, a Gymnasium.

Gruß aus München!

10

One People, Many Sausages

In the last chapter, we looked at how Ludwig I of Bavaria tried to articulate a German identity by building a monument to the great men and women of history who had all spoken some sort of German. It is an intriguing, idiosyncratic panorama of a nation's culture, but, despite its fame at the time, both in and out of Germany, in the long term Ludwig's Walhalla did not become a strong focus for popular national sentiment comparable to the later Hermannsdenkmal (see Chapter 7). Perhaps it was just too highbrow, appealing to a rarefied rather than a general public.

But, almost without meaning to, Ludwig did create another institution which encapsulates German-ness in a way with which everyone, whatever their level of education, can fully engage, and which is even more international in its scope than Walhalla. On 12 October 1810, to celebrate his wedding, the first Oktoberfest was held in his capital city of Munich. It was such a success that it was repeated, and the Munich Oktoberfest is now the largest popular festival in the world—larger, it is claimed, than Carnival in Rio or Mardi Gras in New Orleans. Every year, hundreds of thousands now come to Munich to celebrate something which not only most Germans, but the world enjoys: German beer.

Opposite: "Greetings from Munich!," a 1960s postcard

Glass, silver gilt, amber, and stoneware drinking vessels from the German world

The British Museum has drinking vessels from all round the world, but its German collection is striking for the enormous number of glasses, mugs, tankards and other vessels made primarily for the drinking of beer. Mostly from the sixteenth and seventeenth centuries, they are made of all sorts of different materials, and they come from everywhere in the German-speaking world, from Belgium to the Russian frontier, from the Alps to the Baltic. There are tall glasses from Switzerland, stoneware tankards from Cologne, covered beakers from Austria, silver-gilt mugs from Hamburg and from the German-speaking merchant cities of the Baltic coast, from Lübeck to Riga. Most astonishing of all is the tankard made entirely out of amber—the exotic, expensive, exclusive material found abundantly in East Prussia (see Chapter 3). Looking at this array, it is clear that Germans everywhere not only enjoy beer, but enjoy it in quantity and in style.

They seem to have been doing so for at least 2,000 years. In fact it is almost the first thing that any foreigner mentioned about them. Around A.D. 100 the Roman historian Tacitus, in his *Germania*, talks of the fair-haired, blue-eyed tribes which had given the legions such trouble along the Rhine, of the more distant ones who gathered amber on the Baltic, and of one thing that they all had in common:

> A liquor for drinking is made of barley or other grain, and fermented into a certain resemblance to wine. To pass an entire day and night in drinking disgraces no one.

Later archaeology confirmed Tacitus' observation of heavy, happy, beer-drinking among the German tribes. This is in part why beer later became a touchstone of being German, as Peter Peter, the food correspondent of the *Frankfurter Allgemeine Zeitung*, explains:

> "There is a lot of archaeological evidence that the ancient Germans who heroically fought against the Roman Empire consumed enormous quantities of beer. Many nineteenth-century painters depicted the ancient Germans in a way that combined bear and

> beer: lying on bearskins, swigging enormous quantities of beer from gilded ox horns. So beer in the nineteenth century became a national cause. Look at the enormous nineteenth-century beer halls, especially in Munich: those architects were inspired by Wagnerian dreams of Nordic heroes."

It is rather as though the nineteenth-century English had discovered Boadicea's favourite tipple and made it their national drink.

When the nineteenth-century nationalists, eager to discover authentic German traditions, set to work on the symbolic status of beer, as well as quoting Tacitus they unearthed the Bavarian *Reinheitsgebot*, the Beer Purity Law, first promulgated in 1487 by Duke Albrecht the 4th of Bavaria. This Purity Law became the basis of some very successful myth-making. The nineteenth-century nationalists assumed it was designed to make sure that only clean, unpolluted water was used to brew beer: evidence that the integrity of the national drink had been resolutely defended through the centuries. It is an assumption still widely accepted as true, but Peter Peter thinks otherwise:

> "The German *Reinheitsgebot* meant that you were allowed to use only a limited number of things to make beer—barley, hops, water and nothing else. It was an entirely political thing. It had nothing to do with consumer protection, or stopping people from getting ill—it was simply to prevent them from brewing with wheat or rye, because wheat and rye would be better used for bread."

In other words, the *Reinheitsgebot* was originally connected to another abiding German memory—the fear of famine. Peter's colleague Harald Scholl, of the Munich Slow Food Convivium, takes up the idea of how the notion of beer purity became politicized:

> "It is very interesting that these documents on beer purity were neglected for more than 300 years, and it was only in the nineteenth century, when drinking beer had become a symbol of

pfarrern in vnserm lannde nit gestatt werden sol/außgenomen was die pfarrer vnd gaistlichen von aigen weinwachsen habñ/ vnd für sich/jr pfarrgesellen/priesterschafft vnnd haußgesindt/ auch in der not den kindlpetterin vnd krannckẽ leütn/ vnuärlich geben/das mag jne gestatt werdẽ. Doch geuärlicher weiß/ von schennckens vnd gewins wegen/söllen sy kainen wein einlegen.

Wie das Pier Sũmer vnd Wintter auf dem lannd sol geschennckt vnd praüen werden.

Pier satz.

Item wir ordnen/setzen/vnd wöllen/mit Rate vnnser Lanndschafft/das füran allennthalben in dem Fürstenthumb bairn/ auff dem lannde/ auch in vnnsern Stetten vnd Märckten/ da deßhalb hieuor khain sonndere ordnung ist/ von Michaelis biß auff Georij/ain Maß oder Khopffpiers vber ainen pfenning münchner werung/vnd von sant Jörgen tag/biß auf Michaelis/die maß vber zwen pfenning derselben werung/ vnnd dernenden der Khopff ist/vber drey haller/bey nachgesetzter peene/ nicht gegeben noch ausgeschenckt sol werdñ. Wo auch ainer nit Mertzen/sonder ander Pier prawen/oder sonnst haben würde/ sol Er doch das/ kains wegs höher/dann die maß vmb ainen pfenning schencken/vnd verkauffen. Wir wöllen auch sonderlichen/das füran allenthalben in vnnsern Stetten/Märckten/ vnd auf dem lannde/zü kainem pier/merer stückh/dann allain Gersten/Hopffen/vnnd wasser/genomen vnd gepraucht söllen werden. Welher aber dise vnnsere ordnũg wissentlich vberfarn vnd nit halten wurde/dem sol von seiner gerichtzöbrigkait/ dasselbig Vas pier/ züstraff vnnachläßlich/so offt es geschicht/genomen werden. Yedoch wo ain Geüwirt von ainem Pierprewen in vnnsern Stetten/Märckten/oder aufm lannde/ yezüzeiten ainen Emer piers/zwen oder drey/kauffen/vnd wider

requisita ad cerevisiam.

> German identity, of German nationalism, that the documents resurfaced. Beer was now national, and, so it was said, only we Germans, and not the rest of the world, had defended the purity of beer."

Though the original Beer Purity Law was Bavarian, it was quickly adopted in many other parts of Germany. The devastation of northern Germany—especially the lethal, legendary famines of the Thirty Years' War, and the frequent scarcity of grain for bread, made it seem a valuable regulation for preserving food supplies. It is a measure of how successfully the mythical union of beer and national identity had been fostered that in 1871, during negotiations over German unification, Bavaria made the adoption of the Beer Purity Law a condition of its joining the new German Empire.

Astonishingly, at least to a non-German, the issue arose again at the reunification of 1990. Across Germany the so-called "Brandenburg Beer War," fought out in the courts, lasted for ten years—all over a black beer brewed in the former GDR that contained sugar, something forbidden by the Purity Law.

Regional beers, as Peter Peter describes, are what has defined German towns, cities and localities for centuries.

> "There is a strong tradition of regional brewing in Germany. In Franconia, you find real hand-made beers from very small breweries, brewed with a special barley which is malted. In Bamberg you have a sort of smoke beer, *Rauchbier*, which is very special, and makes you think of an Islay malt whisky with its very distinctive taste. One of the best beers of Munich, called Augustiner beer, was made by the Augustinian monks."

That sense of strong local identity is strikingly apparent on the beer tankards in the British Museum. On one after another, they display the arms of the different cities or the different princes. These drinking cups, made by master craftsmen, often out of precious materials,

---

Opposite: The Beer Purity Law as re-promulgated by Duke Wilhelm IV of Bavaria in 1516

are clearly intended as statements of civic pride. But they also have a very significant function to perform. Legal contracts, trade deals, oaths of allegiance were often concluded by *Zutrinken*, a pledge of good faith—drunk in wine or, more usually, beer—not unlike a handshake, to seal the deal. Out of grand ceremonial tankards like these, the different parties to the agreement would drink in turn, in a public, ceremonial act of assent. Given the size of some of the tankards—several litres in some cases—it seems that Tacitus was not exaggerating when he described the German fondness for passing an entire day and night drinking.

To go with the beer, the other great emblem of Germany's national diet is *Wurst*—the sausage. *Wurst*, like beer, defines Germany's cities and regions, each different sausage with its own ingredients and its particular traditions. In Munich, for example, the local speciality is the *Weisswurst*, to be accompanied ideally by the local beer made by the Augustinian monastery. *Weisswurst* is a white sausage, delicately flavoured, made of minced veal and bacon—heated in water rather than fried, best accompanied by pretzels, and which no true Bavarian would dream of eating after midday. Apparently this is because the *Weisswurst*, made of raw, unscalded meat, was quickly perishable in the days before refrigeration and so had to be eaten at once. Proper taboos resist all technology, and this one, ignoring modern chilling techniques, is still honoured as seriously as a Scotsman insists on salt in porridge, even today. The *Weisswurst* must not hear the church bells strike noon.

A *Wurst* map of Germany would be a mosaic of ungraspable complexity. Apart from the international celebrities, like the Frankfurter, Bavaria alone can field many other stars like the Nuremberger and the Regensburger; then from further afield, there is *Bratwurst* from Franconia, *Bregenwurst* from Saxony, *Pinkel* from Bremen, *Teewurst* from Pomerania, and so on and on. It is claimed there are 1,200 of them. In Germany beer and sausage embody centuries of national, regional and local history, they are living assertions of local diversity, the gastronomic equivalents of the flourishing regional dialects. They have a special place in the regional and local memory—and indeed in the national psyche, as Harald Scholl, food expert, explains:

The display in a Wilmersdorf butcher's shop, 2006

> "The German sausage is history on your plate. Traditionally, manufacturing sausages was a complicated feat of craftsmanship—you needed a lot of experience to mince the meat, to add spices to preserve it, and so on. So it was the pride and privilege of German free cities, and many sausages still bear their names. So we have here some small sausages, about the size of a finger, called Nurembergers. They have cinnamon and other spices added to them: Nuremberg was in regular contact with Venice, and so had privileged access to Oriental spices. And as they were expensive, these sausages are small. Now the name Nuremberger is protected by law all over Europe."

The Nuremberger sausage may not be familiar to non-Germans, but everyone knows the Frankfurter. The blandest, most basic of sausages, usually served in a bun, is available on nearly every street corner across Germany, and across Europe and America as well: smoky, finely minced meat, ground almost to a paste, usually then plastered with mustard or tomato ketchup.

But the humble Frankfurter did not begin like that. It has a high Imperial pedigree. Frankfurt Cathedral was for centuries the place where the Holy Roman Emperor was crowned. As part of the celebrations, an ox was killed and stuffed with sausages made of the most finely—and therefore expensively—minced pork: a great luxury to mark a great event, a sausage that had taken a great deal of work and time, but worth the effort on a great public occasion. Sausages, like people, can come down in the world. The Frankfurter has fallen far.

One of the most fascinating of all regional sausages, says Harald Scholl, also comes from Frankfurt—the *Rindswurst*—a sausage made from pure beef. Why? It is not easy to chop beef, which is a very hard meat, and it needs a lot of work. In the late nineteenth century, Frankfurt was the town with probably the biggest Jewish population in Germany (see Chapter 28). Jews of course could not eat pork sausages like the famous Frankfurters, so as a special treat they ate these finely minced *Rindswurst*, which then became popular with the whole population—a rare instance of Jewish patrimony still present in everyday German food.

In the late nineteenth century, food production became mechanized in Germany, as it did elsewhere, and *Wurst* manufacture, traditionally a cottage industry, fell victim to the trend. New machinery meant any meat could now be minced finely, and, more importantly, cheaply (the process which ultimately dethroned the Frankfurter). The industrial sausage emerged as the staple food of the proletarian poor, especially in Berlin, the fastest-growing city in Europe at the time. It became notoriously difficult to be sure what was actually in a Berlin sausage. Hence the famous—though probably apocryphal—remark by Bismarck, that citizens do not really want to know how either laws or sausages are made.

Fifty years later, the poor quality of Berlin sausages was to have an unexpected consequence. Museums are dedicated to material evidence, and, disappointingly, sausages leave few physical traces. Unlike beer, with its rich legacy of glasses and tankards, sausages have few dishes or utensils exclusively connected to them, and so

The making of blood sausages, detail from *The Month of December*, by Hans Wertinger, *c.* 1525–26

museums struggle to tell the tale of the *Wurst*. Which is why it was with surprise and delight that, a few years ago, the international museum community discovered that we all had a new colleague, the Currywurst Museum in Berlin, located just beside the former Checkpoint Charlie. Its existence speaks of the astounding success of a very late arrival on the *Wurst* scene, not the heir to proud coronation traditions of an Imperial Free City, but the result of food shortages in post-1945 Berlin. Parodying Keynes, you might say that the Currywurst is one of "The Gastronomic Consequences of the Peace." And it is still very much with us—an essential part of the Berlin experience. Harald Scholl:

The Berlin Currywurst Museum, 2010

> "Currywurst was invented with the help of an unknown British soldier, who sold curry powder on the black market in Berlin in the late 1940s. They had only very cheap sausages then, so they decided to camouflage them by sprinkling curry powder on them. It was a time when we were frenetically discovering foreign dishes, so it was interesting having something Indian and exotic, and the Currywurst became a symbol of Berlin—a town that had never had excellent sausages. After the Wall fell in 1989, a lot of Germans discovered Berlin and the Currywurst became an emblem of a young, cool Berlin lifestyle. It is a gourmet tragedy that Currywurst has become the national symbol of German food."

While the *Wurst* tradition can easily be cheapened or commercialized, beer-drinking has retained its place in the public life of the nation, even if not exactly as Tacitus described it. In the nineteenth century emerged another Bavarian tradition which became very popular: the beer hall, vast temples to beer-drinking, full of marble and wood-panelling, grandiloquent celebrations of the national

Hitler speaks in the Bürgerbräukeller, 8 November 1935

drink. The most famous—and biggest—beer hall in Munich was the Bürgerbräukeller. In the 1920s it became a favourite meeting-place for Hitler's growing Nazi party and it is where he launched his infamous but unsuccessful *Putsch* against the city government in 1923. It is also where he gave his annual speech to the *Alte Kämpfer*—the Old Fighters—after he came to power ten years later. The Bürgerbräukeller has been demolished, but the tradition of the beer hall speech, or, these days, more often the beer *tent* speech, lives on and is a skill German politicians still have to master. Peter Peter:

> "These are ideal locations for political gatherings. Nowadays the biggest political speeches in Bavaria are given on Ash Wednesday, in big beer tents. You need to be populist: you should be a little bit aggressive, but you should also make the people laugh, otherwise it will not work."

Beer-drinking is not as popular in Germany as it once was, but the country is still the third-biggest consumer of beer in the world, and

The Oktoberfest in Munich

local beers still reign supreme—as do local sausages. Both suffered after 1945 from an image problem—they were too closely associated with a nationalist image of Germany which the post-war generation wanted to throw off. But, as Peter Peter has found, things are now changing:

> "Now there is a new generation that did not know the problems of the Cold War or the Second World War, for whom it is cool to try these old-fashioned things. It's avant-garde in a certain way to rediscover that even sauerkraut can be an excellent dish. I think a very good symbol of this new Germany is the Oktoberfest. Twenty years ago nobody there would dress in the traditional Bavarian costume. Now everybody does it and it doesn't seem either nationalistic or jingoistic. The Oktoberfest, with its enormous number of beer consumers, is a wonderful example of the new Germany that combines iconic tradition with open-mindedness. It brings people and peoples together more even

Beer drinkers in Munich in traditional costume

> than football. It is not nationalist—it is now a symbol of German hospitality."

To the British observer, Germany is a nation of startling diversity. Regional specialities represent centuries of regional history—different beers and locally distinct sausages, all managed by wider regulations that began 500 years ago. General de Gaulle famously complained of the difficulties of governing a country with 246 varieties of cheese. He should have been grateful he was not attempting one with many, many more kinds of sausage. But these wide variances are, as so often in Germany, contained within an overarching national structure. In a sense, it is a gastronomic analogy to the coins of Chapter 5, and to the entire political functioning of the Holy Roman Empire, which held together much of Germany and Central Europe, despite enormous local variations, for a millennium.

Part Three

The Persistent Past

Politically Germany has long been the epitome of loose association and variable geometry. For nearly a thousand years the Holy Roman Empire of the German Nation held together peoples and states of different dialects, laws and religions. The Hansa was a flexible and outstandingly successful trading association, or free-trade area. Memories of both are still alive, and are talked about as models for Europe today. Different episodes from Germany's past—the Reformation, the Napoleonic invasions and the revolutions of 1848—have left long legacies, down to the present.

Replica of the crown of the Holy Roman Emperors, the "Crown of Charlemagne," made by order of Kaiser Wilhelm II, 1914

11

The Battle for Charlemagne

Among the many precious possessions gathered over the centuries into the Hapsburgs' Imperial Treasury in Vienna, perhaps the most prized is the *Reichskrone*, the Crown Imperial. Heavy with historical and symbolic significance, it is known as the Crown of Charlemagne and was used for nearly a thousand years at the coronation of the Holy Roman Emperors. That crown is not the subject of this chapter. The crown illustrated here is a copy of it, a copy made for the rival German ruling house, the Hohenzollerns, in 1914, and held today in the City Museum in Aachen.

The first section of this book explored the floating frontiers and the many changing versions of Germany that have existed over the centuries, along with its numerous internal divisions. This section is devoted to the memories that unite Germans today, collective memories and understandings which, in spite of those divisions, carry associations of shared experience and common aspirations. So it may seem strange that the object I have chosen to embody such a jointly held idea is, if not exactly a fake, then certainly a replica—but in this instance one perhaps even more eloquent than the original. And, indeed, we shall see that even the original is not what it seems.

Around the year A.D. 400 the Roman Empire in the west began to disintegrate. The authority of the Emperor dissolved. The legions withdrew from Britain, Germany and France, and over much of

DEUS HOC TUTUM STABILI FUNDAMINE TEMPLUM QUOD CAROLUS PRINCEPS CONDIDIT ESSE VELIT + CUM LAPIDES VIVI PACIS COMPAGE LIGANTUR
DIGNUS

western Europe ordered civil society collapsed. Four hundred years later, around 800, one man, Charles, King of the Franks and ruler of most of what is now France and Germany, set about remaking that lost Roman Empire. He built his palace chapel at Aachen to the west of Cologne, using the model of Roman Imperial churches in Constantinople and Ravenna. He transported there sacred Christian relics from Jerusalem and ancient porphyry columns from Rome, remaking pagan Rome on Christian German soil. It is a magnificent example of appropriating different histories to make one new narrative.

His chapel still stands, a noble and domed octagon, three storeys high. It was for centuries the tallest building north of the Alps. It is supported by ancient Roman columns, which hold the lofty rounded arches. This is properly, visibly, the capital church of a new, a *Holy*, Roman Empire. The king who built it, Charles, is known to Germans as Karl der Grosse—Charles the Great. To the French and to us, he is Charlemagne.

During forty years of almost continual fighting, between his accession in 770 and his death in 814, Charlemagne, King of the Franks (who certainly spoke a Germanic dialect), conquered territories running from the Pyrenees in the west to the Elbe and the Danube in the east, and also included much of Italy. In Rome, on Christmas Day 800, he was crowned Emperor by the Pope. For a brief moment it seemed as though the Roman Empire in the West had been reborn, and with it the hope of a return to peace and prosperity.

That hope ended in 843, when Charlemagne's three fractious grandsons inherited the Empire and carved it up among them. Conflict followed, and the rulers of the western and eastern parts of Charlemagne's realm (roughly corresponding to what are now France and Germany) settled to a long tussle for supremacy, bitterly focused on the central territories which lay between them. The struggle between Germans and French to claim Charlemagne's legacy—the right to dominion over western Europe—was fought out over 1,000 years, with Aachen Cathedral standing as a great symbolic prize.

Previous pages: left, Aachen Cathedral, with Charlemagne's octagon in the centre; right, Aachen Cathedral, interior of the octagon

Ninth-century figurine of Charlemagne on horseback in Metz Cathedral

Charlemagne was buried here in the year 814, and over the course of 600 years—from 936 to 1531—thirty Holy Roman Emperors were crowned in this building.

The Emperor who concerns us here is Otto I. He was crowned first in Aachen as King of the Romans. Then, in 962, like Charlemagne, he was crowned by the Pope in Rome as Holy Roman Emperor. The Imperial Crown now in Vienna was probably first worn by Otto in that ceremony of 962, although it was later, and certainly wrongly, held to be the crown of Charlemagne himself. It is an extraordinary confection of gold and precious stones, enamels and pearls, further embellished over the centuries—an arch and cross were added later. It continued to be used in the coronation of Holy Roman Emperors to the very end of the Empire in 1806.

The crown is not circular as you might expect it to be, but made up of eight separate panels—four jewelled, four enamelled—joined to make an octagon. Together they form a jewelled allegory of earthly rule ordained by God. The four enamel plaques show kings: the three Old Testament kings who prefigure Christ—Solomon, David and Hezekiah, all with scrolls carrying extracts from the coronation liturgy—while the fourth shows Christ himself, enthroned between seraphim. Two other panels are studded with an array of coloured precious stones—amethysts and malachite, rubies and quartz, crystal and pearls—while the two tallest panels each carry twelve large stones: the one at the back symbolizes the twelve tribes of Israel, the one at the front the twelve apostles. Over the front panel stands a jewelled cross: on its reverse is an engraved image of the crucified Christ.

The whole object is a mystical, dazzling—literally dazzling—fusion of the spiritual authority of biblical kingship and the sheer power and wealth of the early Middle Ages. But there is more: this is in fact not only a crown; it is the echo of a building, of Charlemagne's chapel in Aachen, and a reminiscence of the majestic Imperial churches in Constantinople and Ravenna. Wherever this crown travelled, and over the centuries it travelled very widely across the

---

Opposite: Karl der Grosse (Charlemagne) from *Twelve Ancestors and Early Kings of the Germans*, 1543

Carolus Magnus/der erst Deutsche Keiser.

Carolus der groß/ein Franck des gblüts
Ein thewrer Fürst/eins edlen gmüts/
Kühn/weis/mechtig/vnd grosser sterck
Das zeigt sein that/vnd all sein werck/
Erlangt von wegn seins hohen rhumbs
Die Monarchey des Keyserthumbs
Wölcher mit ehr/vnd grosser macht
Hat erstlich an die Deutschen bracht
Wölchs auch in ehrn in Deutschen landen

Er hat Deutschland gar hoch erhaben
Erleucht mit vielen thewren gaben
Mit Policey vnd gbewen zirt/
Vil grosser fehrlich krieg gefiert/
Aln vngehorsam vnderbracht
Gut Regiment vnd friden gmacht
Hat Gotseligkeit/vnd kunst geliebt/
Vnd sich in aller tugent geiebt
Gestifftet hoher schulen drey

whole of the Holy Roman Empire, it carried with it resonances of the Aachen chapel and above all of the political and spiritual authority of the man venerated as the Empire's founder—Charlemagne. He himself never wore this crown. But to hold it was to hold his legacy.

Horst Bredekamp, the German cultural historian, explains:

> "In the *German* imperium Charles the Great and Aachen as his palace were taken as the origin of Germany and of German dominion in Europe, or at least central Europe. And, of course, from the French side, it was claimed that not Charles the Great but Charlemagne was the founding father of *French* kingship. This conflict continued all through the Middle Ages. In the eighteenth century Voltaire claimed Charlemagne as a very French ruler. In contrast, nineteenth-century Germany regarded Charles the Great as the great German. This opposition continued until the replica of the crown was made, and is the reason why it was made. What was Charlemagne? Was he the founder of the German imperium or the French one?"

To support these claims, both monarchies, with a pleasingly symmetrical disregard for historical authenticity, incorporated "relics" of Charlemagne in their coronation rituals from the Middle Ages to the end of the eighteenth century—the French using what they claimed was his sword, the Germans the "Crown of Charlemagne."

What did that crown mean as the political and military power of the Emperor waned? To Europe as a whole, it stood as an emblem of divinely ordained authority, all the more potent because the office of Emperor was not hereditary but, like the Papacy, elective. Since both Charlemagne and Otto had been crowned by the Pope himself, it confirmed the primacy of the Emperor among all the rulers of Christendom. Within Germany it was a symbol—and after the addition of the top-piece, a literally overarching symbol—of the widely disparate

---

Opposite: The relics, vestments and insignia of the Holy Roman Empire, Nuremberg, 1470–80

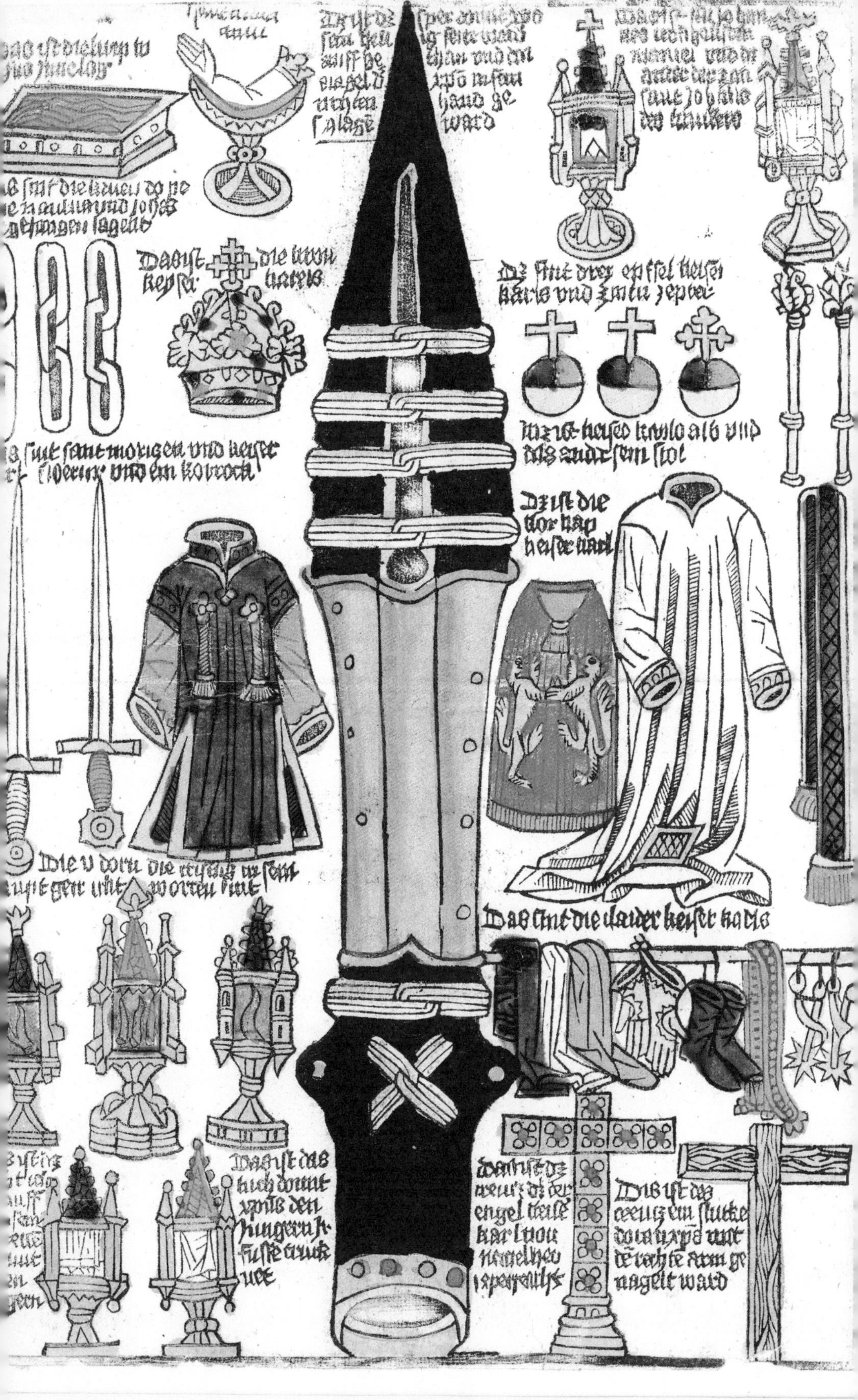

Das sint die cleider keiser karls

territories of the Empire, of the shared vocation of the German lands. It spoke quietly, archaically, imprecisely, of a common inheritance.

As the Emperor, over the centuries, was elected from different families, the crown moved around different German cities. But eventually, around 1500, when the Hapsburgs consolidated their hold on the Empire, it settled in Nuremberg, making that rich and powerful Free City in a very particular sense Imperial, and putting it at the centre of a dream world of German harmony and unity. It was a resonance in which Wagner delighted and which, later, Hitler exploited. Over the course of time, princes of the Empire acquired their own crowns—in Prussia, Great Britain and Poland. But those were crowns of mere kingdoms. There was only one Empire, and so this crown remained supreme.

Then, with the ascent of Napoleon Bonaparte, everything changed. Now French troops did not just attack the Rhineland, as Louis XIV had frequently done, but invaded Italy and occupied Rome. In 1804, Napoleon crowned himself Emperor of the French in Notre-Dame, like Charlemagne, in the presence of the Pope, who had been specially transported to Paris for the occasion. For the first time in over a thousand years, there were two emperors in western

Medal by Bertrand Andrieu, 1806, showing Napoleon and Charlemagne on one side, and their defeated opponents Frederick William III of Prussia and the Saxon leader Widukind on the back

Napoleon's version of Charlemagne's crown, 1804

The Emperor Napoleon I Crowning Himself, by Jacques-Louis David, *c.* 1805–7

Europe. The theatre of the ceremony left no doubt about Napoleon's intentions. At the door of the cathedral, a statue of Charlemagne was erected for the occasion. During the coronation, Napoleon wore "Charlemagne's sword." And as Charlemagne's "real" crown was of course in Germany (the Hapsburgs went to great lengths to keep it out of Napoleon's hands, moving it from Nuremberg to Vienna and beyond), he simply commissioned a *new* Charlemagne crown, on a quite different design. Made in 1804, it is still exhibited in the Louvre, startlingly titled "La couronne dite de Charlemagne" ("The crown said to be Charlemagne's"). There could be no greater tribute to the mythic power of the medieval crown in Nuremberg—or, as R. J. W. Evans explains, no clearer demonstration of the French challenge to the very existence of the Holy Roman Empire:

> "Napoleon destroys the Empire. There's no question about that. Napoleon's claim, when he makes himself Emperor of the French, was quite evidently irreconcilable with the Holy Roman Empire. The Austrian ruler recognizes that, and although he is

> already Francis II, Holy Roman Emperor, he calls himself Francis I, Emperor of Austria. He sees that he just has to have that as a fallback position.
>
> "When the French win the day at Austerlitz in December 1805, it becomes clear that Napoleon is free to act more or less as he wishes on German territory. He has of course lots of allies among the German princes, which leads him to create a Confederation of the Rhine. This is the immediate trigger for the dissolution of the Holy Roman Empire. In the summer of 1806, a proclamation by Francis releases his vassals from their bonds of fealty. He does it because he can see that the next step is that either Napoleon will somehow usurp the Empire, or will create an alternative empire which includes his German vassals. Either way it will be impossible to sustain the Holy Roman Empire."

If the crown was one focus of conflict, the battle for the inheritance of Charlemagne can be read just as clearly in the stones of his chapel in Aachen. In 1794 invading French revolutionary troops hacked the Roman porphyry columns out of the building and took them to Paris. Only some were returned (most of the rest are still in the Louvre), and so those columns still in Aachen that were originally brought from Rome by Charlemagne himself now stand among nineteenth-century replicas. But it was not only columns that were taken to France. In 1801, at the Peace of Lunéville, the whole of Aachen was annexed, incorporated into France, now a French city with a significant symbolic role to play in Napoleon's assumption of Charlemagne's Imperial mantle. After Waterloo and Napoleon's defeat by the Prussians and British in 1815, Aachen could not be restored to its previous status as an Imperial Free City of the Holy Roman Empire, as that empire no longer existed. Instead, it became an integral part of the territory of Prussia. The Imperial chapel of Aachen, long held by the Hapsburgs, coveted by Napoleon, was now in the hands of the Hohenzollerns. Charlemagne was now once again Karl der Grosse, Charles the Great, a German, or perhaps, mischievously, a Prussian.

Opposite: Stained-glass window showing Kaiser Wilhelm I dressed as Holy Roman Emperor, 1888

·WILHELM·I·
·DEUTSCHER KAISER, KONIG VON PREUSSEN·

As the nineteenth century progressed, the Hapsburgs, now emperors simply of Austria, increasingly retreated into their dynastic lands to the south and east. But as Prussian power advanced, so the idea of a German Empire revived until, in 1871, after the Prussian victory in the war against France, Napoleon III, Emperor of the French, was deposed and Wilhelm I, the Hohenzollern King of Prussia, was proclaimed German Emperor in Versailles. You might have imagined that the competition for Charlemagne's legacy had finally been settled. There were still bitter rivalries between Berlin and Vienna, but in essence this was surely now an intra-German discussion (see Chapter 21). But myth is a powerful thing, and this myth of European dominion was too strong for France to abandon. In 1882 a huge bronze statue of Charlemagne and his paladins, by the brothers Charles and Louis Rochet, was erected on the Île de la Cité, at the very doors of Notre-Dame in Paris, near the spot where a Charlemagne statue had been erected for the coronation of the first Napoleon. The Third French Republic, anti-clerical, anti-imperial, which had expelled and exiled Napoleon III after the defeat of 1870, nonetheless wanted the ancient emperor from Aachen to stand at the heart of the national capital, in front of the national church. Defiantly he faces Germany, and the visitor today can see that even on horseback, riding out to war, this bronze Charlemagne wears the octagonal crown which is at the centre of this chapter.

In 2013 the British Museum asked if we could borrow, from the Imperial Treasury in Vienna, Otto's crown, with all its resonances of Charlemagne's authority. Politely, we were refused: the Imperial Crown of the Holy Roman Empire, we were told, no longer travels. But we discovered that we were in very exalted company. A century before, Kaiser Wilhelm II had made exactly the same request, for an exhibition he wanted to organize in Aachen about Imperial coronations. In spite of the close military and political alliance between Berlin and Vienna by that time, Kaiser Wilhelm also was refused. On the eve of the First World War the Hapsburg emperors would not, could

---

Opposite: Charles and Louis Rochet's huge bronze statue (1877) of Charlemagne on the Île de la Cité, Paris

not, part with the crown that carried the aura, spiritual and political, of the first German Emperor.

Horst Bredekamp continues the story:

> "In the replica of the Imperial Crown, in Aachen, a long history is encapsulated—the history of the competition between the Prussian Hohenzollerns and the Austrian Hapsburgs to claim the inheritance of the Holy Roman Empire of the German nation. It is a replica, because when Kaiser Wilhelm wanted to borrow the original, it was not allowed to leave Vienna, where it was kept, to travel to Prussia. And so he had a copy of it made, in order to demonstrate that the Hohenzollerns are the true heirs to the whole tradition of the Holy Roman Empire of the German nation."

The copy of the *Reichskrone* now in Aachen is of very high quality and accurate in every detail, proof of the importance that Wilhelm II attached to his planned exhibition on Imperial coronations. That project was disrupted by the outbreak of war in 1914. By the end of the war, both Hapsburg and Hohenzollern emperors had disappeared. The crown, however, remained, and the story it embodies had still not reached its conclusion. Horst Bredekamp:

> "This copy is an act of resistance against the Austrian claim that the Hapsburgs embodied this *imperium* in their own person.
>
> "It started of course with Otto I, who—or so most research suggests—inaugurated not only the German Empire, but also the myth that the crown goes back to Charles the Great, or Charlemagne. From that moment onward Charlemagne became an object of dispute: French or German?
>
> "But that is in the past. Charlemagne, Charles the Great, today stands for the friendship between France and Germany. That is why the Aachen Prize (the Charles Prize), which is given always to a true European, now plays the major role in the German public's memory of Charlemagne. Charles the Great, if he plays a role in German consciousness, is a great German, not as

a figure for advancing German interests, but for transcending them, elevating German interests to a higher, European, level.

"If I were, in my imagination, to place Charlemagne in a particular setting today, I would locate him in the Cathedral of Reims in 1962, where Adenauer and Charles de Gaulle celebrated the new brotherhood between the French and the German nations. That was a moment at which Charlemagne, Charles the Great, was absolutely present, giving legitimation for both statesmen, in a European way which transcends national interests."

Adenauer and de Gaulle met for that solemn act of reconciliation exactly 1,000 years after Otto I was crowned by the Pope in Rome,

De Gaulle and Adenauer leaving Reims Cathedral, 1962

probably with the original "Crown of Charlemagne." The saga that began in Aachen, the conflicts surrounding the crown of Charlemagne and the struggle for his legacy, was formally consigned to history, and a new and lasting partnership between Germany and France declared to be the keystone of an enduring European order.

There is a final, or near final, sour twist to the story. The "happy ending" of 1962, to which both France and Germany now look back with warmth, had had a very unhappy prelude twenty years earlier, which has—understandably—sunk from the collective memory. Like Napoleon, like Kaiser Wilhelm II, Adolf Hitler was also interested in the legacy of Charlemagne. He had the Imperial Crown brought back from Vienna and restored to Nuremberg, where it had lodged before the Napoleonic invasions, and which was now the site of the spectacular rallies celebrating the Third Reich, the third iteration of the German Empire.

In the early 1940s, when Hitler was trying to win support from the French Right for the war against Russia—or, in his terms, the crusade to defend European values against Bolshevik barbarism—he turned to Charlemagne as the founder of European civilization, whom both

Sèvres plate produced in 1943 for the 1,100th anniversary of the division of Charlemagne's empire

countries could revere. A porcelain plate produced in Sèvres in 1943 shows a small statuette of Charlemagne on horseback. On the other side, an inscription in Latin records:

> The Empire of Charlemagne, divided by his grandsons in 843, Adolf Hitler is now defending, together with all the peoples of Europe, in the year 1943.

Hitler did indeed find French volunteers to fight with Germany on the Eastern Front. They were called the Division Charlemagne.

Riemenschneider's Luke from *The Four Evangelists*, *c.* 1490–92

12

Sculpting the Spirit

In his famous jibe of 1756, Voltaire scoffed at the Holy Roman Empire as being "in no way holy, nor Roman, nor an Empire." It's a great one-liner—Voltaire was good at those—but it will not do. The Holy Roman Empire was in fact, at various stages of its thousand-year existence, emphatically all three. In plain language, the Holy Roman Empire did exactly what it said on the tin: it set out to be the heir of both the Rome of the emperors and the Rome of the popes, and, to a surprising degree, it was. We have already looked at the Empire through its coinage (Chapter 5) and as the creation and legacy of Charlemagne (Chapter 11). In this chapter, I want to look at one particular aspect of its holiness.

From the beginning, in spite of being centred in the Rhineland, the Empire was very Ancient Roman in its military ambitions and its dreams of wide territorial dominion. Charlemagne, transporting choice antiquities from Imperial Rome to his chapel in Aachen, was determined that he and his successors would be *imperator*, in the military and the political sense, their empire universal. The Kaiser would be Caesar, with many of the same attributes and titles. But the Empire was also, from the beginning, Holy. In 800, as we saw in the previous chapter, Charlemagne went to Rome and was crowned by the Pope. The temporal and the spiritual authority of the new realm were to be inseparable—princes of the church were princes of the state. Of the seven electors (all territorial magnates) who chose the Emperor, three were archbishops—of Mainz, Trier and Cologne.

Among the many astonishing things about the Holy Roman Empire, not the least is that this ancient, quintessentially Roman Catholic political structure could, at the Reformation, adapt so successfully that it was able to accommodate—in every sense—a Protestant as well as a Catholic faith, and in large measure retain the allegiance and affection of both. It was a great political achievement, but it was an accommodation bought at great cost. This chapter discusses that painful transition around 1520, which permanently split both the Church and Germany, as it affected the life and the work of one of the most powerful and moving of all European sculptors: Tilman Riemenschneider.

Riemenschneider is relatively little known outside Germany, but he is, I believe, comparable to Donatello in the intensity and subtlety with which he explores the spiritual. His favoured medium was the traditional German material of lime-wood, whose fine grain allowed him to achieve astounding varieties of texture. *The Four Evangelists*, now in the Bode Museum, Berlin, were part of a great carved altarpiece, made for the Magdalenenkirche in Münnerstadt, near Würzburg, and completed in 1492. The tall, many-figured composition, dedicated to St. Mary Magdalene, dominated the east end of the church, with figures soaring towards heaven (and getting quite close to the roof). The sitting figures of the Evangelists, each about two and a half feet high, were at the bottom, just above the altar itself. As the priest celebrated mass, in Catholic theology representing Christ himself, he would be face to face with Matthew, Mark, Luke and John. In their company, he would read aloud the Gospels they had written. Only a few yards away from them, the faithful would kneel. These are sculptures designed to be looked at closely and often, to be lived with as companions, and to be engaged in dialogue every time mass is said or received. In this soaring altarpiece, Riemenschneider provided a sacred framework within which mortal actors could perform their timeless spiritual functions. In that sense it might stand as

---

Opposite: The altar of Münnerstadt church, for which Riemenschneider's *The Four Evangelists* were originally made, with modern reproductions

an emblem of the structure of the entire Holy Roman Empire, itself a sacred framework, punctuated with references to the life and redeeming suffering of Christ, within which transient actors—emperors, princes, merchants—lived out their divinely ordained roles.

St. Luke sits on a low stool, head tilted pensively, his right hand resting on his Gospel, his left patting his faithful attribute-ox, who kneels placidly at his feet. Carved out of one piece of wood—the trunk of a lime tree—the figure demonstrates Riemenschneider's tranquil mastery of technique and materials. Luke's hand, his book and the cloth between them are all demonstrably different from each other in texture, substance and weight, and different again from the folding dewlaps of the ox's neck. But the carving addresses issues beyond surfaces. The draperies suggest that while Luke is at rest, he is not at peace: the heavy gathering of cloth on his shoulder and the zig-zagging folds of his sleeves speak of a burden of unease. From where he sits, he looks down to the altar, on which Christ's sacrifice

Riemenschneider's *The Four Evangelists*: (left to right) Matthew, Mark, Luke and John, 1490–92

will be symbolically re-enacted in the mass. Luke's Gospel alone tells the story of Christ's birth: every day he here watches his death. His face has an expression of meditative melancholy, but, like an attentive dog concerned for his master, the ox turns expectantly, consolingly towards him. This saint is very like us.

The Director of the Bode Museum in Berlin, the art historian Julien Chapuis, is a noted scholar of Riemenschneider:

> "This is the crux of his genius. This is why he was so successful. You cannot look at these works without forgetting that you are looking at wood. We need to remember that at the time this was created, 1490 to 1492, most sculpture in Germany was coloured, gilded and painted. If as a sculptor you know that your figures will be painted, you can rely on the painter to add a blush on the cheeks or add red to the eyes to make the figure look as if it had been crying; whereas if you have to deliver a sculpture that is

going to remain uncoloured, expression is entirely dependent on your ability to control the chisel. And in that Riemenschneider was unsurpassed. He was absolutely matchless in this ability.

"The very light lime-wood is covered with a honey-coloured glaze and you see that the eyes are just marked with a dot of paint and the lips have a slightly reddish tinge to them. But that is all. Everything, the entire expression, is achieved through the manipulation of the lime-wood. If you look closely you can see tool marks pretty much everywhere. The big flat folds, for example, have traces of a different chisel. The texture of the hair, by contrast, is drilled in different directions to allow separate locks of hair to stand out. It is deeply incised to create a rich pattern of light and dark: Riemenschneider was a great master in the use of light as a creative element. You have to imagine that in the church in which these works were displayed, light conditions changed between morning and evening and according to seasons and weather. Often there would be candlelight. The expressions would change continuously.

"The figure of St. Luke for me is outstanding for its introversion and meditative quality. The meaning and form are perfectly matched. He holds the finished gospel on his knee, but he does not hold it directly. A portion of his drapery separates his hand from the book—a centuries-old convention to indicate that you do not touch that which is Holy. The melancholy on the face, the posture of the figure, the drapery, the gestures, all seem to me to suggest the awe that he has for the contents of the book that he has written."

Considering his fame as a sculptor, we have few firm facts about Riemenschneider's early life—not even his exact date of birth. Like Gutenberg, he moved around the great cities of south Germany, and like Gutenberg his career was shaped by the religious economy of the late Middle Ages. He is thought to have learned his trade in Ulm and Strasbourg and then came to Würzburg, the seat of a rich, powerful prince-bishop, where he settled, in 1483, in his early twenties. Two years later he married a wealthy widow (he would go on to marry

Probable self-portrait of Tilman Riemenschneider from the Creglingen altarpiece, 1505–10

three more times), and qualified as a master craftsman. Most of his work was for the church, but he had his own workshop and trained apprentices from other parts of Germany. Although sculpture like his was painstaking, time-consuming work, his workshop was large and the output was huge—nearly 150 altarpieces and other religious sculptures, tombstones and statues. While much is now lost, at least twelve altarpieces survive in the Würzburg area, and many works from much further afield. By the time he carved *The Four Evangelists* in 1492 he was pre-eminent in his field, and with up to forty apprentices ran a large enough concern to become a wealthy landowner with vineyards. He became a prominent citizen in an important prince-bishopric of the Holy Roman Empire. This is an artist thoroughly integrated into the life—religious, economic, political—of his city and his world.

Riemenschneider's flourishing career came at a time of growing religious and political instability. The ideas that would later fuel the Reformation were gaining ground across Germany and causing lively debate. We do not know where Riemenschneider's religious sympathies lay, but Julien Chapuis believes *The Four Evangelists* reveal a sculptor who was himself wrestling with these new, unsettling ideas:

> "In my opinion, one of the most important gains of the Reformation is that intermediaries no longer exist between God and mankind: you could pray directly to God. Every time that mass was celebrated, which was certainly every day, the Elevation of the Host took place with these figures as a background. The host is the symbol for God made flesh, God made man. *The Four Evangelists* represent God made word. Riemenschneider fuses these two dimensions of God by placing these figures behind the Elevation of the Host. And this is why—if you look at Luke's face—I do not want to say he is deeply troubled, but clearly what is in the book does not leave him indifferent. There is great sadness and he caresses the back of the ox's neck, which pricks up its ears, almost as if to say, everything will be all right after all. You have a sense that this is someone close to breaking down, and this extremely personal dimension is what is so striking and moving in these carved blocks of wood—which we can perceive both as blocks of worked wood and at the same time as human beings.
>
> "Riemenschneider is never theatrical. His art does not shout. It articulates convincingly and softly. We recognize our hopes, our weaknesses, our aspirations; what makes us human and also what helps us to become better. His talent resides in making God approachable on a personal level and in that sense he is, if you want, a Reformation artist, even though he worked for the Catholic Church all his life."

The inwardness of the statue of Luke, meditating in private on the significance of the life and death of Christ, certainly corresponds to a strong current of German spirituality around 1500—a personal piety which became a key element in the Reformed, Protestant theology.

When this altarpiece was made, the structures of Church and Empire were secure, even if the practices of the Church, especially its relationship to money, were under attack. The Emperor had under him hundreds of rulers of different territories: some were princes, dukes or counts, but many were bishops and abbots. The church everywhere provided the framework for the spirit, but in many places it also operated as a power in the land. Prince-bishops were to all intents and purposes the local sovereigns, and one such was Riemenschneider's protector, patron and prince, the Bishop of Würzburg. Their worldly status was offensive to a growing number of commentators, and Protestants came to believe that the Church's central spiritual mission had been compromised and corrupted by temporal power. Inevitably, from a mixture of principle and self-interest, some of the Empire's secular dukes and princes agreed, and espoused the Protestant cause. The scene was set for political turmoil, as Joachim Whaley explains, and Riemenschneider was at the centre of it:

> "Artists such as Tilman Riemenschneider, for example, citizen of Würzburg, and city councillor there, would have experienced the Reformation and the years around this period as years of great uncertainty. While the Emperors, Maximilian I and then, from 1519 onwards, Charles V, were keen to maintain Catholicism, some of the princes and cities had rather different aspirations. Many were concerned to promote the reform of the Church, but were above all keen to maintain order in their own territories. The problems that resulted from the Reformation were underlined for many contemporaries by the great uprising, the German Peasants' War of 1525, which seriously threatened the political equilibrium in many parts of Germany."

The Holy Roman Empire was to a high degree conceptually held together by the Roman Catholic faith: whatever the day-to-day realities of power, political functions were formulated and enacted within a theological framework. A comparison with the relationship between the current Chinese state and the traditional, orthodox doctrine of Marxist–Leninist communism is perhaps not entirely fanciful. So when a new and different understanding of the Christian faith arose with the Reformation, the whole *idea* of the Empire was called into question. That was certainly the case in Würzburg. By the 1520s Tilman Riemenschneider was a leading member of the city council. And the bishop was one of the wealthiest and most powerful of the Empire's ecclesiastical princes, a divisive figure, constantly in friction with the local burghers.

In 1525, Europe experienced its largest and most widespread popular uprising before the French Revolution: the German Peasants' War. It was provoked in part by anger about excessive taxation by the princes, a familiar complaint that in itself represented nothing new. What *was* new was the support given to the peasants by a number of leading Protestant clergy. For many this became a revolt against political and economic oppression: there emerged a novel strain of radical egalitarianism which threatened every local hierarchy. The ultimate suppression of the revolt by the authorities was every bit as bloody as the uprising itself. In its mixture of utopian idealism and savagery, the Peasants' War holds a special place in the memories of both the Right and the Left in Germany. It was a major preoccupation of the young Käthe Kollwitz (Chapter 22). In 1525, Würzburg was the site of one of its most important episodes.

It was Tilman Riemenschneider's bad luck to be one of the mayors of Würzburg in the year the revolt broke out across Germany. Along with the town council, he had to decide whether to side with the forces of the bishop or with the far larger peasant armies. Ultimately (they probably had no option) the council opened the gates of the city to the rebels while the cathedral chapter and the bishop withdrew to the fortress on the hill above. Later, once the revolt had been crushed, the bishop re-entered his city in triumph. The spiritual prince then set about reasserting his temporal authority. What actually happened to Riemenschneider at this point is wreathed in the smoke of conjecture, and many accounts, according to Julien Chapuis, are merely wishful myth-making:

> "This is a subject about which there are few facts and a lot of romance. We know that Riemenschneider was Bürgermeister, mayor, of Würzburg on two occasions. He was a member of the

The army of the Swabian League arriving to suppress the peasants at Würzburg, 1525

municipal council for several years, and as the council had suffered under the authority of the prince-bishop of Würzburg, it sided with the peasants in their revolt. There were also pragmatic reasons for this. Würzburg was not an independent city—it had a prince. It might well have wanted the more autonomous status of an Imperial Free City, like Nuremberg or Cologne. So it is not clear that the council's motivation was totally humanitarian.

"It is known that after the failure of the revolt he was arrested. We have no surviving statement from Riemenschneider telling us about his opinions. If you look at the facts that we have, it is possible that he was indeed straightforwardly in favour of the advancement of the peasants. But we cannot prove that. The legend is that he was tortured, that his hands were broken and that, after that, he never carved again. All we know for sure is that

> he did some repair jobs, but nothing significant after the end of the Peasants' War in 1525: we do not know that his hands were broken.
>
> "One would, however, expect a master of his distinction to work into his old age if he could. But to continue receiving commissions, there were expectations of behaviour that an artist had to respect. It was not advisable to voice too much criticism. Even the great Johann Sebastian Bach, 200 years later, signed his letters to his patrons as your most humble and obedient servant. And after the peasants' revolt was quashed by the prince-bishop, Riemenschneider, regardless of his ability as a master, was clearly persona non grata. He had become radioactive to potential patrons who did not want to run into trouble with the prince-bishop."

The Peasants' War ended in blood. Luther, the man who translated the Gospel into the language of the people, who had spoken of all as equal before God, was appalled by the kind of equality for which the people now clamoured. He called on the princes to suppress the revolt ruthlessly. They did.

Whatever the truth about Riemenschneider's involvement in the Peasants' War, it ended his career as a sculptor. German art—and the world—would be the poorer for that. But the consequences for his existing works were, initially at least, less apocalyptic. In France, England and Scotland, the Reformation had a devastating effect on religious art. There, pictures, glass, sculptures were smashed and burnt, monasteries reduced to ruins. But in Germany it was different. Luther took a generous view of the role of art in worship. The decentralized structure of the Holy Roman Empire, with its patchwork of interlocking but independent states, meant that an overarching iconoclasm never took root. Whereas many of Riemenschneider's altarpieces and statues would, in other parts of Europe, have met certain destruction, in the Empire they survived.

As Joachim Whaley points out, the weakness of the central Imperial power meant that in Germany, unlike the rest of Europe, compromise, rather than ideological ruthlessness, won the day:

> "In 1526 it was agreed that each ruler should manage his affairs and his territory as he wished, until such time as the Church Council decided everything, a rather vague formula. Of course, the Church Council never ultimately decided everything, and that led to one compromise after another. Following a last attempt by Charles V to impose his authority and his own religious preference—Catholicism—by force in the 1540s, which was resisted by the princes and failed, a framework agreement was arrived at in 1555, the Peace of Augsburg. This recognized the two Christian confessions, Roman Catholic and Protestant Lutheran, as equally valid within the Holy Roman Empire. That in turn was further elaborated, culminating in the Peace of Westphalia in 1648, which further recognized Calvinism as the third permitted confession. It was an agreement which recognized not only the rights of princes but also and above all the rights of individual subjects to freedom of religion in the context of those three confessions."

The Peasants' War and the Thirty Years' War had resulted, after terrible conflict, in what some historians regard as the ultimate achievement of the Holy Roman Empire: the creation of a political unit which could officially accommodate religious difference. In terms of religious tolerance, neither Britain nor France could compare.

Riemenschneider survived (in some fashion) the Reformation and the Peasants' War, and so (in some fashion) did most of his works, only to fall victim later to a different force—taste. The Münnerstadt altarpiece with *The Four Evangelists* came through the Reformation unscathed. But its beautifully worked varnish was thought too dull, and another artist was commissioned to colour the figures. Then the whole thing went irrevocably out of fashion. The huge altarpiece was dismantled and put into storage. During the disruptions of the Napoleonic Wars, it was split up into its component parts and sold piecemeal. But most of it survived, and the separate parts are now housed in different museums. The *Four Evangelists*—later colour carefully removed—are now safely in Berlin.

In the twentieth century, Riemenschneider's reputation as an artist has steadily risen. The churches that house his sculptures have become tourist attractions. Museums have highlighted his work in special exhibitions. He is seen as a supreme sculptor, working in a peculiarly German medium, lime-wood, but articulating the sensibilities of a continent. He has at last taken his proper place in the story of European art. His reputation as a man, however, has, since 1945, had an astonishing trajectory. In the German construction of national memory, Tilman Riemenschneider has played a surprising role.

As the war ended in May 1945, and Germans wondered what future they had in a Europe they had done so much to destroy, across the ocean in Washington, one of the great Germans of the twentieth century, the writer Thomas Mann, who had fled Hitler's Reich, stood up in the Library of Congress to address his American hosts on "Germany and the Germans" (see Chapter 6). He suggested that after what had been done by "bad Germans," the time had come to identify the "good Germans," the "other Germans." After acknowledging Luther's flawed greatness, especially deploring his part in the defeat of the peasants, Mann went on:

> At that time there lived in Germany a man who has my special sympathy, Tilman Riemenschneider, a master of religious art, a sculptor and wood-carver, widely famous for the faithful and expressive excellence of his works, which ornamented the places of worship all over Germany. He never expected to take a hand in politics, in world affairs—the thought lay far from his natural modesty and from his love for his free and peaceful work. But his heart, that beat warmly for the poor and oppressed, forced him to take that part of the peasants, whose cause he recognized as just and pleasing in the sight of God, against the lords, the bishops and princes, whose favour he could easily have retained. Moved by the great and fundamental contrasts of the time, he felt compelled to emerge from his sphere of purely spiritual and aesthetic artistic life and to become a fighter for liberty and justice. He sacrificed his own liberty for the cause that he held higher

---

Opposite: *The Adoration of the Magi*, by Riemenschneider, 1505–10

> than art and the dignified calm of his existence. It was his influence, chiefly, that determined the city of Würzburg to refuse military service to the "Burg," the prince-bishop, and in general, to assume a revolutionary attitude against him. Riemenschneider paid dearly for it. For after the crushing of the peasant revolt, the victorious powers whom he had opposed took cruel revenge upon him; they subjected him to prison and torture, and he emerged from the ordeal as a broken man, incapable of awakening the beauties in wood and stone.

In this moving, lyrical tribute, it is clear that Thomas Mann believed he had found a soulmate—an artist who, through moral conviction, played the part he could in the great struggle for liberty (though unkind spirits might reflect that sitting out the Third Reich in California was less testing than being in the political thick of the Peasants' War in Würzburg). It is, of course, a view which is not supported by historical evidence. It says much more about Thomas Mann than about Tilman Riemenschneider. But it says even more about the painful difficulty of constructing a German history, of the compulsion to recover—to create—memories that can nourish. It is a problem that

East German five-Mark coin and West German sixty-Pfennig stamp commemorating the 450th anniversary of the death of Riemenschneider

other countries with easier histories, and easier attitudes to them, have rarely had to address.

It was not only Thomas Mann who adopted the lime-wood sculptor as a moral and political hero. Both post-war German states followed his example. The Federal Republic put his work proudly on their stamps. To the German Democratic Republic—as easy-going as Mann in their approach to documentary evidence—Riemenschneider the man was more important. He was obviously everything an artist should be in his fearless commitment to the freedom of the poor from oppression by the powerful. They put him on a coin. In the GDR's construction of a national memory, the sculptor, at once artist, activist and martyr, was a model all might follow—a secular saint for the Socialist state.

Seventy years after Thomas Mann's speech, the question of Riemenschneider's politics remains open and, in some circles, alive. The inwardness of Riemenschneider's art still speaks with the quiet force which has marked much of German spirituality for centuries, strikingly evident in the Pietistic movement in Lutheranism, and still perceptible today in the deep-seated German admiration for modesty and reticence.

Georg Gisze of Danzig, by Hans Holbein the Younger, 1532

13

The Baltic Brothers

Hamburg and Bremen: the last two medieval city-states in Europe, each now an autonomous *Land* within the German Federal Republic, each still with its own local legislature. They are worlds away from the great ex-dynastic *Länder* like the former kingdoms of Bavaria and Saxony. They are the survivors of an outstandingly successful German experiment in the variable geometry of political association, one of the most enduring commercial networks ever established: the Hansa.

If you come out of Cannon Street Station in the City of London and turn left down Dowgate Hill towards the river, you come to a dark, uninviting alley under the railway lines: Steelyard Passage. Walk through the gloom and turn right onto the embankment, and you see a plaque on the wall of the railway bridge. It was unveiled in 2005, and it marks the location of the Steelyard, a thriving commercial trading post founded at the end of the thirteenth century, now completely obliterated by Cannon Street Station. The Steelyard, or *Stahlhof,* was a small piece of Germany in London. It was the English headquarters of the huge German-speaking trading alliance which straddled the North Sea and the Baltic, connected the Rhineland to Russia, and linked scores of cities across northern Europe: the Hanseatic League or the Hansa. Today, a path along the embankment is still called Hanseatic Walk.

Boo Church
Stiliard

The Steelyard, a huge, walled settlement on the Thames, was effectively a gigantic warehouse. Beside it was the quayside with its crane, where ships brought in German wines and exported woollen cloth. There were meeting rooms and houses and a great hall for the 400 German merchants who lived here. They were in many ways a separate community, self-governing, literally a law unto themselves. The plaque says the merchants "inhabited peaceably in the City of London from the 13th to the 19th centuries," which is stretching the truth. The Hansa's control of the English wool trade in the Middle Ages led to some violent confrontations; but there were good reasons for the English to keep the Germans of the Hansa onside. Hilary Mantel, who has researched the activities of the London Hansa for her novels on Thomas Cromwell—whose strong links with the continent frequently ran through the Steelyard—explains why:

> "Given that Germany was not an entity in those days, but a number of independent states, this was as close as one could come to official representation. There was not the division between trade and diplomacy that we might find at a later era so the Steelyard could be described as the face of Germany in England. Economically it was an absolute power-house, because the goods coming in through the Steelyard were noted not only for their usefulness but for their quality. Even in those days, to have goods made in Germany was a guarantee they would work. The German community was favoured partly because, in times of war, it was good to have the Hanseatic League merchants on your side: they commanded a huge fleet, and England of course was always vulnerable to blockade. This was one of England's great weaknesses during the time of Henry VIII: if grain had been cut off, then the country could easily have starved during periods of bad harvests. England was a huge producer and exporter of woollen cloth but she could not necessarily feed herself."

One person who would have walked regularly through the gates of the London Steelyard in the 1530s was the artist Hans Holbein

---

Opposite: Detail from Hollar's *Long View of London* showing the Steelyard

Self-Portrait, by Hans Holbein the Younger, 1542

the Younger. Since arriving in London from Basel, he had built an extraordinary client base in London among intellectuals, courtiers and merchants. He had the patronage of Thomas Cromwell and Anne Boleyn, both sympathetic to the Reformed religion. Hansa merchants in London were the most enviable of non-doms, a wealthy and privileged elite, with access to all the luxuries of the continent. And if they could afford it, they could have their portrait painted by their fellow German-speaker, Hans Holbein.

If I had to choose one object that sums up the Hansa in its heyday it would be Holbein's 1532 portrait of Georg Gisze, a Danzig merchant trading in the Steelyard. Gisze is thirty-three years old, expensively dressed—those red sleeves!—and very keen that the viewer should know who he is. He obligingly holds a letter at an angle that allows us to see it is addressed (in Low German) to: "Dem Erszamen Jergen Gisze to lunden in engelant mynem broder to handen"—"To be handed to my brother, the honourable Georg Gisze at London in England." Above his head, on a slip of paper stuck to the wall with sealing wax, we learn (in Latin this time) that this is an accurate rendering of Georgii Gysenii, in his thirty-fourth year, that his cheeks are just as we see them here, and his eyes just as lively. And, in case we have missed these two clues, painted on the wall to the left is "G. Gisze." The letters on the rack to the right have the return addresses of merchants in Basel: G. Gisze, having ensured we know who he is, clearly wants us also to know that he is assiduous in his business correspondence. He is a serious, successful, educated young man, gaining valuable business experience in the City of London.

The Gisze family, originally from the important Hanseatic trading centre of Cologne, were established merchants in Danzig (now Gdansk), a German-speaking city that owed allegiance to the King of Poland. On the table in front of Georg is a ring with the arms granted to the family by King Sigismund. Together with the letter from his brother, it underlines how much the Hanseatic trading community depended on family links, particularly in the arranging of credit over very long distances. The right-hand side of the picture is entirely about business, the letters from Basel, the account book with its red velvet straps, the pewter inkstand, quill pens, red sealing wax with a signet ring and seal—the stuff of official correspondence. On the other side of the painting, the vase of flowers suggests a different Georg: the carnations are a conventional symbol of betrothal, rosemary of remembrance and hyssop of purity. This is G. Gisze the model fiancé: three years after this portrait was painted he married Christine Krüger, daughter of another successful Danzig merchant—and above his name on the wall to the left is the slightly prissy motto "Nulla sine merore voluptas"—"No pleasure without sadness."

Hilary Mantel knows this picture—and the sitter—well:

> "Georg Gisze was the offspring of a wealthy Danzig family, serving his time at the German house in London, picking up international experience. Georg is looking directly at us. You can read the picture as a love letter. It has been overpainted so his gaze

has been turned slightly to his right, and the right is traditionally where the woman is placed. The carnations indicate that he is engaged; it is as if he is looking at his absentee fiancée, who is back home. If you think trade has no dignity, you have to look at the Steelyard portraits. These are the merchants of the Hanseatic League, this vast international trading organization. They are people of wealth and status, but perhaps not formal political power, and within them Georg is placed as a young man of influence. Holbein's other Steelyard paintings are plainer. They are no-nonsense in style. Often the sitter looks at us full face—like a mug shot done by a genius."

The Hansa's origins lie in the twelfth century. The word originally meant a band of men, with some military overtones, but by the twelfth century it was used to describe the medieval guilds. At its peak in the fifteenth century the Hanseatic League was an alliance of some ninety self-governing German-speaking cities, led by Lübeck and Hamburg, a loose federation that worked in a cooperative fashion. In that way it was very Germanic. Like much of north Germany, it operated outside the control of both the Emperor and the imperial

Lübeck in 1552

institutions. Some member cities, including Danzig and Riga, Stockholm and Bergen, were outside the Empire altogether.

Cornelia Linde, of the German Historical Institute, has made a special study of the Hansa's history:

> "The Hansa was a very strange beast in that it had no officials, no seal, no statutes, no army, no navy, no ships. Those were all individually owned by the merchants. It was very much based on an economy of trust. One element that bound most of the Hansa merchants together was the language they spoke—Low German. Another was family ties: many of the Hansa families you find in the eastern cities originally came from further west, and they often retained connections with cities in the west through intermarriage. So usually somebody in Lübeck would know exactly who they were dealing with in Riga and the chances are they might be in some way related."

That Hansa merchants in London were commissioning portraits from such an eminent and expensive artist as Holbein gives us some idea of how important and powerful the Hansa had become by the

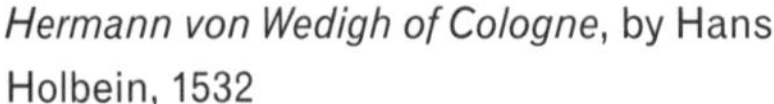

Hermann von Wedigh of Cologne, by Hans Holbein, 1532

Derick Berck of Cologne, by Hans Holbein, 1536

middle of the sixteenth century. The organization itself may have owned little, but it controlled much. Its power was based on a complex web of trading routes spanning the North Sea, the Baltic and the great rivers of northern Europe—linking the Volga to the Thames. But the Hansa cities did not just seek to trade; they also defended trade routes, which is why they themselves raised armed fleets to protect their member cities and, if necessary, to wage war on those who challenged their power and activities. They developed their own system of commercial law, and held a more or less annual meeting, the *Hansetag*—Hansa parliament—in Lübeck to debate important issues. Hanseatic power stretched from Novgorod in north-west Russia right across the Baltic and North Seas to London and eastern England. Cornelia Linde explains how it all worked:

> "What the Hansa did by banding together was basically seek safety in numbers. It was a community of people with common commercial interests. The curious thing is that the cities of Lübeck and Hamburg did not produce anything much themselves. They were just centres in which wares were traded. The

Salt warehouses in Lübeck, some of the few original Hansa buildings still standing today

increasing professionalization of merchants meant that they no longer needed to travel so much themselves. This in turn allowed them to become politically active in the cities where they were based; many Hansa merchants became council members, for example. They had specialist crews to do the travelling, and they had their business partner—a cousin, say—waiting at the other end for the cargo. Working this way, a merchant was not limited to making just one trip to Bergen: he could send ships to London, Riga and Bergen at the same time. Really what the Hansa merchants did was to connect eastern and western Europe."

This is the world Holbein conjures so powerfully in his portrait of Georg Gisze, whose father was, typically, a member of the Danzig town council, and whose letters link Basel to Danzig in one friendly family network of credit and exchange.

But the network went far wider than that. Gisze's vase of symbolic flowers is made of the finest, thinnest Venetian glass, which simultaneously demonstrates Gisze's wealth and Holbein's skill in capturing reflected light. Beside the vase is a small circular brass clock, certainly made in southern Germany, and both sit on a Turkey carpet imported from the Levant. But behind Gisze, hanging from the top shelf, is a reminder of home: a small pendant sphere of amber from the foreshore of the Baltic. Thus was the wealth of the world brought together by the Hansa in the Steelyard.

But in 1532, when the portrait was painted, the Hansa were trading ideas as well as goods, and those ideas were shaped by the fact that most of the great Hanseatic cities embraced the new Reformed faith; and, as so often, religion travelled along trade routes. Hilary Mantel again:

> "Everything in this painting is about communication. And it is about the word in more than one sense because the German merchants in London were importing forbidden bibles, Lutheran works. They were the centre for anyone interested in the word of God in the vernacular. The Steelyard was a very conspicuous self-sufficient community and they were already the focus of intense suspicion, and had been raided. They were a beleaguered community, but nothing was going to stop the profitable trade in forbidden books. Indeed, you simply cannot keep ideas out, and by the 1530s things were moving in their direction. Thomas Cromwell, an evangelical sympathizer, was the coming man and he was steering through a series of laws which would create the break with Rome and set the English Reformation on its course. Holbein, as it turned out, was part of the plan. The German—Hanseatic—merchants at the time of Anne Boleyn's coronation [in June 1533] commissioned him to design a triumphal arch, which was their contribution to this hugely transgressive event: the coronation of the woman whom much of Europe regarded as Henry's concubine. The German merchants, so often out in the cold ideologically, were now at the centre of affairs and,

> after this, anyone who was anyone in Tudor England, up to and including the king himself, would be painted by Holbein. This German painter, who was very much identified with his own countrymen and their vast economic power, would give us many of the cultural icons of the era which we think of as distinctively English."

In the fifteenth century, the Hansa was a powerful presence along the whole east coast of England. As well as London, Boston and King's Lynn, it had depots in Hull, Ipswich and Sandwich. In Germany, its power bases Hamburg and Lübeck were granted free-city status within the Holy Roman Empire. But as England and the Netherlands expanded their trade with the Americas and the Far East, and their shipbuilding, sea power and financial centres developed with it, the Hansa cities found themselves increasingly at a disadvantage. The Baltic could not compete with the Atlantic. Hansa privileges were gradually withdrawn: by Russia in 1594, by Elizabeth I in 1598. By 1604 there were only fourteen member cities left. Cornelia Linde explains that there were other, internal, factors at work:

> "One of the reasons for its demise was that there was no proper structure, so over the course of time the individual merchants turned away from the Hansa, and then it just disintegrated. It was a very slow demise that unfolded over a couple of centuries. We do not even have a proper end date for when the Hansa ceased to exist. One date often mentioned is 1669, the last time the *Hansetag* got together, but it is not as though they declared the official end of the Hansa in 1669. It is just that no decisions were made. They thought they would meet again, but they never did."

London, or rather Holbein, may have provided us with the best portraits that we know of Hanseatic merchants, but England was always on the Hanseatic periphery. The heart was the Baltic. There is no painting that sums up the complex functioning of this north-German merchant world as compactly as *Georg Gisze*, but you can come even closer to its enduring cosmopolitan opulence in a group of three ceremonial tankards dating from the seventeenth century. It was customary in this world to seal a trading contract or confirm a commercial deal by formally drinking beer together—rather as we might now shake hands—and in Lübeck, or Hamburg, or in Georg Gisze's home town of Danzig, you could drink beer in astonishing style (see Chapter 10). All three tankards are extravagant silver gilt, elaborately decorated, conspicuously rich. But the Danzig tankard far outdoes both the others.

Made a little before 1700 by the Danzig goldsmith Daniel Friedrich von Mylius, the barrel of the tankard is given over to a panoramic vision of Belshazzar's Feast in Babylon. King Belshazzar himself sits at the head of a long sloping table, his miniature guests individually modelled in high relief, each feasting happily as, above them, visible to the drinker of the tankard but not yet to them, the Writing on the Wall appears—"Mene Mene Tekel Upharsin," "Thou art weighed in the balance and found wanting"—and God condemns the opulent sacrilege of the feast. This is great goldsmithery for the Protestant rich: power and wealth are allowed, but may be enjoyed only in the fear and admonition of the Lord. And it is a characteristically German form of that message: the words "Mene Tekel" are still used in modern German to pronounce something unacceptable or wrong.

The two other tankards make a quintessentially Hanseatic point. The one made in Lübeck has engraved inside the cover the city emblem of Riga, then part of the Polish–Lithuanian Commonwealth; while the Hamburg beaker, a startling creation that could be mistaken for Art Nouveau, carries an inscription in Russian in Cyrillic script. Together they are wealthy witnesses to the centuries-long supra-national trading community of the Hansa. The German merchant diaspora of the Baltic, the German-speaking populations of Danzig and Riga, Tallinn and Königsberg, survived and flourished until 1945. Then the entire population was expelled or killed. With this, the eastern Hansa was finally extinguished (see Chapter 26).

Opposite: Top left: silver-gilt tankard from Lübeck, 1601–25. Top right: silver-gilt beaker from Hamburg, *c.* 1650. Bottom: silver-gilt tankard from Danzig, *c.* 1680

In England, we have only a plaque on the Thames embankment in London, a warehouse in King's Lynn and some superb Holbeins to remind us of what the Hansa was. But in Germany much stronger traces remain. Ten German cities still call themselves "Hansa cities," and their car numberplates proudly carry an initial H—HB for (Hansestadt) Bremen, HH for Hamburg, HL for Lübeck, and so on. According to the political historian Michael Stürmer:

> "If you ask people from Hamburg or Bremen where their friends and neighbours are and which are their closest neighbours, they would invariably say Britain and Scandinavia."

As late as the 1880s, even though the Hansa was long gone, it is said that children would chant: "Hamburg, Lübeck and Bremen. No one can ever shame 'em. For they are cities free. Where Bismarck has no right to be." The writ of the new German Empire, in other words, had no right to run there. But there was no doubt that the prosperity of these cities depended now on their industrial and Atlantic endeavours, not on their traditional Hanseatic activities. The consequence by 1900 was a growing gulf between the booming Hamburg and Bremen, on the one hand, and Lübeck, whose status waned throughout the nineteenth century.

> Often, the outward and visible material signs and symbols of happiness and success only show themselves when the process of decline has already set in. The outer manifestations take time—like the light of that star up there, which may in reality be already quenched, when it looks to us to be shining its brightest.

The most powerful and famous literary evocation of embedded Hanseatic prosperity comes when it was already in the past. Thomas Mann's melancholy tale *Buddenbrooks*: *Decline of a Family* (published in 1901) captures the traditions and wealth of one great Hanseatic family in its well-to-do twilight.

Lübeck, Thomas Mann's home city, is now incorporated into

The historic centre of Lübeck

Schleswig-Holstein, and no longer autonomous. Hamburg and Bremen, facing the Atlantic, have prospered and are still Free Hanseatic cities and separate *Länder* within modern Germany. (Hamburgers are intensely proud that theirs is a "Freie *und* Hansestadt," while Bremen is merely a "Freie Hansestadt." The distinction, clearly of huge significance, remains to outsiders impenetrably opaque.) Both cities saw themselves, and still do, as republican city-states after the high Roman fashion, governed by consuls and senators, and adopting for public buildings the Roman letters *SPQR*, *Senatus Populusque Romanus*. You can see to this day *SPQH*, *Senatus Populusque Hamburgensis*, on the door of Hamburg Town Hall, and similarly *SPQB* in Bremen. Germany's airline is Lufthansa—the Hansa of the air—with its Senator class for business travel.

Twenty-five years after the fall of the Iron Curtain, the political geography of northern Europe has returned to an earlier pattern. The cultural and linguistic fundamentals may have changed, but trade across the Baltic and the North Sea is once again commonplace. Tallinn, Riga and Gdansk today trade easily with Hamburg, Bremen and London.

Opposite: Hamburg Town Hall: SPQH

S.P.Q.H.

Iron Cross, 1813

14

Iron Nation

> A thousand ladies richly dressed. No lady was without her plume, some were blue like the sky, some were tinged with red, here violet and yellow, there shades of green. The diamonds encircling them caught the sun through the windows and threw dazzling beams around. Each lady seemed to rise out of a gilded barricade, it seemed as if the curtain had risen to show a pageant in another sphere.

This was the British court in the early nineteenth century, as described by Richard Rush, the American ambassador. For millennia, the clearest symbols of power and riches in Europe were precious metals and gemstones. Women were decked in these emblems of wealth and the opulence of power, to be worn with pride and to be looked at with wonder. And the ladies of London rejoiced in them. If, however, the ambassador had been accredited to Prussia, he would have been confronted with a very different scene. At a court ball there he would have seen jewellery of a much more modest sort, such as the simple necklace illustrated on page 252. It is not made of precious metal (no "gilded barricade" here), nor is it decorated with sparkling precious stones: it is plain, black and made of iron. In Prussia, and especially nineteenth-century Prussia, this unglamorous metal, the stuff of swords and helmets, of industry and agricultural

Iron statue of the Great Elector as Saint George, 1680

implements, had become the material of choice for jewellery with a new purpose—not the demonstration of wealth, but of patriotism, a symbol of resistance to the French invader.

This particularly Berlin habit of using iron in unexpected contexts has a long history. It can be seen in this small statuette of the Great Elector of Brandenburg (the forerunner state to Prussia), Frederick William I, who had heroically defended his country against invasion by the Swedes in the 1670s and begun the transformation of Brandenburg–Prussia into a European power. He is shown as the military hero and Christian knight St. George, dressed in Roman armour, triumphing over evil. Mounted on his charger, spear at the ready, he has overcome the dragon which is writhing beneath him. It is standard sculpture rhetoric, conventional in all but one aspect. Anywhere else in Europe, a statue like this would usually have been cast in bronze, with all its noble echoes of Imperial Rome. But this was Berlin, a court notorious for its ostentatious eschewal of luxury. The Great Elector, in the Berlin of the 1680s, is shown in iron. If Saxony was later defined by its production of porcelain (see Chapter 18), in Prussia the nation itself was personified in iron: no frippery, no nonsense. This was the Iron Nation.

The Iron Cross stands firmly in this Prussian tradition. The whole world knows the Iron Cross—rightly—as a symbol of German military prowess. But it also embodies an ideal of the Prussian state and of its citizens, united, understated and resolved. The story begins, though, with the iron jewellery. It is quintessentially German, speaking of a much-prized German virtue, *Bescheidenheit*—modesty. The necklace is restrained, unostentatious. Black-iron evocations of ancient Roman cameos form a circlet of nine oval medallions on three delicate linked chains. It dates from around 1805, the darkest moment of the Napoleonic Wars, when French troops had conquered and occupied almost all the German lands. Emerging from a period of neutrality, Prussia fatefully—probably foolishly—responded to what it saw as Napoleonic provocation and took up arms. The king, Frederick William III, urged a very public rejection of all forms of extravagance, and the adoption of ostentatious frugality. Following the lead of Princess Marianne, the Prussian royal family exhorted its female citizens to hand in their gold and silver jewellery, as a personal contribution to the war effort. In return, they were given iron jewellery like this necklace. Often, it was inscribed "Gold gab ich für Eisen"—"I gave gold for iron"—a public attestation of self-denying loyalty and patriotism. Prussians were to be men and women of iron.

In 1806 the Prussian army was humiliatingly defeated at the battles of Jena and Auerstädt and Napoleon entered Berlin (see Chapter 9). The royal family retreated to Königsberg in East Prussia, now the Russian enclave of Kaliningrad (see Chapter 3), which lies hundreds of miles east of Berlin, and then even beyond, to Memel on the very border with Russia. Königsberg may seem a far-flung outpost but it was central to the soul of Prussia. It was where the Kingdom of Prussia had begun and where in 1701 its first king was crowned. Settled

Iron necklace, *c.* 1805

Iron busts of King Frederick William III and Queen Luise of Prussia, by Christian Daniel Rauch, 1816

in Königsberg, King Frederick William III was forced to admit that Prussia, one of the most successful and enlightened states of eighteenth-century Europe, was now in mortal danger. In public memory, this notion of Prussia in 1806 as defiant, brave and alone still lingers, perhaps not unlike British memories of solitary heroism in 1940 after Dunkirk. The state was now fighting for its survival, led by its king, and beside him the heroic Queen Luise, who became a figure of devotion and inspiration to much of Germany.

Prussia's fightback against the French began in Königsberg. It was about rethinking the state, reorganizing the army, and re-energizing the people. The king declared that "only iron and determination" would save the nation. The women of Prussia who chose to wear iron jewellery were one aspect of that. Then in 1813, as the military tide began to turn in favour of Prussia and its allies, the king suspended all existing military decorations. He ordered a new one to be struck, for those who took part in the war against Napoleon. The Iron Cross was to be awarded to men of all ranks, not just officers—a historic innovation in Prussia, and a brilliant PR stroke. In the fight to free the nation, all Prussians would henceforth be honoured on equal terms, irrespective of wealth or social standing. (It was a system Napoleon had used with the Légion d'honneur in 1804. In Britain, it was not until 1856 that a medal for all ranks—the Victoria Cross—was introduced.) According to Christopher Clark, the author of *Iron Kingdom*, the institution of the Iron Cross fitted neatly into the existing mythology of Prussia:

> "Frederick William declared that the decoration was made of iron because this was a time of abstinence and deprivation. And there is something interesting about this—the link between a particular kind of austerity and the identity of Prussia, the idea that Prussia was a state which could make do. The notion that wives of *Junkers*, wives of Brandenburg aristocrats, would make their own dresses. In this mythical memory of what Prussia was, there is an insistence upon the simplicity and modesty of basic arrangements, and this liking for iron fits into that pattern, that emotional matrix.
>
> "The attraction of iron is of course that it is not a noble metal. It is an everyday material, with which everyday things are made. The king made this clear. When the Iron Cross was created, this was a new kind of military decoration, one which recognized the valour and the gallantry of all ranks, not just of generals and aristocrats, but also men of the line equally, regardless of status, depending only on how they performed their duties."

The Iron Cross, then, was as much an expression of Prussia's self-image of sobriety and resilience as of Frederick William's own iron determination to liberate his kingdom from French occupation. It was, he said, to be "a peculiar distinction of merit, for the duration of the present war." As a decoration, it is strikingly simple, made of cast iron, black with a silver border. There's no inscription, no grandiose assertion of valour, just a crown at the top, above the King's initials "FW," three oak leaves in the centre, and the date of the beginning of the great fightback: 1813. Iron, not a noble metal. German oak, not Roman laurels. It is indisputably an elegant object, but the symbolic impact of an iron cross—as opposed to bronze, silver or gold—is still potent. That symbolism is, however, even more complex than a non-German might think. Horst Bredekamp explains how this Prussian military cross has a much broader significance for Germans:

> "From our point of view, intuitively, iron is the symbol of German steadfastness, a central virtue. That is a perspective that combines very well with the German oak, which everybody knows as a German symbol, connected to the same traditional definition of German character [see Chapter 7]. And then with the iron cross is combined a second metal. The silver border. That represents the queen, Luise, and her ability to symbolize a different aspect of the German character. Silver is connected to sensitivity and weakness—weakness in a good sense, not in a feeble sense: being sensitive, feeling, intuitive, able to develop what the German soul was then meant to be. So you have in the Iron Cross not only strength, and the egalitarian principle, but also the softness of the German soul. That is why the symbol became so charged—because of its incorporation, as we see it, of at least three principles and not only one."

Just to the north-east of Königsberg is the small town of Tilsit. Here in 1807, on a raft in the River Neman, Napoleon met the Tsar and signed a Franco-Russian alliance. And here, in stark contrast to that expansive treaty, Prussia was forced to accept Napoleon's punitive terms for peace. Queen Luise met Napoleon in a final attempt to persuade him to offer a more generous settlement. Napoleon ignored her. Under the terms of the treaty, Napoleon removed around half of Prussia's territory and population—distributed among Russia, Saxony and Napoleon's own family. A huge fine was imposed. The vindictive conditions shocked Europe. They were never forgotten by Prussia. When in 1871 the fortunes of war were reversed, the French

Queen Luise of Prussia pleads with Napoleon, July 1807

were outraged that the Prussians treated them in the same way. But in the process Napoleon had created a formidable foe: Queen Luise spent her remaining years encouraging the Prussian people to hold out until they could recover their dignity and their lands. She was loved and revered by them as the "soul of national virtue." Napoleon, when she died in 1810, remarked that Frederick William had "lost his best minister." And even though the Iron Cross combined strength with soul—the silver that symbolized the queen—four years after her death, the grieving king, to honour her memory, founded the Order of Luise, a medal for the women of Prussia who had given service to Germany. It was limited to a hundred holders and, as with the Iron Cross, was open to all social classes.

The Order of Luise is represented by a small, black-enamelled cross with a sky-blue panel in the centre, bearing the letter "L" surrounded by a wreath of seven stars. Queen Luise, as wife and mother, patriot and example, came to hold a central place in the mythology and the memory of the nation. The Order of Luise survived in unbroken continuity until 1918. The Iron Cross, in contrast, was discontinued in 1815, at the end of the Napoleonic Wars, and was not revived until Bismarck had led Prussia to victory in the 1871 Franco-Prussian War (see Chapter 21).

An object now exhibited in the German Historical Museum in Berlin demonstrates how powerful the memory and the symbolism of the 1813 Iron Cross proved to be: it is shaped like the original decoration, but is much bigger—over three feet across and studded with iron nails. Once again this is iron used in the service of the state:

Cross of the Order of Luise, introduced in 1814

crosses like these were fundraisers for the First World War. From 1915 onwards people could buy a nail, to be hammered into the cross: the money went to the war effort. The nails were of different quality, and price, so that anyone, whatever their income, could help support the war, the poor side by side with the rich, workers side by side with Junkers. Like wearing iron jewellery a hundred years earlier, buying a nail was an act of public patriotism. An iron cross was once again the symbol of a nation united in arms.

For Horst Bredekamp, the creation of the original Iron Cross in 1813 epitomizes a rare and powerful moment in Prussian history, an alliance of Left and Right, of the liberal-intellectual parts of society and the military-authoritarian, a moment when the nation, men and women equally honoured, stood shoulder to shoulder in one common aim, to defeat Napoleon. That social alliance achieved its purpose resoundingly, but it couldn't survive the peace that followed.

> "In the best tradition of the founding idea of the Iron Cross, the Prussian king played the card of authority and also the willingness to bring together all citizens in a new union. They wanted to create a nation but they always wanted to avoid creating a democratic nation. And that is of course why the national movement, after the Wars of Liberation, was destroyed: because the democratic, liberal aspect of the movement became too dangerous. The Iron Cross was the very symbol of a coalition of what we today would call a left–liberal national movement with an authoritarian one, and that coalition had to be broken. And it is because that liberal tendency in the movement of German unification was after 1815 destroyed or suppressed that the revolutions of 1848 occurred."

After Waterloo, the liberals hoped that a new kind of society would emerge, with civic rights guaranteed by a constitution and some form of popular representation. The king had other ideas, and within a few years Prussia had reverted to its old pattern of authoritarian royal rule. Little would change until the upheavals and revolutions of 1848.

The unifying ideals of the Iron Cross soon died in the struggle

Giant Iron Cross with nails, 1915–18

between reaction and reform. It no longer exists as a military decoration, but it lives on in a significant if surprising way in the life of contemporary Berlin. One of the liveliest, buzziest districts of the modern city is named after it, Kreuzberg—Cross Hill. On the top of the hill to the south of the city centre, at the point from which Berliners watched Napoleon's army finally retreat in 1813, the architect Karl Friedrich Schinkel designed a monument to honour Prussia's part in freeing all of Germany from the decades of French invasion and occupation. In the shape of a Gothic cathedral spire, it looks to a British eye very much like the Albert Memorial. It is, unsurprisingly, made entirely out of iron. In twelve tall niches, oversize iron statues represent the key battles in which Napoleon's troops were steadily

GROSS
BEEREN
den 23 August
1813
GROSS
GOERSCHEN
den 2 Mai
1813
DENNEWITZ
Der König dem Volke
das auf seinen Ruf hochherzig
Gut und Blut dem Vater
lande darbrachte den Gefal
lenen zum Gedächtniss den
Lebenden zur Anerken
nung den künftigen Geschlech
tern zur Nacheiferung

driven out of Germany, culminating in the Battle of the Nations near Leipzig in 1813—the largest land battle in Europe before the First World War—and continuing through the Prussian occupation of Paris in 1814 and the final victory at Waterloo in 1815.

On the top of the spire of course is the Iron Cross itself, the symbolic embodiment of the historic wartime Prussian alliance between military power and liberal egalitarianism. The military side of that partnership finally and definitively foundered in Germany's total defeat in 1945, but here in Kreuzberg the liberal aspects are clearly and surprisingly alive. The district has become emblematic of the new multi-cultural, multi-ethnic Berlin, and in the park around Schinkel's monument, on a sunny day, one can hear German and Turkish, Arabic and Russian, spoken as families in hijabs eat ice creams and döner kebabs, paddle in the waterfall and listen to al fresco piano-playing—all in the shadow of the Iron Cross.

Today's happy ending would have astonished those liberals who attended the inauguration of the Kreuzberg monument on 30 March 1821. With the dangers of invasion safely behind them, rulers across Germany quickly decided that they could manage very well without ideas of equality or democracy. Hopes of reform were rapidly and successfully suppressed. The next twenty-five years were to be years of unavailing struggle by the liberals, and to end in the publication of Marx's *Communist Manifesto* and then the humiliating failures of 1848.

Opposite: Etching of the Prussian National Monument at Kreuzberg, by J. M. Mauch after Schinkel, 1823

15

Two Paths from 1848

As Germany celebrated the World Cup triumph of its football team in the summer of 2014, the television screens of the world were filled with black, red and gold. The national colours appeared on rattles and mascots, face paints and flags. For most people, national flags are essentially labels or identifiers, their significance largely ceremonial. But for Germans their national flag—*that* national flag, and those three colours—have a very particular meaning and carry a long history.

In the German Historical Museum in Berlin, there are many flags—with heraldic emblems or coats-of-arms, with eagles sporting one or two heads, flags of sovereigns, states and cities. It is not until the gallery devoted to the revolutions of 1848 that what we know today as the German flag first appears. It is in a quite different category from all that has gone before: for this is the flag not of a particular ruler or an existing state, but of an *idea* for a new state—a united Germany, governed by the rule of law. This is the flag of a state waiting to be born. And in 1848 it nearly was.

After 1815, and the defeat of Napoleon first at Leipzig and then at Waterloo, Germany had quite simply to re-invent itself politically.

Overleaf: One of the tricolour flags of constitutional Germany, *c.* 1848–52

The trauma of French invasion—in some cases leading to occupation for nearly twenty years—had left it unstable and divided. Napoleon had effectively destroyed the Holy Roman Empire, and humiliated both Prussia and Austria. There was no obvious centre of authority or unity that commanded general respect. In 1815 at the Congress of Vienna, guided by the subtle Austrian statesman Clemens von Metternich, the assembled rulers of Europe determined to restore as much as they could of the old, conservative order. The former ruling houses resumed control. The patchwork of the old Holy Roman Empire was rationalized into fewer, larger states. Together they set up the Deutscher Bund, the German Confederation, a loose assembly of sovereign states, an echo of, rather than a replacement for, the Holy Roman Empire, with the Emperor of Austria as president.

Yet for the increasingly educated middle class—the *Bürgertum*—and especially for the young, this return to the authoritarian structures of monarchies and grand duchies, rather than some kind of parliamentary model, was not merely unjust, but unacceptable. The French may have been invaders and oppressors, but they had brought with them the revolutionary ideas of equality and freedom, which were eagerly embraced by many Germans, who hoped, after the final defeat of Napoleon, for a new liberal constitutional order. For them—and they were numerous—the return to the past was intolerable. Professor Jonathan Sperber, a historian of the revolutions of 1848, explains:

> "There was a vacuum of legitimacy following the immense upheavals of the age of the French Revolution and of Napoleon in which the territories had been rearranged and reshaped and the 300 pre-1789 German states had been reduced to thirty-seven. There was a lot of feeling in the population that the existing rulers were not legitimate. They were not their traditional dynastic rulers. They often were of a different religion. Most people in the Palatinate, for example, were Protestants but were being ruled by a Catholic King of Bavaria. And there was a desire for some new form of government that would have a greater legitimacy."

The year 1848 saw unrest and revolution across the whole of Europe. The continent was economically depressed after a run of bad harvests and there was a rash of local conflicts—a serf rebellion in Austria, religious skirmishes in Switzerland. At the turn of the year, political disturbances coalesced into widespread violence: in Italy, in France, in the Low Countries and Austria, conservative regimes faced insurrection and several collapsed. France became a republic, the Austrian emperor abdicated, even the Prussian king, Frederick William IV, granted a constitution. Most important of all, among the delegates to the Parliament of the German Confederation, gathered in Frankfurt, the liberals for the first time were in the ascendant.

It was that Parliament which for the first time declared black, red and gold to be the colours of Germany—a new kind of Germany—united, operating under a legal constitution, and free. The three colours were echoed by three words—"Einigkeit, Recht und Freiheit"—unity, justice and freedom. The new flag and the new national anthem, the "Deutschlandlied," carried the same message. Freedom was to be guaranteed by a constitution, to protect against the arbitrary rule of princes. The flag was to be the flag of the German *people* rather than of a specific *state*. Jonathan Sperber:

> "It is traditionally said that the three colours of the German tricolour—the black, red and gold—date from the uprising against Napoleon and the French occupation in 1813, when a group of volunteers in Prussia wore black uniforms with red buttons and gold trim. The three colours were used as a national symbol on cockades and, increasingly after 1830, as a flag, most famously at the Hambacher Fest [a popular festival of national sentiment] in 1842. It could not be flown publicly. It was illegal, a challenge to the various German governments because it implied that there was both a nation and a popular sovereignty which was set above individual monarchs. One of the first things that

---

Overleaf: Fighting between civilians and soldiers in the Frankfurter Linden Strasse, Berlin, 18–19 March 1848

happened as soon as the revolution began in 1848 was that people took out these black, red and gold flags and began flying them everywhere—in the streets, in government buildings. It was very humiliating to the Prussian authorities. It was a symbol of what people hoped in the spring of 1848 would be a fundamental change in the way things were. The idea embodied in the flag is that the nation should be constituted by the people. There was a German people and they would finally, as a result of their revolution, have their own nation state, their own united Germany, which would encompass within it all the different monarchies, all thirty-seven of them."

The year 1848 was thus different in Germany from elsewhere in Europe. It was not just about throwing off the yoke of unaccountable princely power; crucially, it was about forging a new national entity that would embrace all Germans. It looked as though the flag had found its country. The inspiring, transforming idea was that Germany should not be Prussia or Bavaria, Saxony or Hamburg. Germany—Deutschland—was to be above all these, a new and higher entity and identity, more than the sum of its constituent parts. Jonathan Sperber:

"To express this ideal, they had a new song, the 'Deutschlandlied.' Its initial phrase—'Deutschland, Deutschland über alles' ('Germany, Germany above everything')—was designed to mean that Germany was more important to people than their local monarch, than their city, than their home. It was to be not a regional, but for the first time a national anthem. That was its original purpose. History has distorted its meaning for the outside world. The trouble with the 'Deutschlandlied' is that it is so associated with the Nazis. But it was originally designed as a democratic national song."

The "Deutschlandlied" words by August Hoffmann, and sung to Haydn's melody in praise of the Austrian emperor, was not, then,

August Hoffmann, author of the "Deutschlandlied," 1841

about German domination, but about union, just as the flag was a uniting flag: the different parts of the German-speaking world should be together, united and free under the law. Today, the tainted words "Deutschland über alles" are not sung—their original romantic national sentiment would certainly be misconstrued. Their place has, since the Second World War, been taken by the third verse of Hoffmann's song—"Einigkeit und Recht und Freiheit," the words of the German national anthem today.

The German tricolour flew for less than two years after 1848. The Frankfurt Assembly, weakened by factions and disputes, collapsed in 1850. The German constitutional experiment had failed. The reactionary monarchs recovered their confidence, and the liberals were crushed. Individual rulers reasserted their powers in their different states, Austria reassumed the presidency of the Confederation, and remained the Great Power of south Germany, while Prussia dominated in the north. Everywhere constitutions were watered down. The tricolour was once more suppressed. The status quo had prevailed. Twenty years later, Germany was indeed united, under the leadership of Bismarck's Prussia, with a very different constitution and under the black, red and white flag of the new German Empire. But the memories of those two years, 1848–50, survived, and when that empire in turn collapsed in 1918, the Weimar Republic returned to many of the democratic ideals of 1848, and the black, red and gold flag flew over the Reichstag. The Nazis removed it and replaced it.

Another event in that year of 1848, which was also a failure in the short term, was to have an equally profound long-term political impact on Germany, and an even greater one on the rest of the world: a rich young businessman, and a thirty-year old lawyer-turned-philosopher published a slim twenty-three-page pamphlet in an attempt to energize the members of a new fringe group, the German Communist League. The *Communist Manifesto* appeared just before the popular upheavals in Germany got into their stride. Its authors, Karl Marx and Friedrich Engels, had both had to leave Prussia because of their revolutionary ideas, so the manifesto, written in

The Frankfurt Assembly, 1848

German, first appeared in London, where they could publish freely. Phrases from the *Communist Manifesto* have become the mantra of left-wing politics worldwide and are familiar to even the least politically minded: "The history of all hitherto existing societies is the history of class struggles," and, finally, resoundingly, "Workers of the world, unite!"

Few copies of that original pamphlet now survive, but one is in the British Library. Dull in design, cheaply, densely printed in German Gothic type, it looks flimsy and vulnerable in its faded green paper covers. Nothing about it would suggest the impact it was going to have. Susan Reed, curator of German printed books at the British Library, tells us about the initial print run:

> "It has been reckoned to be at least 2,000, so they would have been circulated not only to members of the league but they would have tried to pass them on . . . We know that a thousand copies

were sent to Paris after the outbreak of revolution and that others were sent to other European countries."

But Marx's *Manifesto*, like the liberal tricolour flag, failed to produce the transformative revolution in Germany that he and Engels predicted. Susan Reed:

"Strangely enough, the ideas in the manifesto don't seem to have circulated very far in Germany in 1848, although it grew very much out of the same soil as the revolution and predicted some of the things that were going to happen. It became rather forgotten in 1848, and it was only really later, in about the 1870s, that it started to be picked up again and republished. Gradually, by the turn of the twentieth century, the *Manifesto* became a canonical text, almost like the prayer book. If *Das Kapital* is the Bible of Marxist thought, the *Communist Manifesto* is the Book of Common Prayer.

"It talks about expropriation of property using rents for state purposes, strong progressive taxes, the abolition of inheritance law, centralization of credit in the hands of a national state bank. It talks about Germany being on the eve of a great bourgeois revolution. And it says that the Communists will support the bourgeois revolution because only by doing that can they then rise up themselves and overthrow the bourgeoisie."

The failures of 1848 haunted both liberals and Communists for decades afterwards, and the memory of that fateful year—when two quite different Germanys might have been born—has been constantly re-examined. Jonathan Sperber again:

"You may know A. J. P. Taylor's famous remark—1848 was when German history reached its turning point and failed to turn—and there is a lot in that. But I think in recent decades we've come to

---

Opposite: Title-page of the first edition of the *Communist Manifesto*, February 1848

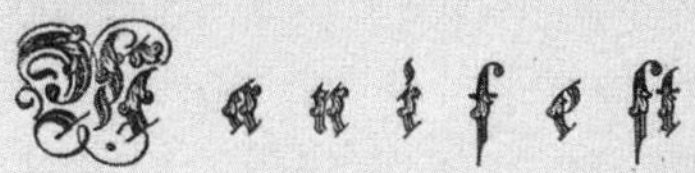

der

Kommunistischen Partei.

Veröffentlicht im Februar 1848.

London.
Gedruckt in der Office der „Bildungs-Gesellschaft für Arbeiter"
von J. E. Burghard.
46, Liverpool Street, Bishopsgate.

look at 1848 somewhat differently. Not as an example of failure of politics, so much as a new opportunity for all sorts of people to become involved in politics—women, for instance. Germany's first feminists all began their political careers in the 1848 revolution. More: a greater proportion of Germans belonged to political parties in 1848 than do today actually—about three or four times as many—and so we see that 1848 marked an explosion of political participation. That left its traces throughout politics. The idea of national unity, once brought into the public sphere, would not go away. Ultimately and ironically it was the Prussian conservative Bismarck and his spiked-helmeted soldiers who would create the national unity which the liberal revolutionaries had envisaged, but it was their idea that brought it to the fore in the first place. So I think historians have tended to have a more favourable take on 1848 recently than they have in the past, and indeed the 150th anniversary of the revolution in 1998 was very widely celebrated in Germany."

After the abdication of the Kaiser in 1918, both Communists and liberals saw—and seized—the opportunity to complete the work begun in 1848. And both did it on the same day. On 9 November 1918, from the balcony of the Reichstag in Berlin, the Social Democrat Philip Scheidemann declared the German Republic, whose constitution would later be worked out in Weimar. Two hours after Scheidemann spoke from the balcony of the Berlin Stadtschloss, Karl Liebknecht, the Communist leader, proclaimed the Free Socialist Republic. The attempt at a Communist state was quashed within a few months, and Liebknecht murdered (see Chapter 22). The liberals of the Weimar Republic were in their turn overwhelmed by the Nazis. Both strands of 1848 had failed again.

Yet in spite of ending in failure the events of 1848 have the same kind of potency in the German historical imagination as 1832 and the Reform Bill have for Britain, or the Declaration of Independence

---

Overleaf: Celebrations at the re-opening of the Brandenburg Gate, 22 December 1989

East Berlin, 1989

Statues of Marx and Engels in the Marx-Engels-Forum, Berlin, with Berlin Cathedral behind

has for the United States: they inform the national debate at every level and set the terms of reference for political engagement. Hostility between the two competing traditions of 1848—liberal/democratic and Marxist—not only weakened the Weimar Republic, but later characterized the two separate Germanys that emerged in 1949. In the West, the Federal Republic claimed descent from the Frankfurt Parliament and its liberal constitution; in the East, the Democratic Republic saw itself as the fulfilment of Marx's proletarian revolution, now that the workers of the world had, finally, united. The industrial city of Chemnitz was proudly renamed Karl-Marx-Stadt.

In 1949 *both* Germanys, the liberal-democratic West and the Marxist East, claimed the revolutionary black, red and gold flag as their own. It flew both in Bonn and in Berlin for ten years, until in 1959 East Germany added its national emblem of the hammer, compasses and circlet of rye, to make clear that the division between the two states was profound and permanent. Thirty years later, after the fall of the Wall, a demonstrator in East Berlin, clamouring for unity, carried the black, red and gold flag in the shape of a united Germany, once again a state waiting to be born, with the slogan: "Wir sind ein Volk"—"We are *one* people." Very 1848.

Germany is now again united under both the flag and the anthem of the liberals in the 1848 revolution. Karl-Marx-Stadt is once again Chemnitz. One might think that the bourgeois liberals of the Frankfurt Parliament had finally triumphed over the princes, and had definitively seen off the proletarian revolutionaries of the *Communist Manifesto*. But Berlin has a knack for accommodating what cannot be reconciled, for living with different and difficult histories. The black, red and gold now flies over a Reichstag bearing the inscription "Dem Deutschen Volke" ("For the German People"). But the Karl-Marx-Allee is still the grandest street in the refurbished eastern half of the city; and at the heart of Berlin, the political centre of Europe's leading capitalist economy, still stand, splendidly positioned, the imposing bronze statues of the authors of the *Communist Manifesto* and the heroes of the German Democratic Republic—Friedrich Engels and Karl Marx. The paths from 1848 continue.

Part Four

Made in Germany

Metalwork, precision engineering, cars, clocks, books and the finest copper-plate engravings: Germans have long been good at making extremely complex things unusually well. Technical training and craft skills have a greater presence in Germany than in other European countries. "Made in Germany," from Gutenberg to the Bauhaus and the Beetle, has always been an acknowledged badge of quality.

A printing press, 1520

16

In the Beginning Was the Printer

For a thousand years, making a book began with the killing of animals to provide parchment, and then required the long, careful labour of a scribe. That all changed in Germany, five and a half centuries ago, when Johannes Gutenberg invented a new kind of movable type and the printing press—and the book as we now know it was born. For many, it is the moment at which the modern world began. It is without doubt the point at which access to knowledge in Europe stopped being the privilege of the few. Gutenberg's invention shaped the Reformation which came sixty years after he began his work, and it changed our politics. In spite of the digital revolution, it dominates the way we organize our thoughts. Reading today on the flat screens of our iPads, we still impatiently flip to the "back page" to discover whodunnit; without any self-consciousness at all we use "bookmarks"; and when sending emails, we select our "font." In the world of advanced IT we remain unashamedly, irrecoverably, the children of Gutenberg.

In this section we are looking at things made in Germany which shaped and transformed not just Germany, but the world. The modern printing press must surely be the greatest of them all. In this chapter we look at how Gutenberg accomplished his revolution and why it could probably have happened only in Germany. The best place to begin is with Gutenberg's bible, published in Mainz in the early

1450s. The example illustrated opposite ultimately wound up in the British Royal Collection and, as a highly prized possession, it has been magnificently bound with the arms of George III (it is now in the British Library). It is the size of a bible one might see today on the lectern of a church. On being opened, it looks at first exactly like an illuminated manuscript: two columns of elegant black text, apparently written in a clear, even hand, are surrounded by painted decorations of foliage and birds, executed in gold leaf and brilliant colours. This is a most beautiful object to look at, as well as being expertly designed to be read.

Gutenberg printed around 180 bibles, of which forty-eight substantially complete copies still survive. Two of them are now in the British Library. Kristian Jensen, a historian of the early printed book, and the British Library's Head of Collections, describes what reveals it to be a printed book, not a manuscript copied down by an unusually consistent scribe:

> "The Gutenberg bible is what a user around 1455 would expect a book to look like. If you want to sell something, you need to make something that your customers will recognize and understand. So Gutenberg produced something that looked just like a traditional book. One of the ways you can tell that it is printed is by looking closely at the ink, which has a very shiny surface. When you write a book by hand, you use a water-based ink. You put your pen into it and the ink runs off. That does not work if you are printing, because the ink will also run off the press and spoil the page. So one of Gutenberg's inventions was an ink which was not ink. What we call printer's ink is actually a varnish, which means that it sticks to its surface and does not run, and that means that it looks different."

Finding the right kind of varnish—Gutenberg borrowed a formula used by painters—was only one of the many practices that he identified and adopted from other crafts. Winemakers and metalworkers, Latin scholars and goldsmiths, all had secrets and skills on which he drew and which he could then combine to make the first printer's

GEN ESIS

Incipit liber Bresith quē nos Gene
In principio creauit deus celū sim võ⁹
et terram. Terra autem erat inanis et
vacua: ⁊ tenebre erant sup faciē abissi:
et spiritus dñi ferebatur super aquas.
Dixitq; deus. Fiat lux. Et facta ē lux.
Et vidit deus lucem ꝙ esset bona: et
diuisit lucem a tenebris· appellauitq;
lucem diem et tenebras noctem. Factū
q; est vespere ⁊ mane dies unus. Dixit
quoq; deus. Fiat firmamentū in me-
dio aquarū: et diuidat aquas ab a-
quis. Et fecit deus firmamentū: diui-
sitq; aquas que erant sub firmamen-
to ab hiis que erant super firmamen-
tum: ⁊ factum est ita. Uocauitq; deus
firmamentū celū: ⁊ factum est vespere
et mane dies secundus. Dixit vero deus. Congregentur aque que sub celo
sunt in locum unū et appareat arida.
Et factum est ita. Et vocauit deus ari-
dam terram: cōgregatiōnesq; aquarū
appellauit maria. Et vidit deus ꝙ esset bonū· et ait. Germinet terra herbā
virentem et facientem semen: et lignū
pomiferū faciens fructum iuxta genus
suū: cuius semen in semetipso sit super
terram. Et factum est ita. Et protulit
terra herbam virentem et facientem semen iuxta genus suū: lignūq; faciens
fructū et habēs unūquodq; sementē scdm
speciē suā. Et vidit deus ꝙ esset bonū:
et factū ē vespere et mane dies tercius.
Dixitq; aūt deus. Fiant luminaria
in firmamēto celi· ⁊ diuidāt diem ac
noctē: ⁊ sint in signa ⁊ tēpora· ⁊ dies ⁊
annos: ut luceāt in firmamēto celi et
illuminēt terrā. Et factū est ita. Fecitq;
deus duo luminaria magna: luminare
maius ut p̄esset diei et luminare min⁹
ut p̄esset nocti: ⁊ stellas· ⁊ posuit eas in
firmamēto celi ut lucerent sup terrā: et
p̄essent diei ac nocti: ⁊ diuiderēt lucem
ac tenebras. Et vidit de⁹ ꝙ esset bonū:
et factū ē vespere et mane dies quart⁹.
Dixit etiam deus. Producant aque
reptile anime viuentis et volatile sup
terram: sub firmamēto celi. Creauitq;
deus cete grandia· et omnē animā viuentem atq; motabilem quā produxe-
rant aque in species suas: ⁊ omne volatile secundū genus suū. Et vidit deus ꝙ esset bonū: benedixitq; ei dicens.
Crescite et multiplicamini· et replete a-
quas maris: auesq; multiplicentur
super terram. Et factū ē vespere ⁊ mane
dies quintus. Dixit quoq; deus. Pro-
ducat terra animā viuentem in gene-
re suo: iumenta ⁊ reptilia· ⁊ bestias terre secundū species suas. Factū ē ita. Et
fecit deus bestias terre iuxta species suas: iumenta ⁊ omne reptile terre in ge-
nere suo. Et vidit deus ꝙ esset bonū:
et ait. Faciam⁹ hominē ad ymaginē ⁊
similitudinē nostrā· ⁊ p̄sit piscibꝫ maris·
⁊ volatilibꝫ celi· ⁊ bestiis vniuersq; terre:
omniq; reptili qd mouet ī terra. Et creauit deus hominē ad ymaginē et similitudinē suam: ad ymaginem dei creauit illū: masculū et feminā creauit eos.
Benedixitq; illis deus· et ait. Crescite
et multiplicamini ⁊ replete terram· et
subicite eam: ⁊ dominamini piscibus
maris· ⁊ volatilibus celi: ⁊ uniuersis
animātibus que mouentur sup terrā.
Dixitq; deus. Ecce dedi vobis omnē
herbam afferentem semen sup terram·
et vniūsa ligna que habēt ī semetipīs
sementē generis sui: ut sint vobis ī escā·
⁊ cūctis aiantibus terre· omniq; volucri
celi ⁊ vniuersis q̄ mouētur in terra· et ī
quibus ē anima viuēs: ut habeāt ad
vescendū. Et factū est ita. Viditq; deus
cuncta que fecerat: et erāt valde bona.

The opening of the Book of Genesis from the Gutenberg bible, 1455

workshop. After that, he had to construct a business model and a distribution system. This man was a great combiner, a great entrepreneur, and there are few places where he could have operated so successfully in the 1450s as in Mainz.

Today in the large square in the city centre, holding pride of place, stands the statue of Gutenberg himself—a powerful if totally imaginary portrait of a tall, bearded figure in bronze. We have no idea what Gutenberg actually looked like, but his fame quickly required an image—and so a likeness was invented after his death, popularized by prints, and spread across Europe. It is the model for this statue. Because of its strategic position on the Rhine, Mainz has been badly knocked about over the centuries. It was systematically bombed in the Second World War. Most of the buildings of the historic city centre clearly date from the 1950s or 1960s, except for the huge cathedral, which was damaged and then expertly restored. It has remained the dominant landmark that Gutenberg would have known well—the seat of the Archbishop of Mainz, one of the most powerful men in Germany. Gutenberg's family home was just a few minutes' walk from the cathedral, and the ruins of his parish church, St. Christopher, still stand.

There had been earlier forms of book-printing in Europe, but they were limited in scope. Carved wooden blocks were widely used to produce single sheets—usually an illustration, sometimes with a bit of accompanying text—a holy image with a prayer, for example. The wood-block was laid face-down on a piece of parchment or paper, and banged with a hammer to make a print—often fairly crude, but acceptable. But carving out of a wooden block has drawbacks for text, especially if the text is a sacred one: if a mistake is made, it cannot be corrected—the work has to start all over again with another block. So as a means of printing anything as large and complex as a book, the technique has serious drawbacks. Gutenberg's press, using movable metal letters, changed all that.

Dr. Cornelia Schneider, Curator of Early Printing at the Gutenberg Museum, describes the process Gutenberg would have used:

Opposite: Statue of Gutenberg, by Bertel Thorvaldsen, 1837, with Mainz Cathedral behind

CROZATIER FUDIT
MDCCCXXXVII

> "There is nothing of Gutenberg's workshop left, nor of any other printer's workshop from the fifteenth century. But at our museum we have re-created an impression of how it might have been in the early days of printing. First the paper is fixed into a frame with little pins, so that when the other side is printed, the sheet can be turned over, reusing the pin-holes so it could be printed on exactly the same part of the paper on the other side. The next step is to ink the type, using two leather dumb-bells, filled with horsehair. You cover them with ink, then you spread it very thinly over the metal letters. Now the letters are in their tray, inked, held in the press above the paper. The press itself is about six, seven feet high, with a huge wooden spiral in the middle, like a giant corkscrew. The corkscrew is tightened, and the type is pressed against the paper. It is hard work, but if the print is clear, it is wonderfully readable. When the future Pope Pius II saw one of these pages, he wrote: 'You could read them without your glasses.'"

One of the reasons why the future Pope found the text so clear was because each letter had been printed with the same level of pressure, the result of Gutenberg's brilliant idea of using a press. Mainz was, and still is, in a major wine-producing region, so he naturally hit upon the idea of using the technology of a wine-press. The screw could be turned to exert very strong but equal pressure across the page, and this was what allowed him to print all the different lines with such regularity and clarity.

The really difficult part of the process was manufacturing all the metal letters needed for any one page. Here again, geography and history were on Gutenberg's side: for millennia, the Mosel and the Saar had been centres of metallurgy. Expertise in the intricate working of metals was on hand, ready to be redirected, as Kristian Jensen explains:

> "Germany was one of the areas in Europe where metalworking skills were developing very fast, so Gutenberg worked in an advantageous technical environment. To make a book, you need

Reconstruction of the Gutenberg press and workshop in the Gutenberg Museum, Mainz

lots of very similar and (in many cases) identical versions of an 'A,' an 'E,' an 'O,' etc. Hundreds of 'E's are needed just for one page, so you need to be able to reproduce the letters many times over. Gutenberg invented a method whereby he could cast from a mould many instances of the same letter. Then you had these hundreds of bits of metal which had to be different in terms of which letter they had on them, but identical in terms of how high they were, because if they were not identical in height, then when you put them together and turn the press, they would break the paper. So he needed to have a method not only of standardizing each 'E,' each 'I,' but of standardizing the body they sat on. This is not at all easy."

Having access to so many movable, separable, letters solved one of the greatest drawbacks of the wood-block: mistakes could be spotted

Imaginary portrait of Gutenberg, 1584

in a proof print, and easily corrected by slotting in the right letter. But, as Kristian Jensen has pointed out, that advantage came at a price. Failure to equalize the height of every element of the movable type would wreck the paper. Cornelia Schneider explains why Gutenberg had no option but to use such a fragile support:

> "He wanted to use parchment, because he wanted to print the Bible and if you are printing the word of God you have to use the most precious material that you can get, which is parchment. But it was impossible to obtain enough parchment to print 180 copies of the Bible: it has around 2,000 pages and for every eight pages you need one sheep or goat. There were simply not enough animals, and so he used paper."

This is not quite as straightforward as it sounds. Good-quality paper of the kind needed for printing could not be bought just anywhere. The best paper was made in Italy, which would involve a long and expensive buying trip. Here again, the location of Mainz played a critical role. Just up the river is Frankfurt, with its two great fairs every year, where Gutenberg could order paper from Italy, knowing it would be delivered at the next fair six months later. So at every step, with every element of technology or materials that went into producing this new, printed bible, Gutenberg was able to source locally.

Even though Pope Pius II could read Gutenberg's bible without his glasses, it is much easier to find one's way around a block of text—especially when reading out loud—if there are chapter headings, and even easier if there is some colour to guide the eye. So to begin with Gutenberg printed chapter headings in red. But then he gave this up. Kristian Jensen explains why:

> "He probably realized that it was more time-consuming and therefore more expensive to print coloured headings than it would be for him or somebody else to pay a scribe to do it later. So he stopped. This is interesting because it shows us that this was very much a financial operation; and Gutenberg was learning how the workflow should be organized in order to make money out of this new process. He also began by printing forty lines per page, but soon moves on to printing forty-two lines per page, to save paper. This was a learning process."

It took Gutenberg and his skilled workers a long time to create enough letters for a bible, about two years. But once the movable type was available, he could print 180 bibles in the time it took a scribe to produce just *one*. Kristian Jensen:

> "Each element in the complex process of producing a book existed already. Gutenberg's genius lay in combining all these various different processes into one coherent work. Presses had been around for a very long time, but the use of a press for printing text was certainly new. Another of his masterstrokes was his use of varnish. Varnish for paintings was a fairly new thing in the fifteenth century, and Gutenberg could see that it was what he needed for his new technique. We can see from the production of the bible that Gutenberg employed more and more people

> working on separate parts of the bible consecutively in order to speed up the process. You needed somebody with engraving skills, somebody with metal-casting skills, somebody with carpentry skills. You also needed somebody as compositor, to put the metal letters together to form words, columns, pages, who was comfortable with Latin. Such a person cannot always have been easy to find, because getting your fingers dirty by putting pieces of metal together may not be what you had in mind when you studied Latin at university in the fifteenth century. Then you needed somebody who would actually ink the type, which is quite hard work because varnish is sticky and stiff; and somebody to put it in the press and actually pull the press, and, finally, somebody to proofread the pages and make sure that they were assembled in the right order into the book."

Such skills and techniques had never before been brought together like this.

Even so, what Gutenberg was selling was still not the finished product: it was an unbound bundle of printed pages, nothing more. It was up to the buyer to have the pages bound and decorated, in colour and by hand, which is exactly what happened, to such splendid effect, with the British Library copy. This system allowed every buyer, wherever in Europe they might be—and the Rhine made possible wide and easy distribution—to decorate their book in the local style with which they, and their readers, were familiar.

The economics of this business model, and of this system of production, although in many ways completely recognizable to the modern eye, were challenging. Gutenberg was a relatively wealthy man, but he needed working capital to acquire the materials, pay the craftsmen and so on. In Mainz he was able to borrow money, and find business partners, though that did not always work out to his advantage. He also had to operate in an economy that is very foreign to us, one that was still as much religious as financial. Kristian Jensen:

> "All the surviving evidence is that people buying big bibles in the fifteenth century would give them to a religious house in order

Indulgence printed by Gutenberg: fill in your name at the bottom. In this instance the purchaser, Paulinus Chappe, has entered his name, date and signature.

> to get prayers for their soul in return. It was not as if religious houses did not have bibles already. They did—many—but this was a very good book to give to a religious house if you wanted to have prayers said for you. So at the other end of the production of the Gutenberg bible, we are still in the world where one of the most valuable things was a prayer for the dead."

Kristian Jensen outlines the complexities of running the first European printer's business (China had had wood-block and movable type printing for some time):

> "Gutenberg was a very clever businessman. But one of the reasons why we know so much about him is because he was often short of money, and this led to him getting into trouble with the law; and if someone gets into trouble with the law, they end up in

archives. Broken promises of marriage, imprisoning senior civil servants from neighbouring cities—Gutenberg sailed close to the wind. He borrowed money, and he went into partnership with somebody who had access to money, a partnership that we know about because it broke down, resulting in a court case in 1455. In the meantime, while he was producing the bible, Gutenberg needed cash flow, which he earned by producing, for example, letters of Indulgence, which were used to confirm that your sins would be remitted. Gutenberg produced what were, in effect, preprinted forms: some gaps were left blank for the name of the person who bought the Indulgence and the date on which they bought it. This was administratively useful for the Church, as it meant it did not need to employ people to sit around writing them out. Indulgence forms are not all that rare, which must mean that Gutenberg printed thousands and thousands of them. So as well as giving the penitent buyer remission of sins in the next world, it gave Gutenberg a handy cash flow."

So at every stage of the process, from prayers for the dead to the remission of sins, late-medieval piety was the financial driver of Gutenberg's technological innovation. And as church schools focused above all on teaching Latin, Donatus' *Latin Grammar*, by far the most popular schoolbook north of the Alps, was another of Gutenberg's cash-cow best-sellers.

Gutenberg's growing business was badly damaged by civil strife in Mainz in 1460. This, however, served merely to encourage the spread of printed books right across Europe. Some of his craftsmen left and took their skills to Cologne and to Italy. William Caxton, for example, came to see what was going on in Cologne, and somewhere around 1470 brought the practice of printing back with him to England. Mainz had provided the perfect conditions for the creation of the printing press: it was also ideally positioned to ensure the unstoppable spread of the printed book.

The great red sandstone cathedral seems to proclaim the historical continuity of this originally Roman city. But, in Gutenberg's day, Mainz was not just a cathedral city—it was a cathedral state, with

A page from the *Latin Grammar* of Aelius Donatus, printed by Gutenberg in Mainz, 1456–58

its own currency and its own laws. Its sovereign, the archbishop, was the senior of the seven rulers who elected the Holy Roman Emperor; in constitutional terms the Archbishop of Mainz was second only to the Emperor himself (see Chapter 5). Situated near the point where the River Main runs into the Rhine, Mainz was at the heart of a cluster of prince-bishoprics and free cities, all of them independent states within the Empire: in the immediate neighbourhood were Strasbourg, where Gutenberg had long lived and developed his ideas, and the busy trading centre of Frankfurt; further to the north were Cologne and the prosperous cities of the Netherlands. This was an area of independent courts, rich cities and international fairs—in other words, an unusually dense concentration of literate customers, providing a ready market for printed books. Skilled craftsmen moved

Panorama of Mainz, 1565

easily from centre to centre in a network of economic activity that only the German-speaking world could offer and to which the great German rivers—the Rhine, Main, Mosel and Neckar—provided an incomparable distribution system. What was made here could be sold across the whole of Europe.

There was therefore from the beginning a large public immediately receptive to Gutenberg's publications in particular, and to the printed book in general. And, crucially, there was no central political authority to control developments. Kristian Jensen explains why this mattered so much:

> "It meant that people who might have found it difficult to do so previously could get access to texts. There is an example from

1400
1900
Johann Gensfleisch
zu Gutenberg
Offizielle
Festpostkarte
Gutenbergfeier
in Mainz
Carl Goebel fec.

> 1485 of a commentary on the missal, which had existed happily in manuscript form for several centuries in German, and then is printed. But as soon as it was printed, it was banned. The Archbishop of Mainz banned not only that commentary, but all translations into the vernacular from Latin and Greek. His argument was: how can you expect people who have not been through a proper university education to make proper sense of this? Unless you've been taught how to understand it, you will get it wrong. But he cannot prevent it from being printed outside his territory. So it is not just the reduction of price that widens access. It is also a question of the type of people who can now have texts to interpret for themselves—outside the controlled environment. The demand for printed books is so strong that type itself becomes a commercial object. You sell type: which means that by 1470/1475 hundreds of people can set up printing workshops. You cannot control it. The way the technique works militates strongly against control by the authorities."

The political fragmentation of the Holy Roman Empire guaranteed a remarkable level of freedom. So when, sixty years later, Luther printed his attack on the sale of Indulgences (those very Indulgence forms which, as well as enriching the Pope, had financed Gutenberg), he found in Germany not only printers to publish it, but—unlike in centralized states such as France or England—printers who could not be stopped.

Opposite: Postcard from Mainz in 1900 celebrating the supposed 500th anniversary of Gutenberg's birth

Self-Portrait, by Albrecht Dürer, 1500

17

An Artist for All Germans

Volkswagen, Adidas, Puma, Mercedes, Lufthansa—famous German companies with famous German logos: the intertwined VW of Volkswagen, for example, the three athletic stripes of Adidas, or the three-pointed star of Mercedes. The logo itself is a German invention: a logotype was a symbol or device cast by printers in order to divide or decorate a page. In this chapter we shall be looking at the first and arguably the most celebrated of all German logos. It dates from around 1500 and it is still recognized and coveted worldwide. The Print Room at the British Museum has many objects bearing this brand. They are some of the best known prints in the world, and on them there are a pair of initials, elegantly designed—a tall "A," with a flat top and a high cross-bar, and inside the legs of the "A," a "D." They are the initials and the logo of Albrecht Dürer.

Dürer is the defining artist of Germany. His images—and his self-image—are known to all Germans. He was a new kind of artist, clearly fascinated by himself, the first great artist in Europe to paint so many self-portraits. He embodies the Renaissance idea of the artist as hero and star, entirely engaged with a new world and a new technology. Dürer was also the first artist to sell his work widely throughout Europe, exploiting for the visual arts the distribution systems that had spread the printed word to markets across the continent (see Chapter 16). But Dürer was a *global* artist too. Like Shakespeare for the English, he was the filter through which many Germans encountered the changing world of Renaissance Europe and the new realms with which it was coming into contact. Like Shakespeare he explored all aspects of life—politics and natural history, religion and philosophy, sex and landscape; also like Shakespeare, he was closely connected to the court, while remaining independent of it. Dürer's art was produced not only for a patron—on occasion the Emperor himself—but for a market. He was a shrewd businessman (yet another similarity to Shakespeare) and a great commercial success. For all these reasons, Dürer has become *the* great German artist. Just as English writers unconsciously quote from Shakespeare, so German artists, right up to the present day, quote from Dürer, almost without knowing it.

Any logo can of course be trusted only so far; and it is disconcerting to discover that, according to experts, a number of the British Museum's prints bearing the AD monogram are actually fakes. Giulia Bartrum, Curator of German Prints and Drawings at the British Museum, explains how you can distinguish the authentic AD from his imitations:

> "I have to say it is with some difficulty. A design as simple as Dürer's AD is very straightforward to copy. It is clear that after Dürer's death, in the later part of the sixteenth century it was copied to stimulate sales of prints once the supply of originals had dried up. The familiarity of that AD monogram to everybody buying prints was such that they would not really worry too much about whether it was strictly one of his works or not: to have something even remotely associated with Dürer was enough. We believe that one of the reasons Dürer went to Venice in 1506 was to find out who was circulating prints with his monogram on them and to do something about it—in effect, to protect his brand. It was clearly a problem in Nuremberg too. At the back of the 1511 edition of his very well-known series of *Apocalypse* prints, he adds a warning: 'Beware all ye thieves and imitators of my work,' telling them

> they would be punished. What is surprising to us is that reproduction of the image itself was clearly of less concern to him than the unauthorized use of the AD monogram. It appears that he didn't object to other artists copying his images; what he really minded was their claiming that they were his."

Prints produced directly for a patron were, naturally, easier to control. Among the highlights of the British Museum Dürer collection is one work remarkable because of its massive size. It is one of the biggest prints ever created, made from 195 separate blocks (see overleaf). It is a gigantic triumphal arch made out of paper, commissioned around 1515 by the Holy Roman Emperor, Maximilian I, and richly decorated with allegorical and historical figures, promoting the benefits of Imperial rule. Maximilian was one of the first rulers to appreciate the potential of printmaking for political propaganda. The triumphal arch in this print never existed—Maximilian could not afford to build it—but he could distribute Dürer's paper image of it, and no fewer than 700 copies were printed in the first edition. They hung in town halls and ducal palaces throughout the Empire, suggesting (very economically) that at any moment the Emperor himself might arrive in triumph.

Dürer's story begins in Nuremberg, a rich Imperial Free City in south Germany. The Gothic castle, where medieval emperors summoned representatives from all over Germany, and where the Crown of Charlemagne was kept (see Chapter 11), still stands guard over the picturesque city, as it did when Dürer was born there in 1471, one of eighteen children. Nuremberg was famous for its metalwork (see Chapter 19), and Dürer's father was a successful goldsmith. The young Albrecht trained first as a goldsmith and then as a painter. But his godfather, Anton Koberger, was instead dedicated to the new technology of printing and was by the early 1490s one of the most successful printers and publishers in Germany. It was prints, with their potential for multiple sales through Germany's wide distribution networks, that turned Dürer from a local artist into a European celebrity, making both his reputation and his fortune.

The house where, for twenty years, Dürer, the master of business

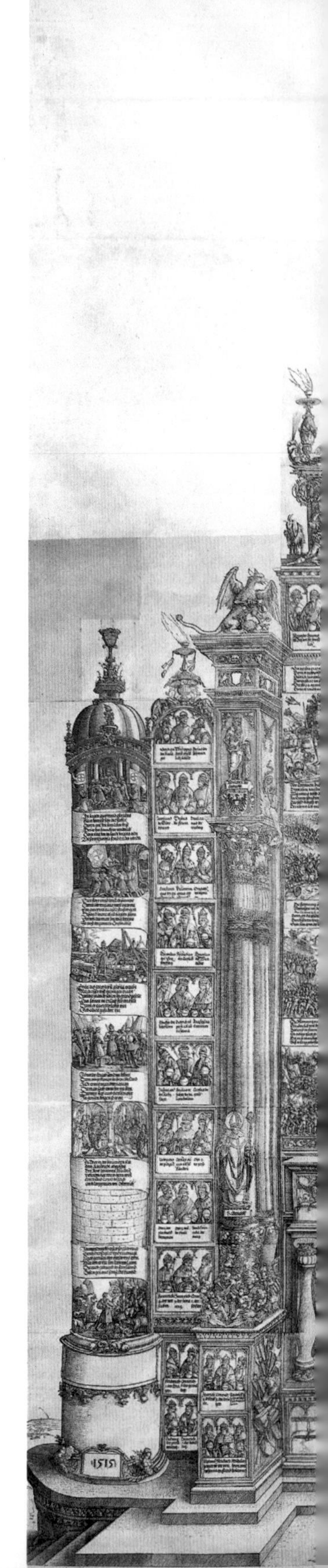

Triumphal Arch of Maximilian I by Albrecht Dürer, 1515–17

Old Nuremberg, rebuilt after 1945, with the castle on the left and Dürer's house on the right

logistics as much as the master of line, ran his business and created his masterpieces still stands. The Director of the Dürer house, Dr. Thomas Schauerte, explains some of the local conditions which favoured Dürer's success:

> "Dürer was born at the right time, in the right place. Around 1500, Nuremberg was in its heyday. There were successful merchants, there were great Renaissance humanists: for example, Dürer's friend the lawyer/scholar Willibald Pirckheimer; there was a lot of wealth within the city, which had trading connections with the entire world—to Venice, to Brussels and Antwerp, to Krakow, to Oslo, all the important trading cities in Europe. These links were very close, and of great benefit to Dürer, much more than to a traditional painter. As he reproduced his artworks by printing, his woodcuts and engravings in a short time were distributed all over Europe."

The fairs, rivers and trade routes of Renaissance Germany disseminated Dürer's images just as efficiently as they did Gutenberg's books.

Dürer's prints were the first great artworks in Europe to be mass-produced, and Dürer was the first great artist to master the new technology of the printing press, raising the status of the woodcut and of engraving on copper sheets to a new level. No one called it information technology then, but that is what it was. They massively expanded the number of images, of all sorts of useful and amazing things, that one person could see in a lifetime.

Dürer and his capable wife, Agnes Frey, travelled together around Germany—and beyond—selling the prints, spreading the fame and the impact of the images. His *Apocalypse*, the first printed book in Western art to be illustrated by a major artist, appeared in 1498. The biblical text was accompanied by fifteen woodcuts, including the celebrated *Four Horsemen of the Apocalypse*. The timing was good. Many people believed the apocalypse, the end of the world, would come in the year 1500, and were curious to see what might be in store. And even when it became clear the world was not going to end, connoisseurs continued to admire and to buy the powerfully expressive images. Dürer published the book himself, investing a lot of capital in the skilled labour needed to produce the wood-blocks. Apocalypse then, as apocalypse now, was good box office: the prints sold so well they provided him with an income for the rest of his life.

Dürer has always been especially admired for his engravings on copper: very difficult, precise painstaking work, and—unlike woodcuts—carried out by the artist himself, working directly on the copper plate. Two of these engravings have long been regarded as supreme in execution and rich in meaning: the great allegorical figure of Melancholy, sitting surrounded by a range of objects and symbols; and the Knight riding bravely out on his horse, flanked by Death and the Devil. Giulia Bartrum explains why they are so remarkable:

> "They have a similar degree of quite astonishing technical accomplishment, and the subjects complement each other. We have the Knight riding through a rocky gorge with the Devil, his faithful

Four Horsemen of the Apocalypse by Albrecht Dürer, 1498

dog running beside him. Behind his horse, on his right side, is Death. But he is brushing off Death. He is purposeful and active. The figure of Melancholy is slumped in a heavy draped costume. Her dog is asleep. She is surrounded by cold geometric objects, and an empty apocalyptic landscape fills the background. You sense that she is not in control of her life, entirely consumed by the struggle to think and create. Either way, she is the complete opposite of the Knight, who rides purposefully forward, while she sits immobile.

"Technically, Dürer here is showing off what he can do best. He is in complete command of the burin—making dots and dashes that conjure light and clouded passages. To be able to do that in black and white is quite astonishing. The degree of difficulty of engraving to this level of sophistication is not to be underestimated. Nobody ever again achieved prints of this complexity. The lines are so well graded. You have to be able to use different types of burin to convey this effect of shadow, the soft texture of the silk robe that Melancholia is wearing, the effect of fur on the back of the Knight's dog, where the hairs all individually move, so that you can see the bones coming through. Dürer does that in all his animals. There were many copyists who later attempted to capture just the appearance of these two images, but nobody again achieved this level of sophistication in handling the burin. Goya used aquatint, Rembrandt could do it in etching, but Dürer was the only one that could make a copperplate engraving like this."

These two prints are famous not just for the supreme skill of their making. They are so well known that they have become, in a sense, twin self-portraits of Germany in her two contradictory aspects—the Knight representing forceful action, Melancholia inward-looking contemplation. It is hard to think of any other European nation that could visualize itself in images of such subtlety and complexity.

Interpretations of the prints and their significance have echoed down the centuries, playing a unique role in the history of German identity, according to Horst Bredekamp:

Melancholia by Albrecht Dürer, 1514

Knight, Death and the Devil by Albrecht Dürer, 1513

"I think that one cannot find two other objects which in the nineteenth century so embodied the self-definition of the German soul, with the results we know. The Knight is in a setting which is extremely hostile, without any possibility of escape, without hope—surrounded by the Devil and a landscape resistant to everything he does. This Knight epitomized the self-definition of the German who, with an iron heart, follows his chosen path in spite of the times. So in this sense the Knight became the symbol of steadfastness, holding to his line, disregarding all enemies or barriers in his way. Melancholia is the opposite. This was taken as a symbol of a German soul which can be defined as the alternative to the Enlightenment as represented by Descartes. Melancholia is the romantic alternative to French rationalism. Here it is not the machine of body and mind that is determinant, but the soul which is the energizing factor for both, mind and body. This was how the German soul was defined—deeper and more complex than in any other nation. And that also implies elements of self-destruction, of disablement from action, of self-reflection, which can lead to madness. So this is a bi-polar definition, so to speak, of the German soul in the nineteenth century, which nowhere can be seen with such clarity—I say that ironically—as in these two pieces."

The power of these two prints and the belief that Dürer expressed qualities quintessentially German led to an extraordinary revival of interest in him in the years after the Napoleonic occupation of Germany. The Dürer house in Nuremberg was opened to the public as a memorial museum in 1828. The only artist with an older memorial house is Michelangelo, in Florence. Dürer, the most cosmopolitan and European of artists, had become part of the German national revival, says Thomas Schauerte:

"One must remember the political situation in Germany at that time, after the Napoleonic Wars. Germany was divided, and a longing for national unity runs through the entire nineteenth century. In 1871 we have a remarkable coincidence: the victory of

> Prussian Germany over France, the founding of the second German empire, and the 400th birthday, celebrated here in Nuremberg, of Albrecht Dürer. They did not believe that could happen by chance. That is the moment when Dürer turned into the national hero."

Being a national hero in Germany (as Bismarck, the architect of the 1871 victory, was to discover—see Chapter 21) may turn out to be a poisoned chalice. Had he been alive in the later nineteenth century, Dürer might have given his curly locks a sceptical shake on being told that *Knight, Death and the Devil* was Richard Wagner's favourite print, and that to Nietzsche it was an image of rare potency. He might well have regarded it as his own personal apocalypse in the twentieth century to learn that the print had been appropriated for Goebbels's propaganda campaigns. The art historian Wilhelm Waetzoldt wrote in 1936: "Heroic souls love this engraving, as Nietzsche did and as Adolf Hitler does today." Like so many of the other achievements and traditions discussed in this book, Dürer's work took on an unwelcome, sinister taint when it was taken up and contaminated by the Nazis: to post-1945 eyes, the Knight could be seen not as a noble, courageous striver, but as a lawless robber-knight who brings Death and the Devil with him. Unsurprisingly, modern German critics have focused their attention on the creative struggles of the other great print—*Melancholia*.

But melancholy is not a proper place to end. Dürer is about the abundance of life, and a new world—not just a new world of printing and communication, but the real New World. When he saw in Antwerp the Aztec treasures sent back to Europe by Cortes after the conquest of Mexico, these creations of a civilization previously totally unknown made a profound impression; he wrote that they were much more precious to him than miracles. From the other side of the world had come the subject of perhaps Dürer's most famous print of all—the *Rhinoceros*. Brought by the Portuguese from India to Lisbon in 1515, it was the first rhinoceros to be seen in Europe since Roman times, and Dürer produced a best-selling woodcut print of it. It is one of his many contributions (though by far the most famous)

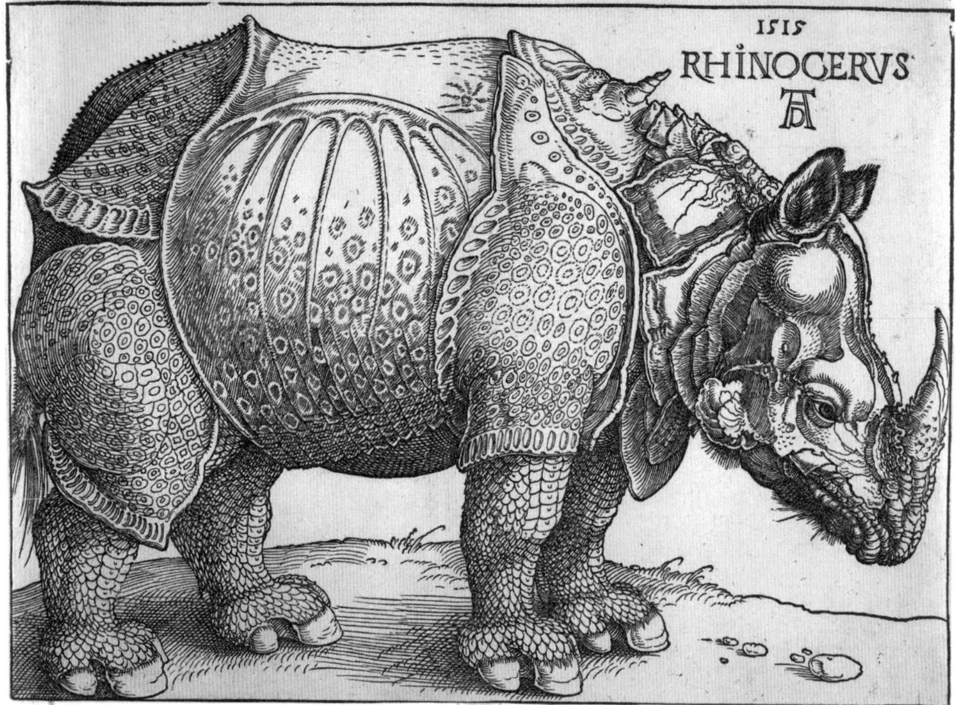

Rhinoceros by Albrecht Dürer, 1515

to the popular world of broadside prints about the wondrous and the strange, alongside the images he produced of monstrous pigs and conjoined twins. To the scientific eye, the *Rhinoceros* has, as Giulia Bartrum explains, something of the aspect of a beast from *Jurassic Park*:

> "Dürer himself had never seen the animal. He was working from a journalist's report which gave a detailed description of its appearance, mentioning the speckly tortoise-like effect on its scaly skin. Clearly there was something in the report which made it sound like a piece of armour, because Dürer gives sections of its skin a distinctly armour-like appearance. It looks very vicious with a sense of incredible power. That's something to do with the way Dürer has squashed this huge creature into a small box,

> which is after all rather how it was seen at the time: it would have been in a cage. Brilliantly, it is represented here with its horn squashed against the front edge of the print, and its tail pushed in at the other side. And he has put very normal whiskers, which he invented, underneath its chin—a detail borrowed from animals that he was familiar with. So the rhinoceros has an appearance which is entirely believable as represented, and has a power to it which gives it frightening authority."

Dürer produced 4,000–5,000 copies of this print in his own lifetime: one of the advantages of woodcuts is they allow a very long print run, even if the detail is often coarse. Given Dürer's pride in his unmatched skill as an engraver on copper plate, given the delightful subtleties of *Melancholia*, he might well have expressed some chagrin that this popular image—a cash-raiser if ever there was one—would become the most instantly recognizable and widely famous of all his works.

Two hundred years later, the Meissen porcelain factory in Dresden decided that it wanted to make a rhinoceros in porcelain as a show-off piece. By that time, other, real, rhinoceroses had been seen. But the factory did not bother with a real rhinoceros. They preferred Dürer's print. Like so many Germans before and since, they saw the world through *his* eyes.

Augustus II of Saxony and Frederick William I of Prussia, by Louis de Silvestre, *c.* 1720

18

The White Gold of Saxony

Eighteen blue-and-white Chinese vases, about four feet high, were in 1717 at the centre of one of the most extraordinary diplomatic deals ever struck between two European rulers. In exchange for a total of 151 pieces of Chinese porcelain, including these vases, the ruler of Saxony gave to the King of Prussia 600 of his best soldiers. In Berlin they were known as the Dragoon Guard, and to this day these vases, still on show in the porcelain gallery in Dresden, are known as the Dragoon Vases.

Augustus the Strong, the Elector of Saxony, was a passionate, in fact an obsessive, collector of works of art of all kinds. But he had one over-riding enthusiasm: he suffered from what was called at the time the *Maladie de Porcelaine*. As his 600 dragoons marched across Germany from Dresden to Berlin, what they thought of the deal—and their porcelain transfer fee—is not recorded; but nothing could better demonstrate the status and value of *weisses Gold*, white gold, as Chinese porcelain was then known. It was as exotic as it was expensive because it was everything that European porcelain was not: hard, durable, translucent, fine-glazed, as near indestructible as porcelain could be and very beautiful. Crucially, no one in Europe could make anything at all comparable.

In 1728, eleven years after that extraordinary exchange of gifts had taken place, another memorable Saxon–Prussian encounter took place. The Prussian king, Frederick William I, visited Dresden, where he was entertained with masques and banquets. Augustus the Strong made a return visit to Berlin and, as protocol demanded, took with him gifts for Queen Sophia Dorothea of Prussia. The *pièce de résistance* was a specially made set of porcelain, including a bowl and dish, now residing in the British Museum. We know it was intended for Queen Sophia because of the Prussian eagle in the centre of each piece surrounded by the letters of her name. The extraordinary thing about this porcelain is that while it is apparently Chinese—delicate and translucent, hard and vitrified—it is not white with blue decoration like the Dragoon Vases traded in 1717. It is white, certainly, but the artwork is in a different tradition, red and green and blue and black and, above all, gold everywhere, gold edging and gold chasing. In the eleven years between the two exchanges of gifts something

Seven of the Dragoon Vases given to Augustus of Saxony in 1717

Meissen porcelain made for Queen Sophia Dorothea of Prussia, 1730

very remarkable had happened. Augustus had found out how to make Chinese porcelain in Europe; more precisely, in his home state of Saxony. He had overseen one of the first great triumphs of modern German chemistry: Meissen porcelain. And Augustus wanted to show off by giving it as a present to his rival and neighbour in Berlin. For the second time (Gutenberg was the first), Germany had replicated one of the triumphs of Chinese technology.

In Andrea Mantegna's *The Adoration of the Magi*, painted around 1500, the oldest of the wise men offers the Christ child the gift of gold in what was for Europeans the most precious container the Orient could provide, a Chinese porcelain cup. In the early eighteenth century porcelain was still as precious as it had been when Mantegna was painting in the late fifteenth century. One reason for this was that no one had managed to discover how it was made. Another was that importing it into Europe from China and Japan was a lucrative monopoly long controlled by the Dutch East India Company. The

Company shipped it to Amsterdam, where much of it passed rapidly into the hands of the House of Orange, which provided the hereditary *stadhouder* of the Dutch Republic.

In the competitive power politics of the German states in the eighteenth century, diplomatic gifts were more than just a matter of form, they were about flaunting one's prestige in relation to the next duke, or prince, or king. Above all, it was important to be able to give something that nobody else could offer, just as today, for example, only the Chinese can give pandas. As Cordula Bischoff, an expert on the politics of porcelain, explains:

> "The diplomatic gift was a sort of a currency in the early modern period and it was vital for every prince to have a special kind of object, perhaps a product of his own manufacture, to offer as a gift. Every prince longed to find something unique, something that only he could give. This could be a natural product, for example the tsars of Russia gave furs or the electors of Hanover bred special kinds of horses, or it could be an item produced in the luxury manufactories, as the French did. The electors of Brandenburg actually had two unique items they could offer as precious gifts: amber, which they found on the Baltic coast [see Chapter 3], and, from the second half of the seventeenth century, Chinese porcelain. They had access to that through their relationship to the House of Orange."

Augustus of Saxony, unluckily, had nothing special to give, only his dragoons. Yet the competition for status was growing more intense. Around 1700, three of the electors of the Holy Roman Empire became kings. Frederick William of Brandenburg declared himself King in Prussia (see Chapter 3). George of Hanover inherited the throne of Great Britain and Augustus himself was elected King of Poland. Even more than electors, kings needed to be able to give grand presents. Being truly royal required the power to bestow truly royal gifts. And Augustus was chronically, notoriously, short of money.

Quite by accident, what seemed the answer to Augustus's desperate situation fell—or rather fled—into his hands. Johann Böttger was an alchemist, one of that breed of persistent and persistently unsuccessful men who had been searching for centuries for the Philosopher's Stone, the magic formula that would metamorphose base metal into gold. In 1701 Böttger had left Berlin in a hurry when King Frederick William wanted to put his boasted alchemical talents to the test and sought sanctuary in Saxony. Augustus saw his chance. He gave asylum to the refugee. He then locked Böttger up, telling him to get on with the job and to fill his Treasury with gold. Ulrich Pietsch, Director of the Dresden Porcelain Collection, takes up the story:

> "Augustus took Böttger as a prisoner and asked him to make gold. Naturally he was not able to do that. His companion Ehrenfried Walther von Tschirnhaus, who was an inventor and mathematician, had also done a lot of experiments to find the recipe for porcelain but had never succeeded. But he encouraged Böttger to make such experiments as well and, in the end, Böttger succeeded. In 1708 he found the right method. The secret is very simple. The Chinese did not work to a recipe. They just took earth from the ground, and that Chinese white clay contained feldspar, quartz and kaolin. Böttger had to find the different ingredients out, and after two years of experimenting he succeeded and discovered what had to be in the paste. He took white clay from Saxony and from other parts of Germany and then he mixed them together. He always took careful notes of what he had used, and of the precise quantities of minerals involved. And after a long time he succeeded."

Wizardry had given way to something recognizable to us as experimental research. And so it was that in Saxony the physics of the implausible Philosopher's Stone, the basis of the legend of Faust and his pact with the Devil, was overtaken by the chemistry of the possible. Beside the River Elbe in Dresden the metamorphosis happened: simple earth was finally transmuted into *weisses Gold*.

Real gold it was not, but Augustus realized pretty quickly that he could turn it into that. At last he had his exclusive diplomatic gift and

Dresden Seen from the Right Bank of the Elbe, by Bernardo Bellotto, 1748

Böttger's red porcelain experiments: (left) Chinese teapot, 1662–1722; (right) Böttger's copy made in Meissen, 1712

weapon but also a potentially lucrative source of income, as Ulrich Pietsch explains:

> "Once the king was convinced that Böttger could produce the same quality as the Japanese and Chinese, he decided to found the manufactory in Dresden. But after some months the laboratory was too small, so he decided to move the manufactory to Meissen, to the Albrechtsburg, where it was secluded, because he wanted to preserve the secret, and the monopoly. At first Augustus commissioned copies of his own oriental porcelain, which quickly made the Meissen manufactory very successful. Everybody wanted to have this porcelain decorated with patterns from China and Japan. But after some years the manufactory became more self-confident, imitated less, and created its own, European forms and decorations. For the first time truly European porcelain was being produced. The whole continent was envious."

All of which explains the European-style Meissen china that Augustus presented to Queen Sophia Dorothea in 1728. It was his *own* china made near his *own* capital, Dresden. Augustus the Strong was now also Augustus the Rich, or at least Augustus the Less Poor. Unlike Gutenberg, who realized and exploited the potential of a mass market in books, Augustus took precisely the opposite view of making porcelain. He wanted it to remain a rarity that only the rich and privileged could afford: its high price would then bring direct and continuing benefit to the Saxon state Treasury—and it did exactly that for 250 years. He vigorously promoted Meissen as a diplomatic tool to generate not only cash but influence. If porcelain could be made to replace gold and silver on the tables of Europe this would pay handsome dividends. State banquets in Saxony featured a rich array of fine porcelain. Gifts were made to other royal houses in the hope that it would encourage others to do the same, and to buy their porcelain in Saxony. But the popularity of porcelain was also driven by other factors, according to Cordula Bischoff:

> "The import of drinks like chocolate, coffee and tea to Europe in the seventeenth century demanded new vessels. They were served hot, which was uncommon before then, and so gold, silver and glass were not very practical. They could have used cups from China or other oriental countries, but these did not appeal to European taste, and were very small. They were also too expensive for everyday use. The fashion for coffee and tea was growing, and very soon even people with no connection to the court could afford to go into a coffee house. Earthenware crockery was used in the beginning, but that chipped easily, and it was just a short step to think of the newly developed Saxon porcelain."

As well as the china dinner service, the tea-set and the coffee-set had arrived.

One of the joys of inventing a new medium lies in the discovery of just how much can be done with it, and as time went on Augustus became more and more ambitious and inventive in showing what extraordinary things porcelain made in Saxony could achieve. It was so strong it could rival not only silver and gold in tableware, but bronze in making sculpture. Meissen started producing small statues, then bigger ones, until Augustus eventually decided to combine every princely extravagance in one.

All great rulers had aviaries and menageries, rare collections of exotic birds and animals gathered from all over the world, maintained at great expense. They were ideal for entertaining and impressing foreign visitors. Augustus decided he would have a *porcelain* aviary and a *porcelain* menagerie. Nothing like them had ever been made before, and they can both be seen today in the palace in Dresden. The smaller birds, brightly painted, plunge and swoop from consoles high on the wall in all kinds of different postures and brilliant hues. On the floor are the larger birds and the animals in white porcelain. These are completely astonishing. One peacock stands tail trailing down from the tree on which it is perched. Another peacock—life size—is shown preening in its pride. This is pushing the material to its physical limits—a huge, unsupported sheet of porcelain to represent the quivering, erect tail feathers. It is technically superb. But this is not just static spectacle. Birds and animals are shown in action—doing what they would do in nature. Playing. Feeding. Killing. Two dogs tumble playfully while a fox makes off with a hen in its jaws. Most sinister of all are the vultures, one shown still clutching in its beak the heart of a parakeet which it is holding in its claws. This is not just a menagerie, this is the theatre of nature, red in tooth and claw but presented here in white—dazzling white—porcelain.

There is no doubt at all who is the star of the show. It is the rhinoceros, or rather the pair of rhinoceroses. One is brown, one is white. They are modelled on Dürer's famous woodcut (see Chapter 17), so famous that the sculptor in Dresden decided not to bother looking at a real rhinoceros but simply to turn into three dimensions that memorable two-dimensional image. The Meissen rhinoceros is a striking fusion of great German achievements—the printing press, the genius of Dürer, the invention of porcelain, all combined and presented in one of the most beautiful cities of eighteenth-century Europe. Ulrich Pietsch:

The porcelain menagerie in the palace in Dresden

> "I think Augustus wanted to show the whole world that he was able to make wonderful porcelain. And he wanted people to commission Meissen porcelain from the manufactory. It was a public relations exercise for the manufactory. That is why his son very often gave gifts to other princes, to push the desire to have Meissen porcelain at their courts. And it worked. Many Italian noblemen for example commissioned Meissen porcelain coffee services with their coat of arms, and much more."

It went on working. By the middle of the eighteenth century porcelain was rapidly becoming a feature of middle-class homes, and not only in Germany. The success of Dresden was copied in porcelain factories across Europe—in Vienna and Paris, Berlin and London. The Meissen factory remained one of the most prestigious parts of German manufacturing right up to the end of the Second World War, when it fell victim to the vast scale of reparations demanded by Stalin to recompense Russia for the destruction of Soviet industry by the

Porcelain rhinoceros, by Johann Gottlieb Kirchner, 1730

Meissen porcelain being decorated with a portrait of Wilhelm Pieck, the first President of the GDR, 1955

Nazis. Large parts of the factory were physically removed, and the collection was carried east. Ulrich Pietsch explains what happened next:

> "In 1945, the porcelain collection was, like all the other artworks from Dresden, moved to the Soviet Union, and came back only in 1957, or about 90 per cent of it came back. In 1962 the porcelain collection was installed in the Zwinger Palace [the royal palace in Dresden] and the manufactory started to produce again, but only for the Western market. You could not buy Meissen porcelain here in the GDR, it was impossible. You could get it only by secret ways. It was strictly forbidden to export porcelain or to take it with you when you left the GDR, so the state could make a lot of money from its export. After the unification in 1990 the Meissen manufactory was really very successful because Meissen was still regarded a status symbol, although now this

> has changed, it is no longer seen as a status symbol, and its luxury status has almost been forgotten."

In a pleasingly consistent twentieth-century twist to the old tradition that porcelain is the prerogative of the ruler, the Meissen factory was commissioned to make official china for Erich Honecker, the last head of the Communist East German state before reunification. Anybody who rules in Saxony must engage with porcelain.

With Gutenberg, Germany proved it could not only emulate Chinese printing but surpass it, and the same was true of Meissen. Today porcelain is no longer the preserve of princes and it is very easy, perhaps too easy, to take it for granted. In any high street store we can buy high-quality porcelain from which we can drink hot coffee without endangering fingers or lips. Three centuries ago, how many soldiers would have been the transfer fee for such a one-pound mug?

Silver masterpiece cup from Nuremberg, late sixteenth century

19

Masters of Metal

What are the sounds of Germany? Most people's list would probably include, in ascending volume, and growing numbers, a Bach cantata, a Beethoven symphony, a Wagner opera and—loudest of all—the roar of the crowds as Germany wins the World Cup. All of them are sounds known round the world, all of them are part of what it means to be German. But just as much a part of German-ness, I would argue, is another sound—the sound of metal on metal, the hum and thrum of the music of precision engineering.

For a collection of such sounds one might propose: the reliably turning engine of a Volkswagen Beetle, that icon of post-war German engineering, twenty-one million sold worldwide (more than the Model T Ford); the clinks of a brass compendium, a high-precision astronomical device from the sixteenth century telling the time, the phases of the moon and much, much more besides; a cuckoo clock from the mid-nineteenth century (in spite of the *Third Man* Harry Lime's disparaging remarks, it was the Germans, not the Swiss, who almost certainly invented it); the tick of a sixteenth-century pocket watch, a German invention from Nuremberg so highly thought of that its supposed inventor's name, Peter Henlein, was inscribed in Ludwig of Bavaria's Walhalla (see Chapter 9); and, earliest, but most important of all, the creaking wood of the Gutenberg printing press, that early synthesis of precision engineering from Germany that would change the world (see Chapter 16). And there are many more candidates for inclusion in this symphony of manual skill.

Nowhere are German design and craftsmanship, artistry and innovation, more evident than in metalwork and engineering. German engineering is admired the world over, and it is something the Germans themselves know they have always been good at—making precision products, based on painstaking training through a centuries-old apprenticeship system, which regenerated the country after the Second World War and still operates today.

Many people, even beyond the world of opera, know that Nuremberg had *Meistersinger* (master singers), a guild of amateur poets and musicians who competed, within strict rules, to create the most beautiful of all possible songs. But Nuremberg, like every other German city, also produced masters in many other arts and crafts, professionals who had trained for years to reach the peak of their skills. And in Nuremberg the most celebrated of all were the metalworkers. Their training was based, as it was all over Europe, on the guild system. Every city had its guilds, covering all aspects of skilled manufacture, from candlemakers and furriers to woodworkers and glassblowers, and including the many smiths: blacksmiths and coppersmiths, silversmiths and goldsmiths. Goldsmiths, needless to say, were the top of the tree.

These guilds were almost secret societies—membership was restricted in order to maintain quality, standards and, every bit as important, prices. The guildmasters trained the next generation of artisans through apprenticeships. You began as an apprentice, spending anything from four to six years as a workshop assistant; then you qualified as a journeyman, and would spend several years wandering from city to city, working for other masters, until you were ready to apply to join the guild as a *Meister,* a master, yourself. And to do this, you had to submit three "masterpieces" which would show you were ready. The word has become debased, loosely applied to anything of high quality. It has lost the sense of struggle and competition. These pieces showed whether—or not—you were fit to be a master. To be a master goldsmith, you had to make a seal, a ring set with a stone, and a cup. In Nuremberg, the cup, which had to be in the shape of a columbine flower, was the most important of the three. There is a splendid example in the British Museum (see page 334), a silver masterpiece cup from the late sixteenth century, thought to be the work of one Martin Rehlein. It is not at all practical. A columbine flower is not a good shape to drink out of. It has six deep lobes, which would make sipping without spilling tricky to say the least. But on each lobe there are finely detailed engravings containing scenes from classical mythology, the symbol of a virtue or a vice, and a Latin inscription. Every available space is decorated, inhabited by a lizard or a beetle or at least by a beautiful wavy line. The point of this cup is, self-evidently, not drinking: it is to show that its maker is a master of his craft, a supreme technician, a man of learning and status. And it implies that you, the viewer, the customer and, if you insist, the drinker, will value these skills highly—and pay for them highly. The Nuremberg masterpiece columbine cup perfectly sums up the status of the German metal craftsman through the ages.

It is unclear where the watch first emerged out of small portable clocks—north Italy and south Germany are both contenders. Germans in the nineteenth century had no doubt; in the Walhalla monument (see Chapter 9) one of its great Germans was the undoubtedly important locksmith and clockmaker Peter Henlein of Nuremberg (1485–1542), identified as inventor of the watch. The reality was more complicated. The first watches were basically small portable clocks, very rare and expensive, which could be worn as pendants or attached to clothing. True pocket watches only developed in the later sixteenth century. A watch by Hans Schniep of Speyer, in the Rhineland, known to be a member of the Speyer Guild of Smiths, is a typical one of the period. Its front and back cases are elaborately pierced, the back with a conventional urn and flower pattern, the front with apertures that reveal the numerals on the silver and enamel dial beneath. The numerals appear twice, in Roman and Arabic forms, with 2 in the "Z" form characteristic of German clocks and watches. It has an alarm that can be set and it strikes the hours.

Overleaf: Nuremberg cityscape, from the *Nuremberg Chronicle*, 1493

NVREMBERGA
S. Laurencius.
S. Sebaldus.

German craft skills developed to such a pitch in part because Germany was uniquely placed to exploit them. Many of the major European overland trade routes passed through the great German cities, like Leipzig and Frankfurt—the great trade fair cities—or Augsburg and Nuremberg, which dominated metalworking up to the eighteenth century, and so attracted the best goldsmiths from all over Germany. Silke Ackermann is director of the Museum of the History of Science at Oxford:

> "The Holy Roman Empire of the German Nation in the sixteenth century was a huge expanse of land, with any number of courts, all competing with each other to have the finest craftsmen. So Germany was completely different from England, where London was always the centre. In Germany, Nuremberg was where the trade routes came together and it was at the time described as 'Quasi Centrum Europae'—more or less the centre of Europe. Every kind of trade passed through Nuremberg, even ivory, everything you could possibly imagine."

The proliferation of small self-governing states inside the legal framework of the Holy Roman Empire made it possible at local level to enforce high standards and—it has to be said—restrictive practices and regulations, such as on the size of the workshops. In London or Paris a successful workshop could expand to take whatever commissions its success brought its way. In the Imperial free cities like Nuremberg and Augsburg, a major commission had to be shared between several workshops, so in consequence they first competed together and then worked with each other to meet the same high standards.

That collegial approach paid off handsomely. It helped to establish German gold- and silversmiths as the best in the world; but it was for the making of scientific instruments that Germany's workers in the other metals were especially renowned. They worked across a whole range of disciplines at the highest level, combining academic, scientific and practical skills with mathematics and creative artistry. Such an intricate piece of workmanship is held by the British Museum: a

Gilt-brass clock-watch, Hans Schniep, *c.* 1590

rectangular object about the size of a small pocketbook, known as an astronomical compendium. Within this one metal box, there is a collection of small instruments which enable you do an amazing number of things. You can tell the time in various ways; it has several types of tiny, elaborate sun dials and right in the centre is a small, very complex astrolabe, the computer of its time, which can be used to locate the planets and stars, keep time by the moon, and so on. It will help you find your direction, a bit like modern satellite navigation, and it has various types of hour systems, since different cities kept time in different ways. Not least, it can be used for casting horoscopes. Silke Ackermann:

> "This is an astronomical compendium made by Johann Anton Linden from Heilbronn in 1596. An astronomical compendium is, basically, the smart phone of the day. It is the universe in a box: it has got everything you would ever want in terms of

time-keeping, in terms of finding your place on earth, in terms of finding the date. It even has compartments for your drawing instruments. Astronomical compendia can come in various shapes and sizes. They are frequently round, and look a bit like a pocket watch hung from a chain from your belt. They can really take any shape you fancy, but this one is very unusual in that it has the shape of a book. Imagine three smart phones put on top of each other like sandwiches. That is the size and the thickness of it. And the variety of instruments in it is absolutely unique. It shows the owner's wealth: he can attract the finest craftsmen. But it also shows that that owner is engaged in the latest scientific discussions. This piece is of the late sixteenth century, an extremely exciting period, when the Copernican revolution had just happened. In 1543 Copernicus's book about the sun being in the centre of the universe was published; it was a huge shock for people, a completely different way of seeing the world. The Pope announced a new calendar, with new Leap Year Rules in 1582 shortly before this instrument was made. Every astronomical and mathematical table needed to be re-engraved. By being the owner of an object like this, you would show that you were engaged in these discussions. We might wonder whether the owner would have understood all the functions. Like people today who have the latest smart phone but use only a fraction of its capability, the owner of an object like this would have had all those instruments, but is unlikely to have used them on a daily basis. It is very much a show-off piece."

Show-off piece or not, it demonstrates that, around 1600, south German precision engineering was intellectually and technically in a league of its own.

The guild system that had worked so well for German craftsmanship survived almost unchanged to the early nineteenth century. Then, as in other European countries, the Industrial Revolution and the mass-production techniques it created put the old craft traditions

Astronomical compendium, by Johann Anton Linden, 1596

under severe strain. The guilds fought hard to stop factories opening, because the cheap goods they produced would undermine their markets. But the tide could not be held back. The historian Bernhard Rieger has a special interest in German economic history of this period:

> "The guild system was no longer really relevant from the middle of the nineteenth century onwards, as the Industrial Revolution gathered pace and divested the guilds of all their traditional

Black Forest cuckoo clock, 1860–80

powers. This started most strongly in Prussia in the early nineteenth century, when the Prussian state initiated a large number of reforms around 1810 as a response to its devastating defeat by Napoleon. One of the things that the Prussians did to stimulate economic development was abolish the powers of the guild; this was really one of the foundations for their Industrial Revolution. As a result of this marginalization of the guilds, pretty well anybody could start a business. It was basically freedom of enterprise and it was on the move throughout much of the nineteenth century."

For the consumer, it was a revolution that affected everything, from precision metal instruments to cuckoo clocks. One cuckoo clock in the British Museum collection, illustrated here, tells a fascinating story of German industrial production. Made in the Black Forest, it looks exactly as one would expect a cuckoo clock to look. It has a case in neo-Gothic architectural style, and a beautifully carved circular pendulum. There is more fine wood-carving on the cuckoo's door and roof gable. The basic construction is simple, but every aspect of the design and the assembly is of remarkably high quality. It is a good example of where some of German industry was heading in the nineteenth century: towards low-end manufacture of consumer goods, but always of high enough technical quality to support a strong reputation for reliability. (Some American cuckoo clocks, for example, were dishonestly promoted as "Made in Germany," then, as ever, a sure indication of mechanical quality.) The rich patron of precision metalwork had been largely replaced by the everyday consumer who wanted a reliable product at a reasonable price. For the last sixty years, *the* German product that has been presented as reliable at a reasonable price, and has come to sum up German engineering to much of the world, is the VW Beetle.

It was Germans who made the first internal-combustion engines in the 1880s, and Germans, notably Gottlieb Daimler and Karl Benz, who built the first working motor cars. Ordinary Germans were not, to begin with, the beneficiaries of this new engineering prowess. Daimler-Benz made fine cars, but they were limousines for the rich. The whole idea of a people's car, like America's Model T Ford, was very slow to take off in Germany. And, according to Bernhard Rieger, the reason why, as for so much else at that time, lay in the economic consequences of the First World War:

> "In the 1920s roughly 85 per cent of the German population could just about afford to go to the cinema once or twice a week. The First World War, in which the middle class had invested and lost a lot of money in war bonds, and then the hyperinflation of the late teens and the early twenties, really wiped out the middle class as a consumer. The vast majority of the population really did not have a lot of money. So the consumer base was geared towards mass consumption; this was a particularly German phenomenon

in Europe after the Second World War. In Britain and France, there was a broader middle class than in Germany. This was very visible when it came to car ownership levels. Britain and France had far stronger, far more developed car ownership than Germany. Auto-manufacturing was not a strength of the Germans until after the Second World War. There was of course a car industry in Germany, but it was a luxury car industry first and foremost."

When he came to power in 1933, Hitler was appalled that German car ownership was so low, although the Weimar government had been working to change this and had already started planning the *Autobahn* network. Motorizing Germany, the Nazis decided, should be a key policy. It would show the strength of the regime, as well, of course, as keeping people happy, and proving that Germany was

Hitler in an early Volkswagen with Ferdinand Porsche leaning over, May 1938

The VW production line at Wolfsburg in the late 1940s

a match for the United States. So Hitler told Ferdinand Porsche to design a robust, easy-to-maintain, reliable car which could be mass-produced for a nation that had very little spare cash. It was to be called the *Volkswagen*, the People's Car. Bernhard Rieger has written its history:

> "Porsche, who secured almost unlimited funds for this design project, set to work, and the result was the car that we now know as the Beetle. It was a high-quality design. It was air-cooled and very sturdy, so you could park it outside: you did not have to have a garage, which would have been very important for consumers who were not so wealthy. Sturdiness was also important because it meant that the car would not require much maintenance, keeping running costs low. So in many ways this was a car that bore the imprint of the material scarcity of the 1930s. It was basically supposed to be a project that would square a circle—mass-motorize

> what was essentially a poor country. Before the Second World War, the car was never produced. The Nazis put together a vast factory in Wolfsburg, but production never happened because the outbreak of the war prevented it. Had production taken place, however, it would have been an economic disaster, because Hitler on one occasion simply sat down and said, 'We will make this car available for under 1,000 Reichsmark.' This was basically a symbolic price, nobody had ever done the sums, and once they started doing the sums in the Third Reich, all the managers effectively had a nervous breakdown, because they all knew it would be economically ruinous."

It was in fact the British who first produced Beetles after the end of the Second World War, for their occupation forces. But no British manufacturer was interested in taking it over: "the vehicle does not meet the fundamental technical requirement of a motor-car. It is quite unattractive to the average buyer" was one of the evaluations made by British car manufacturers in 1945–46. But when the factory was handed back to the Germans, all the elements of the German engineering narrative came together. Out of the economic, social and political wreckage of the failed Nazi state, the new West German democracy, with its new currency, the Deutschemark (see Chapter 27), painstakingly rebuilt its old reputation for quality and innovation, and nowhere more so than in the motor industry. It is a development that was due in large measure to the West German government's insistence on re-creating the apprenticeship system—for no fewer than 342 different trades—to ensure the highest possible industrial standards, whatever the product. Bernhard Rieger explains:

> "The Beetle was never a luxury product, but it shared one aspect of the longstanding reputation of German manufacturing, and that was its quality. Even when it was selling cars faster than it could make them, in the fifties, the company permanently fussed over the quality. Even the CEO read the technical inspection reports in the mid-fifties and fired off memos to his staff to make sure a bumping noise that somebody had detected somewhere

Zeiss apprentices in Jena, East Germany, 1949

> would not reoccur. And the line was simple: our future depends on this very high quality; we cannot afford any weaknesses. There is something psychological about this German pinning of success to the maintenance of high quality. Partly it has something to do with the two experiences of military defeat, with losing everything in the first half of the twentieth century: really it is a compensation for those defeats."

The quality of the work ensured an enormous, world-wide success. We think now of the Beetle as the archetypal German car, which in many ways it was. But it was more than that. It was part of the post-war economic miracle, the *Wirtschaftswunder*, and it was the new *face* of the new Germany—democratic, peaceful, part of the new comity of Western nations. Nowhere was this more the case, says Bernhard Rieger, than in the country that had contributed so greatly to destroying the old Germany—the U.S.A.:

> "There were several developments that turned Germany into the car nation we know. The first is the economic miracle. Real incomes in the fifties and sixties quadrupled and that gave most people totally new types of discretionary spending power. One of the first things that people really wanted to buy was an automobile. The second thing was that the international economy took off and so many of the German car manufacturers—and VW was really in the lead here—turned themselves into export concerns. As early as 1955, Volkswagen sold more cars abroad than at home. That was an incredible success story, and the biggest and the most prestigious foreign market for VW was of all places the United States—the biggest car market in the world. This was because from the early fifties onwards, when Americans thought of West Germany, they didn't think of a former enemy first and foremost, but now of a Cold War ally. So the presence of this Volkswagen Beetle highlighted the success of their own occupation policies and also of their initiatives in the early years of the Cold War. This was very important because it lent the country visibility in the most prestigious market and it basically also contributed to the rehabilitation of this very important label of 'Made in Germany.'"

What began as the humble low-tech Volkswagen company now owns high-tech Audi, with its slogan *Vorsprung durch Technik*, "Progress through Technology"; a catchphrase now as well-known abroad as it is in Germany. But the slogan makes an important point. The twenty-first-century German motor industry has returned to the sixteenth-century origins of Germany's reputation for fine metalworking, to the tradition that links it directly to the masterpiece columbine cup in Renaissance Nuremberg and the virtuoso technical skills of the astronomical compendium. The masters of metal are German.

Opposite: Shipping Volkswagens from Hamburg to the U.S.A., August 1950

A family picnicking beside their Volkswagen in the 1950s

Wolfsburg, 2011

20

Cradle of the Modern

In the post-war chaos of 1919, when Berlin was in the grip of violent fighting between left- and right-wing factions, the newly elected German National Assembly chose to meet not, as might have been expected, in the Reichstag of Berlin, but in the theatre in the city of Weimar. It was a choice of a safer place, but perhaps even more of a safer tradition. Instead of militaristic, authoritarian, imperial Berlin, which had led Germany to war and to failure, the new republic would debate its constitution in the city of two of Germany's greatest authors, Goethe and Schiller, indeed in the very theatre where their works had often been performed. The cosmopolitan humanity of their Weimar classicism, arguably Germany's supreme cultural achievement, would shape and inspire the new Weimar Republic with their intellectual and ethical authority. In 1919 building a better future for Germany began by choosing a better past: not Prussia, but Weimar.

On the wall of the German National Theatre in Weimar today a bronze plaque records that "In this house the German people, through their National Assembly, gave themselves the Weimar constitution of 11 August 1919." The bold, clear lettering was designed by the architect Walter Gropius. And in that same year, 1919, Gropius himself established in Weimar another new institution also inspired by

Opposite: The young Bauhäuslers in Weimar, *c.* 1922

Bronze plaque on the wall of the German National Theatre, with lettering by Walter Gropius

historic German values, the School of Architecture, Art and Design now known throughout the world as the Bauhaus.

This most modern of movements was deeply rooted in tradition. The name itself, Bauhaus (literally "building-house"), refers to the architects' and masons' workshops that were permanent fixtures in German Gothic cathedrals. In the new Bauhaus, Gropius hoped to combine the medieval-guild traditions of communal working with the most rigorous principles of modern design and the enormous potential of industrial production. Old values would produce new works of high quality for an unprecedentedly wide public. Like the Weimar Republic, the Weimar Bauhaus would draw on the values of Germany's past to shape a new society. In fact, Bauhaus reshaped the world. Our cities and houses today, our furniture and typography, are unthinkable without the functional elegance pioneered by Gropius and the Bauhaus.

One object that perfectly sums up the aesthetic of the movement is the cradle in the Bauhaus Museum designed by the 24-year-old student Peter Keler in 1922. Like so many Bauhaus objects, it is made of simple materials—in this instance wood—uses pure geometric

---

Opposite: Newly elected Reich President, Friedrich Ebert, speaking from the balcony of the National Theatre in Weimar, 11 February 1919, with statues of Goethe and Schiller in the foreground

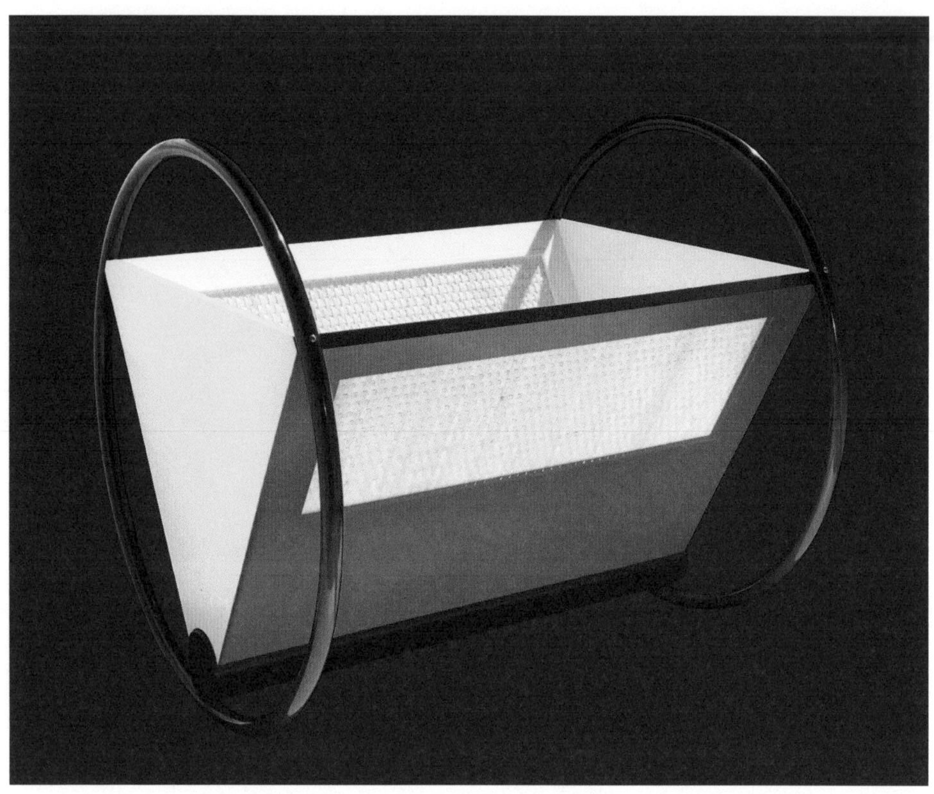

Cradle by Peter Keler, originally designed in 1922 and still in production today

shapes, and is painted in primary colours. The cradle itself is triangular, about a metre long with the two sloping sides almost squares. The apex points downwards, and at either end all three corners of the triangle are held in a large circle. If you push these wooden circles the cradle will rock. But as the centre of gravity is low, especially if bedding and baby are inside, it will not tip over. A beautiful, elegant, practical object, circles, triangles and squares, cheerfully painted in red, yellow and blue—perfect Bauhaus. Any baby lucky enough to sleep in this cradle would imagine the world as ordered, balanced and bright. The curator of the Bauhaus Museum in Weimar, Dr. Ulrike Bestgen, considers the cradle as an epitome of Bauhaus teaching:

> "The principles of the Bauhaus can be seen here in the fact that Peter Keler has put into practice the colour theory of Wassily Kandinsky. To his Bauhaus students Kandinsky taught that

geometric shapes have corresponding colours, that the triangle, for example, corresponds to yellow, the square to red, and the circle to blue—all of which you can see here. You can also see that Keler has closely considered the functionality of the cradle. On each side, there is a wicker panel, for example, to give ventilation, so that the baby will feel comfortable. He manages to harmonize the functional and the formal while studying carefully the nature of materials, in this instance bent plywood. These are the key principles of industrial design which the Bauhaus taught in Weimar. In many ways they are close to the old medieval guild system. The Bauhaus manifesto reads as though they wanted to build a kind of cathedral, where students and teachers and craftsmen live closely together, and work together in a kind of community."

As Gropius wrote in the 1919 Bauhaus manifesto:

> Architects, sculptors, painters, we all must return to the crafts! For art is not a "profession." There is no essential difference between the artist and the craftsman. The artist is an exalted craftsman. In rare moments of inspiration, transcending the consciousness of his will, the grace of heaven may cause his work to blossom into art. But proficiency in a craft is essential to every artist. Therein lies the prime source of creative imagination.
>
> Let us then create a new guild of craftsmen without the class distinctions that raise an arrogant barrier between craftsman and artist! Together let us desire, conceive, and create the new structure of the future, which will embrace architecture and sculpture and painting in one unity and which will one day rise toward heaven from the hands of a million workers like the crystal symbol of a new faith.

If the Bauhaus had a distinctly medieval inspiration, it was determined to function in the modern world of factories. From the beginning Gropius was quite clear: fine arts and applied crafts were two sides of the same coin, and must be combined. So as well as practising

Bauhaus masters on the roof of the Bauhaus building in Weimar, 1926. Left to right: Josef Albers, Hinnerk Scheper, Georg Muche, László Moholy-Nagy, Herbert Bayer, Joost Schmidt, Walter Gropius, Marcel Breuer, Wassily Kandinsky, Paul Klee, Lyonel Feininger, Gunta Stölzl and Oskar Schlemmer.

craftsmen, Gropius invited the artists Johannes Itten, Paul Klee, Lyonel Feininger and Wassily Kandinsky to teach in the new school. The Russian painter Kandinsky, who had pioneered abstraction in Munich before the war, was particularly influential in many areas of the school's teaching. The spiritual and the practical should go together; usefulness was in no way the enemy of beauty; and mass production would carry an artist's or craftsman's creativity at an affordable price to a new, huge public. Peter Keler's cradle was from the beginning designed for industrial production. It is still being manufactured today, and can be bought anywhere in the world online: Gropius would surely be pleased.

As one might expect in a school where "fine" and "applied" arts co-exist, the characteristics of the cradle applied no less to Bauhaus graphic design. What is fascinating is the number of earlier German traditions within which the innovative—revolutionary—Bauhaus comfortably and confidently takes its place. The invitation cards for the 1923 exhibition to promote the work of the school, designed by teachers and students, are some of the Bauhaus's most striking creations (see page 364). Even today they look like the cutting edge

A silver tea-infuser by Marianne Brandt, 1924–29

The metal workshop at the Weimar Bauhaus, 1923

of chic abstraction, taking Kandinsky's theories to new heights of pleasurable refinement. But in their scale, patterning and effect they clearly owe a great debt to a series of small cards which Goethe had produced in Weimar 200 years earlier, to accompany his lectures on his theory of colour—cards which of course Kandinsky knew and studied (see page 147). The Bauhaus baby, slumbering in the Keler cradle, is the unconscious heir not just to German guild traditions, medieval building practices, and Kandinsky's notions of colour and the sublime, but also to the scientific explorations of the Enlightenment and Goethe's investigations in this same city over a hundred years earlier. No revolutionary movement was ever so firmly rooted in the past.

Walter Gropius was determined that the Bauhaus, in spite of its radical principles, should be apolitical, but that was a hopeless, utopian dream in the febrile atmosphere of the Weimar Republic. In

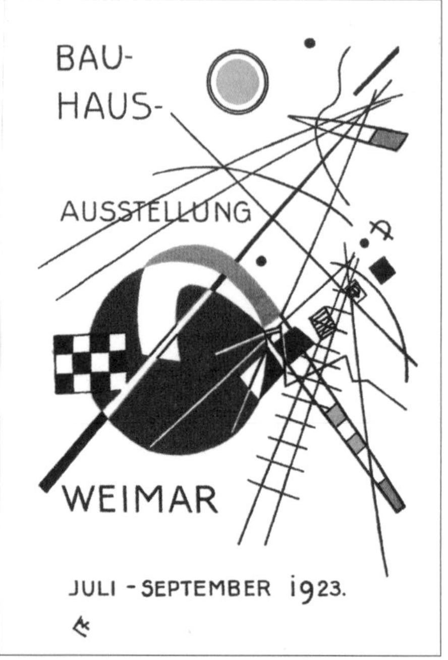

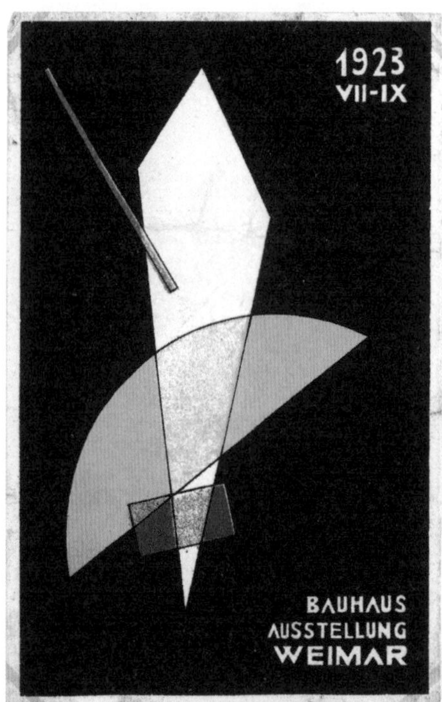

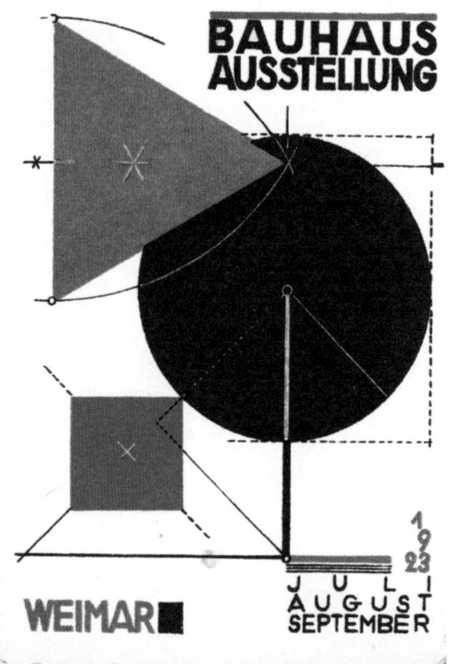

Postcards for the Bauhaus exhibition, Weimar, 1923, by Wassily Kandinsky (top left), Paul Klee (top right), László Moholy-Nagy (bottom left), Herbert Bayer (bottom right)

The Kunstschule, Weimar, built 1904–11, first home of the Bauhaus

The Bauhaus school in Dessau, designed by Gropius in 1926, badly damaged 1945, restored 1976

1924 the Social Democrats lost power in Thuringia. They had funded the Bauhaus from the outset, but their successors were conservative nationalists, who cut the funding by half. So in 1925 the Bauhaus closed in Weimar and moved to Dessau in Saxony. There the political debate intensified. Gropius resigned in 1928. His successor, Hannes Meyer, who moved the school further to the political left, was fired in 1930, and for a while the great modernist architect Mies van der Rohe took over. But the real crisis came when the Nazis won control of Dessau and forced the school to move yet again, this time to Berlin, where in 1933 it closed, condemned by the Nazis as a centre of cultural Bolshevism. Yet if the Nazis hated what the Bauhaus stood for politically, they were much more ambivalent about what it *did*. Ulrike Bestgen takes up the story:

Hitler reclining in a Bauhaus-style steel chair, 1928

"The National Socialists always knew that modernity was very important for them. They needed new industrial designs to maintain their power. They hated the people connected with Bauhaus, but they needed their objects and their technological expertise. There is a famous photograph of Hitler sitting on a steel-frame chair that could have been Bauhaus-designed. And Wagenfeld, one of the most famous of the Bauhaus designers, was able to work during the Third Reich with no difficulties. The problem the Nazis had was not what the Bauhaus designed, but what it stood for—liberty and freedom."

After 1933, although many teachers and students were, like Wagenfeld, able to carry on working, many left Germany to spread Bauhaus ideas and Bauhaus skills across the globe. The "Bauhaus in exile" was especially strong at Yale University, which was where Michael Craig-Martin, the conceptual artist, encountered it and became keenly aware of its principles and purpose:

"They were trying to find a way of integrating all aspects of visual culture, to integrate the teaching of painting with design, furniture design with graphic design, graphic design with typography, typography with architecture—all of these things are intermeshed. And then there is a desire to bring honesty and purity to materials. The material itself will tell you what you should be doing with it, if you look carefully at the nature of the material. This is not meant to be an exclusive thing for wealthy people. This is an attempt to find a way to get beautiful things into the hands of ordinary people."

Pretty well all these ideas are visually articulated in one of the first publications from the Bauhaus: a portfolio of fourteen lithographs by the school's masters published in 1921 and called *New European Graphic Art* (*Neue Europäische Graphik*). A glance at the title page (see page 368) is enough to tell you what is going on. Michael Craig-Martin:

Title-page by Lyonel Feininger of the first Bauhaus portfolio, *Neue Europäische Graphik*, 1921

Opposite: *Figure Design K1*, by Oskar Schlemmer, from *Neue Europäische Graphik*, 1921

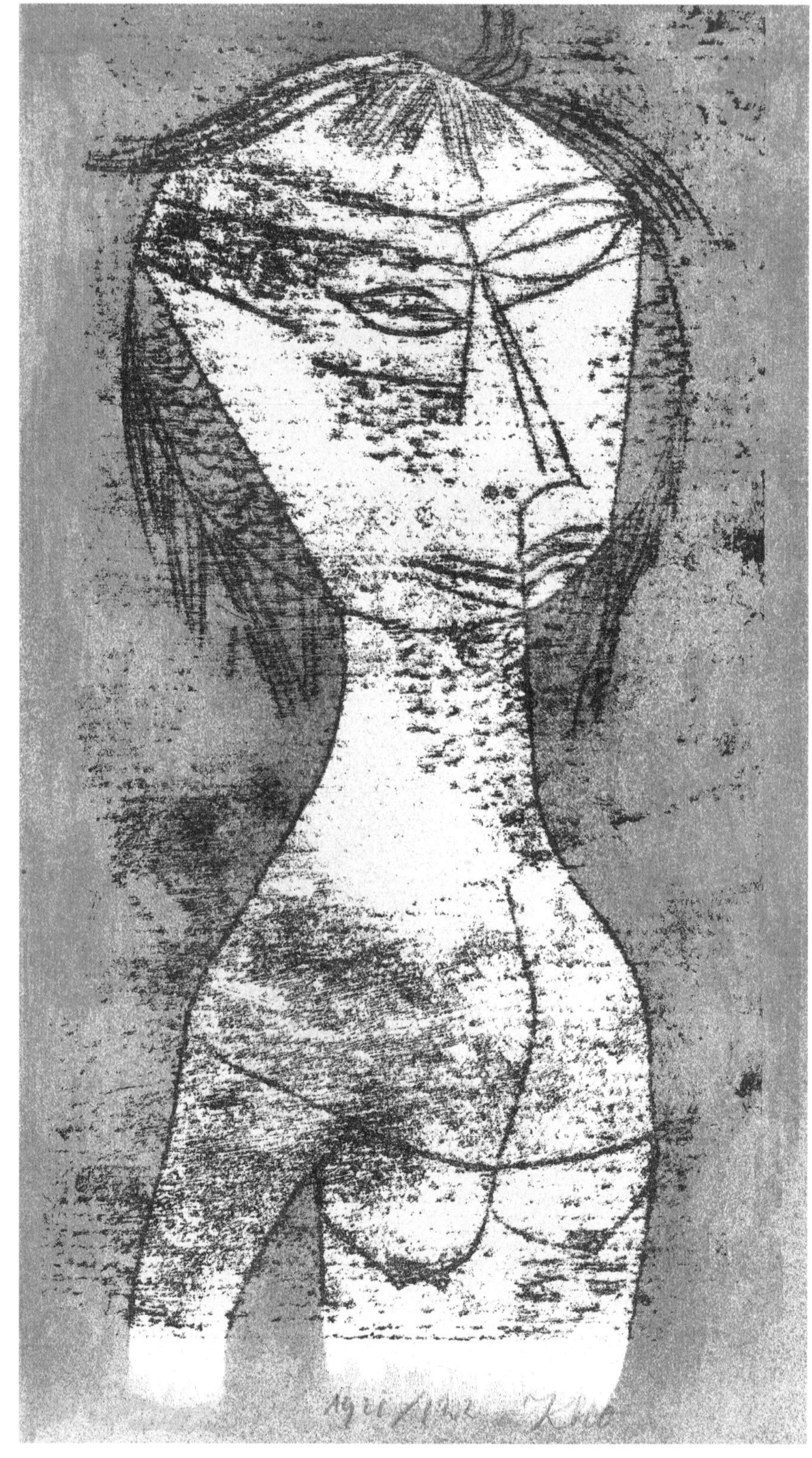

> "A re-viewing of the world is underway. The lettering has been treated in an entirely new way. Every letter has clearly been hand-carved, hand-made. Each one is a different size, the letters overlap each other, there are changes of scale, changes in the weight of the line. It is rich, hand-made looking, graphic, dynamic."

The carefully, playfully crafted letters of the title page, designed by Lyonel Feininger, set the tone for the whole portfolio. Throughout, there is a striking, energizing absence of any consistent doctrinaire address to the world. This is a collection in which Oskar Schlemmer's schematized abstractions of many human figures, *Figurenplan KI* (see page 369)—can sit happily beside Paul Klee's intensely individuated religious engagement with the *Saint of the Inner Light* (*Die Heilige vom inneren Licht*) opposite. But there is one sheet which, more than any other, seems to epitomize the design ideals of the Bauhaus: Johannes Itten's lithograph *The House of the White Man* (*Das Haus des weissen Mannes*), as much a typographic fantasy as an architectural design (see page 372). Michael Craig-Martin:

> "It is like an image that you might present to a client, showing them what a house might be like. It is a geometric house, a cube on a cube on a cube. The windows are all strictly rectangular, there is no framing, no articulation, no element of decoration at all, just the alternation of black and white. It is interesting particularly because Itten was not an architect. He was most famous for his colour theory, but the print is an architectural drawing in black and white. And one of the things that is most striking about it is that we can look at it now and imagine that house being built today. It uses all the features that we associate with modern design. The Bauhaus really created the look of the modern world. One of the striking things about the geometry of this house is its lack of symmetry. Nazi architecture is nearly always symmetrical, an expression of authority. Here we have the opposite. The Bauhaus was viewed by the Nazis as a left-wing venture.

Opposite: *Saint of the Inner Light*, by Paul Klee, from the *Neue Europäische Graphik*, 1921

The House of the White Man, by Johannes Itten, from *Neue Europäische Graphik*, 1921

It is essentially a Socialist vision of what a Utopia could be for ordinary people."

After 1933, there was only one allowable vision of Utopia in Germany, and in that Nazi world there was no room for many who supported the ideas and ideals of the Bauhaus. The textile manufacturer who bought the portfolio, Erich Goeritz, came to Britain in 1934 as a Jewish refugee. He presented it—along with other valuable prints—to the British Museum in 1942, as a mark of his gratitude, but above all to ensure that these products of an earlier, different, nobler Germany would survive. For Michael Craig-Martin, Bauhaus has more than survived. It has triumphed in ways inconceivable in the 1920s:

> "The true inheritor of the Bauhaus is Ikea. Ikea is everything that the Bauhaus dreamed of, mass production of simple, well-designed things, made inexpensively for a mass audience. All the great furniture designed at the Bauhaus is on sale today, and it looks just as modern now as it did in the Twenties. A lot of the designs the Bauhaus wanted to create were not actually manufacturable at that time. You could not bend metal in that kind of way, and you certainly could not mass-produce it. It is only now that we have developed the techniques that allow us to realize their vision."

Inside Germany, the memory of Bauhaus is still strong. But what it means depends largely on which part of Germany you lived in before 1989. Ulrike Bestgen explains:

> "There are two different traditions of Bauhaus, in East and West Germany. In West Germany, the Bauhaus was always a symbol of the truly democratic. For example Bauhaus students and teachers like Gropius went to the U.S. and to Great Britain, and they came back at the beginning of the sixties, or in 1968. They represented democracy. The young Bundesrepublik wanted to be a democratic state, so they adopted the Bauhaus. There was no question about it: the Bauhaus was what they wanted to stand for.
>
> "In East Germany they privileged the tradition of Hannes Meyer, who taught at the Bauhaus in Dessau and was a Communist. His motto was 'the people's need, instead of luxury need' ('Volksbedarf anstatt Luxusbedarf')."

It is easy to see why the GDR would adopt Meyer's view of the central purpose and achievement of the Bauhaus. And one of the beneficiaries of his prominent role in the GDR was the maker of our cradle. After finishing at the Bauhaus, Peter Keler opened his own

design studio. The Nazis banned him from exhibiting his paintings and designs in public, but like some other Bauhaus students he was able to work as a freelance architect and film-set designer until 1945. Under the German Democratic Republic, Keler, supported by Meyer, returned to Weimar to teach at the School of Architecture and Visual Arts, now called the Bauhaus University, retiring as a professor in 1963. A successful return to painting filled his retirement. He died in 1982 after a steady, professional life: like most Germans, neither an exile nor a martyr, though knowing many who were. Today, on the internet, he and his cradle are global celebrities.

In modern, reunified Germany, Bauhaus's mix of philosophical, technical, practical, spiritual, social and aesthetic issues has a profound appeal. Ulrike Bestgen:

> "It is not possible to reduce Bauhaus to a style, or to certain objects, like prefabricated houses or wonderful Bauhaus objects. Bauhaus means a social attempt in design, and that is still a big discussion in Germany, so we have a lot of young designers now referring to the Bauhaus and Bauhaus ideas. Mies van der Rohe told us that the Bauhaus is an attitude, or a kind of philosophy, and that idea is very much alive in Germany."

Opposite: The office of Walter Gropius in the Weimar Bauhaus, 1924

Part Five

The Descent

In 1871, when the German Empire was proclaimed in Versailles, Germany took over France's traditional role as Europe's difficult neighbour too big for its borders. The next seventy-five years saw Germany both inflict and suffer catastrophe on an unprecedented scale. Disasters of these dimensions are hard to grasp. Part Five focuses on the experiences of a few individuals, and on everyday objects, as prisms through which to look at these dark years, the memory of which weighs heavily on every German.

Bismarck handing Germania the sword "Unitas." Woodcut, *c.* 1895

21

Bismarck the Blacksmith

The Hall of Mirrors in Versailles in the 1680s: an astounding display of the new technology of mirrored glass. Reflections of seemingly infinite gardens, glistening chandeliers and, on the ceiling, in a series of grandiloquent paintings, Louis XIV—or is it Mars, God of War?—crossing the Rhine in triumph to attack, defeat and humiliate the Holy Roman Emperor, Leopold I. A bombastic declaration to the world of France victorious; France supreme.

On 18 January 1871, King Wilhelm I of Prussia accepted the crown of the new German Empire and became Kaiser Wilhelm I:

> We, by the grace of God, King of Prussia, do hereby declare that we have considered it a duty to our common fatherland to answer the summons of the united German princes and cities and to accept the German Imperial title, which has not been occupied for more than sixty years.

It was no coincidence that this ringing declaration was made not in Berlin, but in that same Hall of Mirrors at Versailles, before

---

Overleaf: *The Proclamation of the German Empire in the Hall of Mirrors at Versailles*, by Anton von Werner, 1885. Bismarck is shown in white to heighten his prominence (he in fact wore blue). The painting was a gift to him from the Imperial family.

18 Januar

1871.
Prfsin Wilhelm
Prfsin Fr. Carl v.
Prfsin Albrecht
Fr. Leopold Pr.
Alexander Pr.
Louise Prfsin

UNITAS

the Franco-Prussian War was even formally over. After the Prussian military victories over Napoleon III at Metz and Sedan a few months before, this was the ultimate psychological victory: it was the response to two centuries of French aggression, to the loss of Alsace, conquered by Louis XIV, now restored to the German Reich; to Prussia's humiliation and occupation by Napoleon after the battle of Jena; and, perhaps most of all, to the dissolution of the Holy Roman Empire in 1806. That was what the new Kaiser meant when he said that the Imperial title had been unoccupied for sixty years. After two centuries, the wheel of fortune and history had turned. The supreme power in Europe, it was declared in the Hall of Mirrors, was no longer France, but Germany. The Second Empire in France was over: in Germany, a Second Reich was beginning.

The man who had made all this happen, the engineer of this astonishing diplomatic and political triumph, was Otto von Bismarck. Disliked and feared by foreigners, reviled by liberals at home for his authoritarianism, among many sections of the German population Bismarck was a hero. At his death monuments were erected across the whole country by public subscription, but Bismarck could also be brought into your own home. Small statues of Bismarck came in many guises at the end of the nineteenth century, but few are more evocative than the bronze and terracotta figure, about a foot high, showing Bismarck the blacksmith. Bald-headed, sleeves rolled up, wearing a leather apron and wielding his hammer, the middle-aged Bismarck is at his forge, the trusty village blacksmith.

A horseshoe hangs at the base of the anvil, but Bismarck is not shoeing horses. He is making weapons, working the iron which, together with blood, would in his famous remark remake Germany. On the anvil is a sword and beside it, already forged, is a shield bearing the emblem of the Imperial German eagle. At home, on a desk or a mantelpiece, this earnest, hardworking man would stand as a reminder of the struggle that had enabled Germany to take its proper place among the European nations, strong and safe at last from French aggression. Such small statues of Bismarck were produced in huge quantities and distributed as widely as Staffordshire pottery

---

Opposite: Otto von Bismarck as blacksmith

figures of Queen Victoria in Britain. They carried and perpetuated the legend of Bismarck as the champion of German honour and as the unflinching defender of national security.

As we saw in Chapter 14, since the wars against Napoleon, iron had been a key symbol of Prussian identity. Bismarck's association with iron, which led to his portrayal in paintings and sculptures as a blacksmith and to his being called "the Iron Chancellor," goes back to a speech he made nearly ten years before the ceremony in Versailles when he was both the Minister-President and Foreign Minister of Prussia. In this speech, he poured scorn on those who believed that the revolution of 1848 was Germany's great missed opportunity. Nothing of the kind, he said: 1848 (see Chapter 15) was an error, and the future of Germany would be decided on a very different basis:

> The position of Prussia in Germany will not be determined by its liberalism but by its power. Prussia must concentrate its strength and hold it for the favourable moment, which has already come and gone several times. Since the Congress of Vienna in 1815, our frontiers have been ill-designed for a healthy body politic. Not through speeches and majority decisions will the great questions of the day be decided—that was the great mistake of 1848 and 1849—but by iron and blood.

In English we usually talk about "blood and iron" when we quote Bismarck's phrase, but it is important to remember that he put the iron first—a significant difference according to Christopher Clark:

> "Iron, this very widely used element, signifies warfare and military conflict, because iron is what weapons are made of. That is what Bismarck meant when he said the struggle for Germany would be won in the future not by parliamentary speeches and rhetoric and newspaper articles, but by iron and blood. By the time Bismarck was speaking, iron meant much more than just weapons. It also meant the might of an industrial power. This would have been scarcely visible at the moment that Bismarck uttered those words, at the very beginning of the Industrial

Revolution, which in Germany only kicked off in the 1850s and '60s. But when it did happen, it happened with extraordinary speed. The swift expansion of German military might was absolutely remarkable. The Germans overtook almost everybody else, and that had a lot to do with iron. There is no doubt that Bismarck's wars against Austria and France, in 1866 and 1870, could not have been fought in the way that they were without the sophistication and power of the Prussian industrial economy. So iron came to signify not just weapons but girder bridges, railway lines and the kind of industrial power you need to sustain a war using sophisticated armaments."

The miniature anvil of our small village blacksmith represents the greatest industrial economy on the Continent.

Otto von Bismarck was an archetypal member of the Prussian land-owning nobility, the Junkers, who would have been incredulous, if not appalled, at being represented as manual workers. He was born in 1815, just before the Battle of Waterloo and the Congress of Vienna, which created the German Confederation of cities and princely states that succeeded the Holy Roman Empire (see Chapter 15). As the first serious demands for German unification were being made by both liberals and radicals in the 1830s, Bismarck was studying law at the University of Göttingen. He gave up his studies, spent a year as a reserve army officer, and then went home to manage the family estate in Brandenburg. And there the story might have ended. But in 1847 friends who were members of a conservative political faction arranged for him to be chosen as a representative in the new Prussian Parliament in Berlin. There he made a name for himself as a reactionary royalist. His biographer, Jonathan Steinberg, explains Bismarck's response to the revolutionary events of 1848:

"He was delighted to see the revolution come to an end, partly of course because he opposed it politically but also because he saw that its failure created opportunities for him. He was extremely ambitious and managed, in 1854, at the age of thirty-nine, and with no diplomatic preparation, to get one of the best jobs in the

> diplomatic service—Prussian ambassador to the Bund, the German Confederation in Frankfurt, an office in which he learned his trade and developed his theories. Had the revolution been successful, Bismarck would never have been able to take such a job."

It was in Frankfurt that Bismarck first encountered and understood the political dynamics of the wider German middle class, the Bürgertum, and how he could direct its energies. For most of the next decade Bismarck held a series of ambassadorial posts, moving on from Frankfurt to St. Petersburg and Paris. In his own famous phrase, he became aware of the art of the possible. As his pragmatism and his understanding of politics grew, he came to realize there were fundamental weaknesses and inconsistencies amongst Europe's great powers, which could be exploited to unify Germany without sacrificing Prussian power and status. In August 1862, on a visit to London, he revealed his plans to his host, Benjamin Disraeli. Jonathan Steinberg describes what Bismarck said:

> "'I shall soon be compelled to undertake the conduct of a Prussian government. My first care will be to reorganize the army with or without the help of the *Landtag* [the Prussian Assembly]. As soon as the army shall have been brought into such a condition as to inspire respect, I shall seize the first best pretext to declare war against Austria, dissolve the German Confederation, subdue the minor states and give national unity to Germany under Prussian leadership. I have come here to say this to the queen's ministers.' They were stupefied. On the way home, Disraeli accompanied the Austrian ambassador and when they got to his residence, as they parted, Disraeli said to him, 'Take care of that man, he means what he says.' Disraeli was right to take him seriously: Bismarck did exactly what he said he was going to do."

Having set out his programme, Bismarck started putting it into action the following year. When the King of Denmark died in November

1863, he allied Prussia with Austria to manoeuvre Denmark into two violent—if short—wars to claim the Duchy of Schleswig for Prussia, with Austria coming off second-best and getting the lesser prize of Holstein.

Three years later, in 1866, Bismarck turned on Austria and outmanoeuvred her again, after ensuring the neutrality of France and the support of Italy. In alliance with the southern German Catholic states, including Bavaria and Württemberg, Austria went to war to win back her position of leadership in Germany. It was a disaster, all over in seven weeks—it was the first time the word *Blitzkrieg*, a lightning war, was used. Bismarck now created a new North German Confederation that excluded Austria and gave Prussia the leading role in German affairs, with himself as Confederation Chancellor—the Iron Chancellor.

Europe was amazed at what this "artist" of politics had found "possible." Having vanquished Austria, the traditional leader of the German world, Bismarck could now deal with France, the historic arch-enemy. The Spanish throne became vacant and there were tough negotiations between France and Prussia about who should fill it. Bismarck created the crisis he wanted by rewriting a diplomatic note to suggest that both the Prussian king and the French foreign minister had insulted each other. Within days the French had obligingly declared war. Bismarck wrote in his memoirs:

> I always considered that a war with France would naturally follow a war against Austria. I did not doubt that it was necessary before the general reorganization of Germany could be realized.

The rapid and total military victories over the disorganized French led the "blacksmith" and his king to Versailles. Just as Bismarck had predicted in 1862, the new German Empire had been forged, in iron and blood.

In spite of all the diplomatic and military successes, Bismarck's relations with his king, now his emperor, were never plain sailing. In fact, they were fractious, at times childishly so, punctuated by tantrums on both sides. One of their many bitter quarrels took place just before Wilhelm's speech in the Hall of Mirrors. In 1701 the Elector of Brandenburg had had to make do with the title King *in* Prussia, rather than King *of* Prussia; now Wilhelm wanted to be called Emperor of Germany; Bismarck knew this would enrage the other monarchs in the Confederation, so he insisted on German Emperor. Wilhelm would merely be first among equals in the unified, but federated, German Reich. Wilhelm screamed that he was losing everything and fumed to his son that he was giving up "the radiant Prussian crown for this filth-crown." He did not speak to Bismarck for three weeks. But he gave way:

> We assume the title in the hope that the German people will be granted the ability to enjoy the reward of its ardent and self-sacrificing wars in lasting peace, within boundaries which afford the fatherland a security against renewed French aggression which has been lost for centuries.

There are many portraits of Wilhelm I in his new role of German Emperor (see page 205), but none that speaks as powerfully and as subtly of the complexities of his position, of the intrigue and politics, and his relationships with his chancellor and his family, as the life-size head-and-shoulders portrait that now hangs in the German Historical Museum in Berlin. In a coloured oil print, the emperor, impressively whiskered and covered with military medals and decorations, looks out with steady blue eyes, severe yet benign. But as you look at the portrait you realize that the surface is strangely disrupted. At regular intervals vertical strips of wood painted on each side stand about a quarter of an inch proud of the surface. Facing the picture head-on, you see only Kaiser Wilhelm. But if you move to the left, Bismarck appears; move to the right, and his son, the Crown Prince Friedrich, comes into view.

The triple portrait was made as a novelty, a celebration both of the dynasty and of what it owed to the services of Bismarck. But it can be read in a much more interesting way. Standing to the left, there are many points at which you can see both Bismarck and Kaiser Wilhelm together. Bismarck merges into the Kaiser; the Kaiser becomes another manifestation of Bismarck. Given the tensions that we know existed in their relationship, it is a moving and a very powerful evocation of the fact that somehow these two men continued to work together. As Kaiser Wilhelm famously said: "Prussians need only fear God and Bismarck."

The relationship between Kaiser Wilhelm and his son, the Crown Prince Friedrich, that shows itself when the picture is viewed from the right is no less shifting or complex. Friedrich was married to Queen Victoria and Prince Albert's daughter Victoria, and in matters of domestic politics was a liberal. He wanted to move Germany away from the centralized authoritarian structures of Bismarck to a model closer to a British parliamentary tradition. In 1888, when this portrait was made, he had just come to the throne, and liberals hoped that a new Germany was about to be born. But the picture contains another subtle trick. When you look at Bismarck and Kaiser Wilhelm together, Crown Prince Friedrich is completely invisible, which is of course exactly what Bismarck would have wanted. Between the military triumphs of 1871 and Kaiser Wilhelm's death in 1888, Bismarck deployed his cunning, persistence and toughness to ensure that Crown Prince Friedrich was kept, as he is from this perspective of the portrait, firmly out of sight. The manipulation of the artist precisely matches the manoeuvring of the political maestro.

In 1871, Bismarck had become Chancellor of the German Empire, the most powerful political and economic figure in the new Reich. Over the next twenty years he shaped modern Germany. He moved almost immediately against the Catholic Church, which he believed was too powerful and too influential in German politics, and attempted to clip its wings in what was known as the *Kulturkampf*, the Cultural Battle, a policy that was poisonous, destructive and ultimately a failure. He introduced import tariffs to protect German industry, and established Europe's first welfare state with a series of laws on health, accident disability insurance and old-age pensions. These policies too were double-edged, designed to see off the demands of the liberals and the Left. To many Germans today, he remains, as he was in life, a destructive, divisive figure, who

ruthlessly thwarted the development of a coherent social democratic movement, with dreadful consequences in the twentieth century. But his status as uniter of Germany was unassailable. The little statue of the blacksmith is merely one example of the standing he enjoyed. In 1871 a Stralsund fish merchant renamed his pickled herrings in his honour, and "Bismarck herrings," a staple of low-income households, entered the everyday language.

At the same time Bismarck realized that the new Germany had upset the delicate balance of power in Europe. He expended considerable time brokering a series of treaties and deals to ensure that balance was restored, and that there was no war in Europe. When in

Triple portrait, *c.* 1882. From the left: view of Bismarck. From the right: view of Crown Prince Friedrich. (Facing page) from the centre: view of Kaiser Wilhelm I.

1876 a crisis arose in the Balkans, for example, he told the Reichstag that German involvement would be futile: "At the end of the conflict, we should scarcely know why we had fought." Germany remained at peace, and prosperous. He protected the Reich from its inherent geographic weakness, encirclement by its enemies, by concluding a treaty with Russia in 1887, which left France, Russia's ally, out in the cold. Bismarck was able to achieve all this not just because he was a shrewd politician, but because Kaiser Wilhelm lived for ninety-one years, as Jonathan Steinberg explains:

Overleaf: Bismarck monument (now destroyed) in front of the Reichstag, *c.* 1900

BISMA

> "Wilhelm I was born in 1797. Had he lived his biblical three score and ten, he would have died in 1867, before the unification of Germany. Friedrich III would have come to the throne as a youngish man and he would have fired Bismarck. He in fact did not come to the throne in 1867, nor in 1877, nor in 1887, because the old man would not die, and as long as Wilhelm I was there—he died in March 1888 at the age of ninety-one—Bismarck had a job. So the whole of Bismarck's career rested absolutely on the longevity of the old man."

The triple portrait, fusing Bismarck and his master, reflects a profound historical truth.

For German liberals, 1888 was the great year of hope that, under the new Emperor, Friedrich III, everything could be changed. But only ninety-nine days after succeeding his father, Friedrich III himself died of throat cancer. Even to this day Germans refer to 1888 as the *Dreikaiserjahr*, the Year of the Three Emperors. Friedrich was succeeded by his wilful son, Wilhelm II, an Emperor whom not even Bismarck would be able to manage. It was soon clear that he and his chancellor would agree on little. Wilhelm disliked Bismarck's cautious foreign policy, believing, in the famous phrase of one of his later ministers, that Germany needed "a place in the sun." The final break came over Bismarck's attempt to enact stringent anti-Socialist laws. The Iron Chancellor resigned and retired to his estate at Friedrichsruh, near Hamburg, waiting for the call to return. It never came. The epitaph on his tombstone reads "A true German servant of the Emperor Wilhelm I." His departure was seen by many as a foolish move by a wayward Kaiser: *Punch* magazine's classic cartoon of the affair was captioned "Dropping the Pilot." The new Kaiser believed he no longer needed a pilot, that he could steer the ship himself, which he did—but on a course that would never have been countenanced by Bismarck and which led to disaster.

In 1919 it led precisely back to Versailles, where in the Hall of Mirrors a peace treaty was imposed on Germany which was designed to ensure that France was, once again, the dominant power in continental

Europe. In 1815 the peace arrangements of Europe had been designed to set limits on the expansionist habits of France; in 1919 their purpose was to control Germany in a similar way. But after the Congress of Vienna France had been welcomed back into the Court of Europe; in 1919 the victorious powers insisted on declaring Germany guilty, with consequences which ran for the next thirty years.

"Dropping the Pilot," *Punch*, March 1890

Self-Portrait, by Käthe Kollwitz, 1904

22

The Suffering Witness

Can one mother holding her dead child stand for the suffering of a continent and a century? It is a question that was vigorously, painfully debated when, in 1993, Helmut Kohl, as Chancellor of the recently reunited Germany, decided to dedicate a memorial to the Victims of War and Tyranny in the Neue Wache (the New Guardhouse), an austere neo-classical building in the heart of Berlin. The stark, undecorated rectangular space contains only one object. In the centre, under an oculus open to the sky, stands a statue of a mother holding—shielding—her dead son. It is an enlarged version of a sculpture made by Käthe Kollwitz, a sculpture which now silently speaks to all visitors to the Neue Wache of the tens of millions of deaths caused by war and tyranny in the twentieth century.

The life and death of the printmaker and sculptor Käthe Kollwitz were shaped by, and closely mirror, the history of Prussia. Her lifetime coincided almost exactly with its 1860s triumphs under Bismarck, as it united all Germany under its leadership, and its physical devastation, its elimination as a state, and its removal from the map of Europe after 1945. Kollwitz was born in 1867 on the easternmost edge of Germany, in Königsberg in East Prussia, the historic city where

Overleaf: Cast of the *Mother and Son* in the Neue Wache, by Harald Haacke after Käthe Kollwitz, 1993. "To the victims of war and tyranny."

DEN OPFERN VON KRIE

ND GEWALTHERRSCHAFT

the Elector of Brandenburg in 1701 crowned himself king, and where Immanuel Kant had reshaped European philosophy (see Chapter 3). Daughter of a prosperous and politically radical businessman, and granddaughter of an equally radical Lutheran pastor, she was from childhood concerned (consumed might be the more accurate word) by issues of social justice.

Both parts of this radical and religious inheritance are evident in her work. Her art—and she is, I believe, one of the greatest German artists—explores the consequences of a systemically unjust society, using the traditional Christian imagery of suffering. But she refashions it to her particular purposes. In Kollwitz's art, there may be sacrifice; it is not clear that there is ever redemption.

Her husband was a doctor among the poor in 1890s Berlin, where she taught at the Women's Academy of Berlin Artists' Association. The Kollwitzes' flat in Prenzlauer Berg, then a working-class district of Berlin, was small, so she could not work with large canvases or use oil paints. Instead Käthe Kollwitz specialized as a printmaker. Throughout her life, she produced several self-portraits—illustrated on page 396 is one made in 1904, when she was thirty-seven. It is one of the grandest, and survives in only a few impressions. The head is shown in a range of browns, from flesh to deep shadow—a handsome woman in deep thought, her eyes fixed on something just to the right of the onlooker, calm and determined. By this time she was already deeply involved with the lives and hardships of the working-class people among whom she was living, and above all with the role and responsibilities of women. As she wrote in 1941:

> I got to know the women who would come to my husband for help, and incidentally also to me. I was powerfully moved by the fate of the proletariat and everything connected with its way of life . . . But what I would like to emphasize is that compassion and commiseration were at first of very little importance in attracting me to the representation of proletarian life; what mattered was simply that I found it beautiful.

The impact of this contact with working-class women is very evident in her first great public success, the etching series she produced in the mid-1890s, *The Silesian Weavers' Revolt*. The subject was suggested by a play by her friend Gerhart Hauptmann about the 1844 uprising by weavers in the Prussian province of Silesia—a protest brutally put down by the authorities. Kollwitz saw the banned play at a private performance in 1893 and was deeply moved.

The young German writer Daniel Kehlmann has long admired Kollwitz's work.

> "She had this great capacity of compassion and I think it's not sentimental compassion, it's real deep-felt compassion and to put that into something visual, she draws on very old images in the German subconscious. The Thirty Years' War, and the *Bauernkriege* [Peasants' Wars], this whole long period of incredible violence and destruction I think is in some way still etched into the German collective memory, and it was even more before the big catastrophes of the twentieth century. Before she had to react to actual catastrophes happening, she was already all about compassion and poor people being attacked and poor people suffering."

Kollwitz's series of etchings accompany rather than illustrate Hauptmann's play, and the most powerful of them shows a scene not in the play at all (see page 403). It is about the consequences of the men's struggle on the lives of the women and children. In the shadow to the side sits the weaver himself, idle, as are his looms. But in the foreground, compelling our attention, is the weaver's wife, her head in her hands. All the light in the etching falls on the bed of her sick, starving child. A mother looking at a baby destined to die, lying in a crib filled with light, while a shadowy father can be made out in the gloom behind: everything in this composition reminds the viewer of a *Nativity*. Part of Kollwitz's power is her ability to use that familiar formula to show not the Virgin's delight in the newborn child, come to redeem, but this mother's despair, responsible for a life she is powerless to save. The social has crystallized in the personal, and

Kollwitz has found the controlling metaphor for her politics and her art: our duty to nurture and defend each other is analogous to a mother's protective love for her child. And, in each case, the consequence of failure is death.

Kollwitz's *Weaver* prints were exhibited in Berlin in 1898. When Gerhart Hauptmann saw them, he said, "Her silent lines penetrate the marrow like a cry of pain; such a cry was never heard among the Greeks and Romans." The exhibition organizers were so impressed by the work that they put her name forward for a gold medal in official recognition of her achievement, but the Kaiser's advisory committee turned her down—the state would not honour her "in view of the subject of the work, and its naturalistic execution, entirely lacking any mitigating or conciliatory elements." In other words, this art was political, and it showed life, unacceptably, as it really was.

The poet Ruth Padel, who has written powerfully about conflict and creativity, believes Käthe Kollwitz was one of those rare artists who can create beauty from pain and suffering:

> "She was drawn to the alertness of suffering, so that her aesthetic sense meshed together almost completely with her emotional and social sense. She does not commemorate, she faces pain. She is not aestheticizing pain, she is looking at it, which is actually very rare. She finds it always of course in the individual, because if you are going to make a really good work, a work that lives, you cannot just take an abstract theme like war or revolution. You go in via the particular. These were patients coming to her husband's clinic, the poor who had no money for medicine, whose children were dying and starving, but she found beauty in that. And I think there is a kind of fierceness here. It is saying, this is here, suffering is in the world, you cannot escape it. You know you cannot look away. This is art you cannot look away from."

It is clear that this print bears witness as much to what was actually happening in Berlin at the time as to the events in Silesia fifty years earlier. In spite of Bismarck's social reforms, which laid the foundations of the modern German welfare state, and a huge programme

Need, from the series *The Silesian Weavers' Revolt*, by Käthe Kollwitz, 1897

of works aimed at improving public hygiene and health, hundreds of thousands of people in Berlin in the 1900s were living in dire conditions of serious overcrowding with the inevitable consequences for health. Trades unions and their demands were opposed by government and employers alike, and strikes across Germany were, like that of the weavers in Silesia, violently broken. Turning once again to history to explore the present, Kollwitz embarked on her second great cycle of prints illustrating attempts by the poor to take control of their own destiny. This time she chose the Peasants' War of the

1520s (see Chapter 12). It is an event which holds a particular place in German memory. The widespread uprising, which some believed was inspired by the writings of Luther, was disowned by him and totally crushed. Kollwitz was interested in the impact of social unrest on the individual family, and above all on the women. She made a sketch of herself with her son Peter as a model for the print *Need*. It was to be chillingly prophetic.

Yvonne Schymura, Kollwitz's biographer, takes up the story:

> "When the war broke out in 1914, Kollwitz was in Berlin. Her older son, Hans, was twenty-two years old and she helped him find a place in the army. Her younger son, Peter, was hiking in Norway and he returned on August 6th with a wish to volunteer. He was not full age—you had to be twenty-one—so he needed permission from his father to be a military volunteer, and his father refused. Käthe Kollwitz persuaded her husband to give permission. So when the son died, which happened ten days after he left Berlin, there was not only grief, there was of course also guilt."

Peter's death in Belgium in October 1914 changed and determined the rest of Kollwitz's life. "There is in our lives a wound," she wrote, "which will never heal, nor should it."

She fell into a deep depression and began trying to make a sculpture as a memorial to her son and his comrades. She could not bring herself to complete it, and destroyed it in 1919. Meanwhile, her antipathy towards the callous militarism of the state boiled over into full-blooded hostility to the war, and fervent pacifism. When the war was in its final days and the government appealed to old men and boys to enlist, she made her own public counter-appeal: "There has been enough of dying . . . let not another man fall!"

In 1924 she published another cycle of prints, simply entitled *Krieg* (*War*). Unlike those by other artists, like Otto Dix, they showed nothing of battle or destruction, only scenes of the home front—of mothers and children and the heartbreak and hardships endured through what she called "these unspeakably difficult years." The prints are

The Sacrifice, from the series *War*, by Käthe Kollwitz, 1924

hard to look at, starkly black and white, faces tortured with grief and fear and horror. As a woman's witness to war they are unmatched. The first in the series—*The Sacrifice*—reflects her own feelings of guilt and grief about the fate of her son Peter: a naked young woman, possibly a self-portrait, eyes closed, mouth set in a line of sadness, holds out her sleeping baby, safely cradled in her arms, yet at the same time ready to be plucked from them: how willingly, blindly, we walk into war. Another print—*The Mothers*—shows a circle of women, their arms clasped round each other, trying to protect their children, whose faces peep out in terror.

In Germany after 1919, in spite of the huge numbers of losses—around 1.8 million people—there were few monuments to the war dead, or rituals of public mourning. How could you publicly commemorate a war humiliatingly lost, followed by a bitter, imposed

The Mothers, from the series *War*, by Käthe Kollwitz, 1924

peace? How should you honour those who died in vain? Like no other artists of the time, Kollwitz in her *Krieg* prints gave voice to the sense of personal loss felt by ordinary Germans—the loss of sons, fathers, brothers, lovers, the loss of a whole generation, the loss of political stability, of territory, of individual dignity. A woman's response to a man's war. Her own response to a death she could and should have tried harder to prevent.

It was a response, according to Ruth Padel, that ultimately enabled her to complete her memorial to her dead son, Peter. Her first idea had been to show a mother and father kneeling at the head and foot of their son's corpse. When she abandoned it, she wrote in her diary in June 1919, "I will come back. I shall do this work for you and the others." Ruth Padel:

"It took her eighteen years in all. It was finished in 1932, and it did not show Peter. It just showed the parents grieving. It is in a cemetery in Belgium, a very public monument, called *The Grieving Parents*. She gave them her face and that of her husband, but later she realized that she had not finished her own mourning. I think for her perhaps the act of creating was very close to the act of mourning because both involve a kind of reparation, but also an acknowledgement of loss. And these two, just like her aesthetic and her social feelings, were so close together."

Among the great memorials of the Western Front, Kollwitz's two kneeling, grieving parents have a unique pathos. Separated and

The Grieving Parents, by Käthe Kollwitz, 1925–32. Installed in the cemetery at Roggevelde, Belgium, in 1932 and transferred to the German War Cemetery at Vladslo, Belgium, 1956

Karl Liebknecht speaking from a balcony at the House of Representatives at a Spartacist demonstration, Berlin, November 1918

isolated by their suffering, husband and wife are unable to comfort each other. He is frozen with pain, she overwhelmed.

In the immediate aftermath of the First World War, Germany was in political and social turmoil. The Kaiser had gone, there was no central authority, Socialist revolutions overturned the old order in cities and states across the Reich, princes and dukes fled or abdicated. The Imperial army was disbanded and right-wing paramilitary irregulars, known as *Freikorps,* roamed the streets keeping order by whatever means they saw fit. Gun-law was the order of the day. Berlin in particular was a battleground of hostile groups of Left and Right. The capital was too dangerous for politicians to meet and debate and so the freshly elected National Assembly had to gather in Weimar, where it drafted a constitution for the new republic of that name (see Chapter 20).

In November 1918 in Berlin, the Spartacist League tried to

establish a Communist government. Its leaders, Karl Liebknecht and Rosa Luxemburg, were arrested and murdered by the combined action of the Social Democrats and the *Freikorps*. Liebknecht was shot in the back to make it look as if he were trying to escape custody. Rosa Luxemburg quickly became a martyr-icon of the left-wing struggle around the world. The anniversary of Liebknecht's death is still a key commemoration in the revolutionary calendar. For Käthe Kollwitz, it was another turning point in her life: it forced her to examine in depth her own left-wing beliefs and decide what kind of socialism, social democratic or Communist, pacifist or activist, she really wanted.

She went to see Liebknecht's body and then produced a striking image of his mourners with the title *From the Living for the Dead . . . Remembrance of 15 January 1919*. It shows the body of Karl Liebknecht in a simple white shroud, surrounded by his followers and

Memorial for Karl Liebknecht, 15 January 1919, by Käthe Kollwitz

supporters, their faces blank with grief and disbelief. The visual language is tougher than in Kollwitz's earlier etchings. Inspired by her friend Ernst Barlach, a fellow sculptor and printmaker (whom we shall meet again in Chapter 29), she here opted for woodcut with its harsher contrasts of light and dark, and its bolder, simplified forms. Black against brilliant white, Liebknecht's head seems surrounded by a halo. In the foreground are four men leaning over the body, like the disciples lamenting the dead Christ. Among them is Kollwitz's icon for all society: a mother and her baby, bending forward in reverence to the dead man. Once again, a traditional Christian iconography is appropriated to an entirely secular purpose.

According to Yvonne Schymura, Kollwitz made it clear at the time that her sympathy for Liebknecht was personal, not political:

> "In the early Weimar years, Käthe Kollwitz worked a lot for the Workers' International Relief and made a lot of posters for them, which they sold to earn money for their campaign. She made the woodcut of Karl Liebknecht, although she did not like him when he lived, and did not like him even when he died. But his family asked her to make a print about him and so she did. And, as she did, she started seeing him not as a political enemy, but as a man, as an important man for social democracy or communism. She worked a long time on this image and it is still a very famous one today."

The following year she wrote in her diary that, as an artist, she felt she had the right to portray Liebknecht in this sympathetic way, and to dedicate the woodcut to the workers who supported him, without herself being a political follower. As her diary reveals, she had now become clear where she herself stood on the question of activist revolutionary communism:

> "Were I still young I would surely be a communist, even now something tugs me over to that side. But I'm in my fifties, I have lived through the war and seen Peter die—and the thousand other young men. I am horrified and shaken by all the hatred in

The Call of Death, from the series *Death*, by Käthe Kollwitz, 1934–37

> the world. I long for the kind of socialism that lets people live, and I find that the earth has seen enough of murder, lies, misery, distortion. In short, of all these devilish things. The communist state that builds on that cannot be God's work."

Throughout the 1920s and 1930s much of Käthe Kollwitz's output was a continuing reflection on the war and its aftermath, lived out in the irresoluble conflicts of the Weimar Republic. She publicly opposed the rise of Hitler and, along with Einstein, other intellectuals and artists, was a signatory to the "*Dringender Appell für die Einheit*" ("Urgent Call for Unity"), encouraging the voters to reject the Nazis in the 1932 elections. Unsurprisingly, once they came to power, the

Nazis banned her from exhibiting, and forced her to resign from the Academy of Arts. Her work, however, was never officially classified as "degenerate" (see Chapter 24), and was even used anonymously in Nazi propaganda. She was appalled, but refused to protest because it might land her in trouble or, even worse, because the Nazis might retaliate by putting her name to it and so suggest that she endorsed their views.

In 1935 she produced her last cycle of prints—eight lithographs called simply *Death*. The one illustrated on page 411 is the final one, *The Call of Death*. It depicts her own death, her self-portrait as an old woman leaning forward with her left arm raised, her right moving towards a disembodied hand that reaches down to her from above. It is recognizably the same woman as in the self-portrait of thirty years earlier, but transformed and diminished by the experiences of those three dark decades. It could almost be a self-portrait of Germany in these years.

This was hardly welcome to the Nazi regime, dedicated as it claimed to be to the rebirth of a cleansed and pure nation. She was visited by the Gestapo, who raised the spectre of the concentration camp. However, her international profile meant she was left in relative freedom. The Second World War delivered the final blow: the death of her grandson on the Eastern Front in 1942 followed by her evacuation from Berlin the following year. When she died in the last weeks of the war, in April 1945, her birthplace, Königsberg, had been largely destroyed and was in the hands of the Russians. In the following months, the entire German population there which had not already fled was expelled or killed and the city became Russian sovereign territory (see Chapter 26). It remains so today. Seven hundred years of Prussian history had ended.

But during the 1930s she was still working, and still working through the sorrow of 1914. On the anniversary of Peter's death, 22 October 1937, she wrote in her diary:

> I am working at a small sculpture which has developed out of my attempt to make a sculpture of an old person. It has become something like a *Pietà* [Mary with the dead Christ]. The Mother

Pietà, by Käthe Kollwitz, 1937–38/39

> is seated and has her dead son lying between her knees, in her lap. There is no longer pain, only reflection.

Kollwitz had not included Peter in the memorial sculptures of 1932—the focus was the parents' separate griefs. Now she created a private memorial for him and herself together.

Although the form derives from religious imagery, there is nothing Christian in this sculpture. The son is not, like Jesus, presented to the viewer for contemplation or adoration. He is not resting, as in Michelangelo's *Pietà*, on his mother's knees, but is huddled between her legs. His knees are drawn up so far that he is almost totally enclosed by his mother's body. She does not show him to us, but attempts to shield him, although dead, from further harm. The pathos of that futile gesture is extreme. Nothing in this image suggests sacrifice to achieve a higher purpose. There is no hint of salvation, merely a response to slaughter. Ruth Padel again:

> "I came to Käthe Kollwitz's work because I was writing a book about conflict and creativity and about how perhaps creativity comes out of trauma. Some artists can identify with trauma in such a way that they can make really extraordinary art that also speaks to other people. The poet Emily Dickinson says, 'After great pain, a formal feeling comes.' "

On 14 November 1993, in the pouring rain, the President of Germany, Richard von Weizsäcker, came to the Neue Wache to rededicate it as the central National Memorial to the Victims of War and Dictatorship. It was a low-key ceremony with no formal speeches, even though this place over the years had been a memorial to three different wars—it was the Prussian memorial to the Napoleonic Wars, the Weimar memorial for the First World War, and finally the Soviet memorial for the victims of fascism and militarism in the Second World War. Now the building was to commemorate "the

---

Opposite: President Richard von Weizsäcker, 14 November 1993

victims of war and tyranny"—all wars and tyrannies—and here, in the centre of the plain slate floor, under the oculus open to the wind, rain and snow, as well as to the sun, is a larger version of that sculpture created in 1937 by Käthe Kollwitz, who was herself both witness and victim.

President Weizsäcker read out a statement from Helmut Kohl, the German Chancellor, explaining why this sculpture had been chosen: "because the principles that underlie the creative work of this great artist are indissolubly linked with our concept of the state . . . which is founded on those same principles." It was, I think, a great insight on the part of Kohl to see the analogy between Kollwitz's image of a mother protecting her child and the state's recognition of its duty to defend all those over whom it has power.

As Ruth Padel says, Kohl's choice of Kollwitz's sculpture was not universally welcomed:

> "Helmut Kohl chose this image as a memorial to the victims of war and dictatorship in Berlin, as capital of the reunited Germany. He faced a lot of criticism. People said a woman mourning her son does not do justice to the victims of the Holocaust, the mass deaths of the Second World War, only to those of the First. But I think Kohl was brilliant in persisting in his choice, because actually people can only identify with the personal. So there it stands, light versus dark. It is in the open air, the light comes down and it is surrounded by empty walls. It sums up the suffering of everybody in all wars. If this were found in a Neolithic tomb, it would still be relevant, because it is about a grown-up mourning a child. It was a kind of political genius of Kohl to see that this would stand when other things fall away. There is no contextualizing, with any particular clothing or prop. There is just the little face of the dead child, turned up to the mother, the mother's hand over her eyes but yet looking at the child, helpless. It is the embodiment of grief and loss."

The two Germanys that were the heirs to the destruction of the Second World War reflected their different attitudes to the bitter inheritance in the way they approached the work and person of Käthe Kollwitz, says Yvonne Schymura:

> "She is the most important female artist in Germany of the twentieth century. She represents the history of the twentieth century with all its suffering. There are three museums for Käthe Kollwitz alone, there are hundreds of schools, streets and squares named after her. But the re-examination of her work started with reunification. Before that there was something like a competition between East Germany and West Germany over the correct interpretation of her life and art: is she a Socialist artist (as the East wanted) or is she (as the West argued) an artist of all humanity? They fought over it for years. She was of course both."

5000
Fünftausend Mark
Hunderttausend Mark
R·01207990
Reichsbanknote
ZWANZIG MILLIARDEN MARK
Berlin den 1. Oktober 1923
Reichsbankdirektorium
20 MILLIARDEN MARK
F 675082
1000
1000
Deutsche Reichsbahn
08280
Einhundert Milliarden Mark
Dieser Schein wird an allen öffentlichen Kassen wie gesetzliche Zahlmittel angenommen; er kann vom 1. Dezember 1923 ab zur Einlösung aufgerufen werden.
Berlin, den 27. Oktober 1923.
Deutsche Reichsbahn
№ 006697
Eine Billion Mark
(Eintausend Milliarden)
Dieser Schein wird an allen öffentlichen Kassen wie gesetzliche Zahlmittel angenommen; er kann vom 1. Dezember 1923 ab zur Einlösung aufgerufen werden.
27. Oktober 1923.
Der Reichsverkehrsminister
REICHSBANKNOTE
EINHUNDERT MILLIARDEN MARK
ZAHLT DIE REICHSBANKHAUPTKASSE IN BERLIN GEGEN DIESE BANKNOTE DEM EINLIEFERER. VOM 1. FEBRUAR 1924 AB KANN DIESE BANKNOTE AUFGERUFEN UND UNTER UMTAUSCH GEGEN ANDERE GESETZLICHE ZAHLUNGSMITTEL EINGEZOGEN WERDEN
BERLIN, DEN 26. OKTOBER 1923
REICHSBANKDIREKTORIUM
100
REICHSBANKNOTE
FÜNFZIG MILLIARDEN MARK
zahlt die Reichsbankhauptkasse in Berlin gegen diese Banknote dem Einlieferer. Vom 1. Januar 1924 ab kann diese Banknote aufgerufen und unter Umtausch gegen andere gesetzliche Zahlungsmittel eingezogen werden.
Berlin, den 10. Oktober 1923
REICHSBANKDIREKTORIUM
FÜNFZIG MILLIARDEN
2000
Reichsbanknote
MARK
AD 8
100000
V 49
10000

23

Money in Crisis

The First World War brought one particular word to prominence for Germans: *ersatz*. Literally, it means "substitute," but in the popular mind it soon came to mean "artificial." Germany had run out of many of the essentials of daily life long before the end of the war. The Allied sea blockade meant there were large numbers of things you simply could not get. There was *ersatz* rubber from petroleum, *ersatz* tea from raspberry leaves, *ersatz* coffee from acorns. There was even *ersatz* clothing and underwear—made from paper. It sounds quite innovative, even erotic, in the twenty-first century, but it horrified Berliners. Above all, there was not enough metal—any kind of metal. Early on in the war small-denomination Reichsmark coins began to disappear rapidly, as metal was needed for other purposes. By 1919 all the low-value denominations had vanished. Enter the *ersatz* Mark and the *ersatz* pfennig, usually made not from metal, but from paper.

It was called *Notgeld*—emergency money—and in the British Museum is one of the great collections of this temporary currency. There is a great deal of it because, as there was no longer an effective national currency for the lower denominations, every town and city had to make its own. High-value notes from the Reichsbank continued to circulate. *Notgeld* is the small change of daily life: that is what

Opposite: Banknotes from the hyperinflation, 1922–23

Mainz fifty-Pfennig *Notgeld* with Gutenberg monument on the right, 1921

Bremen seventy-five-Pfennig *Notgeld* with harbour scene, 1923

Müritz fifty-Pfennig *Notgeld*, 1922

makes it so interesting. As the central state faltered, regional memories and loyalties revived, and the diversity that had marked coinage of the eighteenth-century Empire (see Chapter 5) found an exuberant twentieth-century parallel in colourful explorations of local identity and civic pride. An example from Mainz promotes the city's attractions, including its statue of Gutenberg; Bremen boasts its fine international harbour; the Baltic resort of Müritz depicts the chic seaside fun on offer there; while Eutin honours its famous son, the composer Weber, with designs including a music score. Some places opt for the historical angle: Bordesholm promotes its abbey, a great religious centre; Eisenach highlights its Protestant tradition with an image of Martin Luther translating the New Testament.

Looking through these notes is like flicking through a travelogue of Germany, each town presenting its distinctive aspect most likely to appeal to the curiosity of the visitors and the pride of the local inhabitants. But the interest of these notes is not just topographical. They present a remarkable survey of the public mood in the years 1919–23, as the Weimar Republic struggled into life; of the issues that alarmed,

Eutin fifty-Pfennig *Notgeld* commemorating the First World War dead and the composer Weber with music from *Oberon*, 1921

fascinated and preoccupied the population. You can chart the continuing desire to honour those who fell in the war. There is a note from Hamburg and Bremen nostalgically showing Bismarck and the lost German colonies in Africa; another from Gramby, which was in danger of being removed from Germany in the plebiscite in the Danish-speaking area of Schleswig-Holstein, requested by Denmark and monitored by Britain and France. There are nasty anti-Jewish jokes,

Bordesholm fifty-Pfennig *Notgeld* with monks, 1921

Eisenach fifty-Pfennig *Notgeld* with portrait of Luther, 1921

Bremen seventy-five-Pfennig *Notgeld* with lost African colonies and Bismarck, 1921

Gramby one-Mark *Notgeld* depicting the local plebiscite deciding whether to be part of Denmark or Germany, 1920

Bielefeld linen thousand-Mark *Notgeld*, 1922

Beverungen seventy-five-Pfennig *Notgeld*, with anti-Jewish cartoon, 1921

disturbing hints of popular prejudice, and much, much more. These notes are a compendium of German memories, hopes and fears in the early 1920s.

Intriguingly, in yet another demonstration of regional diversity, not all *Notgeld is* paper. In Meissen and Dresden the *Notgeld* was made out of porcelain (needless to say, it rapidly became a collector's item); in Bielefeld, the great textile centre, it was linen or silk, and inevitably, in some places, it was a piece of sausage. This is German localism reaffirmed in a powerful way at a time of crisis. And in some sense it was, according to Mervyn King, former Governor of the Bank of England, a hopeful message—people trusted their *local* currency above the national one:

> "The German *Notgeld* is fascinating because it raises the question of why we do not let people produce their own notes. The answer has typically been the fear that people might suddenly find their money to be worthless; if banks issued their own notes, you needed to live pretty close to the head office so that if bad news about the bank came in, you could rush over there and get your money out in the form of gold coins; it was essential to be able to make your claim on the assets of the bank quickly. But *Notgeld* is an example where, in circumstances where the state could not produce adequate supplies of money or guarantee the value of it, communities decided to produce what in effect were IOUs. The great political thinker Hayek advocated that anyone should be allowed to print money, without the state monopoly on currency we have today. The drawback to that idea is that people want to feel that the unit they use to measure things has a stable and uniform value. But that is not a knockdown argument and, of course, the world economy as a whole, in which different countries around the globe have their own currencies, functions perfectly well."

Some of the most distinguished *Notgeld* came from Weimar, the birthplace of the Bauhaus art and design movement, where in the early 1920s the aesthetic and functional world was being entirely

Fifty-million-Mark *Notgeld*, designed by Herbert Bayer in Weimar, issued 25 July 1923

Bocholt twenty-five-Pfennig *Notgeld* with Rathaus, 1918

Tiefurt twenty-five-Pfennig *Notgeld* with an amended quotation from Goethe's *Faust*, 1921

reimagined (see Chapter 20). The Weimar notes were designed by Herbert Bayer of the Bauhaus. There are no historical or touristic themes on these notes. Just pure function, clear communication, bold design. Bayer used strong colours and then simply words and numbers in characteristic typography. Form uncompromisingly follows function. This *Notgeld* is an aesthetic manifesto for modernism. Bayer had only two days to design these notes in 1923, but he realized this was a rare chance to present Bauhaus typography and design to a mass public who would have no option but to use them. Advanced modernist design would reach every household within hours. *Notgeld* gave Bauhaus a previously unimaginable degree of public exposure.

Clarissa von Spee, a curator at the British Museum who comes from North-Rhine Westphalia, has explored some striking examples of *Notgeld* in the collection:

> "Clearly one of the things you can do with *Notgeld* is to show your local sights, the buildings, the landscapes you are really proud of. The British Museum has *Notgeld* from my home town—Bocholt in Westphalia. Bocholt's landmark is the Renaissance town hall, a building typical of the region, and that is what they chose for the money. There is also a note from Tiefurt, just outside Weimar, where the Duchess Anna Amalia of Saxe-Weimar had her summer residence. It is where she entertained Goethe and had long talks and walks with him. The note adapts a quotation from Goethe's *Faust*, which reads: 'Zu wissen sei es jedem der's begehrt, der Zettel hier ist 25 pfennig wert,' meaning: 'Let everybody know who wants to know it, that this bit of paper is worth'—and in the *Faust* it is 100 crowns, but here it says that this bit of paper is worth 25 Pfennigs."

This is *Notgeld* as a literary joke, using Goethe to question the very value of the emergency paper currency on which he is quoted. In such an emergency banknote, its makers are teasing, playing with Goethe, with financial instability and with local memory: it is a confident, stylish, culturally buoyant way of addressing hardship. When it comes to

Top and centre: Hamelin fifty-Pfennig *Notgeld* with Pied Piper, 1918

Bielefeld ten-Pfennig *Notgeld* with turnip, 1919

the currency for Hamelin, the obvious choice is of course not Goethe but the Pied Piper and the rats. Clarissa von Spee explains:

> "The rats appear again and again on notes from Hamelin. On a fifty-Pfennig note from 1918 you see the rats sitting on the numerals. And on the back of this one you see the Pied Piper leading the children out of the city. One of the recurrent themes then of the *Notgeld* is literature with a local connection, whether it's Goethe in Weimar or the legend of the Pied Piper in Hamelin. The language is often quite ribald, there is an undertone of humour, irony, taking the serious times lightly. But not always. The British Museum collection also contains a small note from Bielefeld. It is an early one, from 1917, the so-called turnip winter, when people were so short of food they fed on little else but turnips. A weeping turnip accompanies the inscription on the side, 'Durchhalten den Not ist Kriegs Gebot,' meaning, 'Enduring hardship is the law of war.'"

There is no humour about this at all. It is redolent of a much darker tone that leads into one of the key issues in Germany in the early 1920s—reparations and the demands of the victorious powers. The *Notgeld* addresses that too. Clarissa von Spee:

> "We have notes from Bitterfeld, a coal-producing area close to Berlin. On the back of the notes are trains carrying coal, heading first of all for Cologne—you can see Cologne Cathedral in the background—and then to the left you can see the Eiffel Tower. This is coal being taken from Germany to France, and it tells us very precisely that from April 1920 to March 1921 28.1 million tons of coal were exported. Of this, 67.1 per cent went as reparations. Only 11.5 per cent was sold on the world market."

This *Notgeld* speaks of the deep anger many felt about the fact that the coal Germany produced could not be used to earn foreign currency; instead a huge two thirds of it was devoured as reparation payments, mostly to the French.

Bitterfeld fifty-Pfennig *Notgeld* with train carrying coal to France, 1921

Overall there were more than 160,000 issues of *Notgeld*. They reflect the social and political tensions and anxieties of the Weimar Republic—the militarist, the pacifist, the hedonist, the racist. But what they do not reveal is the huge financial threat that loomed ahead, just around the corner. This intriguing emergency money, representing small sums, was about to be overwhelmed by one of the most catastrophic and destructive inflations in history. The great hyperinflation was ignited by a combination of Germany's post-war economic weakness and the difficulties of making the reparation payments demanded by the victorious Allies. In April 1921 the reparations bill was assessed at the colossal sum of $33 billion. By May that year the industrialist Walther Rathenau had become Minister of Reconstruction, with the job of paying the reparations, and he feared that they spelt the end of any sort of stability for the Mark. Rathenau wrote:

> The majority of statesmen and financiers think in terms of paper. They sit in their offices and look at papers which are lying in

> front of them and on those papers are written down figures which again represent papers . . . they write down noughts, and nine noughts mean a milliard. A milliard comes easily and trippingly to the tongue but no one can imagine a milliard. What is a milliard? Does a wood contain a milliard leaves? Are there a milliard blades of grass in a meadow? Who knows! If the Tiergarten were to be cleared and wheat sown upon its surface, how many milliards would grow? Two milliards?

A milliard is the equivalent of a billion, or a thousand million: the figures are terrifying. Indeed the whole situation became terrifying. There was inflation fever and Germany suffered a kind of collective madness. In June 1922, Rathenau was assassinated. That sent the Mark down to 300 to the dollar. A month later, when the first reparation payments were due, it fell to 500 to the dollar. By late October, with the second payments due, it collapsed to 4,500 to the dollar. By April 1923 hyperinflation had exploded. It is a chilling experience, even today, to handle the notes that resulted (see page 418)—1,000 Marks, 10,000 Marks, 100,000 Marks, 1,000,000 Marks. And then, in words, "Eine Billion," "Ein Hundert Milliarden" Mark. By November 1923 there were twelve trillion Marks to the dollar. Some wag at the British Embassy in Berlin noted that the number of Marks to the pound equalled the number of yards to the sun. By the end of the year, the cost of an egg was five hundred thousand million times more than it had been in 1918. People famously wheeled their banknotes around in barrows, not so much to go shopping as to take worthless cash to the bank to exchange it for ever higher denominations of worthless cash. In 1921 there were 120 billion Marks in circulation. Two years later, it was nearly five hundred million trillion—beyond comprehension. A five-hundred-million-Mark note might buy a loaf of bread.

Most Germans have a family memory of the terrors of hyperinflation, like the senior civil servant who would race home with his monthly salary so that his wife could buy a few grams of butter before it all became junk paper again. Mervyn King explains how such a disaster can come about:

"What happens is that the government finds itself in a position where, for one reason or another, it feels the only way it can finance its budget deficit is to print money. And then people start to expect that it will print more and more money. Their beliefs about where inflation will go rise. They try to get rid of money to buy things as soon as they get money into their hands. The speed at which money changes hands goes up. That starts to push up prices even faster. The government prints more money and you get into a vicious circle in which very, very quickly prices are rising at a speed almost impossible to imagine. Nowadays we think of inflation at around 2 per cent a year. That means that prices double in about forty years. Prices doubled in the German hyperinflation every three and a half days. Those photographs of people carrying money in wheelbarrows: they all go back to the willingness of the government to finance its budget deficit not by conventional means—either by taxation or by borrowing and

Woman fuelling a stove with hyperinflation banknotes, c. 1923

Papiergeld! Papiergeld!

(Karl Arnold)

„Brot! Brot!"

Letzte Zuflucht

Immer höher gehn die Wogen.
Und die Herren Theologen
wissen auch und künden's gern,
daß, warum und inwiefern:

Sehn wir doch, wie die Maschinen
uns beherrschen und bedienen;
und das färbt denn prompt wie Krapp
auf die Metaphysik ab.

Statt der sittlichen Begriffe
gibt's nur noch der Selbstsucht Kniffe.
Ach, kein Mensch glaubt mehr an Gott …
So erklärt sich der Bankrott.

Alle glauben heiß und brünstig
einen Gott, der ihnen günstig
und im letzten Notfall da:
Deus ist's ex machina.

— Diese Ansicht, meine Lieben,
scheint mir etwas übertrieben.
Bloß sein Bild, wie man ihn faßt,
ward dem Zeitgeist angepaßt.

Ratatöskr

— 140 —

Woman raising her starving child out of a sea of paper money, crying: "Bread! Bread!" Cartoon from *Simplicissimus*, June 1923

> making a promise to repay—but simply by printing banknotes, and that is what they did."

The German hyperinflation was not the worst in history: that honour belongs to the more recent Zimbabwean crisis of 2008–9, when prices doubled every day. But one of the strange things about hyperinflation is that it can end as quickly as it starts. In November 1923 the Weimar government appointed Hjalmar Schacht as Commissioner of Currency. He had a simple plan: he introduced a new currency, the Rentenmark, using as collateral/guarantee the value of properties owned by the government in Germany. The exchange rate at the point of introduction was one trillion old marks to one new Rentenmark. Schacht's policy worked with remarkable speed. He stabilized the currency in a matter of months, which, says Mervyn King, is just what you would expect:

> "It was a credible promise to put the budget in order; to raise whatever taxes were necessary to cut back on spending and a commitment not to print money to finance the budget deficit. From the vicious circle of prices rising uncontrollably, a virtuous circle was triggered, where because people believed that the budget deficit would be controlled, they became willing to hold on to their money again. What happens in hyperinflation is that people just do not want to hold money. There is no point: it becomes valueless in the time it takes to drink a cup of coffee. What all hyperinflations tend to have in common is that they start when governments lose control of their budget and the hyperinflation ends as soon as a government is put in power that is determined to manage its budget properly. And then immediately, even before they have been able to reduce the rate of growth or the money supply, inflation comes down very rapidly. Within months."

That is exactly what happened in Germany. The Rentenmark brought stability and confidence, and the economy began to recover. Yet the memory of the hyperinflation, of those banknotes overprinted with zero after zero, is even now painfully, powerfully alive, a guiding force through the decades at the Bundesbank and now at the European Central Bank, as Mervyn King explains:

> "That memory plays into the enormous weight that Germany places on the word 'stability.' Stability is the watchword for economic policy, both fiscal policy and monetary policy. And Germany is rightly very much aware that you play with this at your peril. Stability is to be guarded very carefully. It is the essence of successful economic policy."

There was another, more immediate consequence of this catastrophic financial episode. The hyperinflation provided the ideal context for right-wing parties, especially the Nazis, to exploit the feelings of xenophobia and discontent which many Germans harboured after the humiliation of the Versailles Treaty and the disasters brought on by reparations. The parliamentary system of government introduced by the Weimar Republic was accused of betraying the German army—the famous "stab in the back"—by forcing it to surrender though it had not been defeated. Hyperinflation had added to feelings of resentment and ill-treatment which festered long in the collective memory. Fear, insecurity, xenophobia and prejudice opened the door to the Nazis, with their quack solutions and racist explanations. And, of course, hyperinflation was used by the Nazis to promote their ideology, that it was all the fault of the Jews. The luckless Rathenau, who had tried to meet Germany's reparations commitments, was a Jew; the Weimar government was a "Jew government," and hundreds of republican and left-wing supporters, Jewish or not, were attacked, beaten up or, like Rathenau, assassinated.

The Rentenmark seemed to offer respite from this terrifying spiral of disinformation and violence: the new stability might have heralded a return to political normality. A British diplomat observing the trial of Hitler after the attempted Munich *Putsch* of 1923 reported: "Hitler's greatest enemy is the Rentenmark. It is impossible to overestimate the beneficial effect of the stabilisation of the currency on the Bavarian and, I suppose, also on the whole German outlook."

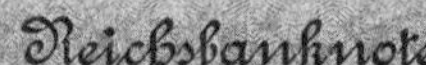

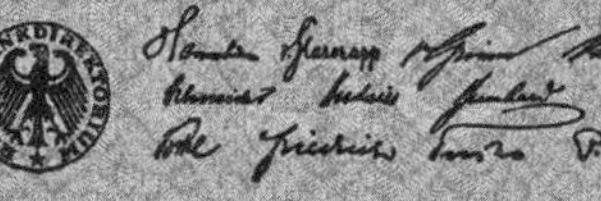

Hundred-million-Mark note, 1923. The reverse is stamped with Nazi propaganda, 1927

But the evil of hyperinflation was not finished yet. Once the currency was stabilized, there was the question: what to do with the old worthless hyperinflation banknotes? You could of course burn them to keep warm (page 432), but the Nazis characteristically had a solution, and a brilliant one: use them for propaganda. The hundred-million-Mark banknote was preserved and turned into an election leaflet in 1927. On the reverse, overprinted, is an anti-Semitic cartoon. A huge, radiant swastika hangs in the sky, in the shape of a comet, above a caricature of a Jewish financier, with hooked nose and huge grasping hands, who cowers before it. His hat has fallen to the ground as he staggers backwards. The text reads: "God the righteous! Another new comet!," then in German: "Germans! With this scrap of paper the Jew has cheated you out of your honest money. Give him your answer . . . Vote Völkisch Sozial," a party closely aligned to the Nazis.

This dazzlingly dishonest object is a powerful political weapon, a single sheet of paper with two simple messages: on the banknote side, an enduring reminder of the failure of the Weimar government to defend German interests and prosperity; on the other, the scapegoat whose fault it has all been, and whose removal will provide a solution. In 1927, when it was devised, the economy was recovering, and the threat from the extreme right wing seemed to be in retreat. The next economic catastrophe, the Great Depression of the early 1930s, would give objects like this and the murderous ideas they embodied a new, revitalized potency, too great to be held in check by the Weimar Rentenmark.

24

Purging the Degenerate

"She was thrown out before everybody else. She came over with 250 pots and 250 paintings and she had had some very bad experiences before she arrived. It dominated my life. It wasn't talked about but it was the most important thing about her."

Frances Marks is talking about her mother, the ceramic designer Grete Marks, who in 1936 left Germany to settle in England. Like many, Grete Marks left because she was Jewish: but she left also for a very particular reason—her pottery was politically dangerous. This chapter is about the inanimate victims of Nazism, the works of art that had no place in the new Germany of the Third Reich, and about the fate of Grete Marks.

On 10 May 1933, just over three months after Hitler was appointed German Chancellor, a group of Nazi students—egged on by Joseph Goebbels, the Minister for Popular Enlightenment and Propaganda—organized a bonfire of books that were considered "un-German"—incompatible with Nazi ideals. Similar bonfires were lit at the same time in university towns across Germany. The books included works by Erich Maria Remarque, who wrote the anti-war best-seller *All Quiet on the Western Front*; by authors held to be

Opposite: Ceramic vase by Grete Marks, *c.* 1930

Nazis burning books in Berlin, 1933

internationalist or left wing, like H. G. Wells and Bertolt Brecht; by Jewish writers and scholars like Heinrich Heine, Karl Marx and Albert Einstein; and even by Erich Kästner, the author of the children's whodunnit *Emil and the Detectives*, whose pacifist views were deemed unacceptable. Kästner was the only author present in the Berlin crowd as his books burned. The bonfire was held on what is now Bebelplatz, a square in the centre of Berlin, and in the middle of Bebelplatz there is now a memorial: a large glass plate set in the cobbles. Through it, far below street level, one can see rows of bookshelves, bare, white and empty, enough to accommodate the roughly 20,000 books burnt that day. The conflagration was an arresting, unforgettable opening to the Nazi campaign to redefine what was and was not German, the start of a process designed to purify all German culture and rid the Nazi state of art that was deemed threatening—or, to use their word, *entartet*, "degenerate." It is an event which lives in the German memory as a moment of high shame. Beside the memorial

Grete Löbenstein (later Marks), *c.* 1925

on the Bebelplatz is inscribed Heine's famous and prophetic remark of 1821: "This was merely a prelude: where they burn books, they end up burning people too."

Books were soon followed by other forms of artistic creation—music and paintings, sculpture and ceramics. Which explains why one of Grete Marks's vases is now in the British Museum (see page 438). It is a pleasing thing to hold and to touch: about a foot high, it is in the shape of two swelling, roughly spherical gourds placed one on top of the other, held together by an applied curving handle. The rounded forms flow serenely into each other and hint at African pottery shapes, but the cool green glaze with bold splashes of red-brown are unmistakably oriental. This is the work of someone who has looked at the ceramic traditions of the world and from them created a work of simple subtlety, but—and this is the surprise—has done so using a robust pottery that can be mass-produced by a factory.

Grete Marks (the name of her second, English husband—in Germany she was known as Grete Löbenstein) had in 1920 trained in Weimar at the Bauhaus school of design (see Chapter 20). She was quickly successful in carrying through its basic principle of creating good design that could be industrially—and therefore cheaply—produced. She opened her own factory at Marwitz, just north of Berlin, in 1923 and was soon acclaimed as one of the leading producers of modern ceramics. Her factory employed over a hundred people and she exported all over the world. A contemporary magazine in 1932 described it as "a workshop [that] designs its products so that you really get your money's worth of good taste." Two years later that "good taste" was under public attack, disparaged as degenerate. In 1934 Grete Marks had to sell her factory to a Nazi-approved owner. In 1936, like so many Jews who were able to, she left Germany.

The Nazi credo famously laid great stress on racial purity, on being Aryan or Nordic, on bearing the physical signs held to be characteristic of true full-blooded Germans. As Hitler said in 1937:

> A shiningly beautiful type of human being is growing up, a type whom we saw last year appear before the world in the Olympic Games [held in Berlin in 1936] in its radiant, proud, physical beauty and health. Never was humanity in its appearance and in its feeling nearer to antiquity than today.

As with human beings, so with art: the truly German characteristics of both were to be identified, admired and emulated. The chillingly simple task of the political leaders was, in the human and artistic world, to sift the pure from the impure, to cleanse the tradition, and to create the new, better Germany.

But in both cases—human and artistic—this turned out to be very difficult. Just as most of the Nazi senior leadership did not look especially Aryan, even less "a shiningly beautiful type of human being," so in the pantheon of German culture it proved hard to identify with confidence the desired *German* tradition. So the emphasis was often not so much on what parts of the tradition were truly German, as had been the case when a new German identity was being sought after the Napoleonic Wars (Chapter 7), but more frequently, and more xenophobically, on what was not. So, Mendelssohn and Mahler—Jews—were swiftly identified and rejected. Luther and Dürer were cited as safe models. Goethe was problematic. Although obviously a giant, he was worryingly cosmopolitan, interested in Asian cultures, and too many of his heroes were sensitive and scrupulous, incapable of resolute action. Although Hitler greatly admired the *Faust* drama, much of Goethe's work was politely parked. The leading characters of Schiller's plays, on the other hand, could be interpreted as true German heroes—courageous and self-sacrificing, while Heine's poetry did just the opposite—it was ironic, mocked German pretensions and shortcomings, and he was of course Jewish. So Heine, author of the famous poem and song, the "Lorelei," was airbrushed out of German cultural history. The "Lorelei" itself was too popular to suppress; its authorship simply became "Anonymous."

In this brave new Nazi world, ideal art would celebrate ideal beauty. So, for the official arbiters of taste, Greek and Roman heroic sculpture scored high, while anything that distorted, diminished or reordered the human form—abstraction, cubism—was suspect. If that reordering used African or other alien models, it was beyond the pale. And if there was, as well as all that, in the work—or in the artist—a hint of Bolshevism or Jewishness, then the work was "degenerate," not fit to be shown to the German public. The battle-lines were drawn. And in the front line, improbably, was our vase in the shape of two gourds.

The Great Depression in the early 1930s severely depressed the German and world markets for modern ceramics. That, the growing anti-Semitism and the witch-hunt against "degeneracy" in art had persuaded Grete Marks in 1934 to sell her ceramics factory at a knock-down price to the Nazi-backed State Artisans' Group. This gave the Nazis a splendid opportunity to attack her and her work. Pottery like this—with its evident debt to Chinese ceramics, its African shapes, its loose brush-splashed glaze suggestive of modernist painting (a hint of Kandinsky?), and the maker's link to the Bauhaus with its deplorable left-wing politics—was never going to be a vase in which a good Nazi would arrange his flowers. The new owners created what they called the *Schreckenskammer*, the Chamber of Horrors, a showroom in the factory dedicated to displaying degenerate ceramics.

In an article in his propaganda newspaper *Der Angriff* (*The Attack*), Goebbels published a picture of the Grete Marks vase, with some of her other works—pottery which, it was claimed, had "lost the simple, vernacular beauty that belongs to the German countryside and the German people." The new designs by her successor, the Nazi-approved Hedwig Bollhagen, on the other hand, were characterized as "noble forms which show how far we have moved on." Comparing the two women's work, the article asked: "Two races find different forms for the same purpose: which is more beautiful?" The answer was meant to be quite clear.

What Goebbels apparently did not realize was that several of these "more beautiful," "more German" forms were actually not by Hedwig Bollhagen, but by the Jewish, Bauhaus-educated Grete Marks herself, designs held over from the time when she had owned the factory. The absurdity of the idea of a "degenerate vase" is compounded by the confused dishonesty of the process of identifying that "simple vernacular beauty that belongs to the German people."

Zwei Rassen fanden für denselben Zweck verschiedene Formen. Welche ist schöner?

Article in *Der Angriff* by Joseph Goebbels comparing ceramics by Grete Marks with those of the Nazi-approved Hedwig Bollhagen, 1934

The racist, xenophobic tone of the 1934 confrontation in the Chamber of Horrors, and in the pages of *Der Angriff*, between the "degenerate" pottery of the Jewish Grete Marks and the "wholesome" works of Hedwig Bollhagen was a foretaste of a much bigger exercise to come. Three years later, a pair of huge exhibitions was organized in Munich, in a setting specially designed for the purpose. Chris Dercon, Director of Tate Modern, was previously director of the Haus der Kunst, which was built specifically to exhibit the healthy, German arts and is now a public gallery:

> "The Haus der Deutschen Kunst was a concept of Hitler's and it was supposed to show the Aryan-ness and the ideals of German culture. So in July 1937 they opened the exhibition of great German art. And a day later the propaganda exhibition, *Degenerate Art*, was opened a couple of hundred metres away from the Haus der Deutschen Kunst, in the Hofgarten. The exhibition of degenerate art was visited by many, many more people than the great German exhibition."

The *Degenerate Art* exhibition consisted of works, mostly from public collections, selected to show the debased and distorted anarchy that had destroyed true beauty. The Nazi authorities organized group visits and encouraged attendance, so that as many as possible might see—and be repelled by—the perversions that passed as modern art.

Six hundred and fifty paintings were deliberately jammed higgledy-piggledy around the exhibition rooms. They were grouped according to themes, such as "demeaning to religion"; "Jewish artists"; works "insulting to German women, soldiers and farmers." They were adorned with derogatory slogans and captions: "Nature as seen by sick minds"; "The ideal—cretin and whore"; "Revelation of the Jewish racial soul." Of the 112 artists exhibited, only a handful were Jews. Some of Germany's (indeed Europe's) greatest artists featured in the exhibition—Chagall, Kandinsky, Klee, Otto Dix,

The *Degenerate Art* exhibition, Munich, 1937–38

Joseph Goebbels visiting the *Degenerate Art* exhibition, February 1938, after it moved to the Haus der Kunst in Berlin

Cover of the *Degenerate Art* exhibition catalogue showing modern sculpture, *c.* 1912, by Otto Freundlich

Five Women, by Ernst Kirchner (1913), exhibited at the *Degenerate Art* exhibition, 1937

Opposite: Parade on the first "Day of German Art," Munich, 18 July 1937

Approved art: Adolf Wissel's *Kahlenberg Farming Family* (1939) (above) was purchased by Hitler for the Reich Chancellery; Adolf Ziegler's *The Four Elements: Fire, Earth, Water, Air* (1937) (below) was exhibited in the 1937 German art exhibition and afterwards hung by Hitler over his fireplace.

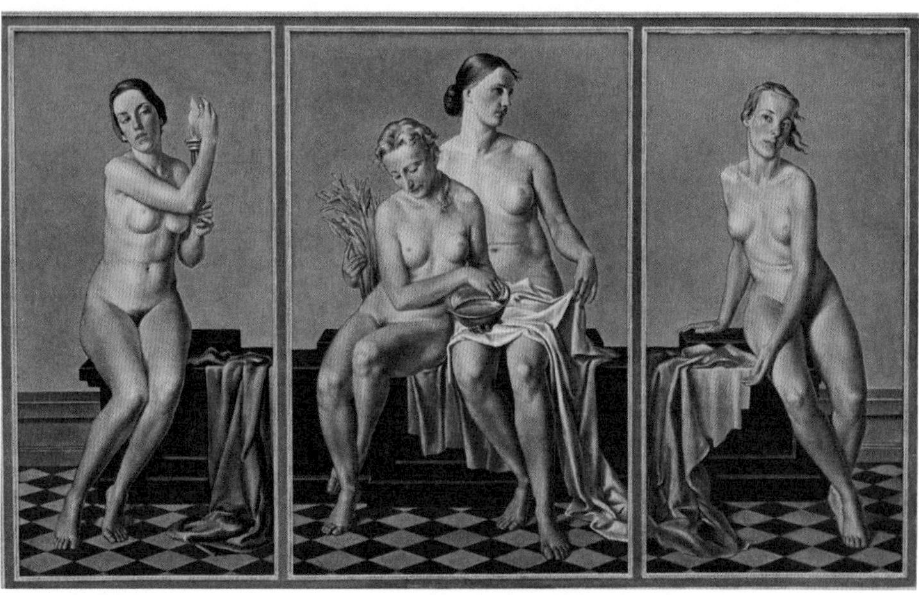

Max Ernst, Kirchner, artists whose works are today seen as central to twentieth-century European art—were exhibited as examples of degeneracy.

On the other hand, it was essential for people to understand what was noble and truly German. So the other exhibition displayed officially approved artists like Oskar Graf, Adolf Ziegler and Adolf Wissel, now mere historical curiosities. It was opened by Hitler with the words: "From now on, we shall wage a relentless war of purification against the forces that remain bent on undermining our culture." That war of purification intensified once the exhibition of degenerate art was over. But there remained the central question: what to do with all the paintings, drawings and prints in public collections? Chris Dercon explains:

> "The list of degenerate-art objects grew bigger and bigger over time. In 1937, before the opening of *Degenerate Art*, they counted about 6,000 objects. Shortly after that there was a list of 16,000 objects, and at the end there was a list of about 20,000–21,000 objects. In 1938 the Nazis floated a law saying that the theft of degenerate artworks from public institutions was legally perfectly acceptable."

The Nazi high command purloined those works they fancied—Goering, for example, selected a van Gogh and a Cézanne. The rest were either sold to raise cash for the Nazi coffers or destroyed. Around 4,000 of them were burnt by the Berlin fire brigade. The loss to Germany and the world was enormous. Even today, Germany's galleries contain surprisingly little great early twentieth-century art, because of what was seized, sold and destroyed. Perhaps one example suffices: the Folkwang Museum in Essen lost fifteen Egon Schiele works, twelve by the Bauhaus artist Oskar Schlemmer and no fewer than 518 by the German-Danish Expressionist Emil Nolde. Bought legitimately at the Nazi sales, many of the "degenerate" works removed from German museums are now to be found in the public collections of other countries. The Kunstmuseum, Basel, has a rich

holding, and the British Museum has an etching by Nolde which still bears on the reverse the stamp of the Lübeck Art Gallery, from which it was removed as degenerate. The stamp is a poignant witness to enforced exile, like the invalid passport of a citizen stripped of his statehood.

But a fate far worse than exile awaited some of the artists of the 1937 Munich show, and some of the public who viewed it. The catalogue of the *Degenerate Art* exhibition makes, even today, disturbing, sickening reading. It is only a short guide, but in language that is uniformly violent and shrill it identifies the categories of artistic perversion which require rooting out: cultural anarchy; artistic Bolshevism; Marxist propaganda; formal abstraction with works made of merely a few lines; pacifist representations of the horrors of war; Jewish-Bolshevik distortions; Negroes and South Sea Islanders presented as ideal human types; the choice of idiots, cretins and paralytics as models. Chillingly, as you read it, you realize that while this is talking about *objects*, these are also the categories of *people* whom the Third Reich had, since the opening of the first concentration camp in Dachau in 1933, been imprisoning or preparing to eliminate—Jews, Communists, pacifists, the mentally and physically disabled, the racially despised. From works of art to people was a short step.

The link is even clearer in the follow-up exhibition, organized later that year and held at the Deutsches Museum in Munich: *Der Ewige Jude*, *The Eternal Jew*. Opened by Goebbels, it presented Jewish history and religion as a long global conspiracy, combining the extremes of usury with the horrors of Bolshevism. The exhibition poster perfectly resumes this next step in the process of identifying degenerate art. It shows a tall Jewish man, whose facial features are a grotesque caricature. In one hand he holds gold coins, in the other a whip. His clothes could not be further from the conventional dress of the integrated German Jew. This man is

---

Opposite: *Vikings*, by Emil Nolde, 1922. The reverse (inset) bears the stamp of the Lübeck Museum.

The Eternal Jew exhibition, Munich, 1937

from Eastern Europe, probably Poland or Russia, an alien. The title of the exhibition is in fake Hebrew lettering—once more alien and un-German. Under his arm he carries the shape of the USSR, cut out as though from a jigsaw, stamped with the hammer and sickle. The Jew—the poster and the exhibition proclaim—is an outsider, bent on extortion and Bolshevism. The final twist is that the exhibition was held in the Deutsches Museum, a museum not of art or history, but of science. Racial prejudice was presented as objective, scientific truth.

It is easy, in the context of mass crimes, to overlook the fact that they are the sum of individual sufferings, endlessly multiplied and repeated, but always particular. What became of the woman who created the vase described earlier—Grete Löbenstein? After she came to England, she remarried, becoming Grete Marks, the name by which she is now better known. She went to work in Stoke-on-Trent, for

The Eternal Jew exhibition poster, 1937

the Minton pottery, where she had her own studio, but the arrangement did not work out. She parted company with Minton's after six months. Frances Marks takes up the story:

> "She was a formidable woman and she was a woman who wanted to be recognised as an artist and it was never possible in England really."

The hundreds of pieces of pottery she had brought with her from Germany were never exhibited:

> "We had a huge Victorian house with church windows and so the pottery was kept in boxes something like twenty feet high and I never saw the pottery until she died, when my father put out a few pieces."

After Grete's death, her husband and family presented a selection of her work to the British Museum, which is how the vase that Goebbels so loathed comes to be in Bloomsbury. But it was not simply the pottery which Grete Marks put away and hid:

> "She lived for being an artist. And certainly, from the age of eleven, she and I fought constantly, although not very effectively. It is enormously difficult to evaluate what bits of my mother's behaviour were because she was a refugee and about what had happened in Germany, and what bits were her personality. The most painful thing is not knowing what she was really like, and not knowing about her past. I did not dare touch it. It was dynamite, so I had learnt not to touch it. It was so painful to her. I never, I never asked her about Germany. It was a taboo area."

Grete Marks was—as she would have acknowledged—one of the lucky ones. She survived, she found a life elsewhere. But the memory of the events, never articulated, never exorcised, continued to wound her—and still distress her daughter to this day.

In Germany now, the memory of how the Nazis manipulated culture and history, exhibitions and museums, is strong. It has left an enduring hostility to any government censorship, and produced a passionate commitment to artistic freedom, expressed with an energy rarely found in other European countries. "Where they burn books, they end up burning people too."

JEDEM DAS SEINE

25

At the Buchenwald Gate

Weimar today is a beautiful city, much loved by tourists. War damage to its buildings has been carefully made good. Visitors come in large numbers to pay homage to Goethe and Schiller in their respective houses, to imbibe the spirit of Enlightenment expressed in Weimar classicism, or to admire the significant Bauhaus collection in the Museum (see Chapters 8 and 20).

About ten miles outside the city lies the charming forest landscape of Ettersberg. Goethe used to walk there, in its tranquil woodland and rolling hills—his lover Charlotte von Stein lived nearby—so for German walkers this landscape was traditionally enlivened by literary associations, a little like Wordsworth's Lake District for the English. Nowadays, walkers here are not in search of literary memories, but it is a tourist destination of a different kind. On one side of the road are the remains of a fence, and what looks like a gate-lodge to a large estate, the German name of which means beech wood, but which the world knows better as Buchenwald.

This place, charmingly set in the forest, is a place of national shame and international reflection. This is where the noble, humane traditions of German civilization—literary and legal, ethical and musical—were brought to nothing. The cruelty and injustice enacted here were part of a process which ended in the destruction of entire

Opposite: The Buchenwald gate viewed from outside the camp

cities and societies from the Atlantic to the Urals, in death camps like Auschwitz, in the systematic murder of the Jews, and the killing of millions.

Buchenwald was not itself an extermination camp, although 56,000 prisoners died here and it was a significant step on the road to Hitler's "Final Solution" and the extermination camps. The entrance gate to Buchenwald merits close attention: it speaks of a particular kind of perversion and brutality, of a sadism of the spirit, yet it is also

Approach to the gatehouse and watchtower of Buchenwald camp

a quiet assertion of dignity. The two sides of this gate are two aspects of Germany in the 1930s.

It is not enough merely to look into this camp. One has to go in, through this gate, and then look out in order to read the motto, boldly lettered in iron, which every prisoner who arrived at Buchenwald read as they looked back at the world from which they were being removed: *Jedem das Seine* (*To Each What They Are Due*). Among those who read that motto as they looked back were the

The replica Buchenwald gate in situ, viewed from inside the camp

writers and future Nobel laureates Elie Wiesel and Imre Kertész; Ernst Thälmann, leader of the German Communist party; Jorge Semprún, Spanish Communist resistant and writer; two prime ministers of France, Léon Blum and Paul Reynaud; Bruno Bettelheim, the child psychologist; and Dietrich Bonhoeffer, a leading Protestant theologian and a key member of the anti-Hitler resistance. All read the words on the iron gate: *Jedem das Seine—To Each What They Are Due*.

The words proclaim an ideal of justice: they are the German translation of the Roman law maxim *Suum Cuique*, incorporated not just into German law but legal systems across Europe. The study of Roman law was one of many areas in which, from the middle of the nineteenth century on, the universities of Germany had led the world. The words resonate in other spheres too. In 1701, on the eve of his coronation, they were adopted by the first King of Prussia (see Chapter 3) as the motto of the Order of the Black Eagle, freshly created as the highest Order of Chivalry in his new kingdom. He had *Suum*

Gold ducat of Frederick I of Prussia with the legend *Suum Cuique*, 1707

Cuique inscribed on his coinage to encapsulate the code of honourable aristocratic behaviour to which the Prussian state aspired. And Johann Sebastian Bach set these words, in their German form, to music in a cantata composed for the twenty-third Sunday after Trinity (BWV 163): *Jedem das Seine* was first performed in November 1715, just a few miles away from Buchenwald in the Schlosskirche in Weimar.

Could any three German words have a nobler lineage? Or carry a greater freight of artistic, ethical, political and intellectual aspiration and achievement? Yet those words are in this place. In a particularly acute way, the Buchenwald gate, a few miles from Weimar, raises the central question of modern German history: how can these different components of the German story fit together? How could all these humane traditions collapse?

"To each what they are due" is a phrase open to many interpretations. Classically, it has been an affirmation of justice. For the inmates it must have seemed a taunt, a riddle, designed to humiliate. Each day, as they left to work in the armaments factories, watched over by SS guards, they read on the gate, *Jedem das Seine*. And however interpreted, the SS clearly wanted to ensure that these words could never be ignored. The historian Mary Fulbrook is a member of the Buchenwald Memorial Foundation Board, which has been researching this particular issue:

Concerto - a 2 Violini 1 Viola. 2 Violoncello. S. A. T. B. e Continuo

Aria

Nur jedem das Seine

> "The side facing the inmates, from which you could actually read the inscription, was repainted annually—eight times through the eight years of the camp's existence, repainted red to make sure it was visible to all the prisoners inside; whereas the outside, the back of the sign that you saw as you were coming into the camp, was only painted when it was first put up and never repainted. So it was clearly very important for the SS that the prisoners should be able to see this clearly in bright red letters all the time as they stood in the parade ground in front of it. And that is, I think, unique. The *Arbeit Macht Frei* (Work Makes You Free) signs in Auschwitz, Dachau or Sachsenhausen face you as you come into the camp. They were for people entering. This one was specifically designed for the prisoners within to look at on a daily basis."

Today Buchenwald is a memorial to its victims, and to all Nazi Germany's victims in camps everywhere. Buchenwald was not the first and was by no means the worst, but through this gate passed all the different categories of victims who, as time went on, were incarcerated or exterminated throughout the camp system: dissident Reich Germans (i.e., from inside Germany's 1939 frontiers), other Germans from outside the Reich, Roma, Slavs, homosexuals, the homeless, the mentally ill, Jehovah's Witnesses and, by far the greatest in number, Jews. *Jedem das Seine* here meant slave labour, torture, murder, unspeakable medical experiments and the Holocaust. Daniel Gaede is one of the guides to the camp memorial. He explains who was sent to Buchenwald and why:

> "In the beginning it was a conflict, you might say, between different Germans, those wearing the SS uniform and anybody who was a Communist or a Jehovah's Witness or designated as Jewish. In the end, people came from nearly everywhere in Europe and so you can compare the history of Buchenwald with the general history of the continent. As soon as a country was occupied, people from that place would come to Buchenwald. So in the

Opposite: Extract from Cantata BWV 163, by J. S. Bach, 1715. The words "Jedem das Seine," from which the cantata takes its title, appear in the tenth stave.

Prisoners inside Buchenwald camp as it was liberated, 1945

beginning they were brought from Austria, then from Poland, later from France, from Belgium, the Netherlands. British people and U.S. pilots who were caught in France were brought also to Buchenwald, as the Allied forces entered France. Polish people, and from the other countries which were occupied, the Czech Republic, many people from the Soviet area. They were treated even less well than all the others because, from the perspective of the Nazis, they did not have the same right to live. It was also meant to kill quite a number of the different groups like Jewish prisoners or homosexuals. The main function of the camp here was work, to support industry, the arms industries for example, and to work outside in villages, in factories, so there were lots of connections with the local population, which is totally different to the extermination camps in occupied Poland."

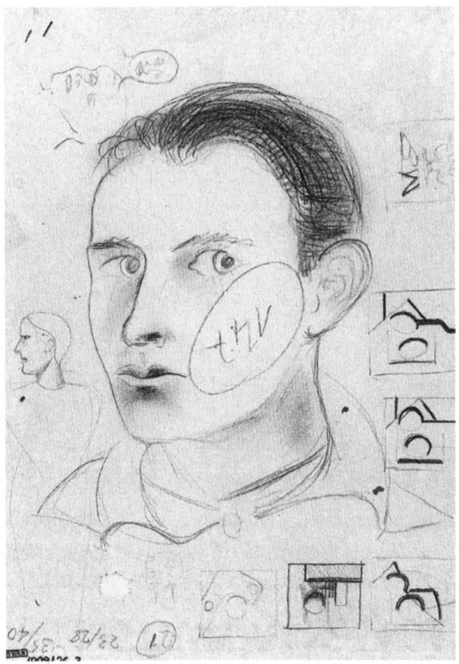

Self-Portrait, by Franz Ehrlich, drawn between 1934 and 1937, while in custody

Franz Ehrlich's poster for the Bauhaus exhibition in Basel, 1929

Walking through the Buchenwald gate is disconcerting: it is not so much a gate as a door, a very domestic door, with a handle, far too everyday, you would think, to contain what lay inside. It does not slam dramatically shut as prison gates should: it gently clicks to. The bold, clear and, it must be said, elegant lettering style of that motto, *Jedem das Seine*, also disturbs. It is at eye level, and it is unquestionably an aesthetic creation, the letters carefully shaped and spaced. It is in fact a splendid example of Bauhaus typography (see Chapter 20). The motto was intended to assert the right of the SS to brutalize and murder whom they chose. But the lettering, inspired by the Bauhaus, which the Nazis loathed as left-wing and cosmopolitan, was a subtle, coded protest against this monstrous assumption. It can be read as an assertion of dignity, eloquent and powerful, against everything this camp—and all the camps—stood for.

It was designed by Franz Ehrlich, a committed Communist who studied at the Bauhaus under Klee, Kandinsky and Gropius. He was imprisoned as early as 1934 for conspiracy to commit high treason and sent to Buchenwald shortly after it opened. It was a year later that the SS, who ran the camp, ordered Ehrlich to design the inscription. Perhaps simply because as a craftsman he wanted, even in these circumstances, to produce something of which he could be proud, perhaps out of a spirit of subtle resistance, he chose to work his letters in a characteristic Bauhaus script. The SS failed to see this, or to grasp its full implications. Many inmates would certainly see—and understand. Mary Fulbrook of the Memorial Foundation for Buchenwald explains:

> "Franz Ehrlich had come out of the Bauhaus and he specifically chose for his design this really artistic, beautiful, almost dancing font, with strong Bauhaus influences, which was in the Nazi view *entartete Kunst*, degenerate art, the kind of stuff they'd just been banning. So, in a sense, Ehrlich putting it in that typeface was saying: actually there is another Germany, there is another tradition. We will still persist. Our spirit lives on despite all. So you can interpret that as subtle subversion of the gate's intention. It is a uniquely artistic sign. If you look at other signs, in other camps, they are just very basic capital letters, or badly produced—you know, the spacing isn't right. The *Arbeit Macht Frei* signs are not artistic productions. This is.
>
> "But as well as the form, the sense of the words could also be subverted. The way in which it was read by some of the prisoners was completely turned round. There is for example a poem written under the title 'Jedem das Seine,' written in 1943 by one of the prisoners, Karl Schnog, who inverted the meaning, saying: in due course you too will get your just deserts, one day we will be free and then we will have justice, we will take revenge against you, the SS. So the prisoners too could see it the other way round, that in the long run it might be that the SS would get what was due to them, that justice would be meted out to them."

In April 1945, when the Americans liberated Buchenwald, they brought more than a thousand citizens from neighbouring Weimar to see for themselves, in person, what had been done in their name,

German civilians taken into Buchenwald by U.S. military police, faced with a prisoner as he was left hanging by the guards, April 1945

and to confront the evidence: the piles of corpses and the emaciated survivors. The American commander-in-chief, General Eisenhower, was determined that Germans should see what he and his soldiers had seen. Visiting Ohrdruf, a sub-camp of Buchenwald, he famously said:

> The things I saw beggar description. The visual evidence and the verbal testimony of starvation, cruelty and bestiality were so overpowering. I made the visit deliberately, in order to be in a position to give first hand evidence of these things if ever, in the future, there develops a tendency to charge these allegations to propaganda.

One might imagine that liberation would mean the end of Buchenwald as a place of suffering, but just five months later, in August 1945, Buchenwald went back into service as a prison camp—this time run by the Russians, as one of the ten camps in their occupation zone. It officially became part of the Gulag system in 1948. Twenty-eight thousand people were held there: a quarter of them died, and were buried in mass graves around the camp. The prisoners were supposed enemies of Stalinism, some of them former Nazis, but many went there apparently because they were victims of identity confusion or arbitrary arrest. The memorial of Buchenwald is their memorial, as it is that of the prisoners and victims of the Nazis.

The complexity of what happened in Buchenwald after the summer of 1945 is reflected in the complexity of responses to it and to all the camps in the two Germanys that emerged from the Second World War. What sort of memories were encouraged or permitted in the zone occupied by the U.S., the UK and France—West Germany—as opposed to the Soviet zone—East Germany? Daniel Gaede has been able to reflect on this over long years of meeting visitors from both:

> "I met adults who had been raised in the East (the GDR), and at school they had to write about the liberation of the camp. They asked at home what happened and got the information that the army of General Patton arrived here April 11, and then the camp was freed. And they proudly presented that in school and got very bad marks—because that was the wrong version. According to the official narrative, the Communists in the camp liberated themselves and only two days later U.S. troops arrived here—surprised to find the camp already in the hands of the prisoners. It was the time of the Cold War and to speak about imperialist forces liberating Communists was a little bit difficult.
>
> "But we have to keep in mind it was also very difficult in West Germany to speak about Communists as resistance fighters against the Nazis. The Communist party in West Germany was illegal, and quite a number of those who had been imprisoned by the Nazis here in Buchenwald were put into prison again in West Germany because they still continued to work as Communists."

The differences went even deeper than that. Buchenwald was one of several concentration camps which were declared memorial sites to the victims of Nazi terror by the East German government in the 1950s. As Daniel Gaede points out, the response to the camps in West Germany was very different. In the 1950s, Dachau, just outside Munich, was actually still being used as a camp—for German refugees expelled from the territories in the east (see Chapter 26), who had to live in the same blockhouses as the concentration camp inmates had ten years before. And although the notorious Bergen-Belsen had formally become a cemetery for the thousands who died there, there was no mention of *who* was buried there, or that they were Nazi victims. West Germany was slow to acknowledge the implications of its Nazi past and to memorialize the victims of the Third Reich. So why did the East German authorities decide so early to make Buchenwald into a monument? Daniel Gaede offers his view:

> "Buchenwald was where Ernst Thälmann, the leader of the German Communist party, had died and been cremated: so this was his martyr's grave, so to speak. But the small group of Communists in control of the state was well aware that they were not governing seventeen million anti-fascists. They knew that the majority of the population had either actively supported, or at least participated in, the Nazi project for society, and so it was not possible to have an open discussion about history. But to show that this new government held the legacy of the fight against the Nazis, it was important to have commemoration places like Buchenwald, where Communists had indeed played a very important role within the camp history. Therefore it became the national monument where every generation should go to understand that they have to continue this fight for a better world in terms of socialism and anti-capitalism and so on. In West Germany people were claiming—look how the people in the East abuse history. At the same time many in the West tried to forget, and not to make visible, how their own careers in the administration, in the military, in the police, had continued after the war. They had good reason

> to give the impression that it was not necessary any more to talk about the past—because they didn't want to speak about their own biographies."

This question of individual biographies, and individual responsibilities, takes us back to Franz Ehrlich's gate. *Jedem das Seine*: to each what is due *to* them. But how much is it reasonable to expect *from* someone when they are confronting a regime of terror? The subsequent biography of the designer of the motto on the Buchenwald gate is eloquent of the dilemmas which every adult in Germany who survived the years between 1930 and 1950 had to confront. Ehrlich, who may have designed that gate as a kind of protest, who many want to believe was asserting in its very making an alternative German tradition, was released from Buchenwald in 1939. We do not know why (many prisoners were amnestied on Hitler's birthday that year), but we do know that he went on to have a career as a designer under the Nazis—a career which continued until the end of the war. What compromises did he choose to make? After 1945 he continued to work in the GDR, not surprising for a former active Communist. But when, after 1990, the Stasi archives were opened (see Chapter 2), it emerged that Franz Ehrlich had been an active informant, spying on his fellow citizens. Anybody who is not German must feel grateful not to have had to face such circumstances and such choices.

Entering Buchenwald today one is confronted by a huge empty space, like an enormous, sloping parade ground. At the end are trees and, beyond the trees, gently rising hills, where today windfarm turbines spin slowly against growing crops. On the face of it there is nothing to see here at all. There is simply a site and a memory. The purpose of Buchenwald today is not just to preserve that memory, but to explore it, and to explain and discover its significance for Germany and for the world.

More than any other object in this story of Germany, the Buchenwald gate, erected almost within sight of Weimar and everything for which Weimar stands, brings us back to the unanswered, perhaps unanswerable question: how could it happen? How did the great

Aerial view of Buchenwald camp, 2010. The rectangles mark the sites of the former huts.

humanizing traditions of German history—Dürer, Luther's bible, Bach, the Enlightenment, Goethe's *Faust*, the Bauhaus, and much, much more—fail to avert this total ethical collapse, which led to the murder of millions and to national disaster? These are the questions with which every German today has to struggle. The gate, and its designer, leaves us all with another question too: what would we have done?

Part Six

Living with History

"In Germany, for a long time, the purpose of history was to ensure it could never happen again."

—MICHAEL STÜRMER

How does a nation recover from extreme trauma? How do perpetrators—and the heirs of perpetrators—address their responsibility? And how are lives put together when everything has been lost? This final part examines the years from *Stunde Null* (Hour Zero), as the Germans call 1945, to the present, as Germany has tried to rebuild itself physically, economically and morally.

Refugee handcart from East Pomerania, probably early twentieth century

26

The Germans Expelled

In 1945, as the Second World War was drawing to a close, and during the first years of peace, Europe experienced its worst refugee crisis ever. It was possibly the biggest forced population movement in history—larger than anything that had happened in Stalin's Russia, comparable in scale to the almost simultaneous partition of India and Pakistan. All in all, by 1950, between twelve and fourteen million Germans had either fled or been forced from their homes in Central and Eastern Europe. Most had nowhere to go. Outside Germany, little is known about this. Inside Germany, it is part of almost every family's history.

In the German Historical Museum in Berlin is a small handcart pulled by one of those refugees from Eastern Pomerania, in what is now Poland, into Germany at the end of 1945. It is about the size and the shape of a child's cot, on four wheels. It is roughly made out of crudely hewn wood with a handle to pull it by: the kind of farm cart that has been used for centuries to carry cabbages and potatoes from the field to the barn, and from the barn to the market.

Like most traditional farm implements it is extremely hard to date—and in fact a cart like this could very well have been used for exactly the same purposes—to carry vegetables, or to flee from an advancing army—in exactly the same part of Germany 300 years earlier, during the Thirty Years' War. Piled high with bedding, clothes and food, there would be very little space to carry anything else from the farms and towns where the refugees, and their families before them, had lived for centuries.

Before January 1945, in what was then eastern Germany—Prussia, Pomerania—people could be shot on sight by the Nazi authorities for using one of these carts. To flee west at that point was weakness, capitulation absolutely forbidden. But once the Wehrmacht began to pull back in the face of the Soviet advance, and once people discovered what followed it—robbery, murder, mass rape, the unsurprising revenge for the terrible things the German army had done in Russia—the civilians fled. They simply upped and left behind everything that they could not carry or pile onto one of these carts. Conditions quickly became chaotic as kilometres-long queues of refugees tried to force their carts through the snow. As most men were either in action or dead, the carts were pulled largely by women, hoping to stay ahead of the advancing and avenging soldiers from the east. Casualties were particularly high when the Soviet army got within reach of the trekkers, who were picked off by low-flying aircraft, even rolled over by tanks.

This was only the beginning of an enormous movement of populations. At the Potsdam Conference in the summer of 1945, the USSR, the U.S. and the UK redrew the map of Europe. The borders of Poland were moved hundreds of miles to the west. The Sudetenland was returned to Czechoslovakia. Königsberg, the home of Kant and refuge of the Prussian monarchy in 1807, became part of the Soviet Union (see Chapter 3). Everywhere German-speaking people—even if settled for centuries—became objects of hatred and persecution. To avoid an explosion of ethnic killing, the occupying powers saw only one solution. The Potsdam Agreement stated:

> The Three Governments, having considered the question in all its aspects, recognize that the transfer to Germany of German populations, or elements thereof, remaining in Poland, Czechoslovakia and Hungary, will have to be undertaken. They agree that any transfers that take place should be effected in an orderly and humane manner.

Refugees resting against their loaded cart, Tempelhof, Berlin, 1945

Refugees with handcarts, East Prussia, spring 1945

Georg Kastner

Behind the bland words lay a brutally simple fact: people who spoke German would be moved to what was now deemed to be German territory, if necessary against their will. As Churchill put it, this would be the "most satisfactory and lasting" solution, "There will be no mixture of populations to cause endless trouble. A clean sweep will be made." That "clean sweep" was not very clean: the death toll attributable to the expulsion is estimated at over two million civilians. There were virtually no lorries or cars available, and horses were scarce. For almost everyone, the only way of transporting their possessions was the handcart.

Andreas Kossert, a historian of the post-war expulsions who works with the German Historical Museum, describes what such an object represents:

> "It is a universal, material expression of having been forced to leave your home. It could well have been made in the nineteenth century and it is typical of one phase of the migration. Carts like this were mostly used in spring and summer 1945, when Polish and Czech authorities legalized the expulsion of German civilians. Before the Potsdam Treaty in August 1945, Polish authorities wanted to get rid of as many Germans as possible, so as to have a better negotiating position. Fourteen million Germans were expelled and lost their homes, which meant that, at the end of the war, one quarter of all surviving Germans were victims of expulsion. Altogether one quarter of German territory was lost in 1945, territory which had for many centuries belonged to Germany. Not all of the refugees were country people. They arrived initially in the areas which were closest to their homes. So, for instance, Pomeranians or East Prussians arrived in northern Germany while the Sudeten Germans from Czechoslovakia arrived in Bavaria or Saxony. But later on the allies distributed them all over Germany. So up to ten million refugees lived in West Germany and about four million in the Soviet-occupied zone—later the GDR."

Opposite: Refugees leaving Königsberg, January 1945

Many of the refugees were forcibly assigned to parts of Germany which they had never before seen, or perhaps even heard of. Much of it was in ruins, barely able to accommodate its own returning population, let alone the millions flooding in from the east and the south, speaking in strange accents and dialects. It is—in a rough parallel—as though the entire population of Canada had been forcibly repatriated to Britain at the end of 1945.

How were these new arrivals to be fed or housed? In this new context, as in the old, the handcarts were valuable. Andreas Kossert:

> "Most of the carts went on being used after the war, because the people who arrived in West Germany as refugees and expellees had to survive. They had to grow vegetables and find places to live, and move around within West Germany. So this was actually an item of transportation that was used for many, many years, and that remained with families for decades."

Unsurprisingly, the immigrants were not at all welcome. They may all have been of German descent, but after long separation they had habits which seemed alien and often uncouth; they were competing for scant resources, and most hoped they would soon return home. But there was, in this case, an extra edge to the tensions. Andreas Kossert:

> "The arrival of the Germans from the east was a reminder to Germans that they all had lost the war together. There was serious conflict between the West Germans and the refugees. The West Germans tried to forget as soon as possible about their own responsibilities for the war. The refugees had no return ticket—they were staying, for ever, and they asked very unwelcome questions: Why were we the ones who have been expelled, while you can still sit in your farms and in the social environment you're used to? Why did we—but not you—pay the bill for Hitler?"

For a long time, it seemed to some that this forced migration might be merely temporary. One of the significant ingredients of West German politics was the *Bund der Vertriebenen*—the Federation of Expellees. Throughout the 1950s and 1960s, the *Bund der Vertriebenen* pressed the West German government to demand the return of land and property confiscated after the war, especially in Poland and what is now the Czech Republic. Slogans of the Federation like "Wroclaw is Breslau and Breslau is German," referring to the capital of Silesia, long a German city but after 1945 part of Poland, soured relations with those two countries and raised the spectre of long and bitter battles—if only in the international courts. In 1970 the West German Chancellor, Willy Brandt, tried to settle the matter by declaring that the border drawn up by the Allies at Potsdam, along the Oder and Neisse rivers, was the final non-negotiable eastern border of Germany. The claims and counter-claims persisted, but Brandt's position prevailed, embodied in the *Ostverträge*, the Eastern Treaties, a supreme diplomatic achievement that settled the question. This peaceful resolution was definitively endorsed in the unification of 1990. As the generation which pulled the handcarts dies out, the political force of any campaign for return of property or territory dwindles. The focus of the Federation's activity is now increasingly the preservation of the popular culture of Sudeten, Silesian or Pomeranian Germans. Germany's eastern frontiers are now peaceful boundaries within the European Union.

It could be argued that the Potsdam decision to move entire populations had at last solved the centuries-old question of where "Germany" was. For most of the nineteenth century, the favoured answer would have echoed Arndt's famous song—"Wherever the German tongue is heard, there is a German's fatherland" whether Hamburg or Breslau, Cologne or Danzig. It was this attitude that determined membership of Ludwig of Bavaria's Walhalla (Chapter 9). But given the vast geographical dispersal of German speakers, it was an answer twentieth-century nationalism had not been able to accommodate peacefully. For Eastern Europe the 1945 solution, brutally simple, reversed Arndt's terms: German speakers should live—only—within the borders of an internationally determined state. Germany's frontiers would no longer float.

If the handcart embodies the closing down of one old discussion, it also sits at the centre of a new one. Abigail Green, reviewing the shifting focus of German historians over the last decade or so, observes:

> "I suppose the most significant recent debate has been about trying to deal with the experience of Germans as victims, as well as perpetrators, during the Second World War period, and how that could be brought into the national narrative."

Like the huge numbers of victims killed in the bombing of German cities, the millions of expellees from Eastern Europe have until recently been under-commemorated and under-studied. Is this because Germans consider these events as just retribution for evil deeds? The suffering of those deported, however, cannot be denied. The pathos of the handcart is powerful and real. The expellees force the awkward question: when a state has done so much wrong, how are we to respond to the suffering its citizens endure as a result? If we assert a communal guilt, can we nonetheless plead for individual compassion? These are questions that preoccupy Andreas Kossert:

> "Now, seventy years after the end of the war, almost every family in Germany is affected by it. But it is only gradually becoming a topic of collective memory in Germany, because until very recently the issue was associated with a right-wing, revisionist position, or that was the general perception. In many families there was total silence and not a word about the loss, the mourning of parents or grandparents. But all of a sudden it's now entering the centre of society. Here in the German Historical Museum we have only this cart on show, telling the story of fourteen million Germans, one quarter of the German population. I think there's still much more to be done on what it means for German collective memory."

A proposal to build a memorial to the expellees in central Berlin is now under discussion.

Model stage set for the first German production of Brecht's *Mother Courage*, 1949

Andreas Kossert is right when he says that in the German Historical Museum there is only one refugee cart from the great migration exhibited to tell the story. But only a few yards away from it is another wagon, also designed to be pulled by hand, also surrounded by scenes of recent warfare and evident displacement—but this handcart is much smaller. It is a model of the stage set for the first performance in Berlin in 1949 of one of the most famous German plays of the twentieth century—Bertolt Brecht's *Mutter Courage und ihre Kinder*, or *Mother Courage and Her Children.*

Brecht fled Nazi Germany in 1933 and was in Stockholm in 1939 when Hitler invaded Poland. Brecht's response to the outbreak of war was to write perhaps this most famous of his plays, certainly one of his most performed. He set it not in his own time, but in the Thirty Years' War, the conflict which from 1618 to 1648 devastated Germany and traumatized its people, and has always haunted the national imagination (see Introduction). Brecht wrote the play in a matter of weeks, as Hitler's armies and aeroplanes smashed their way

across Poland. He intended it to be a condemnation of all wars, and he used the Thirty Years' War as the setting precisely because it had so nearly destroyed the very idea of Germany 300 years earlier. War, famine and plague had in some areas killed over half the population. Brecht was reacting to what he saw in 1939, but with disconcerting prescience he was writing a drama that would be played out in real life by millions over the next five years.

Mother Courage is an archetypal figure, a camp follower, selling food and other necessities to soldiers; essentially a black-marketeer

The Pillage and Burning of a Village, from *The Miseries of War* by Jacques Callot, 1636

and a war profiteer. Her wagon dominates the play. It rolls from scene to scene. Unlike Mother Courage's own children, it outlives everything. By the end of the play, Mother Courage, dehumanized by war, viewing her children's deaths as a necessary, if regrettable, business cost, has almost become one with her wagon: both are merely machines for survival, for keeping going. Brecht's aim, to show her as a knowing participant in the evil business of war, little better than the warmongers and looters themselves, was lost on the audience when the play was first performed in Berlin in 1949. To his

German plague mask, middle of the seventeenth century

irritation, they saw above all her suffering and her failure, and they were moved to compassion, as indeed are most theatregoers to this day.

The actor Fiona Shaw, one of the most powerful interpreters of the role, reflects on how sorry we are meant to feel for Mother Courage, so complicit in her own catastrophe:

> "Brecht is undermining the classical rule of the heroine as somebody whose moral compass you might want to follow, by creating a woman whose own survival—on the surface—is the only thing that matters to her. But in fact of course emotionally she is not surviving.
>
> "Mother Courage becomes very rich and in a way we feel pleased that she is doing well, but the reasons for her doing well

Helene Weigel hauling her cart in the 1949 production of *Mother Courage*

are terrible. And this constant pull is asking us what we feel about ourselves. At the very end of the play, she has been off doing a little deal somewhere and comes back to find that her daughter Kattrin has been shot. Her last child is now dead, so she's alone and she could buckle—perhaps then we could feel sorry for her. But she doesn't feel sorry for herself. She ties herself to the cart and drags it, yet again following the soldiers.

"But it is to no end, and there is an existential issue here. There is no god, there's no religious future, there's no emotional future, and yet she keeps on pulling the cart. I find it hard to believe that Brecht isn't sympathetic to that problem."

We know that for many refugees the response to that existential predicament was a simple one: work. As Andreas Kossert points out:

> "The refugees and expellees contributed quite remarkably to the economic miracle in the 1950s and '60s. For instance, they brought engineering skills, special technologies and so on. And you have also to bear in mind that the big cities were mostly destroyed and so the refugees provided the manpower to help rebuild Germany, and especially West German cities."

The huge Volkswagen factory at Wolfsburg (see Chapter 14), supreme symbol of the economic miracle of the 1950s, was in very large measure staffed by refugees.

The murderous violence of the German occupation of eastern Europe was the subject of much reflection in the decades after 1945 in prose, poetry and painting. Anselm Kiefer's illustrations to and meditations on Paul Celan's poem "Todesfuge" ("Fugue of Death") with its famous line, "Der Tod ist ein Meister aus Deutschland" ("Death is

Your Golden Hair, Margarete, by Anselm Kiefer, 1981

a master from Germany") are the epitome of a profound engagement with pain, loss and shame. Celan was a German-speaking Romanian Jew, whose family perished in the Holocaust. His use of the word *Meister* has all the resonance of skill carefully acquired that was discussed in Chapter 14.

Any considered remembering of the expulsions could not take place until after reunification and the definitive settling of Germany's eastern borders. For Andreas Kossert, when it came, it exerted a new—and very different—influence on German foreign policy and its relations with its European neighbours:

> "I think what really made Germans more aware of their own history was the conflict in former Yugoslavia in the 1990s. We watched expulsions on television screens in Germany, and all of a sudden we realized, we remembered, this was part of our own experience. I think this made people, even politicians, more aware that we had to take action, because ethnic cleansings are not, cannot be justified."

A *Trümmerfrau* stacking bricks in Hamburg, 1946–47

27

Beginning Again

In 1945 nearly eight million Germans had been killed or were missing, over 10 per cent of the population; two thirds of them from the armed forces. Germany's key cities were in ruins; not just the industrial centres but also many of its medieval and baroque treasures, like Nuremberg and Dresden. And what the bombs had not devoured, the firestorms generally had.

Eight million homes were destroyed or damaged across Germany, nearly half the roads, railways, and water, gas and electricity supplies had gone. The economy was similarly in total collapse. Such destruction and suffering had only been seen once before, at the end of the Thirty Years' War in 1648 (see Chapter 26). That catastrophe was held to have affected German economic life for centuries. And yet within a generation of 1945 West Germany's cities had been almost completely rebuilt and her economy was the fourth largest in the world. West Germany was hailed as a model of economic revival. And, for the first time in decades, the world learned a positive German word: *Wirtschaftswunder*, the economic miracle. How did this come about? The answer is: by human hand. It was people—largely women—who made the miracle.

In the centre of Dresden, for example, the destruction was almost total: two and a half square miles of one of the most beautiful cities in the world had simply vanished. The inhabitants who survived the

bombs then had to survive much more: little or no food, no fuel, no transport, in many cases no houses and no streets. And everywhere there was rubble. The question was how to rebuild the country, how to create confidence in some kind of future: not easy when a quarter of German territory had been removed and the people who lived there expelled westwards, adding to the confusion and the pressure on the collapsed infrastructure. Nor was it made any easier by the Allies' original aim of dismantling Germany's industrial base and making it a primarily agricultural economy, an ambition successfully achieved in parts of the Soviet zone.

For ordinary Germans the first priority was to clear the streets and make houses habitable where it was possible, make new ones where it was not and repair the utilities. But how? A fifth of the nation's men were dead, many were injured, traumatized, incapable of working: who was going to embark on the Herculean task of simply clearing the rubble from the endless ruins? You can see some of that rubble today in the German Historical Museum in Berlin, but it is rubble that has been transformed by the sculptor Max Lachnit into an arresting sculpture of the head and shoulders of a young woman (see page 496). Slightly over life size, it is a mosaic of hundreds of polished marble and basalt fragments. With a red head scarf tied at her neck, her expression is composed, almost impassive and reflective. She is a *Trümmerfrau*: a rubble woman, and this sculpture is made out of the very rubble that she and millions like her cleared from the streets of every German city and town. Without these women, the *Trümmerfrauen*, life in Germany would have been unbearable. Their strength, emotional and physical, put the country back on its feet.

Rebuilding Germany was a double task, psychological as well as physical. In Britain the "spirit of the Blitz" came from the population's conviction that they were the victims of a war that was not of their making. But while many Germans in 1945 certainly felt they were victims, there was little public discussion of the issue. Rather,

---

Opposite: The ruins of Dresden, with the damaged spire of the Kreuzkirche. Bellotto had painted the same church damaged by the Prussians two hundred years earlier. See Introduction, pages xxii–xxiii.

Sculpture of Dresden *Trümmerfrau* made from ceramic fragments, by Max Lachnit, *c*. 1945

there was a silence, based perhaps on the shame of what they had allowed to be done in their name. There was no public outpouring of anger over the devastation of Hamburg or Dresden in the way that there was in other European countries over the destruction of their cities. In his essay "Air War and Literature" ("Luftkrieg und Literatur"), W. G. Sebald observes that the traumatic destruction of so many ordinary houses hardly appears in post-war German literature. Pondering this silence, a kind of willed amnesia, he hypothesizes it may be because many Germans felt this terrible obliteration of their towns was just retribution for the crimes of their state.

Whatever the cause, for a long time there was little discussion. The *Trümmerfrauen* just got to work. Between 1945 and 1946 the

Allied powers, in both West and East Germany, ordered all women between fifteen and fifty years of age to participate in the post-war clean-up. They were organized into small groups and if they had any tools at all they were mostly small picks and winches. They demolished the buildings by hand, brick by painstaking brick, clearing them of mortar and then stacking the bricks and stones in a *Trümmerwagen*, a rubble cart. They salvaged everything that was reusable, from washbasins to electric cables; they rebuilt their homes, and rebuilt their cities by hand. Almost every able-bodied woman was recruited to the task.

In the shadow of Lachnit's image of a Dresden *Trümmerfrau*, in the German Historical Museum, I interviewed one of her sisters. Helga Cent-Velden was eighteen when the Russian army reached Berlin and put her to work:

> "First of all, we were divided into two groups and we were sent down Tiergartenstrasse. Everything was very badly damaged, there was rubble everywhere and weapons and ammunition which the soldiers had left behind. And the man in charge said this is where you'll start clearing up, right beside a huge bomb crater, and he said whatever isn't dangerous, throw it into the crater. Everything else—there were shells and bazookas lying about—he said, throw those into the water which was a run-off from the Tiergarten Lake.
>
> "Then I was called to do the real rubble clearance. I was taken to Potsdamer Strasse and I went to this building that was destroyed, collapsed. Though one part was still standing, the rest had gone and it was piled high with rubble. A woman came up to me and said, 'So, you've been assigned to me and we've got to clear this place up. This was where I used to work—it's a shop. We've got to clear all the rubble away so that it can be rebuilt.' But there was nothing there, no roof, nothing. Even so, it had to be rebuilt. And men came with tubs, to cart off the rubble, and it took us about nine months to clear all the rubble out of that building. Some of it was in huge lumps which also had to be carried away. I can't even remember if I even had a hammer or a

chisel to do the job but I do remember how glad we were when they gave us gloves to work with!"

She also remembers, with an emotion still audible in her voice, that this hard manual work entitled her to a higher food ration, particularly welcome to her family. There are few public monuments in Germany to the achievements of women like Helga Cent-Velden. Lachnit's *Trümmerfrau* must stand in memory of them all.

What is so astonishing is the speed at which the *Trümmerfrauen* were able to make Germany habitable again. Empty bombsites were still common in Britain in the 1960s; episodes of television series were filmed on them as late as the 1970s. In Germany a few half-destroyed buildings were deliberately left as memorials, like the Kaiser Wilhelm Memorial Church (the Gedächtniskirche) in West Berlin, reminders of the crimes of the Third Reich and the price paid by people even more than by buildings. By the late 1950s, however, much of Germany (especially West Germany) had been rebuilt. Germans perhaps realized constant work was helpful if they were not to confront uncomfortable truths.

And there were uncomfortable truths a-plenty, not least in the economy, which in 1945 was also in ruins for the second time in twenty-five years: inflation was rampant and barter frequent, and no one trusted the currency. The Reichsmark so painstakingly reconstructed in 1924 after the great hyperinflation had again collapsed. In theory the Reichsmark remained the currency of occupied Germany, but the Allies could not allow the old notes and coins, emblazoned as they were with swastikas, to continue in circulation. They hastily printed and minted new Allied Occupation Marks and coupons for buying necessities like bread and potatoes. In practice even this currency was unsustainable. The four occupying powers could all see that a new currency was needed but were completely unable to agree what form it should take. And so eventually the three Western powers, the U.S., the UK and France, decided to go ahead on their own. In 1948, on Sunday, 20 June, the newly created Bank Deutscher

---

Opposite: Young *Trümmerfrauen* clearing away the ruins of the publishing house Scherl, Berlin, 1945

Länder in Frankfurt, the Bank of the German States, the forerunner of the Bundesbank, introduced not a new Reichsmark, but the Deutsche mark—the D-Mark (see page 502).

Helmut Schlesinger is a German economist and a former president of the Bundesbank. In 1948, when the Deutsche mark was introduced, he was just beginning his Ph.D. in economics at the University of Munich and he remembers what life before the D-Mark was like:

> "We had a double economy. The official economy with fixed prices, where you could buy bread or potatoes with coupons and the prices were fixed at the level of 1936. The fees of the university could be paid in Reichsmark, even taxis could be paid in Reichsmark, so this was the one part of the economy. The other part was the barter economy. Well, as a student you had nothing to barter. There was also a black economy. Most people didn't have much to trade. Coffee, tea, American medicaments, etc., and the Germans had to pay with cigarettes, or whatever they could use."

This is something Helga Cent-Velden remembers well—how little there was and how important it was to have the right work permit and ration card:

> "It was really hard work and as far as I can remember, we were paid 48 pfennig an hour, but the most important thing was that because we were doing heavy work, we got what they called a heavy-labour food ration card so we got a lot more than many people did. For example, a housewife's card only entitled her to 1,200 calories a day. As *Trümmerfrauen*, we got nearly double that, 2,200 calories. And if you added that to the rations the rest of the family had, we could get by."

It was the third time in history that Germany had given itself a national currency called the Mark. The first had come after the unification of Germany in 1871. That version of the Mark had collapsed in the hyperinflation of 1921–23. The second, the Reichsmark of the Weimar Republic, continued through the catastrophes of 1945. Given

Map of occupied Germany with detail of divided Berlin, 1945

From top to bottom: The first Deutsche mark, 1948. Ten-Deutsche-mark note with front design inspired by Dürer, 1977. Hundred-Ostmark note with street scene in East Berlin (front) and Karl Marx (back), 1975. Five-Ostmark note depicting Thomas Müntzer (front) and a combine harvester (back), 1975. Fifty-Ostmark note depicting Friedrich Engels (front) and an oil refinery (back), 1971

this history you might think it was strange that in 1948 the decision was taken to use the name Mark again. But it was a familiar name, and whatever its historical failings the Mark had helped to define the nation since the unification of 1871. Perhaps, given modern Germany's rare capacity to use its history constructively, the very name also carried with it a warning, and served as a lesson from the past: a lesson that German economic and financial managers based in the Bundesbank took to heart over the following decades as they turned the new Deutsche mark into one of the most successful currencies in economic history.

The arrival of the D-Mark was contentious, but not just for the man in the street. Economic doubts were compounded by political ructions. The plan to replace the Reichsmark was carried out in secret, and the D-Mark launched without warning in the three Western occupation zones. The Russians were furious and would not allow it to be used in areas under their control. Its introduction in West Berlin was the spark for the Berlin Blockade. Within a month a rival currency, often known for convenience as the Ostmark, was introduced in the Soviet zone. This remarkable sequence of events was historically almost without precedent: two new currencies, the D-Mark and the Ostmark, led to two new states. The D-Mark unquestionably primed the pump for the economic miracle in the Western zones; but it also helped split Germany in two for the duration of the Cold War.

From the start the two currencies were clearly the products of two entirely different states and states of mind, two different views of history. The coins of both East and West show the German oak but the West German coins also showed the German eagle and later featured images of the post-war political leaders who shaped and rebuilt West Germany: Konrad Adenauer, Ludwig Erhard and Willy Brandt. These were safe heroes to a man. In the East the coins were lighter in weight and bore Soviet-style images of manual production, wheat sheaves, work tools and so on. But it is in the banknotes, illustrated on page 502, that we really see the difference. It is as if West Germany could not find a shape, an acceptable image for the past. It ducked recent history entirely and the illustrations on its notes went back to the Renaissance and the work of Albrecht Dürer: German people, portrayed by the great German artist. But in the East there was an ideological imperative to convey the struggle that had led to the triumph of the proletariat. These notes have contemporary images of education, housing and industry on one side and on the other Socialist heroes such as Thomas Müntzer, the leader of the sixteenth-century German Peasants' War, Clara Zetkin, an early Communist, and Marx and Engels. And so for nearly forty years two banknote visions of Germany faced each other across the Iron Curtain: Dürer, an icon of European culture, with an old-fashioned sailing ship, versus Engels with a modern oil refinery.

By the time the D-Mark powered the West German economy through the 1980s it had become the very symbol of West Germany and her economic success, and it was an object of desire for many East Germans as well—even more stable than the U.S. dollar and effectively unchallenged until 1989. When the Berlin Wall fell and the reunification of Germany was suddenly no longer an aspiration but an imminent reality, it was currency union that caused the economy to falter for the first time since 1948. After the fall of the Berlin Wall, all East Germans were given 100 Deutsche marks *Begrüßungsgeld*—welcome money—just for coming to visit the West. That alone cost nearly four billion Marks, although—as Helmut Schlesinger observes—it was trivial compared to the cost of merging the two currencies. The bankers and economists recommended a 2:1 exchange rate between the East and West Marks, a rate they thought very generous given the relative strength of the economies. Chancellor Helmut Kohl had other ideas: he took the essentially political, not economic, decision to convert the East German Mark at a level even further above its real value. Anything else would have devastated the finances of the East German population and might even have threatened reunification. In an act of great political courage he announced a 1:1 exchange rate for wages, interest and rent.

Above all, Kohl realized he had to move fast. Helmut Schlesinger was at this point deputy chairman of the Bundesbank (and was later to become its president, from 1991 until 1993). Dealing with the consequences of the currency conversion fell to him:

S-BAHN

Begrüßungsgeld

Sa, 2.12.89

8.00-12.00 h

Finanzamt

für Körperschaften

Schöneberger Str. 2-4

AUSGANG

DORT

Poster directing visitors to West Germany to pick up their "welcome money," December 1989

"For us at the Bundesbank, it was clear this exchange rate was too generous. But that was the decision and now we had to act to prevent an inflationary spiral in our country and so we had to put up interest rates, etc. This was a poor financial situation, which, together with establishing a banking system, could work under Western conditions, and all this was constructed in negotiations across a period of six weeks. After six weeks, we had to sign the draft of the treaty. We all knew that there was a very narrow window politically in which we could bring together the Americans and the Russians. We understood we had to do it quickly and risk making some mistakes."

There were recriminations and the immediate result was the first significant inflation in the post-war German economy. But the strength of that economy was proven: by the end of the 1990s it was again surging ahead. And it was at this point that the most remarkable event of all took place: on 1 January 2002 the Germans gave the D-Mark away—the D-Mark, *the* symbol of a democratic, peaceful, successful post-war Germany. It was replaced by the Euro with many regrets but hardly a murmur, given up in exchange for lasting political security. The new currency, it was assumed, would lock Germany for ever into an economic and political structure designed to ensure peace in a continent ravaged twice in a century by wars with Germany. The Euro was in essence the price which France demanded for its consent to German reunification. It appears that most Germans understood that abandoning the D-Mark for the Euro would allay its neighbours' concerns about the new enlarged state's predominance, and were willing to make this enormous commitment to the European Union.

What, I wondered, did Helga Cent-Velden, the Berlin *Trümmerfrau,* make of all this? She approves of the bargain Chancellor Kohl struck:

"When the Wall came down things didn't all go as we wanted them to but overall we got an extraordinarily stable Germany and I feel we have this and Europe to thank that we've had no more war in central Europe. And that's absolutely the most important thing of all—that I can now believe in Europe."

What is perhaps most striking about Germany after 1945 is that it has sought a new identity not through high politics on the world stage—internationally it is often described as a political pygmy—but through its economy and its place in a new Europe, which it has helped forge out of the ruins of the old Europe it did so much to destroy.

From the time of Charlemagne onwards, German identity was for almost a millennium defined in the wider context of Europe through the Holy Roman Empire and her place in it; as time passed, an increasingly dominant place. The Empire had acted as a security network both for Europe as a whole and for Germany within it (see Chapter 5). By the eighteenth century the kings of Sweden, Denmark, Poland, Prussia, Hungary and Britain were all represented in the Imperial Diet in Regensburg, and so in some measure guarantors of stability in Europe. It was an equilibrium that could not survive the aggression first of Napoleon and then of the militarized Prussian state.

So there was a historical appropriateness that it should be France and Germany which set out in 1952 to re-create that security network through what ultimately became the European Union. The wheel has come full circle in that the EU is, in a sense, a new edition of the Holy Roman Empire: economic and secular, not religious; pan-European, not Roman; binding most of the continent into a framework of security and joint consultation, with France and Germany jostling for seniority. It is an old pattern. Is this long historical precedent part of the reason why Germany has so few problems with the idea of a confederal supranational EU? And why the UK, with its very different history, has so many?

28

The New German Jews

By 1945, Germany had murdered over eleven million people in Europe: political prisoners, Roma, homosexuals, the disabled, but in numerical terms, overwhelmingly—around six million—Jews. Of all German memories, the Holocaust is now the most present and the most intractable. Centuries of Jewish presence and culture were annihilated. After concentration camps like Buchenwald (see Chapter 25) and the extermination camps like Auschwitz, it seemed that the story of Jews in Germany must come to a full stop at the end of the war. Why would any Jew in 1945, or in 1965 for that matter, see any part of their future in Germany? But here is a remarkable fact: Germany today has the fastest-growing Jewish population in Western Europe, now numbering several hundred thousand. Most are immigrants. Rabbi Mendel Gurewitz, who in the late 1990s moved from the United States to live near Frankfurt-am-Main, is one of them:

> "You know, before I came here, I said how can we live in such a country? I decided when I came here not to think about it too much because, if you meet older people here in the streets, you right away start to have thoughts. There was a Jewish history, a very Jewish history, here in Germany, and it's a shame just to decide, because of Hitler, they don't want the Jews here any

The arrival of the Torah scrolls at the new Munich synagogue, 2006

more, that you should completely close that country, close it for the Jews. If we do that, we are going to do what Hitler wanted to do. I think we should do the opposite of it. I come from a religious Hasidic movement which sends people all over the world and we look for the most challenging places to live. So that's why I came here with my wife. Now thank God I have lived here for sixteen years, my kids grew up here. We're really happy here."

For many centuries Germany had treated its Jewish population with more tolerance than most Western European countries. England, France and Spain, for example, had at various times expelled their entire Jewish populations. The German lands were not immune from this. Local crises would often see the Jewish community scapegoated and expelled, as in Nuremberg in the 1350s and Regensburg in 1513; but the extreme political fragmentation meant that there was always a Jewish population in some part of Germany, and those who were expelled from individual territories often returned later when the situation had changed. In the eighteenth and nineteenth centuries individual Jews rose to positions of trust and prominence in the German lands, as in Britain and France. Joachim Whaley says that this is often forgotten today:

"The history of the Jews in Germany before the modern period is really often written in the light of the tragic history of the Jews in the twentieth century, and that I think has had a distorting effect. Normally one finds three things being mentioned as characteristic of this early history. Firstly the expulsion of the Jews from many German towns in the late fifteenth century, secondly Luther's famous anti-Semitic pamphlet of 1543 on the Jews and their lives, and thirdly the account of the arrival of the young Moses Mendelssohn in Berlin in October 1743, where the Berlin guard entered in his log that today the Bosentaler Tor saw the arrival of six oxen, seven pigs and one Jew.

"These three things are often taken as emblematic, a prehistory which seems logical in view of what happened later in

Moses Mendelssohn, 1771

> Germany in the twentieth century. In fact, however, the real story is a very different one. Most princes utterly ignored Luther's views and we see from the middle of the sixteenth century onwards a steady growth of small Jewish communities throughout the Holy Roman Empire, a trend which was encouraged by many rulers. They welcomed Jews as craftspeople, as traders and as merchants, they welcomed them also as money lenders, a profession which didn't otherwise exist and on which there was a prohibition for Christians. The Jews were by and large protected by rulers because they were seen to be good for craft and trade activity."

Many do still regard Luther's anti-Semitism as a formative influence on his compatriots over the centuries. We can see, however, just how integrated at least some Jews were within the Holy Roman Empire from a beautiful pouch now in the British Museum. It is a bag for phylacteries, or tefillin, tiny scrolls inscribed with verses from the Torah, worn at morning prayers in the synagogue. It is a luxury

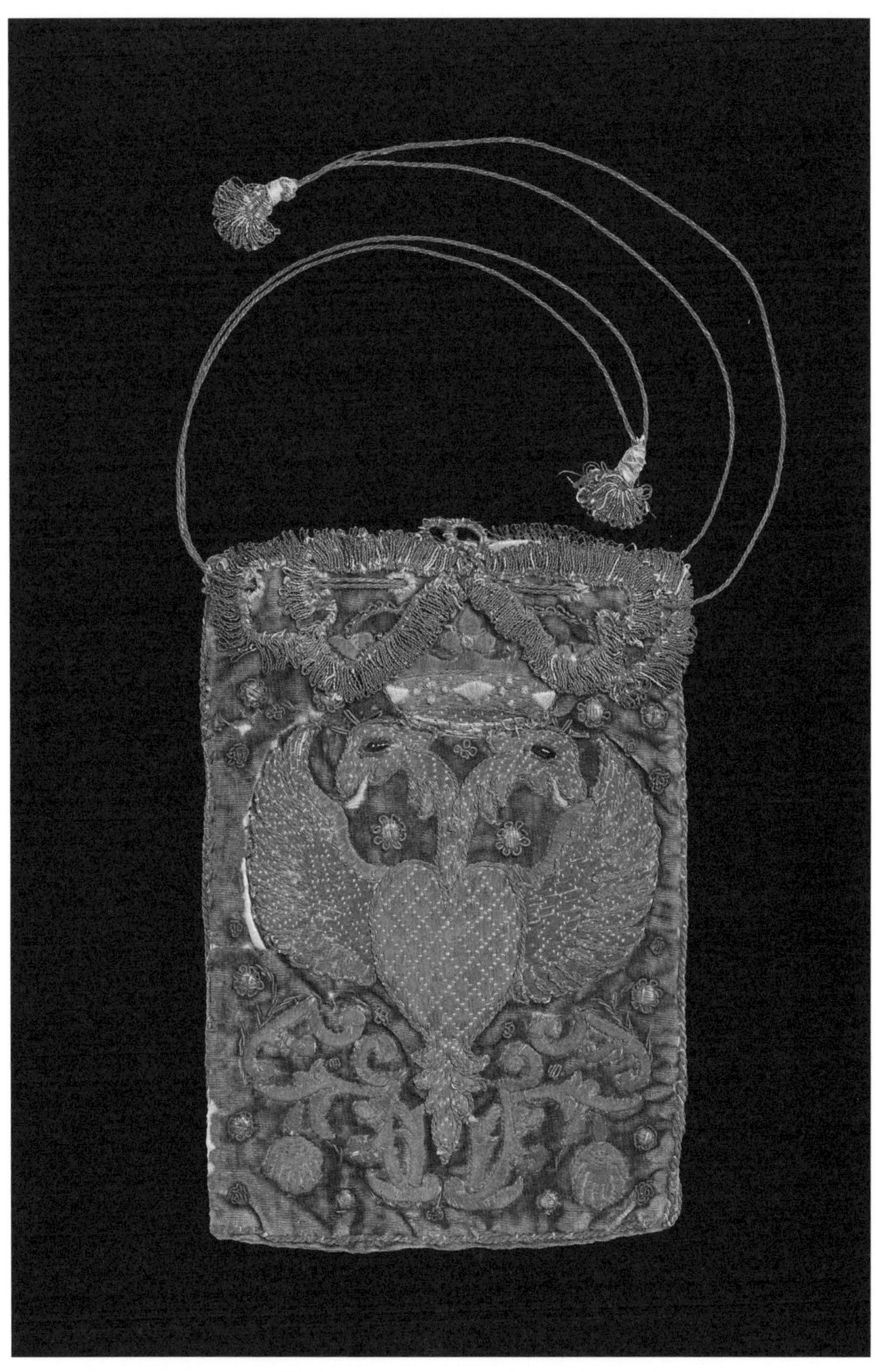

Eighteenth-century tefillin bag with the arms of the Holy Roman Empire

Jews trading with Christians, Nuremberg, 1731

object that speaks of wealth and refinement, and at the same time it is a declaration of loyalty to the Emperor. It is made of green velvet finely embroidered on one side with gold and silver thread and in the centre is the double-headed eagle of the Holy Roman Empire. We do not know to whom it belonged or which town it is from, but it was certainly made in the eighteenth century. The eagle shows that its owner declared himself a subject of the Emperor, the formal protector of all Jewish communities. The pouch makes a very public statement of political inclusion.

Discrimination against Jews certainly existed in Germany in the eighteenth century but it was becoming ever less oppressive. A number of princes actively encouraged Jewish settlement—in Mannheim and Berlin, for example, Frederick the Great permitted the first synagogue in Potsdam (a stone's throw from his Palace of Sans Souci) and remarked: "To oppress the Jews never brought prosperity on any government." Everywhere Jews in theory, and often in practice, had legal rights, which they did not enjoy in many other parts of Europe. They could petition both local and Imperial courts and swear oaths on the Torah rather than the Bible. Many Jews were as poor as their Christian neighbours but the so-called *Schutzjuden*—court Jews—who worked as financiers to the royal courts of the Empire had economic power which they had not wielded since the medieval expulsions and restrictions. Jews were also active in intellectual life: there was a Jewish Enlightenment which challenged many of the traditional attitudes of the Orthodox rabbis. A leading figure was the philosopher Moses Mendelssohn (grandfather of the composer Felix), who translated the Old Testament Pentateuch into German. He may have been counted into Berlin with six oxen and seven pigs, but he became known as the German Socrates, respected and admired far beyond the Jewish community.

There were still restrictions on Jewish life and a widespread assumption that Jews would in the end convert to Christianity, which was a continual source of resentment. In many cities and states, Jews were obliged to pay a special tax. Even Frederick the Great obliged Berlin Jews wanting to marry to buy porcelain from his new royal factory.

And then there was the Frankfurt Ghetto, the major ghetto in Germany, where the *Judengasse*—Jews' lane—was walled in. There was a curfew at night on Sundays and on Christian holidays. It had been built for a few hundred inhabitants, but by the middle of the eighteenth century it housed around 3,000. Goethe, who was born not far away, knew it well and wrote about it:

> The confinement, the dirt, the swarm of people made a disagreeable impression, even when observed only from outside the gate. And yet they were also human beings, energetic, agreeable. Their obstinacy in sticking to their own customs, one could not deny it respect. Moreover, their girls were pretty.

Notwithstanding, Germany's Jews were sometimes distinctly better treated than other minorities, a point underlined by Joachim Whaley:

The *Judengasse*, Frankfurt, in the nineteenth century

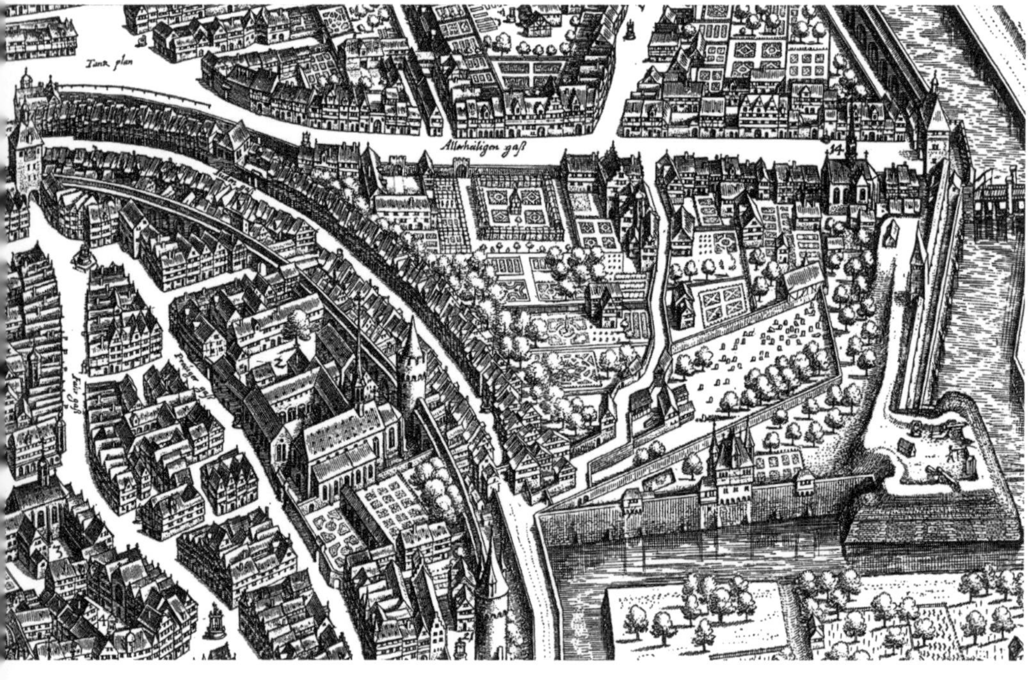

Detail from a 1628 map of Frankfurt, by Matthäus Merian, showing the curving *Judengasse*

Amschel Rothschild Jnr (Frankfurt)

"In Hamburg for example there were tensions but no riots. In fact there were riots against Catholics in Hamburg in the early eighteenth century but there was never an anti-Semitic riot in this whole period, even though Hamburg had one of the most important Jewish communities in the whole of the Empire. It's by and large a protected population. It's seen as a useful population. There's certainly no integration of the Jews. Yet on the other hand there is spatial integration in the sense that the Jews by and large (except in certain centres like Frankfurt) did not live in formally designated ghettoes. So the story of German anti-Semitism is one that doesn't start I think with the expulsions of the fifteenth century, the anti-Semitic diatribe of Luther in the 1540s, but it's rather a story which starts with German modernity in the nineteenth century. There is no long pre-history to the tragedies of the twentieth century. The Holocaust does not have roots that go back in German history into the late Middle Ages."

Carl Rothschild (Naples) (top left); James Rothschild (Paris) (top right); Nathan Rothschild (London) (bottom left); Salomon Rothschild (Vienna) (bottom right)

The ability of Jews to prosper in the Holy Roman Empire is illustrated by the story of the best-known and most successful of all Jewish families, the Rothschilds. They were Frankfurt Jews who lived in the *Judengasse*, where Mayer Amschel Rothschild established his bank in the 1760s, around the time when Goethe described the ghetto. He was a court Jew who financed the nearby Landgrave of Hessen-Kassel. His banking empire was built through his five sons, four of whom he sent out to set up banks across Western Europe, in London, Paris, Naples and Vienna, so that they were not reliant on Germany alone for all their business. They developed a huge and successful network of partners and agents across Europe, financing governments during the Napoleonic Wars, and managing to transfer gold across the continent without it falling into the wrong hands. The German armies fighting Napoleon in 1813 and 1814 were largely paid for by subsidies from London, managed by the Rothschilds. Four of the brothers were elevated to the rank of baron by the Emperor of Austria after the Congress of Vienna, one key reason being the role they had played in financing the wars. In 1848 (see Chapter 15) their mother, Gutle Rothschild, Amschel's widow, reportedly said: "There will be no war in Europe. My sons will not finance it." The Rothschilds were compulsive, diligent and spectacular art collectors. Among the great paintings they bought was the famous Tischbein portrait of Goethe (Chapter 8), which Baroness Salomon de Rothschild donated to the Städel Museum in Frankfurt in its centenary year of 1887.

One of the most obvious signs that Jews had "arrived" in German society was building their place of worship, the synagogue; a very public manifestation of their presence in a town or city. In 1916, in the middle of the First World War, the Jews of Offenbach, a suburb of Frankfurt, opened a splendid new synagogue, a large domed building that could accommodate many hundreds of people. Its site was at a powerfully symbolic address in the town centre: on the corner of Goethestrasse and Kaiserstrasse. In the political and cultural life of Germany, Jews were now confidently, publicly, prominent. According to the Jewish architect Alfred Jacoby, who was born in Offenbach after the Second World War, this marked the high point

The Offenbach synagogue at the junction of Goethestrasse and Kaiserstrasse in 1930

of Jewish assimilation. In spite of the war, the future for the Jews looked settled:

> "On the opening in 1916 the Rabbi said, 'And we are now part of society here. We have arrived in paradise.' He said that in 1916. It shows how strong the pressure on a Jew to be accepted and to be part of the society was at the time. It was more important than thinking, we're in the middle of a war. What are we doing here? You know, it was very strange."

The situation, however, was not quite as serene as the Rabbi suggested. In that same year, 1916, the notorious *Judenzählung* (counting of the Jews) was introduced in response to populist suggestions

Jewish friends on holiday in Bavaria, 1920, in traditional Bavarian costume

(entirely unfounded) that Jews were avoiding military service. And in the political and economic crisis after 1918, Jews and especially leading Jewish politicians (Chapter 23) were scapegoated, and in the case of Walter Rathenau assassinated.

The Offenbach synagogue was desecrated and burnt in *Kristallnacht* in 1938, and its congregation was later deported and murdered. But the story of the Jews and their synagogue in Offenbach was not at an end. The section of the German Historical Museum in Berlin devoted to the years immediately after 1945 contains objects of every imaginable kind—newspapers and magazines, clothes and machinery, and models of housing schemes, schools and hospitals. Among the architectural models one in particular stands out. It is much the least finished, much the least elaborate. It is made entirely out of cardboard and sits on a sheet not much larger than an A4 piece of paper. Around the edge of the rectangle, the cardboard has been turned up to represent the retaining wall defining the site. Most of the ground

Model of the first post–Second World War synagogue built in Offenbach, 1955

has been loosely painted with green and brown paint to suggest a garden with walkways through flowerbeds and shrubbery. Right at the back of the site are two interconnected buildings, not much bigger than matchboxes in the model. Only on close inspection is it possible to see that on the wall at the front of the site and above the door on the front building is the Star of David. This is the architect's model for one of the first synagogues to be built for a Jewish community in Germany after Auschwitz. It was designed by Hermann Zvi Guttmann for the Jewish community in Offenbach around 1950. But who, at that date, were the members of such a community? Rabbi Mendel Gurewitz:

> "It was a bunch of people who survived the Holocaust, not many Germans, they were mostly from Poland. They came here to Offenbach. If you asked any one of them, did you think you would stay here? No. They were here on the basis that 'We're just staying while we're looking for a place to move'—to America, or to Israel. No one wanted to stay here. But it was the idea of some of the people who lived here in Offenbach: we need to build a synagogue, at least for now. So they built a beautiful little synagogue, which was very small, but for them it was big because they never thought anyone else would ever come here."

As Rabbi Gurewitz reminds us, there were many thousands of Jews in transit after the war and many did leave Europe for America, Canada, Australia and, of course, Israel. But not all wanted to leave—Europe was, after all, their home—and not all could leave. Alfred Jacoby's father was a case in point:

> "My father studied to be an engineer after the war. His brother left in 1948, to New York. And my father always wanted to go there, but he was sick. In '48 he had a kind of sealed tuberculosis that wouldn't allow him to travel. The Americans took one x-ray and said, 'Well, we're very sorry, but we'll have to deny you a visa.'"

And so Alfred Jacoby's father stayed on in Offenbach and became a leading member of its small Jewish community, which slowly came to the realization that perhaps staying on was after all an option. It was a big decision to take, but, having taken it, there were other big decisions—such as what to do about the old synagogue that had opened with such fanfare in 1916 and had been expropriated during the Nazi period.

In the end the decision was clear. Although Offenbach council had offered it back to the Jewish community, the old synagogue was not for them: it was too big now; their community was so small and not expected to grow. The building was also sullied by the Nazi years; it would be too hard to use again, and it was too exposed in its position right on the corner of two of Offenbach's best-known streets. A new, less conspicuous building was needed. A site was made available by the local authorities, across the street from the old synagogue, and a new building, based on our model, was inaugurated in 1956. Alfred Jacoby again:

> "It was very rudimentary. It had eighty seats. It had a multipurpose room for having a meal or gathering, and it had a flat for the only member of the earlier community who had come back after the war, who was the caretaker. And that was it. It was as far from the street as possible; it looks as if the architect squashed the building as far as he could to the back of the site. You see this need to camouflage in many German cities. Around that time the Zionist Movement sent a man to Munich and he advised Ben-Gurion to issue a ban on living in Germany. That had only been done once before in Jewish history, in Spain in 1492 when the Jewish rabbis declared that Spain was banned as a place for Jewish people to live. I think architecture is always a medium of expressing such things, such questions about how to behave and what the best way is to live in. And here the impulse was, 'I'd better hide myself, cover my intentions.' If you look at the legal documents drawn up within the community in this period, very many had a passage which said their ultimate aim was to

> facilitate emigration. In other words, the message was: will the last one to leave turn off the light and give back the key."

But the Offenbach Jewish community endured and remained. What is more, there were hundreds of thousands of Jews still locked up in Europe behind the Iron Curtain, especially in the Soviet Union. For them the idea of emigrating to Israel, even if it had been possible, was not always attractive. So during the 1960s and 1970s there was a trickle of emigrants for whom Germany seemed less alien than the Middle East—and to whom Germany wanted to offer atonement. And then, in 1990, when the Soviet Union collapsed, the floodgates opened, as Rabbi Mendel Gurewitz remembers:

> "I was born in New York. We didn't buy any German products. Coming to Germany was taboo. So the Soviet Jews, why did they come here? When the iron gates broke, a lot of them went to Israel. But they felt that Israel wasn't the right climate, especially the older people, they could not live in such a heat. So they were looking for another place that would welcome them and probably the only other country that welcomed them besides Israel was Germany. The Germans, because of what they did in the war, wanted to repopulate the Jews, so they were ready to give them a pension and certain rights. So then all of a sudden the small Jewish community of Offenbach became big because a lot of Russian Jews moved here."

Two hundred thousand Jews moved to Germany after Helmut Kohl, in 1990, agreed to grant them immediate asylum and offered them financial assistance and every facility to integrate into the country. Those Russian Jews chose Germany in the full knowledge of what had happened fifty years earlier, to the bemusement of many Jews elsewhere in the world. What this has meant for the Jews in Offenbach is that their assumption in the 1950s that they would remain a small and semi-hidden community has been entirely overturned. It has grown hugely since 1990 and the synagogue has had to grow with

The synagogue in Offenbach as extended in 1998

it. It has needed not just new space for worship but for social gatherings and, above all, for children. The man who designed the new, enlarged building is the architect Alfred Jacoby:

> "You have a new multi-purpose hall, you have a kindergarten and so on. In fact our kindergarten is interesting because it is a completely interreligious kindergarten with a Jewish base. We have one third Muslim children, one third Christian children and one third Jewish children, yet children will all sit and sing Jewish festival songs and so on. It actually works.
>
> "But mainly the building now faces the city. This was very important—that I should take that away, the fence we were hiding behind, and make the synagogue a civic building within the context of the whole city again."

Synagogues like the one in Offenbach have been the physical representation of the relationship between Jews and Germans throughout history. There are today disturbing anti-Semitic incidents in Germany as in other European countries, but the Jews of Offenbach are now "back on the street" in full view of their host nation. Seventy years after the application of the "Final Solution to the Jewish Problem," hundreds of thousands of Jews have chosen to leave their liberated Eastern European homes and settle in the country that once tried to exterminate them.

29

Barlach's Angel

In Britain, we know what Remembrance Day is all about. We have been commemorating what our soldiers died for—freedom, democracy, independence—every year since 1919. Every town and village has had its ceremony, the sounding of the Last Post, the two minutes' silence. Gathered round cenotaphs throughout Britain and the Commonwealth, we have a well-established ritual to remember our losses and the high price of victory.

In Germany, there is no annual remembrance of the First World War, or the even more terrible conflict of the Second World War. What ceremony could be devised to commemorate a war that Germany lost, and of which Germany had, in the peace negotiations, been declared guilty? And yet, notwithstanding, in 1918 Germany had 1.8 million war dead, almost double the number for the whole British Empire. It is not that Germany has no monuments to its older wars. As in every other European country, there are statues galore of triumphant kings and generals: for instance, the 250-foot-high *Siegessäule* (Victory Column) in Berlin's Tiergarten, celebrating Prussia's nineteenth-century victories over Denmark, Austria and France (see Chapter 1); unembarrassed pride expressed in bronze and stone. But 1918 was different. Germany was defeated and then internationally assailed by accusations of starting the war and by demands for

Opposite: Barlach's *Hovering Angel* as it hangs in Güstrow Cathedral today

Güstrow Cathedral

reparations. It was destabilized at home by riots, attempted coups and the corroding claim of a "stab in the back"—the assertion that the German army was never defeated, but was betrayed by the politicians. In such circumstances, how *could* one commemorate the First World War and its huge human cost?

In the Protestant cathedral in Güstrow, a small town just over 100 miles to the north of Berlin, is one answer. No soaring column or gleaming mausoleum in the nation's capital. Instead, there is here a life-size, hovering figure in bronze, suspended horizontally from the cathedral ceiling, often referred to as an angel. The figure hangs above the old baptismal font, the traditional Christian symbol of forgiveness of sins and newness of life. Underneath is a circular wrought-iron fence like a garland of laurels; the angel is set apart, and above. The angel's lips are closed, soundless. Here, war is internalized, its horror and dread made all the greater by being mute. The angel's eyes are closed, perhaps unable to contemplate the pain and suffering. The figure is the work of the sculptor Ernst Barlach. The angel has been described as a "memorial but not an admonition." Barlach himself said it was about the attitude we should take to war: *Erinnerung und innere Schau*, recollection and inner reflection.

Ernst Barlach is so closely associated with Güstrow that it now calls itself Barlachstadt Güstrow, Barlach Town. He was, however, born in the far north of Germany, in Holstein, in 1870, settling in Güstrow in 1910. Like many artists and poets of the time, Barlach was at first an enthusiastic supporter of the First World War. Like them, he believed that a new society would be forged in the fire of war, and although well over forty years old, he joined up in 1915. The war was indeed a turning point for Barlach, but for quite a different reason. He was appalled by his experiences at the front and became a staunch pacifist. Like the English poet Wilfred Owen, Barlach was overwhelmed by "the pity of war," and, like him, he tried in his art to find an authentic response to its horrors and its futility. In 1916 he was invalided out and thereafter, for the rest of his life, pacifism was a determinant force in his sculpture. His war memorials are perhaps the nearest German equivalent to the British war poets' laments.

Barlach's first commission for a war memorial was in 1921. It was for the Nicolai Church in Kiel, in his native Schleswig-Holstein. He called it *Mother of Sorrows* (*Schmerzensmutter*): a lone woman in a cloak, with her hands clasped in front of her face, and an inscription in the local north German dialect: "My heart bleeds with grief but you give me strength." She is the Virgin Mary, she is a woman of Kiel, she is every mother, enduring without understanding the loss of her son. The statue was controversial, deemed pacifist, unpatriotic, focused on the grief of those who remain, rather than the heroism of those who died. It survived the Nazi era, to be destroyed by an Allied bomb in 1944, but is the subject of a moving tribute by the English poet Geoffrey Hill—"In memoriam, Ernst Barlach"—who warmed to Barlach's focus on a mother's sorrow, simply said in dialect.

Barlach's *Mother of Sorrows* in the Nikolaikirche, Kiel (destroyed 1944)

A short distance from Güstrow's cathedral is the Ernst Barlach Museum. The rooms and garden of what was his studio are filled with his drawings and sculptures—those, that is, which survived the Third Reich. A gallery contains the models for Barlach's war memorials, from towns and churches across Germany; a chorus to the cost of war, for both its participants and its survivors. I know of no comparable room in Britain or France. Barlach's war memorials—all of them—refuse national sentiment or any hint of death in war as noble or admirable. Rather, they are a sharing of grief and a summons to contrition. Volker Probst is the Director of the Barlach Foundation, and a scholar of his work:

Ernst Barlach in his studio next to his sculpture *Mother and Child,* 1937

> "Barlach developed a new type of war memorial. There is no heroism, no glorification of death or war. Instead, in his war memorials for Magdeburg, Güstrow, Hamburg and Kiel, you find an exploration of pain, death, mourning and grief. Barlach's angel is a timeless symbol of peace and non-violence."

By the mid-1920s Barlach was a national figure and his anti-war views were well-known. The fact that he lived in Güstrow led the town to commission him in 1926 to create a war memorial there as part of the cathedral's 700th-anniversary celebrations: the result was the *Hovering Angel*, an evocation of a mother looking west, to the killing fields of Flanders, grieving serenely, perpetually, for her dead son.

One of the most striking features of the *Hovering Angel* in Güstrow Cathedral is its face. Students of German art can immediately recognize the features of another anti-war artist, Käthe Kollwitz, a

Self-Portrait, by Käthe Kollwitz, 1923

Head of Barlach's *Hovering Angel*

close friend of Barlach's and an apposite model: she had lost her son Peter on the Western Front in October 1914 (see Chapter 22). Barlach's pacifism echoed her own, and they developed a close spiritual bond. She echoed his simplicity of style in her own works. (Barlach encouraged her to use woodcut, as she did to great effect in her tribute to the memory of the Communist leader Karl Liebknecht, illustrated on page 409.) Barlach admitted later that she must have been in his mind when he made the cast for the angel—the rounded face with the deep-set eyes, the full lips of the slightly down-turned mouth. The angel is Kollwitz and at the same time, like the earlier *Mother of Sorrows*, it embodies, in its expression of contemplative sorrow, something of all mothers' grief. That, however, was not what Barlach's critics saw. They railed against the angel's Slavic features, the "degenerate" style and the message, which they read as pacifist and defeatist: there is not the slightest suggestion in this monument that the dead lost their lives for a just or worthwhile cause.

The sculpture immediately attracted the scorn of local patriots and right-wingers. The Nazis loathed it, and once they came to power

---

Opposite: The original cast of Barlach's *Hovering Angel* in Güstrow Cathedral, *c.* 1930s

they made it clear that the Angel would have to go. What they wanted was something like Georg Kolbe's Stralsund war memorial—beautiful and strong male figures, holding a sword, proudly facing the foe above the inscription: "You did not fall in vain."

Barlach received death threats from local Nazis. Exhibitions were cancelled. After 1933 his sculptures and art were removed from public places. In 1937, the Nazis held an exhibition of "degenerate art" in Munich (see Chapter 24) to promote public revulsion against what Goebbels called "the perverse Jewish spirit." Although Barlach was neither Jewish nor politically active, his style, message and works were unacceptable. Two of his works were included in the Munich exhibition. In the same year, on 23 August 1937, on the orders of the Nazi authorities, the Angel was removed from Güstrow Cathedral.

When the statue was taken down, it left a space for reflections that go beyond words. Every year, on that day, a silent ceremony is held in the cathedral, as Pastor Christian Höser explains:

> "We meet to remember the removal of the Angel and to consider how deeply our people erred and strayed. The depth of that error cannot be grasped through words, but a sculpture like this helps us to focus on it, and to learn from it; with God's help and by our own actions, we seek to find ways of transforming this dark inheritance into a means of reconciliation. That is the challenge of the statue today."

The sculpture was taken away to Schwerin, and in the early 1940s Barlach's peaceful bronze Angel was melted down by the Nazis to be used as metal for the war effort. Barlach himself died a year after its removal from the cathedral.

So, if the statue of the angel ended up as war matériel, what is it that now hangs above the font in Güstrow? It is a fascinating story. After Barlach's death in October 1938, two years after the removal of the statue, some of his friends and supporters, helped by a dealer who

---

Opposite: Georg Kolbe's *Warrior Memorial*, Stralsund, 1934–35

1914–1918
IHR SEID
»NICHT«
UMSONST
GEFALLEN

had suspiciously good relations with the Nazi authorities, located the plaster mould the artist had originally used to cast the statue, which was still held in the foundry in Berlin. Aware that the bronze Angel from Güstrow was likely to be destroyed, they then cast a second bronze from the plaster. Sometime during the war the plaster mould was itself destroyed by bombing, but the second bronze, identical to the original, survived, hidden in a village near Lüneburg in north Germany. After the war, Barlach's estate finally agreed that it should go on display. But there were commercial conflicts to resolve and by this time Lüneburg was in the West, and Güstrow was in East Germany. So in 1951, after much to-ing and fro-ing, the Angel was given to the Antonite Church in Cologne. It still hangs there, very much as Barlach had intended, but with one addition. On the slab in the floor below it, they added to the dates 1914–1918, the years 1939–1945. The Angel's symbolic power and its history, the Cologners believed, would enable it to carry the added burden of all the losses and deaths of the entire Nazi period.

The question persists: if the second version of the Angel is now in Cologne, what is it that today floats with such mystery and potency above the font in Güstrow Cathedral? Christian Höser explains:

> "In the 1950s there were exploratory conversations about whether the second cast, which went to Cologne, might not come to Güstrow, to hang in the place for which Barlach had conceived it. But in the 1950s the Cold War was going through a very hot phase. In addition, the GDR was not at all clear what the proper official Communist attitude to Barlach's art and ideas should be: the debate inside the GDR was very challenging."

In spite of doctrinal disagreements within the Communist leadership about the legitimacy and meaning of Barlach's message, in spite of the barriers which the Cold War had erected between the two Germanys, a copy of the Cologne cast was made and in 1953 the third

---

Opposite: The second cast of Barlach's *Hovering Angel* in the Antonite Church, Cologne

1914 - 1918
1939 - 1945

incarnation of Barlach's bronze Angel was installed in the cathedral in Güstrow. It was an extraordinary achievement of dialogue, a striking acknowledgement of the sculpture's symbolic significance to people all over a deeply divided Germany.

On 13 December 1981, on a bitterly cold day nearly thirty years after the Angel returned to Güstrow, the West German Chancellor, Helmut Schmidt, was on an official visit to East Germany. It was a significant step in normalizing relations between the two German states. At Helmut Schmidt's request he and the GDR leader, Erich Honecker, visited Güstrow Cathedral, to stand together beneath the Angel. There they were addressed by the Bishop of Mecklenburg. Ernst Barlach, he said, represented for both leaders and both states a shared memory, a shared past. Helmut Schmidt thanked the bishop and responded with these words:

> "I want to thank you for your welcome and for what you have said. And when you say that Barlach is our shared memory and our shared past, I would like to express that somewhat differently and say, he can also be our shared future."

What Erich Honecker thought of that sentiment is unrecorded, but neither he nor Schmidt could have imagined that within a decade the two Germanys would be reunited and Barlach's statue would indeed represent a shared past and a shared future—in a shared country.

In the sixty years since it returned, Barlach's Angel has become the symbol of Güstrow, outlined on motorway signposts, a hook for drawing in tourists in large numbers. It has not left the city for over thirty years. So its temporary absence on loan to an exhibition at the British Museum in 2014 was an event of great local significance. Volker Probst leads the Barlach Foundation, the legal owner of the Güstrow Angel:

> "This angel has been lent two times. In 1970, for the hundredth anniversary of Barlach's birth, it was in Moscow and Leningrad; and in 1981 it was at the large exhibition of Barlach's work in Berlin. But the coincidence of two anniversaries—one hundred years

Helmut Schmidt and Erich Honecker meeting under the *Hovering Angel* in Güstrow, December 1981

> since the beginning of the First World War and twenty-five years since the reunification of Germany: these made it a good moment to take Barlach's Angel to London."

The final decision on whether the sculpture should travel to London for exhibition in 2014 was rightly taken by the congregation of Güstrow Cathedral. Pastor Höser:

> "When Helmut Schmidt and Erich Honecker met here in 1981, a new moment in German history was triggered by the Angel. And now, after reunification, the two parts of Germany can still meet here and, with the help of the Angel, can converse. The theme of reconciliation is always present in our country. But we need it as a theme for Europe too: that is why it is important for us to give the Angel to London."

There can be few objects which embody so much of German twentieth-century history as this sculpture from Güstrow: war fever in 1914, pacifism in the 1920s; the Expressionist art world of Käthe Kollwitz; the destruction of "degenerate art" by the Nazis; the dubious compromises that dealers were nonetheless able to strike with the Third Reich; the Western Front in the First World War, and the bombing of Berlin in the Second; the post-war division of Germany and the dialogues that were possible in spite of it; the continuing painful and difficult conversations between Germany and the world in the quest for resolution and reconciliation. All of these have shaped the Angel and given it ever deeper and wider meaning. Like Germany itself, it has been dishonoured, destroyed, dismembered and refashioned. But it has always carried in itself the survival of an ideal, and the hope of renewal.

In the British Museum it will for a few months be part of another set of discussions about the links between Germany's past and its future. But the last word, or in this case the last silence, must be for Pastor Höser:

> "While the sculpture is away, we decided not to put up any replacement, but to leave a void. That void, and our response to it, will be part of the London exhibition. I hope we can use it to address the questions it raises: are we ready to assume responsibility, are we willing to put ourselves on the line in the cause of reconciliation?"

30

Germany Renewed

We began this journey through Germany's past at the Brandenburg Gate, now the nation's favourite setting for popular celebrations. I want to end it in the Reichstag, seat of the German Parliament and site of Germany's national deliberations. Both buildings have been shaped and reshaped many times, and witnessed great historical events. Both are invested with lasting symbolic significance. These two extraordinary buildings carry in their very stones the political history of the country.

The two are only a couple of hundred yards apart, today a popular tourist stroll—though for most of the last seventy years a difficult or impossible walk, for they were separated after 1945 by the boundary between the Soviet and the British zones of the occupied city, the fault-line of the Cold War that in 1961 became the Berlin Wall (see Chapter 2). Today the Wall has gone, leaving so little trace in this part of the city that tourists puzzle over where it must have been. Surprisingly that memory, though still live and bitter, has virtually no physical presence at the spot which was for decades its iconic centre.

Other memories, however, are all around. Clearly visible, just one block to the south, is the Holocaust Memorial to the Murdered Jews of Europe (pages xlii–xliii), designed by the architect Peter Eisenman and completed in 2005, which, without tower or spire, nonetheless commands completely its urban surroundings. On the other side of

DEM

The Reichstag as restored by Norman Foster after 1992

the road, among the trees of the Tiergarten Park, close to both Gate and Parliament, are three much more modest and more recent monuments to those other groups whom, like the Jews, the Nazis killed simply for what they were: the physically and mentally disabled; homosexuals; and the Sinti (or Roma).

These memorials are here, in this place, by design: the decision to erect them was taken by Parliament after much deliberation. Thus, as parliamentarians make their way to the Reichstag, they are daily reminded of that terrible chapter of Germany's past. That memory will, it is hoped, inform their every debate. And the memorials are not just for the politicians—the intention was to shape the thinking of every citizen too, and to address the visiting world that comes in growing numbers to admire the new heart of this buzzing city. It is, as I said at the beginning of this book, hard to think of any international parallel to such an exercise in painful self-recollection. Has it worked? Christopher Clark believes that it has:

> "The Third Reich, not just as a regime but with the assistance of hundreds of thousands of German citizens, commits crimes of such immensity and such barbarity that there is no gainsaying. There is no going back from the acknowledgement that these events impose a moral burden on the German nation. But what's remarkable after 1945 is the extent to which this is accepted, the guilt is internalized and becomes part of the German national identity. The awareness of a moral burden, of guilt for the horrific crimes of the Third Reich, drives deep roots into German national feeling and I think that's a unique feature of the German polity today, this self-critical awareness of having been morally contaminated by the misdeeds of a regime."

The approach to the Reichstag itself is less solemn. Partly as a result of being so near the Wall, the area around was little developed, and the Reichstag stands now in an informal meadow on which football alternates with sunbathing and holiday snaps. It is an unexpected setting for the grandiloquent palace erected in the 1880s to house the Parliament of the new, united German Empire proclaimed at

Versailles in 1871. It is a typical building of late-nineteenth-century Europe, Roman Imperial in its (originally more decorated) architectural vocabulary, almost British Imperial in its monumental confidence, while its original square central dome gave it a peculiarly German swagger. Clearly this is the Parliament of a state that takes itself very seriously.

In the years following 1871, however, it became equally clear that this new state was reluctant to take its Parliament at all seriously. Bismarck disliked the slow, obstructive process of legislation with its necessary compromises, and he systematically blocked its exercise of real power. The young Kaiser Wilhelm II was as impatient with its claims of democratic legitimacy as he was with so much else. There was constant squabbling, the final tussle between Kaiser and Reichstag being played out over the words proposed to appear on the façade: "Dem Deutschen Volke"—"For the German People." The Kaiser was strongly opposed to such a formulation, with its implication that ultimate authority did not reside with him, and proposed instead "Der Deutschen Einigkeit"—"For German Unity." In 1916, in the middle of the First World War, the parliamentarians finally carried the day. The modernist architect and typographer Peter Behrens designed the lettering, and the bronze, melted from French cannon captured in the war against Napoleon, added a historical—and bellicose—twist to the resolutely democratic and modernist inscription.

Two years later, after the Kaiser had abdicated and when the war was nearly at an end, from a balcony below Behrens's bronze letters, the Social Democrat politician Philipp Scheidemann proclaimed the new German Republic on 9 November 1918. For the next fifteen years this building would house the Parliament of the Weimar Republic, and over it flew not the black, red and white flag of Hohenzollern Prussia, but the black, red and gold of the Liberal Parliament of 1848 in Frankfurt (see Chapter 15). The Reichstag had become a real, democratic Parliament "for the German people," unconstrained by monarchical power—though now under constant attack from both Left and Right.

For the past 140 years the Reichstag has been the central building

The Reichstag on fire, 27 February 1933

of German history, its use, misuse and disuse reflecting the state of Germany in every sense. Its construction was funded by the huge indemnity exacted from France after the victory of 1871. The famous Reichstag fire of 27 February 1933, a few weeks after Hitler had come to power, was blamed by the Nazis on an unemployed Dutch Communist. It not only severely damaged the building: it marked the end of democratic Germany, giving the Nazis the pretext to persuade President Hindenburg to approve what were known as the "Reichstag Fire Decrees," laws they used to abrogate key rights guaranteed by the Weimar Constitution, and so imprison, and in many cases eliminate, opponents from all sides. The building was not fully restored—the Nazis had always disliked its liberal associations—and under Hitler his puppet Parliament met at the nearby Kroll Opera House.

The damage done by the 1933 fire was rapidly overtaken by British and American bombs after 1940. As the war drew to a close Stalin

The Soviet flag over the ruins of the Reichstag, 1945

chose the Reichstag, despite the Nazis' dislike of it, as the prime symbol of fascist Berlin. To capture it before May Day 1945 became something of a Soviet obsession, and huge numbers of men were sacrificed in the bloody and protracted hand-to-hand struggle, which finished with Red Army soldiers planting the Soviet flag on its bombed-out roof—a photograph which passed around the world and is still firmly lodged in the global memory as marking the final triumph of the Russians in the Second World War. Like Berlin itself, like the whole of Germany, the building had taken a terrible pounding: it is a tribute to the strength of its structures that it survived at all. The violent Russian chapter of the building's history can still be read today; indeed it can hardly be avoided. The restored building preserves in its public areas the graffiti scrawled in Cyrillic script by triumphant Russian soldiers. Among the predictable abuse and obscenity, "Hitler Kaputt" is perhaps the most suitable to print. Visitors may explore the others at their leisure.

Russian graffiti from 1945 preserved in the restored building

After 1945 the building languished—made usable, but hardly used, on the very edge of the western half of the city. The Federal Parliament now sat not in Berlin, but in Bonn. Much of the nineteenth-century sculptural decoration, deemed neither expressive nor exuberant, was removed in a restoration in the 1960s, and it was a simpler, utilitarian, indeed essentially provisional Reichstag that was the site in 1990 of the Treaty of Reunification between the two Germanys. It was resolved that the Reichstag building should, as after 1871, be the seat of the Parliament—now the Bundestag—of the newly reunited Germany. An international competition for the fundamental renewal of the building was launched, and in 1992 the British architect Norman Foster was commissioned. The willingness to choose a non-German was in itself a strong statement of the resolute internationalism of the reunited state. But for the Reichstag building to be a worthy home for the new pan-German Bundestag, it needed not just to be changed physically: the very *idea* of the building, disparaged by the Kaiser and despised by the Nazis, soiled by the intrigues around the fire and diminished by post-war neglect, had to be made new. The building and its scars of honour and shame had to be reinvented, as a tribune fit for the representatives of a free people. It had to be reborn, and it was.

The *Wrapping of the Reichstag*—the work of the artist Christo and his wife, Jeanne-Claude—is perhaps the most unexpected episode in the biography of this building. During two weeks, from 24 June to 7 July 1995, 90,000 square metres of silver fabric enveloped the entire building. Millions came to watch as the old Reichstag, with all its disputed or contaminated past, disappeared from view. When it emerged from its huge silver chrysalis, it was a building transformed, able now to become what Germany needed it to be.

Monika Grütters, now Federal Minister of Culture, was an MP at the time, closely connected to the project:

> "It was only after Christo had wrapped the Reichstag—the building, the ruin—and opened our eyes to the true topography of this building, that we understood that it is in fact our house, the house of an entire population, a democratic building in which

The Reichstag wrapped by Christo and Jeanne-Claude, June 1995

> Parliament, the representatives of the people, sit. And something of the spirit of this happening survives today.
>
> "The building at last became popular, touching passers-by. Suddenly it was more than just a building fulfilling a function, which it had only done half-heartedly because of its difficult history. It recovered its central position and, however absurd it may seem, it was Christo that did that through his wrapping—which was exactly his aim. In a few weeks, the wrapping of the Reichstag put years of history in a proper perspective."

It is hard to think of an equivalent re-appropriation of a building by its public anywhere. It was a process that continued during its subsequent, carefully managed, metamorphosis under Norman Foster:

> "I felt very strongly that the fabric as it emerged should preserve the scars of war, of civic vandalism if you like, of history, and

> that there should be a very clear demarcation between what was a record of the past in terms of a visible museum, the traces of history—that those graffiti, obscene or otherwise, should be an integral part of the fabric, and would convey messages of its past and its rebirth with clarity."

Monika Grütters believes that for those working in the building, Foster's approach has been entirely successful:

> "I am particularly conscious of the Russian Cyrillic graffiti, found inside the building, which come from the days in late April, early May 1945. They were written by soldiers of the Red Army, and in a simple, entirely compelling way they remind us that not long ago we were living under a dictatorship and were caught up in what was a collapse of humanity, before this building was able to recover its democratic dignity."

The "reborn" Reichstag was in one very visible aspect different from all previous states of the building. Over the chamber in which the MPs meet is a luminous, lofty glass dome, circled by walkways which allow the visitor to look down on the parliamentarians as they debate. It is an eloquent architectural metaphor: every day, without constraint, citizens can literally oversee their politicians. To a public brought up in the surveillance state of the GDR, with folk memories of the Nazis, or even merely with experience of police tactics in the Cold War Federal Republic, this is a heady statement of civic freedom. It was below this dome that in January 2014 Chancellor Merkel, responding to the revelations about U.S. surveillance by Edward Snowden, asserted the need for citizens and Parliament to keep the security services under control (see Chapter 2). Monika Grütters:

> "The cupola is an inviting place where visitors can walk above the chamber, the citizens are above while we parliamentarians sit below. And so, at last, the words on the façade 'To the German People' ('Dem Deutschen Volke') have taken on their real meaning."

Inside Foster's cupola

Norman Foster, reflecting on his work, goes even further:

> "It's about the relationship between the public and politicians and re-defining that in a way which is unique. It has become a symbol of a city. It has gone beyond that and become a symbol of a nation."

In its 140 years the Reichstag has in fact been the symbol of many Germanys: the newly united Empire of the 1880s; the Weimar Republic's doomed liberal democracy, which perished in the 1933 fire; the fascist Nazi Reich which, like the building, was destroyed and then conquered by the Soviets and their Western allies; and the 25-year-old parliamentary democracy of today. Thanks to Foster's restoration every one of these memories is still present and active in the building. How far these noble architectural metaphors do in fact affect the behaviour of politicians is of course a matter "For the German People."

Berlin is a city that dreams in architecture. In that respect the Reichstag is but one example of this city's capacity to conjure new identities, or remember several pasts as it builds and rebuilds its historic centre. The Brandenburg Gate is modelled on the entrance to the Acropolis and decorated with sculpture echoing the Parthenon metopes: there could be no clearer declaration of Prussia's determination in the 1780s to make Berlin the new Athens. At the other end of Unter den Linden, sixty years later, that same dream of Berlin as the city of learning and art led Frederick William IV in the 1840s to designate the island opposite the Schloss "a sanctuary for the arts": the Museum Island, a Parnassus on the Spree, where museums in the form of classical temples, linked by colonnades, would allow the visitor to revisit the world of antiquity. Both Gate and Island speak of many nineteenth-century Germans' conviction of their similarities to the Ancient Greeks: separate tribes cherishing different identities yet working together, devoted to learning, spreading over vast areas (the Greek Mediterranean diasporas of Alexandria and Constantinople

Berlin's Museum Island from the air

are often likened to the German cities of the Baltic and Eastern Europe). It was a fantasy the Prussians shared with the Bavarians (see Chapter 9), part of a new national self-definition as the freedom-loving Germans/Greeks, against the aggressive imperial French/Romans. Yet it sat strangely, even at the time, with Prussia's concurrent ambitions of military strength. And in today's context of Berlin's economic hegemony over southern Europe, this architecture asserting an essentially Greek Germany must surprise and distress some Mediterranean visitors.

A few hundred yards west of the Museum Island, the buildings of Unter den Linden propose another, earlier dream of Germany—the Prussian Enlightenment, as imagined (and in large measure realized) by Frederick the Great. The long process of renovation is now nearly complete. Christopher Clark explains what these meticulously restored buildings mean:

> "I suppose one could say that what we're looking at here is a kind of architectural restatement of a particular vision of the Prussian state's mission in history. The Prussian state never defined itself solely in terms of military prowess. It was also what the

The "Forum Friedricianum" (Bebelplatz): (left to right) the Opera, St. Hedwig's Church, the University library

Prussians called a *Kulturstaat*, a state designed and intended to pursue cultural objectives. You can see this in this extraordinary space that they call the Forum Friedricianum, a trio of very fine buildings built during the reign of Frederick the Great. In one corner St. Hedwig's church, an extraordinary monument to inter-confessional tolerance in a Protestant state, to allow the Catholics to build a very substantial cathedral in the centre of the town. On one side, the library which was semi-public. Normal people could go into this library and read the books there. On the other side the opera. A statement about tolerance, about books, about music. That's what Berlin was about, among other things, and it's in a sense to recover that sense of Prussia as a state of culture that these reconstructions have been happening."

But, as so often in Berlin, there is a worm in the bud. In the centre of this noble square, a glass panel set into the cobblestones looks down on empty bookshelves. It is a memorial to yet another Germany. It was here, in May 1933, that Nazi students brought books from that "semi-public" library and burnt them (see Chapter 24).

The Forum Friedricianum and the Museum Island witness to

Reconstructing memory, August 2014: the Stadtschloss being rebuilt on its former site and that of the Palast der Republik

Prussia's belief in itself as a *Kulturstaat*. To many Germans, however, and to most of the rest of Europe, it was above all a militarist state. Opposite the Royal Palace, on Unter den Linden, Schinkel's Neue Wache (New Guard House, see Chapter 22) and the exuberant rococo Armoury speak just as powerfully of the central role of the army. Even before the Nazi seizure of power in 1933, the bellicose Prussian leadership was, in the view of many, driving Germany down a disastrous road of aggressive expansion. As most Germans would be quick to point out, Prussia was never the whole of Germany.

At the eastern end of Unter den Linden is the most contested of all Berlin's "sites of memory." Long the object of the vista from the Brandenburg Gate, reconstruction here is still vigorously in progress, and even more vigorously debated. Here stood the Stadtschloss, residence of the Hohenzollern kings and Kaisers, demolished by the GDR in the 1950s. In its place from the mid-1970s stood the Palast der Republik, seat of the Parliament at the GDR, itself demolished—to much protest from East Berliners—in 2006. On this site, the buildings of both the old Prussia and the GDR, memories of distant triumph and recent experience, have both been obliterated. Their traces and their shadows remain. After long discussion the Bundestag voted to build a replica of the old Stadtschloss, which is now rising fast. The vista down Unter den Linden will once again end as the Electors of Brandenburg intended. But this "old" building hopes to be about a very modern Germany. It will house the world-famous Berlin collections of art from Africa, Asia, Oceania and the Americas. This time it will be the palace not of a militaristic Prussian dynasty, but of a new Germany and its capital's relationship with the world beyond Europe. Once again Berlin is building a dream: this time of a peaceful, enriching dialogue of cultures—European and Mediterranean on the Museum Island, the rest of the world in the Schloss whose meaning will now be as ambiguous as the Munich Siegestor with which this book began. The complex German past is here once again being reshaped by its monuments and memories.

Paul Klee, *Angelus Novus*, 1920

Envoi

One of the central arguments of this book has been that history in Germany is concerned not only with the past but, unlike other European countries, looks forward. So it ends with two works of art which reflect on both past and future.

In 1920, a few months before he joined the Bauhaus in Weimar (see Chapter 20), Paul Klee made what became one of his most compelling works, the "Angelus Novus," by the complex oil transfer method of printing which he had developed. It was a moment when Germany was addressing the consequences of the First World War and had embarked, in the Weimar Republic, on a hopeful path to the future. Twenty years later, just before the fall of France in the summer of 1940, the philosopher Walter Benjamin, a Jew born in Berlin but then living in exile in Paris, wrote his *Theses on the Philosophy of History*, one of them a now famous paragraph inspired by Klee's work:

> A Klee painting named "Angelus Novus" shows an angel looking as though he is about to move away from something he is fixedly contemplating. His eyes are staring, his mouth is open, his wings are spread. This is how one pictures the angel of history. His face is turned toward the past. Where we perceive a chain of events, he sees one single catastrophe which keeps piling wreckage upon

> wreckage and hurls it in front of his feet. The angel would like to stay, awaken the dead, and make whole what has been smashed. But a storm is blowing from Paradise; it has got caught in his wings with such violence that the angel can no longer close them. This storm irresistibly propels him into the future to which his back is turned, while the pile of debris before him grows skyward. This storm is what we call progress.

Klee died in Switzerland at the end of June 1940, just as France was being over-run. Exactly three months later, having escaped from France but believing he would be sent back, Walter Benjamin took his own life.

Gerhard Richter is, like Paul Klee, Tilman Riemenschneider and Caspar David Friedrich, a master of reflective silence, in which time is suspended and past and present fuse. He is also, like Dürer and again like Klee, a virtuoso of many technologies. In 1977 he took a photograph of his daughter Betty looking over her shoulder at one of his paintings hanging on the wall behind her. That painting was itself an imprecise, grey rendering of an old press photograph. In 1988 he transformed the photograph of Betty into a painting, from which he later derived this lithograph. Thus, over many years, many different media have been deployed, moments of seeing and re-seeing have occurred, to distil this portrait of a figure whose attitude is impossible to decipher with precision or to articulate with clarity. In its very making it is a complex meditation on events and their recording. It would not, I think, be doing violence to Richter's art to read it as a metaphor for Germany's subtle, shifting, obsessional engagement with its past.

Richter and his daughter embody much of that past. Brought up near what is now the Polish border, his childhood was lived under the Nazis and disrupted by the war. He studied afterwards in the devastated city of Dresden. Like the central figure of Christa Wolf's *Divided Heaven*, he fled the GDR just months before the Berlin Wall was erected in 1961. Betty, who turns away from her father (shyness?

distraction? indifference? revulsion?), was brought up in West Germany, part of a generation that grew up in a country committing itself to excavating a shameful past, publishing and where possible punishing the crimes of her parents' and grandparents' generation—and honouring their victims.

Betty inhabits a space still animated by her father's works, although his painting is no longer discernible in the dark wall behind her, just as all Germans live in the presence—growing fainter, but still commanding—of the deeds of their predecessors. What Betty makes of her father and his generation, we cannot know. But, in a moment, this young woman will turn to face us, and the future.

Acknowledgements

This book is the result of many people's work on three strands of a single project—*Germany: Memories of a Nation.* The first was conceived as a temporary exhibition, to be presented at the British Museum between 16 October 2014–25 January 2015. Sponsored by Betsy and Jack Ryan, and supported by the Salomon Oppenheimer Philanthropic Foundation, the exhibition set out to look at Germany's challenging history from the standpoint of the new Germany created after the fall of the Berlin Wall. Different aspects of that history were explored in the second strand, a radio series—collaboratively developed by the British Museum and BBC Radio 4. The third strand is this book.

At the British Museum, Rosalind Winton, supported by Joanna Hammond and Sam Stewart, nurtured series and book in every stage of their development, while Max Easterman and Christopher Bond shaped the programme scripts with their gifted writing skills. My sincerest thanks are extended to Clarissa von Spee and Sabrina Ben Aouicha for bringing curatorial knowledge and expertise to the exhibition (overseen by Carolyn Marsden Smith and Alasdair Hood), and to the other parts of the enterprise. My greatest debt goes to Barrie Cook, my principal interlocutor, curator of the exhibition, who with apparently limitless knowledge has provided guidance, encouragement and, especially valuably, restraint, at every stage of the project.

Jane Ellison, Commissioning Editor of BBC Radio 4 and Joanna Mackle, Deputy Director of the British Museum, have guided their respective teams over three years to bring *Germany: Memories of a Nation* into being. Without their energetic clarity neither the programmes, with their accompanying website, nor this book would have been achieved.

At the BBC Tony Hall, the Director General and Gwyneth Williams, Controller of Radio 4, gave their blessing and encouragement to this happy partnership between two public-service organizations. In the Documentaries Unit, BBC Radio and Music, Paul Kobrak, master of sound, travelled extensively with me in Germany, and produced programmes which his rigorous curiosity did much to shape. John Goudie throughout guided us with invaluable editorial sense, and indispensable support was provided by Clare Walker, Anne Smith and Sue Fleming. The programmes were supported by a BBC website, for which I extend my thanks to Rhian Roberts and Greg Smith, as well as the Head of Web at the British Museum, Matthew Cock.

This book owes its existence to the indefatigable professionalism and patience of Stuart Proffitt, Publishing Director of Penguin, whose boundless intellectual energy helped transform scripts into book chapters. My warm thanks also go to the Penguin team—Marian Aird, Andrew Barker, Chloe Campbell, Donald Futers, Mark Handsley, Rebecca Lee, Cecilia Mackay, Rita Matos, Michael Page and Kit Shepherd—who enabled the book to be published to mark the 25th anniversary of the fall of the Berlin Wall.

My final thanks go to all the expert contributors who feature both in this book and the radio series that accompanied it—their knowledge guided our research and shaped the project's structure. As well as contributing to one of the programmes, Professor Bernhard Rieger made valuable comments on the later chapters of the book. Finally, Dr. Detlef Felken of CH Beck, the German publisher of this book, has throughout put his knowledge of German history at our disposal, making many creative suggestions and saving us from errors. Those that remain are mine.

To all those involved in the creation and development of *Germany: Memories of a Nation* in each of its manifestations, I extend my warmest thanks.

—Neil MacGregor
Director, The British Museum
October 2014

Bibliography

General

Applebaum, Anne, *Iron Curtain: The Crushing of Eastern Europe 1944–1956* (2012)

Cambridge Modern History, several vols.

Craig, Gordon A., *Germany 1866–1945* (1981)

Evans, Richard J., *The Coming of the Third Reich* (2003), *The Third Reich in Power* (2005), *The Third Reich at War* (2008)

Howard, Michael, *The Franco-Prussian War 1870–71* (1961)

Kehlmann, Daniel, *Measuring the World* (2007)

MacCulloch, Diarmaid, *Reformation: Europe's House Divided 1490–1700* (2003)

Roberts, Andrew, *Napoleon the Great* (2014)

Schama, Simon, *Landscape and Memory* (1995)

Scruton, Roger, *German Philosophers: Kant, Hegel, Schopenhauer, Nietzsche* (2001)

Whaley, Joachim, *Germany and the Holy Roman Empire*, 2 vols. (2012)

Wilson, Peter H., *Europe's Tragedy: A History of the Thirty Years War* (2009)

2. Divided Heaven

Fulbrook, Mary, *Interpretations of the Two Germanies, 1945–1990* (2000)

Garton Ash, Timothy, *The File: A Personal History* (1997)

Hertle, Hans-Hermann, *The Berlin Wall* (2007)

Miller, Roger Gene, *To Save a City: The Berlin Airlift, 1948–1949* (2000)

Schulte, Bennet, *The Berlin Wall: Remains of a Lost Border* (2011)

Wolf, Christa, *Divided Heaven* (1965)

3. Lost Capitals

Davies, Norman, *Vanished Kingdoms: The History of Half-forgotten Europe* (2011)

Egremont, Max, *Forgotten Land: Journeys Among the Ghosts of East Prussia* (2012)

Evans, R. J. W., *Rudolf II and His World: A Study in Intellectual History, 1576–1612* (1973)

Kafka, Franz, *The Metamorphosis and Other Stories* (2000)

4. Floating City

Fischer, Christopher J., *Alsace to the Alsatians?* (2012)

5. Fragments of Power

Ebert, Robert R., "'Thalers,' patrons and commerce: a glimpse at the economy in the times of J. S. Bach," *Bach* 16 (1985), 37–54

Wilson, Peter H., *The Holy Roman Empire, 1495–1806* (2011)

Wines, Roger, "The Imperial Circles, princely diplomacy and imperial reform 1681–1714," *Journal of Modern History* 39 (1967), 1–25

6. A Language for All Germans

Bainton, Ronald H., *Here I Stand: A Biography of Martin Luther* (2009)

Brady, Thomas, Jr, *German Histories in the Age of the Reformations, 1400–1650* (2009)

Edwards, Mark U., Jr, *Printing, Propaganda and Martin Luther* (2005)

Gardiner, John Eliot, *Music in the Castle of Heaven: A Portrait of Johann Sebastian Bach* (2013)

Sanders, Ruth H., *German: Biography of a Language* (2010)

7. Snow White vs. Napoleon

Koerner, Joseph Leo, *Caspar David Friedrich and the Subject of Landscape* (1990)

Pullman, Philip, *Grimm Tales: For Young and Old* (2013)

Vaughan, William, *Friedrich* (2004), *German Romantic Painting* (1994)

Zipes, Jack, *The Brothers Grimm: From Enchanted Forests to the Modern World* (2002)

8. One Nation Under Goethe

Bisanz, Rudolf M., "The birth of a myth: Tischbein's 'Goethe in the Roman Campagna,'" *Monatshefte* 80 (1986), 187–99

Boyle, Nicholas, *Goethe: The Poet and the Age* Vol I (1991), Vol II (2000)
Gage, John, *Goethe on Art* (1980)
Goethe, Johann Wolfgang von, *The Sorrows of Young Werther* (2012)
Moffitt, John F., "The poet and painter: J. H. W. Tischbein's 'Perfect Portrait' of Goethe in the Campagna (1786–87)," *The Art Bulletin* 65 (1983), 440–55
Robson-Scott, W. D., *The Younger Goethe and the Visual Arts* (2012)
Williams, John R., *The Life of Goethe* (1998)

9. Hall of Heroes

Bouwers, Eveline G., *Public Pantheons in Revolutionary Europe: Comparing Cultures of Remembrance, c. 1790–1840* (2012)
Green, Abigail, *Fatherlands: State-Building and Nationhood in Nineteenth-Century Germany* (Cambridge, 2001)

10. One People, Many Sausages

Dornbusch, Horst D., *Prost! The Story of German Beer* (1997)
Tlusty, B. Ann, *Bacchus and Civic Order: The Culture of Drink in Early Modern Germany* (2001)

11. The Battle for Charlemagne

Brose, Eric Dorn, *German History 1789–1871: From the Holy Roman Empire to the Bismarckian Reich* (1997)
Coy, Jason Philip, Benjamin Marschke and David Warren Sabean (eds.), *The Holy Roman Empire Reconsidered* (2010)
Forrest, Alan, and Peter H. Wilson, *The Bee and the Eagle: Napoleon, France and the End of the Holy Roman Empire, 1806* (2009)

12. Sculpting the Spirit

Chapuis, Julien (ed.), *Tilman Riemenschneider, c. 1460–1531* (2004)
Mann, Thomas, *Death in Venice, Tonio Kröger, and Other Writings* (1999)

13. The Baltic Brothers

Holman, Thomas S., "Holbein's portraits of the Steelyard merchants: an investigation," *Metropolitan Museum Journal* 14 (1979), 139–58
Lindberg, Erik, "The rise of Hamburg as a global marketplace in the seventeenth century: a comparative political economy perspective," *Comparative Studies in Society and History* 50 (2008), 641–62
Lloyd, T. H., *England and the German Hansa 1157–1611* (1991)
Tate Gallery, *Holbein in England* (2006)

14. Iron Nation

Clark, Christopher, *Iron Kingdom: The Rise and Downfall of Prussia, 1600–1947* (2007)
Dwyer, Philip G. (ed.), *The Rise of Prussia, 1700–1830* (2000)
Friedrich, Karin, *Brandenburg–Prussia, 1466–1806* (2012)
Gayle, Margot, and Riva Peskoe, "Restoration of the Kreuzberg monument: a memorial to Prussian soldiers," *APT Bulletin* 27 (1996), 43–5
Haffner, Sebastian, *The Rise and Fall of Prussia* (1998)
Koch, H. W., *History of Prussia* (1987)
Paret, Peter, *The Cognitive Challenge of War: Prussia 1806* (2009)

15. Two Paths from 1848

Hewitson, Mark, *Nationalism in Germany, 1848–1866: Revolutionary Nation* (2010)
Levin, Michael, *Political Thought in the Age of Revolution, 1776–1848: Burke to Marx* (2011)
Namier, L. B., *1848: The Revolution of the Intellectuals* (1944)
Rapport, Mike, *1848: Year of Revolution* (2014)
Sperber, Jonathan, *The European Revolutions, 1848–1851* (2005)

16. In the Beginning Was the Printer

Füssel, Stephan, *Gutenberg and the Impact of Printing* (2005)
Jensen, Kristian, *Incunabula and Their Readers: Printing, Selling and Using Books in the Fifteenth Century* (2003)
Weidhaas, Peter, *A History of the Frankfurt Book Fair* (2007)

17. An Artist for All Germans

Bartrum, Giulia, *Albrecht Dürer and His Legacy* (2002)

19. Masters of Metal

Rieger, Bernhard, *The People's Car: A Global History of the Volkswagen Beetle* (2013)
Seelig, Lorenz, *Silver and Gold: Courtly Splendour from Augsburg* (1995)
Thompson, David, *Watches* (2008)

20. Cradle of the Modern

Bergdoll, Barry, and Leah Dickerman, *Bauhaus 1919–1933: Workshops for Modernity* (2009)

21. Bismarck the Blacksmith

Augstein, Rudolf, *Otto von Bismarck* (1990)
Darmstaedter, Friedrich, *Bismarck and the Creation of the Second Reich* (2008)
Röhl, John C. G., *Wilhelm II* (3 vols, 1998–2014)
Steinberg, Jonathan, *Bismarck: A Life* (2012)

22. The Suffering Witness

Prelinger, Elizabeth, *Käthe Kollwitz* (1992)

23. Money in Crisis

Coffing, Courtney L., *A Guide and Checklist of World Notgeld 1914–1947 and Other Local Issue Emergency Monies* (2003)
Fergusson, Adam, *When Money Dies: The Nightmare of the Weimar Hyper-Inflation* (2010)

24. Purging the Degenerate

Fischer-Defoy, Christine, and Paul Crossley, "Artists and art institutions in Germany, 1933–1945," *Oxford Art Journal* 9 (1986), 16–29
Goggin, Mary-Margaret, "'Decent' vs 'Degenerate' art: the National Socialist case," *Art Journal* 50 (1991), 84–92
Hudson-Wiedenmann, Ursula, and Judy Rudoe, "Grete Marks, artist potter," *Journal of the Decorative Arts Society 1850–the Present* 26 (2002), 100–19
Levi, Neil, "'Judge for yourselves!': the 'Degenerate Art' exhibition as political spectacle," *October* 85 (1996), 41–64

25. At the Buchenwald Gate

Browning, Christopher, *Ordinary Men* (1992)
Goldhagen, Daniel Jonah, *Hitler's Willing Executioners: Ordinary Germans and the Holocaust* (1997)
Kershaw, Ian, *Hitler* (2009)

26. The Germans Expelled

Douglas, R. M., *Orderly and Humane: The Expulsion of the Germans After the Second World War* (2012)

27. Beginning Again

German History in Documents and Images, *Occupation and the Emergence of Two States (1945–1961): 3. Reconstituting German Society*, http://germanhistorydocs.ghi-dc.org/subpage.cfm?subpage_id=163

28. The New German Jews

Elon, Amos, *The Pity of It All: A Portrait of the Jews in Germany, 1743–1933* (2002)

Gilbert, Martin, *The Holocaust: The Jewish Tragedy*, 1989

29. Barlach's Angel

Paret, Peter, *An Artist Against the Third Reich: Ernst Barlach, 1933–1938* (2007)

30. Germany Renewed

Beevor, Antony, *Berlin: The Downfall 1945* (2007)

Index

Page numbers in italics indicate illustrations

Illustrations and Photographic Credits

Every effort has been made to contact all copyright holders. The publishers will be happy to make good in future editions any errors or omissions brought to their attention.

Frontispiece. Gerhard Richter, *Betty*, 1991 (detail). Offset print on lightweight cardboard, with a layer of nitrocellulose varnish, mounted on plastic, framed behind glass. Copyright © Gerhard Richter

p. xxvi. The north side of the Siegestor, Munich. Photo: ullstein bild—imagebroker/Siepmann

p. xxviii. The south side of the Siegestor, Munich. Photo: istockphoto.com

p. xxix. (*left*) The Arc de Triomphe, Paris. Photo: akg-images/De Agostini Picture Lib./G. Dagli Orti

p. xxix. (*right*) Constitution Arch, Hyde Park Corner, London. Photo: Julie Woodhouse/Alamy

pp. xxxii–xxxiii. Bernardo Bellotto, *The Ruins of the Kreuzkirche in Dresden*, 1765. Oil on canvas. Gemäldegalerie Alte Meister, Dresden. Photo: akg-images/Erich Lessing

p. xxxv. Georg Baselitz, *Inverted eagle painted over with colours of the German flag*, 1977. Etching. Copyright © Georg Baselitz, 2014. Photo copyright © The Trustees of the British Museum (2013,7043.16)

p. xxxvi. Jacques Callot, *The Hanging*, from the series *The Miseries and Misfortunes of War*, *c.* 1633. Etching. Photo copyright © The Trustees of the British Museum (1861,0713.788)

p. xxxvii. Adolph Menzel, *Allegorial Figure of Germania Sitting on a Rock*, 1846–57. Wood engraving. Photo copyright © The Trustees of the British Museum (1913,0404.10)

p. xxxviii. Children's cut-outs of Hitler and soldiers. Colour print, 1933–43. Photo copyright © The Trustees of the British Museum (2012,7020.80)

p. xxxix. Hamburg after an Allied air raid, summer 1943. Photo copyright © akg-images/ullstein-bild

p. xl. Peter Fechter's body beside the Berlin Wall, 1962. Photo: akg-images/picture-alliance/dpa

pp. xlii–xliii. View of the Reichstag and quadriga of the Brandenburg Gate from the Holocaust Memorial, Berlin. Photo: Herbert Knosowski/AP/PA Photos

pp. 4–5. The Brandenburg Gate, Berlin. Photo copyright © Massimo Ripani/SIME/4Corners

p. 6. The Stadtschloss, Berlin, 1896. Photo: akg-images

p. 7. Friedrich Jügel after Ludwig Wolf, *Napoleon's Entry through the Brandenburg Gate*, *c.* 1806. Coloured engraving. Photo copyright © Deutsches Historisches Museum, Berlin (1988/996.3)

p. 9. The Siegessäule (Victory Column), Berlin. Photo: Shutterstock

p. 10. Albert Speer, model of the proposed Congress Hall for Berlin, 1939. Photo: akg-images/ullstein-bild

p. 12. The Palast der Republik, Berlin, 1976. Photo: akg-images/Straube

p. 13. Erich Ott, Medal of Reunification, 1989–90. Cast bronze. Photo copyright © The Trustees of the British Museum (1991,0412.1)

p. 14. The Fernsehturm (Alexander Tower), Berlin. Photo: Shutterstock

p. 15. World Cup fans at the Brandenburg Gate, June 2014. Photo copyright © Corbis UK/Reuters

pp. 18–19. White crosses by the River Spree opposite the Bundeskanzleramt (Federal Chancellery building), Berlin. Photo: DDP/Camera Press

p. 20. Christa Wolf, *Der geteilte Himmel (Divided Heaven)*, 1963. Front cover of the first edition. Copyright © Landeshauptarchiv Sachsen-Anhalt

pp. 22–3. Aerial view of the Berlin Wall, 1980. Photo copyright © Peter Marlow/Magnum Photos

p. 25. Wetsuit manufactured by VEB Solidor Heiligenstadt, 1987. Neoprene. Deutsches Historisches Museum, Berlin (Kte 90/786). Photo copyright © The British Museum

p. 27. Friedrichstrasse Station, 1956. Photo: akg-images

p. 29. Model of the border crossing at Friedrichstrasse Station, East Berlin, 1970. Wood, metal, tin plate, enamel. Photo copyright © Deutsches Historisches Museum, Berlin (SI 90/384)

p. 32. Christa Wolf at her writing desk, 1980s. Photo: akg-images/ullstein-bild/Barbara Köppe

p. 33. Carnival float with figure of Edward Snowden at the Rosenmontag (Rose Monday) festival, Mainz, 2014. Photo: akg-images/picture-alliance/dpa/Fredrik von Erichsen

p. 35. Angela Merkel's speech at the Bundestag, 29 January 2014. Photo: Hans Christian Plambeck/Laif/Camera Press

p. 36. Joachim Gauck, 1992. Photo: Waltraud Grubitzsch/DPA/Press Association Images

p. 38. Tankard with cover, 1640–60. Carved amber with silver gilt mounts, manufactured in Königsberg. Photo copyright © Trustees of the British Museum (WB.229)

p. 40. Karolinum, Prague. Photo: Mariusz Świtulski/Alamy

p. 41. The west façade of Kaliningrad Cathedral, *c.* 1998. Photo: akg-images/Volker Kreidler

p. 42. (*left*) Immanuel Kant, *Kritik der praktischen Vernunft* (*Critique of Practical Reason*), 1788. Title-page of the first edition. Photo: courtesy of the Thomas Fisher Rare Book Library, University of Toronto

p. 42. (*right*) Plaque near Kant's tomb, Kaliningrad. Photo: Shutterstock

p. 43. Königsberg Castle, *c.* 1905. Photo: akg-images

pp. 44–5. Friedrich Probst after Friedrich Bernhard Werner, *View of Königsberg*, 1740. Coloured engraving. Photo copyright © Photo Scala, Florence/BPK, Berlin, 2014.

p. 46. *Amber Fisherman on the Amber Coast.* Illustration from Johann Wilhelm Meil, *Spectaculum Naturae & Artium [...]*, Berlin, 1761. Photo: akg-images/Imagno/Austrian Archives

p. 47. (*left*) Detail of the sun from the base of a tankard, 1640–60. Carved amber, manufactured in Königsberg. Photo copyright © Trustees of the British Museum (WB.229)

p. 47. (*right*) The coat of arms of the Swedish Royal House of Vasa, detail from the cover of a tankard, 1640–60. Carved red and white amber, manufactured in Königsberg. Photo copyright © Trustees of the British Museum (WB.229)

p. 48. *The Coronation of Frederick I King in Prussia, 1701.* Illustration from Johann von Besser, *Preuße Krönungsgeschichte*, 1712. Photo: akg-images

p. 49. (*left*) Samuel Theodor Gericke (attr.), portrait of Frederick I as Frederick III, Elector of Brandenburg, after 1701. Oil on canvas. Märkisches Museum, Berlin. Photo: akg-images

p. 49. (*right*) Antoine Pesne, portrait of King Frederick I of Prussia, eighteenth century. Oil on canvas. Staatliche Schlösser und Gärten, Potsdam. Photo: Bridgeman Images

p. 51. The Amber Room at Tsarskoye Selo, Russia, *c.* 1930. Photo: akg-images

p. 52. Manhole cover in Kaliningrad. Photo: Deposit Photos

p. 54. Adriaen de Vries, *Rudolf II Introducing the Liberal Arts to Bohemia*, 1609. Bronze relief. The Royal Collection, Windsor Castle. Photo: The Royal Collection Trust, copyright © Her Majesty Queen Elizabeth II, 2014/ Bridgeman Images

p. 55. The old town square, Prague, 1922. Photo: Mary Evans/Süddeutsche Zeitung Photo

p. 56. Hans Fronius, portrait of Franz Kafka, 1937. Woodcut. Copyright © Ch. Fronius, Vienna. Photo copyright © The Trustees of the British Museum (19780121.309)

pp. 60–1. Herman Saftleven, *Rhine Landscape with Landing Stage*, 1666. Oil on board. Kunsthistorisches Museum, Vienna. Photo: akg-images

p. 62. The astronomical clock, 1843, Strasbourg Cathedral. Photo: Bildarchiv Monheim GmbH/Alamy

p. 63. Anton Johann Kern, portrait of Johann Wolfgang von Goethe, 1765. Oil painting, formerly in the collection of Leipzig University, destroyed in the Second World War.

p. 65. Isaac Habrecht (manufacturer) and Conrad Dasypodius (designer), the Strasbourg Clock, 1589. Gilded-brass clock with automata. Photo copyright © The Trustees of the British Museum (1888,1201.100)

p. 66. View of the cathedral and rooftops of Strasbourg. Photo: Shutterstock

p. 68. Anon., *Imachio Crisiverus französischer Calender-Spiegel, oder Prognostikon Trost und Begleitungs-Reymen*, broadside on the French occupation of Alsace, *c.* 1678. Photo copyright © The Trustees of the British Museum (1857,0214.406)

p. 69. Anon., after Ludwig Pietsch, *Goethe in Strasbourg: On the Platform*, 1870. Coloured print. Photo: akg-images

p. 71. Angelika Kauffmann, portrait of Johann Gottfried Herder, 1791. Oil on canvas. Goethe-Museum, Frankfurt. Photo copyright © David Hall—ARTOTHEK

p. 72. A. Matthis Elberfeld, *Deutschlands Einheit* (*Germany's Unity*), 1870. Lithograph. Photo copyright © The Trustees of the British Museum (1871,1209.4543)

pp. 74–5. Anon., *Strasbourg after the Bombardment*, 1871. Lithograph. Photo copyright © Scala, Florence/BPK, Berlin, 2014.

p. 77. Anon., *Vive l'Alsace!* Illustration of the statue of Strasbourg in the Place de la Concorde, Paris, from *Le Petit Journal*, 7 February 1904. Photo: Artmedia/Heritage Images/TopFoto

p. 78. (*top*) Half-thaler of Sophia, Electress of Hanover, 1714. Silver, minted in Hanover. Photo copyright © The Trustees of the British Museum (C.3595)

p. 78. (*bottom*) Five-guinea coin of George I, 1716. Gold, minted in London. Photo copyright © The Trustees of the British Museum (E1946,1004.657)

p. 81. (*top*) Thaler of Leopold I, 1700. Silver, minted in Tirol, Austria. Photo copyright © The Trustees of the British Museum (1920,0907.318)

p. 81. (*bottom*) Gulden of Friedrich Adolf, Count of Lippe-Detmold, 1714. Silver, minted in Brake. Photo copyright © The Trustees of the British Museum (1848,0804.22)

p. 83. (*top*) Thaler of Joseph I, 1705–11. Silver, minted in Cologne. Photo copyright © The Trustees of the British Museum (1935,0401.15433)

p. 83. (*centre*) Ten-ducat coin of Hamburg, with view of the city, 1689. Gold, issued in Hamburg. Photo copyright © The Trustees of the British Museum (1865,0218.1)

p. 83. (*bottom*) Ducat coin of St. Alban, 1744. Gold, minted in Prioz of St. Alban. Photo copyright © The Trustees of the British Museum (1919,0214.223)

p. 84. Thaler of the Abbess of Quedlinburg, 1704. Silver, minted in Berlin. Photo copyright © The Trustees of the British Museum (G3,Germ.1094)

p. 85. (*top*) Thaler of Lothar Franz von Schönborn, 1697. Silver, minted in Bamberg. Photo copyright © The Trustees of the British Museum (1935,0401.5692)

p. 85. (*centre*) Half-thaler of Lothar Franz von Schönborn, 1696. Silver, minted in Mainz. Photo copyright © The Trustees of the British Museum (1847,1117.192)

p. 85. (*bottom*) Twelve-ducat coin of Duke Friedrich II, 1723. Gold, issued in Altenburg. Photo copyright © The Trustees of the British Museum (G3,Germ.1116)

p. 87. Thaler of Leopold I, 1673. Silver, minted in Wismar. Photo copyright © The Trustees of the British Museum (G3,GerC.2078)

p. 92. Lucas Cranach the Elder, portrait of Martin Luther, 1529. Oil on wood. Photo copyright © Deutsches Historisches Museum (1989/1547.1)

p. 93. Lucas Cranach the Elder, portrait of Katharina von Bora, 1529. Oil on wood. Photo copyright © Deutsches Historisches Museum (1989/1547.2)

p. 95. Martin Luther, *Disputation zur Erläuterung der Kraft des Ablasses* (*The Ninety-Five Theses*), 1517. Deutsches Historisches Museum, Berlin (R63/685). Photo: Bridgeman Images

pp. 96–7. Hans Sebald Beham, *Luther before the Emperors and Electors at the Diet of Worms*, 1521. Woodcut. Photo: akg-images

p. 98. Workshop of Lucas Cranach the Elder, portrait of the Elector Frederick III of Saxony, 1532. Oil on panel. Copyright © The Trustees of the British Museum (SLPictures.271)

p. 99. View of the Wartburg Castle and Eisenach. Photo: akg-images/euroluftbild.de

pp. 102–3. Martin Luther, *Biblia, das ist, die gantze Heilige Schrift: Deudsch*, pub. Wittenberg, 1541. Front endpaper showing portraits of Martin Luther and Johann Bugenhagen, with facing page showing inscriptions by Luther from the 23rd Psalm. Photo copyright © The British Library Board (679.i.15)

p. 106. Workshop of Lucas Cranach the Elder, *The Creation of the World*, illustration from Martin Luther, *Biblia, das ist die gantze Heilige Schrifft, Deudsch*, pub. Wittenberg, 1534. Woodcut with later hand-colouring. Herzogin Anna Amalia Bibliothek, Weimar. Photo copyright © Klassik Stiftung Weimar

p. 110. *Die deutsche Bibel*, edition with comments by Abraham Calov, published in Wittenberg, 1681. Title-page with autographed note of ownership by J. S. Bach. Concordia Seminary, St. Louis, Missouri. Photo: akg-images

p. 112. Ludwig Emil Grimm, illustration for *Snow White*, from the Brothers Grimm, *Kinder- und Hausmärchen* (*Tales for Children and the Home*), pub. Berlin, 1825. Photo: Mary Evans/Süddeutsche Zeitung Photo

p. 115. Caspar David Friedrich, *The Chasseur in the Forest*, 1814. Oil on canvas. Private collection. Photo: akg-images

p. 116. The Brothers Grimm, *Kinder- und Hausmärchen* (*Tales for Children and the Home*), Berlin, 1815. Title-page and contents page. Photo copyright © Deutsches Historisches Museum (R 92/963-1)

pp. 118–19. Caspar David Friedrich, *The Solitary Tree* (*Village Landscape in Morning Light*), 1822. Oil on canvas. Nationalgalerie, Staatliche Museen zu Berlin

p. 121. Georg Friedrich Kersting, *At the Sentry Post* (*Theodor Körner, Karl Friedrich Friesen and Christian Ferdinand Hartmann*), 1815. Oil on canvas. Nationalgalerie, Staatliche Museen zu Berlin. Photo copyright © Scala, Florence/BPK, Berlin/Jörg P. Anders, 2014

p. 122. One-Pfennig coin, 1949. Bronze, issued by the Government of Germany. Photo copyright © The Trustees of the British Museum (2005,1111.315)

p. 125. The Brothers Grimm, *Rapunzel*, 1857. Broadside with illustrated borders by Otto Speckter. Photo: akg-images

p. 126. Caspar David Friedrich, *Graves of Fallen Freedom Fighters*, 1812. Oil on canvas. Kunsthalle, Hamburg. Photo: Bridgeman Images

p. 127. The Hermannsdenkmal (Hermann Memorial), Detmold. Photo: akg-images/Euroluftbild.de

p. 129. Poster for the Walt Disney film *Snow White*, 1937. Photo: akg-images/Album/Walt Disney Productions

pp. 132–3. Johann Tischbein, *Goethe in the Roman Campagna*, 1786–87. Oil on canvas. Städel Museum, Frankfurt am Main. Photo: Artothek/Bridgeman Images

p. 134. Anon., Goethe's birthplace, Frankfurt am Main, 1832. Coloured engraving. Photo: akg-images

p. 135. Goethe's puppet theatre. Photo copyright © Freies Deutsches Hochstift/Frankfurter Goethe-Museum, David Hall

p. 137. Johann Wolfgang von Goethe, speech made on Shakespearestag, 14 October 1771. Manuscript. Photo copyright © Freies Deutsches Hochstift/Frankfurter Goethe-Museum (Hs-2421)

p. 139. Johann Wolfgang von Goethe, *Die Leiden des jungen Werthers* (*The Sorrows of Young Werther*), pub. Leipzig, 1774. Title-page of first edition. Private collection. Photo: Antiquariat Dr. H.-P. Haack, Leipzig

p. 140. Johann David Schubert (probably decorator) for Meissen, cup with illustration of Werther, from a set, *c*. 1790. Porcelain with enamel colours and gilt. Photo copyright © Victoria and Albert Museum, London (1328E-1871)

pp. 142–3. J. C. E. Müller after Georg Melchior Kraus, *Weimar from the North-West*, 1798. Coloured engraving. Staatliche Kunstsammlungen, Weimar. Photo: akg-images

p. 145. Jochen Ersfeld, replica of Stephenson's *Rocket*, *c*. 1992, similar to the one owned by Goethe, now lost. Goethehaus, Weimar. Photo copyright © Klassik Stiftung Weimar, Museen (Kat. 202—KKg/00636/001)

p. 146. Johann Wolfgang von Goethe, *Zur Farbenlehre* (*On the Theory of Colours*), 1810, plate 1. The Pierpont Morgan Library, New York. Photo copyright © Pierpont Morgan Library/Art Resource/Scala, Florence, 2014

p. 147. Christoph Erhard Sutor, three colour theory cards, from Johann Wolfgang von Goethe, *Beiträge zur Optik* (*Contributions to Optics*), 1791. Goethehaus, Weimar. Photo copyright © Klassik Stiftung Weimar, Museen (GFz 035—037)

p. 148. Carl Vogel von Vogelstein, *Faust Conjuring the Spirits*, detail from *Scenes from Goethe's Faust*, 1840. Oil on canvas. Palazzo Pitti, Florence. Photo copyright © Scala, Florence/BPK, Berlin, 2014

p. 150. Statue of Goethe based on the portrait by Tischbein, at the Goethe Bar, Terminal 1, Frankfurt Airport. Photo: courtesy Frankfurt Airport press office

p. 152. The Walhalla viewed from the River Danube, copyright © epa european pressphoto agency b.v./Alamy

p. 155. Angelika Kauffmann, *Crown Prince Ludwig, in the Costume of the Knights of St. Hubert*, 1807. Oil on canvas. Neue Pinakothek, Munich. Photo: akg-images

pp. 156–7. Anon., after Ludwig Bechstein, *The gods entering Walhalla, the Final scene from Das Rheingold*, *c.* 1876. Engraving. Photo: akg-images

p. 159. (*left*) Johann Gottfried Schadow, bust of Frederick II of Prussia (Frederick the Great), 1807. Marble. Walhalla-Verwaltung, Donaustauf. Photo copyright © Herbert Stolz

p. 159. (*right*) Konrad Eberhard, bust of the Empress Maria Theresa, 1811. Marble. Walhalla-Verwaltung, Donaustauf. Photo copyright © Herbert Stolz

pp. 160–61. (*top*) Ludwig Michael von Schwanthaler, southern pediment frieze depicting Germania and the creation of the German Confederation, 1832–42. Marble. Walhalla-Verwaltung, Donaustauf. Photo copyright © Herbert Stolz

pp. 160–61. (*bottom*). Ludwig Michael von Schwanthaler, northern pediment frieze depicting the Battle of the Teutoburg Forest, 1832–42. Marble. Walhalla-Verwaltung, Donaustauf. Photo copyright © Herbert Stolz

p. 163. Bernhard Grueber, *Interior View of the Walhalla*, 1842. Colour lithograph. Photo copyright © Deutches Historisches Museum (Gr 2004/189)

p. 164. (*left*) August Wredow, bust of Catherine the Great, 1831. Marble. Walhalla-Verwaltung, Donaustauf. Photo copyright © Herbert Stolz

p. 164. (*right*) Johann Nepomuk Haller, bust of King William III of England, 1816. Marble. Walhalla-Verwaltung, Donaustauf. Photo copyright © Herbert Stolz

p. 165. (*left*) Wilhelm Matthiä, bust of Johannes Gutenberg, 1835. Marble. Walhalla-Verwaltung, Donaustauf. Photo copyright © Herbert Stolz

p. 165. (*right*) Ernst Friedrich Rietschel, bust of Martin Luther, 1831. Marble. Walhalla-Verwaltung, Donaustauf. Photo copyright © Herbert Stolz

p. 168. The Nazis honour Adolf Rothenburger's bust of Anton Bruckner in the Walhalla, 1937. Photo: Interfoto/akg-images

p. 169. The Prime Minister, Horst Seehofer, unveiling Bert Gerresheim's bust of Heinrich Heine in the Walhalla, 2010. Photo: akg-images/picture alliance/dpa/Armin Weigel

p. 171. Wolfgang Eckert, bust of Sophie Scholl with plaque to the Resistance, 2003. Marble. Walhalla-Verwaltung, Donaustauf. Photo copyright © Herbert Stolz

p. 173. Landolin Ohmacht, bust of Erwin von Steinbach, 1811. Marble. Walhalla-Verwaltung, Donaustauf. Photo copyright © Herbert Stolz

p. 174. Anon., "Gruß aus München!" ("Greetings from Munich!"), 1960s. Postcard. Private collection. Photo: Arkivi UG, All Rights Reserved/ Bridgeman Images

pp. 176–7. German drinking vessels (*left to right*): Silver parcel-gilt tankard, 1601–25, manufactured by Engelbrecht II Becker in Lübeck (WB.128); stoneware "pinte" tankard, *c.* 1530s, manufactured in Cologne (1895,0116.8); amber tankard, 1640–60, manufactured in Königsberg (WB.229); stoneware jug with pewter lid, 1598, manufactured by Jan Baldems Mennicken in Raeren, Belgium (1887,0617.43); enamelled glass "humpen" beaker, 1625, manufactured in Bohemia (1855,1201.133); enamelled "Wiederkom" glass, *c.* 1650, manufactured in Switzerland (S.841). Photo copyright © The Trustees of the British Museum

p. 180. The *Reinheitsgebot* (Beer Purity Law) promulgated by Duke Wilhelm IV of Bavaria, 1516. Photo: akg-images

p. 183. Butcher's shop, Wilmersdorf. Photo: ullstein-bild/TopFoto

p. 185. Hans Wertinger, *The Month of December* (detail showing the making of blood sausages), *c.* 1525–6. Oil on panel. Germanisches Nationalmuseum, Nuremberg. Photo: Bridgeman Images

p. 186. The Currywurst Museum, Berlin. Photo: akg-images/ullstein-bild/ Schöning

p. 187. Adolf Hitler making a speech in the Bürgerbräukeller, Munich, 8 November 1935. Photo: akg-images/ullstein-bild

p. 188. Oktoberfest, Munich. Photo: akg-images/ullstein-bild/CARO/Kaiser

p. 189. Men in traditional costume drinking beer, Munich. Photo: ullstein bild/ akg-images

p. 192. Bernhard Witte and Paul Beumers, replica of the Holy Roman Emperor's crown, 1914/15. Pearls, gold, enamel, gemstones. Rathaus, Aachen. Photo copyright © Anne Gold, Aachen, courtesy Städtische Museen, Aachen (Inv. CK3)

p. 194. Aachen Cathedral. Photo: Bildarchiv Monheim/akg-images

p. 195. Interior of the Palatine Chapel, Aachen Cathedral. Photo: Hemis/Alamy

p. 197. Anon., figurine of Charlemagne on horseback, ninth century, horse restored in the eighteenth century. Bronze with traces of gilding. Cathedral of Saint-Étienne, Metz. Photo copyright © RMN-Grand Palais (Musée du Louvre)/Droits réservés

p. 199. Peter Flötner, portrait of Charlemagne from *Ancestors and Early Kings of the Germans*, *c.* 1543. Broadside with hand-coloured woodcut and letterpress. Photo copyright © The Trustees of the British Museum (E,8.292)

p. 201. Anon., *The Relics, Vestments and Insignia of the Empire*, 1470–80. Print. Photo copyright © The Trustees of the British Museum (1933,0102.1)

p. 202. Bertrand Andrieu, medal depicting Napoleon and Charlemagne, 1806. Bronze. Photo copyright © The Trustees of the British Museum (1898,0102.76)

p. 203. (*left*) William Biennais after Charles Percier, the imperial crown of Napoleon, based on Charlemagne's, 1804. Copper, gold and silver, set with cameos. Musée du Louvre, Paris. Photo copyright © RMN-Grand Palais/ Jean-Gilles Berizzi

p. 203. (*right*) Jacques-Louis David, *The Emperor Napoleon I Crowning Himself*, *c.* 1804–7. Pen and ink drawing. Photo copyright © RMN-Grand Palais (Musée du Louvre)/Thierry Le Mage

p. 205. Window for the arms room of Kiel Castle depicting Kaiser Wilhelm I, *c.* 1888. Stained glass and lead. Photo copyright © Deutsches Historisches Museum, Berlin (KG 97/57)

p. 206. Charles and Louis Rochet, statue of Charlemagne with his paladins Roland and Olivier, 1877. Bronze. Île de la Cité, Paris. Photo: Yvan Travert/ akg-images

p. 209. Konrad Adenauer and Charles de Gaulle at Reims Cathedral, 1962. Photo: Keystone France/Gamma/Camera Press

p. 210. Sèvres porcelain factory, plate bearing the image of Charlemagne, 1943. Porcelain. Musée de l'Armée, Paris. Photo copyright © Paris—Musée de l'Armée, Dist. RMN–Grand Palais/image Musée de l'Armée

p. 212. Tilman Riemenschneider, *Saint Luke*, *c.* 1490–92. Limewood. Bode Museum, Berlin (Inv. 403). Copyright © Staatliche Museen zu Berlin—Skulpturensammlung und Museum für Byzantinische Kunst/photo: Antje Voigt

p. 215. The modern high altar with some of Riemenschneider's original elements, Church of Mary Magdalen, Münnerstadt. Photo by Bruce White, courtesy National Gallery of Art, Washington, DC.

p. 216. (*left*) Tilman Riemenschneider, *Saint Matthew*, *c.* 1490–92. Limewood. Bode Museum, Berlin (Inv. 402). Copyright © Staatliche Museen zu Berlin—Skulpturensammlung und Museum für Byzantinische Kunst/photo: Antje Voigt

p. 216. (*right*) Tilman Riemenschneider, *Saint Mark*, *c.* 1490–92. Limewood. Bode Museum, Berlin (Inv. 404). Copyright © Staatliche Museen zu Berlin—Skulpturensammlung und Museum für Byzantinische Kunst/photo: Antje Voigt

p. 217. (*left*) Tilman Riemenschneider, *Saint Luke*, *c*. 1490–92. Limewood. Bode Museum, Berlin (Inv. 403). Copyright © Staatliche Museen zu Berlin—Skulpturensammlung und Museum für Byzantinische Kunst/photo: Antje Voigt

p. 217. (*right*) Tilman Riemenschneider, *Saint John*, *c*. 1490–92. Limewood. Bode Museum, Berlin (Inv. 405). Copyright © Staatliche Museen zu Berlin—Skulpturensammlung und Museum für Byzantinische Kunst/photo: Antje Voigt

p. 219. Tilman Riemenschneider, *Self-Portrait*, *c*. 1505–10, detail from the predella of the Marienaltar, Herrgottskirche, Creglingen. Photo copyright © Volker Schier

p. 223. *The Conquest of Würzburg by the Swabian League*, illustration from the *Bamberger Burgenbuch*, *c*. 1527. Coloured woodcut. Copyright © Staatsbibliothek Bamberg (RB.H.bell.f.1, fol. 68). Photo: Gerald Raab

p. 227. Tilman Riemenschneider, *The Adoration of the Magi*, relief for an altar-panel (?), 1505–10. Lime-wood. Photo copyright © The Trustees of the British Museum (1852,0327.10)

p. 228. (*left*) Five-Mark coin designed by Heinz Rodewald, commemorating the 450th anniversary of the death of Tilman Riemenschneider, 1981. Nickel-silver, minted East Germany, 1981. Photo: Matd13

p. 228. (*right*) Sixty-Pfennig stamp commemorating the 450th anniversary of the death of Tilman Riemenschneider, 1981. Issued by the Deutsche Bundespost, West Germany. Photo: Kayatana Ltd

p. 230. Hans Holbein the Younger, portrait of George Gisze of Danzig, 1532. Oil on panel. Copyright © Gemäldegalerie der Staatlichen Museen zu Berlin—Preußischer Kulturbesitz (Ident. Nr. 586)/photo: Jörg P. Anders

p. 232. The Steelyard (*Stahlhof*) in London, detail from Wenceslas Hollar's *Long View of London*, 1647. Photo: Bridgeman Images

p. 234. Hans Holbein the Younger, *Self-Portrait*, 1542. Pastel on paper. Galleria degli Uffizi, Florence. Photo: Bridgeman Images

pp. 236–7. Elias Diebel, *Panoramic View of the Free City of Lübeck*, facsimile of the 1552 original, published by Johannes Geffcken in 1855. Colourized lithograph. Photo: Paulus Swaen Gallery, Indian Rocks, Fl.

p. 238. (*left*) Hans Holbein the Younger, portrait of a member of the Wedigh family, probably Hermann Wedigh, 1532. Oil on wood. Bequest of Edward S. Harkness, 1940, Metropolitan Museum of Art, New York (Acc. no. 50.135.4). 16⅝ × 12¾ in. (42.2 × 32.4 cm), with added strip of ½ in. (1.3 cm) at bottom. Photo copyright © The Metropolitan Museum of Art/Art Resource/Scala, Florence, 2014

p. 238. (*right*) Hans Holbein the Younger, portrait of Derick Berck, 1536. Oil on canvas, transferred from wood. The Jules Bache Collection, 1949,

Metropolitan Museum of Art, New York (Acc. no. 49.7.29). 21 × 16¾ in. (53.3 × 42.5 cm). Image copyright © The Metropolitan Museum of Art/Art Resource/Scala, Florence, 2014

p. 239. Salt warehouses, Lübeck. Photo copyright © Guido Cozzi/4Corners

p. 243. (*top left*) Tankard with cover, 1601–25. Silver parcel-gilt, manufactured by Engelbrecht II Becker of Lübeck. Photo copyright © The Trustees of the British Museum (WB.128)

p. 243. (*top right*) Beaker, 1642–58. Silver, parcel-gilt, manufactured by Johann Berendt Brockner of Hamburg. Gift of Princess Louise, Duchess of Argyll. Photo copyright © Victoria and Albert Museum, London (M.98-1926)

p. 243. (*bottom*) Tankard with cover, *c.* 1670–1700. Silver-gilt, manufactured by Daniel Friedrich von Mylius of Danzig. Gift of Dr. W. L. Hildburgh, FSA. Photo copyright © Victoria and Albert Museum (M.6-1964)

p. 245. Aerial photograph of Lübeck. Photo copyright © SZ Photo/euroluftbild.de/Bridgeman Images

p. 247. SPQH sign on the door of the banqueting hall, Rathaus, Hamburg. Photo copyright © Tim Brüning/T. B. Photography

p. 248. The Iron Cross, 1813. Photo: Private collection

p. 250. Gottfried Leybebe, statue of the Great Elector as St. George, 1680. Iron. Skulpturensammlung, Berlin (Ident. Nr. 856). Copyright © Skulpturensammlung und Museum für Byzantinische Kunst der Staatlichen Museen zu Berlin—Preußischer Kulturbesitz/photo: Antje Voigt

p. 252. Necklace, *c.* 1805. Cast iron. Photo copyright © The Trustees of the British Museum (1978,1002.108.a)

p. 253. (*left*) Christian Daniel Rauch, bust of Frederick William III, King of Prussia, after 1816. Cast iron, painted black with gold-plating. Copyright © Stiftung Stadtmuseum Berlin (Inv. Nr. KGM 85/49)/photo: Michael Setzpfandt

p. 253. (*right*) Christian Daniel Rauch, bust of Luise, Queen of Prussia, after 1816. Cast iron, painted black with gold-plating. Copyright © Stiftung Stadtmuseum Berlin (Inv. Nr. KGM 85/50)/photo: Michael Setzpfandt

p. 256. Jean-Charles Tardieu, *Napoleon I Receiving Queen Luise at Tilsit in 1807*, 1808. Oil on canvas. Châteaux de Versailles et de Trianon, Paris. Photo: akg-images/visioars

p. 257. The Order of Luise, *c.* 1866/1918. Silver and enamel. Photo copyright © Deutsches Historisches Museum, Berlin (O 262)

p. 259. Anon., metal cross with nails, 1915–18. Iron, wood and brass. Photo copyright © Deutsches Historisches Museum, Berlin (MK 73/195)

p. 260. J. M. Mauch after Karl Friedrich Schinkel, architectural drawing for the Prussian National Monument, 1823. Etching. Photo: akg-images

pp. 264–5. The Imperial War Flag used by the German naval forces between 1849 and 1852. Linen and wool. Photo copyright © Deutsches Historisches Museum, Berlin/S. Ahlers (Fa 77/64)

pp. 268–9. *Battle between Civilians and Soldiers in the Frankfurter Linden Strasse in Berlin on 18 and 19 March 1848*, detail from a broadside, 1848. Coloured lithograph. Photo: akg-images

p. 271. C. Hoffmeister after E. Fröhlich, portrait of August Heinrich Hoffmann, 1841. Coloured etching. Photo: akg-images

p. 273. Ludwig von Elliot, *View of the Interior of the Paulskirche during the Frankfurt Assembly*, 1848/49. Coloured lithograph. Photo: Horst Ziegenfusz, copyright © Historisches Museum Frankfurt (C 10472, K 349)

p. 275. Karl Marx and Friedrich Engels, *Manifest der Kommunistischen Partei* (*The Communist Manifesto*). Title-page of first edition, 1848. Photo copyright © The British Library Board (C.194.b.289)

p. 277. Demonstrator with banner at a rally in East Berlin, 9 December 1989. Photo: Lutz Schmitt/AP/PA Photos

pp. 278–9. Crowds at the Brandenburg Gate, Berlin, December 1989. Photo: dpa/Corbis

p. 280. Ludwig Engelhardt, monument to Karl Marx and Friedrich Engels, 1986. Bronze. Karl-Marx-Forum, Berlin. Photo: akg-images/Pansegrau

p. 284. Charles de Bovelles, illustration of a printing press, from *Aetatum mundi septem supputatio*, 1520. Woodcut. Private collection. Photo: Bridgeman Images

p. 287. The opening of Genesis, from Johann Gutenberg's 42-line Bible, pub. Johann Gutenberg, Johann Fust and Peter Schoeffer, Mainz, 1455. Printed on paper, hand-illuminated in Erfurt. Photo copyright © The British Library Board (C.9.d.4, f.5)

p. 289. Bertel Thorvaldsen, statue of Johann Gutenberg, 1837. Bronze. Gutenbergplatz, Mainz. Photo: ullstein-bild—Dietmar Scherf/akg-images

p. 291. Reconstructed Gutenberg press and workshop. Gutenberg Museum, Mainz. Photo: akg-images/Erich Lessing

p. 292. André de Thevet, portrait of Gutenberg, 1584. Cabinet des Éstampes et des Dessins, Strasbourg. Photo: De Agostini Picture Library/M. Seemuller/ Bridgeman Images

p. 295. Indulgence completed by hand in Braunschweig, for contributions to the war against the Turks, printed by Johann Gutenberg, 1454. Parchment. Herzog August Bibliothek, Wolfenbüttel

p. 297. Aelius Donatus, *Ars Minor*, *c.* 1456–8, folio salvaged from an early binding, printed by Johann Gutenberg in Mainz. Vellum. Photograph courtesy of Sotheby's, Inc., copyright © 2011

pp. 298–9. Franz Behem, *View of Mainz*, 1565. Kölnisches Stadtmuseum, Cologne (G 1209). Copyright © Rheinisches Bildarchiv Köln/photo: Wolfgang F. Meier (2009.03.18, rba_d012689)

p. 300. Carl Goebel, postcard issued to celebrate Gutenberg's 500th anniversary, 1900. Photo copyright © Scala, Florence/BPK, Berlin, 2014

p. 302. Albrecht Dürer, *Self-Portrait*, 1500. Oil on panel. Alte Pinakothek, Munich. Photo: akg-images

p. 306–7. Albrecht Dürer, *Triumphal Arch of Maximilian I*, 1515–17. Woodcut. Photo copyright © The Trustees of the British Museum (E,5.1)

p. 308. View of Nuremberg showing Dürer's house. Photo copyright © Reinhard Schmid/4Corners.

p. 310. Albrecht Dürer, *The Four Horsemen of the Apocalypse*, 1497–8. Woodcut. Photo copyright © The Trustees of the British Museum (E,3.121)

p. 312. Albrecht Dürer, *Melancholia*, 1514. Woodcut. Photo copyright © The Trustees of the British Museum (E,2.107)

p. 313. Albrecht Dürer, *A Knight, the Devil and Death*, 1513. Woodcut. Photo copyright © The Trustees of the British Museum (1868,0822.198)

p. 316. Albrecht Dürer, *Rhinoceros*, 1515. Woodcut. Photo copyright © The Trustees of the British Museum (E,2.358)

p. 318. Louis de Silvestre, portrait of Augustus II and Frederick William I of Prussia, *c.* 1720s. Oil on canvas. Gemäldegalerie Alte Meister, Dresden. Photo: akg-images

p. 320. Qing Dynasty, Kangxi period, seven dragoon vases, *c.* 1662–1717. Porcelain with underglaze-blue decoration. Copyright © Porzellansammlung, Staatliche Kunstsammlungen Dresden (Inv. Nr. PO 1011, PO 1010, PO 9448/PO 1013, PO 9172, PO 1014/PO 2064, PO 1017, PO 9130). Photo: Jürgen Lösel

p. 321. Meissen porcelain factory, porcelain made for Queen Sophie Dorothea of Prussia, 1730. Photo copyright © The Trustees of the British Museum (Franks.67)

pp. 324–5. Bernardo Bellotto, *View of Dresden from the Right Bank of the Elbe*, 1748. Oil on canvas. Gemäldegalerie Alte Meister, Dresden. Photo: akg-images/Erich Lessing

p. 326. Chinese stoneware teapot (*left*), Yixing, Kangxi Period (1662–1722), with imitation of it (*right*) by Johann Friedrich Böttger, *c.* 1712. Copyright © Porzellansammlung, Staatliche Kunstsammlungen Dresden (Inv. Nr. PO 3884, PE 6859 a/b). Photo: Klaus Tänzer

p. 329. The porcelain menagerie manufactured by Meissen for Augustus the Strong, early 1730s, installed in the Zwinger, Dresden. Copyright © Porzellansammlung, Staatliche Kunstsammlungen Dresden

p. 330–1. Gottlieb Kirchner, *Rhinoceros*, 1730. White porcelain, manufactured by Meissen. Copyright © Porzellansammlung, Staatliche Kunstsammlungen Dresden (PE 56). Photo: Herbert Jäger

p. 332. Meissen artisan decorating an urn with a copy of a portrait of President Wilhelm Pieck, 1955. Photo: Bundesarchiv, Koblenz/Allgemeiner Deutscher Nachrichtendienst—Zentralbild (Bild 183-32361-0033)

p. 334. Masterpiece cup, late sixteenth century. Silver, manufactured in Nuremberg. Photo copyright © The Trustees of the British Museum (WB.103)

pp. 338–9. Michael Wolgemut, *View of Nuremberg*, from the *Nuremberg Chronicle*, 1493. Photo: akg-images/ullstein-bild

p. 341. Hans Schniep, clock-watch with alarm, *c.* 1590. Gilt-brass and steel. Photo copyright © The Trustees of the British Museum (1958,1201.2213)

p. 343. Johann Anton Linden, astronomical compendium, 1596. Gilt and silvered brass. Photo copyright © The Trustees of the British Museum (1857,1116.1)

p. 344. Johann Baptiste Beha, Black Forest cuckoo clock, 1860–80. Wooden-cased and weight-driven. Photo copyright © The Trustees of the British Museum (1995,0112.2)

p. 346. Adolf Hitler and Ferdinand Porsche at the Volkswagen factory at Fallersleben (later Wolfsburg), 26 May 1938. Photo: akg-images/ullstein-bild

p. 347. VW Beetle production line, Wolfsburg, 1940s. Photo copyright © Hulton-Deutsch Collection/Corbis

p. 349. Günther Paalzow, photograph of a group of apprentices at Zeiss, Jena, 1949. Photo: Bundesarchiv, Koblenz/Allgemeiner Deutscher Nachrichtendienst—Zentralbild (Bild 183-S89614)

p. 350. VW Beetles for export to the U.S.A., Hamburg, 1950. Photo: akg-images

p. 352. Jupp Darchinger, photograph of family picnicking beside a VW Beetle, 1950s. Photo: J. H. Darchinger/Friedrich-Ebert-Stiftung

p. 353. The new-style VW Beetle, Wolfsburg, 2011. Photo: DDP/Camera Press

p. 354. Anon., *Bauhaus Students and Their Guests, Weimar, c.* 1922. Gelatin silver print. Bauhaus-Archiv, Berlin (Inv. 3844/4)

p. 356. Plaque with lettering designed by Walter Gropius, 1922. Deutsches Nationaltheater, Weimar. Copyright © DACS, 2014

p. 357. Reich President Ebert speaking from the balcony of the National Theatre, Weimar, 11 February 1919. Photo: akg-images

p. 358. The Bauhaus cradle, 2014, manufactured after an original design by Peter Keler, 1922. Wood, metal, wicker. Photo copyright © The Trustees of the British Museum

p. 360–1. Anon., *Masters on the Roof of the Bauhaus Building*, Dessau, 1926. Gelatin silver print. Musée national d'art moderne/Centre de création industrielle, Centre Georges Pompidou, Paris. Photo: Bauhaus-Archiv, Berlin (Inv. Nr. F2003/46)

p. 362. Marianne Brandt, tea-infuser, 1924–29. Silver with ebony handle. Copyright © DACS, 2012. Photo copyright © The Trustees of the British Museum (1979,1102.1)

p. 363. Anon., *Metal Workshop at the Bauhaus, Weimar*, 1923. Photograph. Photo: akg-images

p. 364. (*top left*) Wassily Kandinsky, *Postcard No. 1 for the Bauhaus Exhibition in Weimar*, summer 1923. Colour lithograph on card. Copyright © ADAGP, Paris and DACS, London, 2014. Photo: Bauhaus-Archiv, Berlin (Inv. Nr. 922)

p. 364. (*top right*) Paul Klee, *Postcard No. 4, for the Bauhaus Exhibition in Weimar*, summer 1923. Colour lithograph on card. Photo: Bauhaus-Archiv, Berlin (Inv. Nr. 923)

p. 364. (*bottom left*) László Moholy-Nagy, *Postcard No. 4, for the Bauhaus Exhibition in Weimar*, summer 1923. Colour lithograph on card. Copyright © Hattula Moholy-Nagy/DACS, 2014. Photo: Bauhaus-Archiv, Berlin (Inv. Nr. 2414)

p. 364. (*bottom right*) Herbert Bayer, *Postcard No. 11 for the Bauhaus Exhibition in Weimar*, summer 1923. Colour lithograph on card. Copyright © DACS, 2014. Photo: Bauhaus-Archiv, Berlin (Inv. Nr. 3586/4)/Markus Hawlik

p. 365. (*top*) The Kunstschule, Weimar. Photo: akg-images/Stefan Drechsel

p. 365. (*bottom*) The main building of the Bauhaus, Dessau. Photo: akg-images/Florian Profitlich

p. 366. Heinrich Hoffmann, *Hitler Sitting on a Steel-Frame Chair in Berchtesgaden, Summer 1928*. Bayerische Staatsbibliothek, Fotoarchiv Hoffmann. Photo: BSB München/Bildarchiv (Bild-Nr. hoff-6843)

p. 368. Lyonel Feininger, title-page of *Neue Europäische Graphik*, 1921. Print. Copyright © DACS, 2014. Photo copyright © The Trustees of the British Museum (1942,1010.30.+)

p. 369. Oskar Schlemmer, *Figure Design K1*, from *Neue Europäische Graphik*, 1921. Lithograph. Photo copyright © The Trustees of the British Museum (1942,1010.30.12)

p. 370. Paul Klee, *The Saint of Inner Light*, from *Neue Europäische Graphik*, 1921. Colour lithograph. Photo copyright © The Trustees of the British Museum (1942,1010.30.6)

p. 372. Johannes Itten, *The House of the White Man*, 1920. Lithograph. Copyright © DACS, 2012. Photo copyright © The Trustees of the British Museum (1942,1010.30.4)

p. 374. Lucia Moholy, *Walter Gropius's Director's Office*, 1924–25, reproduced in *Neue Arbeiten der Bauhauswerkstätten*, 1927. Copyright © DACS, 2014. Photo: akg-images

p. 378. Anon., after Guido Schmitt, *The Blacksmith of German Unity*, *c.* 1895. Engraving. Photo: akg-images

pp. 380–81. Anton von Werner, *The Proclamation of the German Empire in the Hall of Mirrors at Versailles in 1871*, 1885. Oil on canvas. Bismarck Museum, Friedrichsruh. Photo: akg-images

p. 382. Anon., figurine of Otto von Bismarck as a blacksmith, *c.* 1900. Terracotta and bronze. Photo copyright © Deutsches Historisches Museum, Berlin (PL 2009/3)

p. 390. Albin Förster, *Lamellenbild*, turned to show a portrait of Kaiser Wilhelm, *c.* 1882. Wood and board. Photo copyright © Deutsches Historisches Museum, Berlin (AK 99/318)

p. 391. (*left*) Albin Förster, *Lamellenbild*, turned to show a portrait of Otto von Bismarck, *c.* 1882. Wood and board. Photo copyright © Deutsches Historisches Museum, Berlin (AK 99/318)

p. 391. (*right*) Albin Förster, *Lamellenbild*, turned to show a portrait of Crown Prince Frederick, *c.* 1882. Wood and board. Photo copyright © Deutsches Historisches Museum, Berlin (AK 99/318)

pp. 392–3. View of Reinhold Begas's statue of the Bismarck monument in front of the Reichstag, Berlin, *c.* 1901. Photochrome. Photo: akg-images

p. 395. John Tenniel, "Dropping the Pilot," caricature of Otto von Bismarck and Kaiser Wilhelm II from *Punch, or The London Charivari*, 29 March 1890

p. 396. Käthe Kollwitz, *Self-Portrait*, 1904. Lithograph. Copyright © DACS, 2014. Photo copyright © The Trustees of the British Museum (1951,0501.73)

pp. 398–9. Käthe Kollwitz, *Pietà*, cast made by Harald Haacke, 1993. Bronze. Neue Wache (New Guard House), Berlin. Photo: Dieter E. Hoppe/akg-images, copyright © DACS, 2014

p. 403. Käthe Kollwitz, *Mother and Dead Child*, from the series *The Silesian Weavers' Revolt*, 1897. Lithograph. Copyright © DACS, 2014. Photo copyright © The Trustees of the British Museum (1951,0501.74)

p. 405. Käthe Kollwitz, *The Sacrifice*, from the series *War*, 1923. Woodcut. Museum of Modern Art, New York (470.1992.1). Copyright © DACS, 2014. Digital image copyright © The Museum of Modern Art, New York/Scala, Florence, 2014

p. 406. Käthe Kollwitz, *The Mothers*, from the series *War*, 1923. Woodcut. Philadelphia Museum of Art, Philadelphia. Copyright © DACS, 2014. Photo: Art Resource/Scala, Florence

p. 407. Käthe Kollwitz, *The Grieving Parents*, 1925–32. Granite. Vladslo German War Cemetery, Diksmuide, Belgium. Copyright © DACS, 2014. Photo: David Crossland/Alamy

p. 408. Karl Liebknecht giving a speech from a balcony of the House of Representatives at a Spartacus League demonstration, Berlin, November 1918. Photo copyright © SZ Photo/Bridgeman Images

p. 409. Käthe Kollwitz, *In Remembrance of Karl Liebknecht, 15 January 1919*, 1919–20. Woodcut. Copyright © DACS, 2014. Photo copyright © The Trustees of the British Museum (1984,1006.2)

p. 411. Käthe Kollwitz, *The Call of Death*, from the series *Death*, 1934–7. Lithograph. Copyright © DACS, 2014. Photo copyright © The Trustees of the British Museum (1951,0501.80)

p. 413. Käthe Kollwitz, *Pietà*, 1937–38/39. Bronze. Käthe-Kollwitz-Museum, Berlin. Copyright © DACS, 2014. Photo: akg-images

p. 415. Dedication of the Neue Wache (New Guard House) by President Richard von Weizsäcker, Berlin, 14 November 1993. Photo: akg-images/ullstein-bild/Weychardt

p. 418. Hyperinflation banknotes from the years 1922–3. Photo: akg-images

p. 420. (*top*) Fifty-Pfennig *Notgeld*, 1921, issued in Mainz. Photo copyright © The Trustees of the British Museum (2005,1111.103)

p. 420. (*centre*) Seventy-five-Pfennig *Notgeld*, 1923, issued in Bremen. Photo copyright © The Trustees of the British Museum (2006,0405.1414)

p. 420. (*bottom*) Fifty-Pfennig *Notgeld*, 1922 , issued in Müritz. Photo copyright © The Trustees of the British Museum (1984,0605.4402)

p. 421. Fifty-Pfennig *Notgeld*, 1921, issued in Eutin. Photo copyright © The Trustees of the British Museum (2006,0603.259)

p. 422. (*top*) Fifty-Pfennig *Notgeld*, 1921, issued in Bordesholm. Photo copyright © The Trustees of the British Museum (1984,0605.3903)

p. 422. (*bottom*) Fifty-Pfennig *Notgeld*, 1921, issued in Eisenach. Photo copyright © The Trustees of the British Museum (1961,0609.108)

p. 423. Seventy-five-Pfennig *Notgeld*, 1921, issued in Bremen. Photo copyright © The Trustees of the British Museum (2006,0405.1723)

p. 424. (*top*) One-Mark *Notgeld*, 1920, issued in Gramby, Denmark. Photo copyright © The Trustees of the British Museum (2006,0405.1505)

p. 424. (*centre*) Thousand-Mark *Notgeld*, 1922, issued in Bielefeld. Linen. Photo copyright © The Trustees of the British Museum (2006,0405.1426)

p. 424. (*bottom*) Seventy-five-Pfennig *Notgeld*, 1921, issued in Beverungen. Photo copyright © The Trustees of the British Museum (1984,0605.3890)

p. 426. (*top*) Fifty-million-Mark banknote, 1923, designed by Herbert Bayer, issued in Thuringia. Photo copyright © The Trustees of the British Museum (2013,4146.1)

p. 426. (*centre*) Twenty-five-Pfennig *Notgeld*, 1918, issued in Bocholt. Photo copyright © The Trustees of the British Museum (1925,0713.353)

p. 426. (*bottom*) Twenty-five-Pfennig *Notgeld*, 1921, issued in Tiefurt. Copyright © The Trustees of the British Museum (1984,0605.4727)

p. 428. (*top and centre*) Fifty-Pfennig *Notgeld*, 1918, issued in Hamelin. Copyright © The Trustees of the British Museum (1984,0605.4169)

p. 428. (*bottom*) Ten-Pfennig *Notgeld*, 1919, issued in Bielefeld. Copyright © The Trustees of the British Museum (1957,0701.100)

p. 430. Fifty-Pfennig *Notgeld*, 1921, issued in Bitterfeld. Copyright © The Trustees of the British Museum (1961,0609.717)

p. 432. A woman using banknotes to fuel a stove, *c.* 1923. Photo: IAM/akg-images

p. 433. Karl Arnold, "Papiergeld! Papiergeld!," cartoon from *Simplicissimus*, 11 June 1923. Coloured print. Copyright © DACS, 2014. Photo: Bayerische Staatsbibliothek München/Bildarchiv (Bild-Nr. port-010085)

p. 436. Hundred-million-Mark banknote, 1923, overstamped on the reverse with a Nazi propaganda cartoon after 1924. Photo copyright © The Trustees of the British Museum (2006,0405.1628)

p. 438. Grete Marks, ceramic vase, 1923–34. Earthenware. Copyright © The Estate of Margarete Marks. All Rights Reserved, DACS, 2014. Photo copyright © The Trustees of the British Museum (1995,0504.6)

p. 440. Nazi supporters burning books in Berlin, 10 May 1933. Photo: akg-images/Imagno

p. 441. Anon., portrait of Margarete Heymann-Löbenstein (later Heymann-Marks), *c.* 1925. Gelatin silver print. Photo: Bauhaus-Archiv Berlin (Inv. Nr. 10716)

p. 444. Comparison of Grete Marks with Hedwig Bollhagen, photograph from the article "Jewish Ceramics in the Chamber of Horrors," published by Joseph Goebbels in *Der Angriff*, May 1935

p. 446. (*top*) The *Degenerate Art* exhibition, Munich, 1938. Photo copyright © SZ Photo/Scherl/Bridgeman Images

p. 446. (*bottom*) Joseph Goebbels visiting the *Degenerate Art* exhibition, Berlin, 1938. Photo: akg-images

p. 447. Front cover of the *Degenerate Art* exhibition guide, 1937, featuring Otto Freundlich's sculpture *Large Head (The New Man)*, 1912. Photo: akg-images

p. 448. Ernst Ludwig Kirchner, *Five Women*, 1913. Oil on canvas. Wallraf-Richartz-Museum, Cologne. Photo akg-images/De Agostini Picture Lib

p. 449. Parade on the first Day of German Art, Munich, 1937. Photo: akg-images/Imagno/Austrian Archives

p. 450. (*top*) Adolf Wissel, *Kahlenberg Farming Family*, 1939. Oil on canvas. Property of the German Federal Republic. Photo: akg-images

p. 450. (*bottom*) Adolf Ziegler, *The Four Elements: Fire, Earth, Water, Air*, 1937. Reproduced in *Die Kunst im Dritten Reich*, 10 October 1937. Bayerische Staatsbibliothek, Munich, Abteilung Karten und Bilder (Inv. 15766). Copyright © Adolf Ziegler, EKS and Marco-VG, Bonn. Photo: BPK, Berlin /Scala, Florence

p. 452. Emil Nolde, *Vikings*, 1922. Etching. Copyright © Nolde Stiftung, Seebüll. Photo copyright © The Trustees of the British Museum (1980,1108.1)

p. 454. *The Eternal Jew* exhibition, Munich, 1937. Photo: akg-images

p. 455. Hans Stalüter, poster for *The Eternal Jew* exhibition, 1937. Photo copyright © Deutsches Historisches Museum (1990/1104)

p. 458. The gate of Buchenwald, viewed from the exterior. Photo copyright © J. M. Pietsch, Spröda

pp. 460–61. The gatehouse and watchtower of Buchenwald. Photo: akg-images/ullstein-bild/Scherhaufer

p. 462. The replica gate at Buchenwald, viewed from the inside of the camp. Photo copyright © Sammlung Gedenkstätte Buchenwald, Weimar

p. 463. Ducat of King Frederick I of Prussia, 1707. Gold, issued in Berlin. Photo copyright © The Trustees of the British Museum (G3,Germ.c.183)

p. 464. Johann Sebastian Bach, *Nur jedem das Seine (To Each Only His Due)*, BWV 163, 1715. Manuscript. Staatsbibliothek zu Berlin—Preußischer Kulturbesitz (Bl. 1r, T. 1-17). Photo copyright © Scala, Florence/BPK, Berlin, 2014

p. 466. Jewish prisoners inside a barrack at Buchenwald after its liberation, November 1945. Photo: akg-images/ullstein bild

p. 467. (*left*) Franz Ehrlich, *Self-Portrait*, 1935–36. Pencil drawing. Copyright © Stiftung Bauhaus Dessau. Photo: Bauhaus-Archiv, Berlin (Inv. Nr. 1999/26.3v)/Markus Hawlik

p. 467. (*right*) Franz Ehrlich, poster for the Bauhaus exhibition at the Gewerbemuseum Basel, 1929. Colour lithograph. Copyright © Stiftung Bauhaus Dessau. Photo: Bauhaus-Archiv, Berlin (Inv. Nr. 7308)

p. 469. German civilians view Buchenwald after its liberation, 1944. Photo: Keystone/Getty Images

p. 473. Aerial view of Buchenwald camp, 2010. Photo: Euroluftbild.de/akg-images

p. 476. Refugee cart from East Pomerania, first half of the twentieth century. Iron, wood, wire, textile, string. Deutsches Historisches Museum (AK 2009/113). Photo copyright © The British Museum

p. 479. (*top*) Gerhard Gronefeld, *German Refugees Resting against Their Wagon in Tempelhof, Berlin*, 1945. Deutsches Historisches Museum, Berlin. Copyright © The Estate of Gerhard Gronefeld. Photo: Bridgeman Images

p. 479. (*bottom*) Refugees with handcarts, East Prussia, spring 1945. Photo: akg-images

p. 480. Refugee trek in a town square near Königsberg, January 1945. Photo: Interfoto/akg-images

p. 485. Model of stage-set for the 1949 production of Bertolt Brecht's *Mother Courage* at the Deutsches Theater, Berlin. Replica, *c.* 1970. Glass, wood, canvas, metal. Photo copyright © Deutsches Historisches Museum (SI 71/1)

pp. 486–7. Jacques Callot, *The Pillage and Burning of a Village*, from the series *Les Petites Misères de la guerre* (*The Little Miseries of War*), 1632–35. Etching. Photo copyright © The Trustees of the British Museum (1861,0713.754)

p. 488. Plague mask, seventeenth century. Leather, glass, velvet. Photo copyright © Deutsches Historisches Museum (AK 2006/51)

p. 489. Helene Weigel as Mother Courage, Berlin, 1949. Photo: Willi Saeger. Copyright © Scala, Florence/BPK, Berlin, 2014

p. 490. Anselm Kiefer, *Dein goldenes Haar, Margarete*, 1981. Watercolour. Copyright © Anselm Kiefer/White Cube. Photo copyright © The Trustees of the British Museum (1983,1001.19)

p. 492. Woman stacking bricks, Hamburg, 1946/7. Photo: akg-images

p. 494. Dresden after the Allied bombing, *c.* 1943. Photo: Corbis

p. 496. Max Lachnit, *Trümmerfrau*, *c.* 1945–56. Plaster, tesserae. Copyright © The Estate of Max Lachnit. Photo copyright © Deutsches Historisches Museum (Pl 96/3)

p. 498. Women clear away the ruins of the publishing house of Scherl, Berlin, 1944. Photo copyright © SZ Photo/Scherl/Bridgeman Images

p. 501. Atlanta Service, *Map of Occupied Germany Showing the Four Allied Areas*, *c.* 1945. Photo copyright © Deutsches Historisches Museum (Do2 90/2544)

p. 502. (*1st row*) One-Deutsche-mark banknote, 1948, issued in West Germany. Photo copyright © The Trustees of the British Museum (2006,0405.1630)

p. 502. (*2nd row*) Ten-Deutsche-mark banknote, 1977, issued by the Deutsche Bundes-bank, West Germany. Photo copyright © The Trustees of the British Museum (1979,1128.1)

p. 502. (*3rd row*) Hundred-Ostmark banknote, 1975, issued by the Staatsbank, East Germany. Photo copyright © The Trustees of the British Museum (1979,1128.1)

p. 502. (*4th row*) Five-Ostmark banknote, 1975, issued by the Staatsbank, East Germany. Photo copyright © The Trustees of the British Museum (1986,1227.9)

p. 502. (*5th row*) Fifty-Ostmark banknote, 1971, issued by the Staatsbank, East Germany. Photo copyright © The Trustees of the British Museum (2006,0405.1636)

p. 505. Poster promoting *Begrüßungsgeld* (welcome money), 1989, issued by the Finanzamt für Körperschaften. Photo copyright © Deutsches Historisches Museum (Do2 96/1622)

p. 510. The arrival of the Torah at the new synagogue, Munich, 2006. Photo: Corbis/Reuters

p. 512. Anton Graff (after), portrait of Moses Mendelssohn, 1771. Jewish Museum, Berlin. Photo: akg-images/Erich Lessing

p. 513. Tefillin bag with arms of the Holy Roman Empire, eighteenth century. Green velvet with embroidery. Photo copyright © The Trustees of the British Museum (1893,0522.1)

p. 514. Jews trading with Europeans, detail from the frontispiece of Johannes Jodocus Beck, *Tractatus de juribus Judaeorum*, pub. Nuremberg, 1731. Photo: Bridgeman Images

p. 516. (*top*) Houses on the *Judengasse*, Frankfurt, in the nineteenth century. Photo: akg-images

p. 516. (*bottom*) Detail of the *Judengasse,* from Matthäus Merian's plan of Frankfurt, 1628. Photo: Bridgeman Images

p. 517. Anon., after Moritz Daniel Oppenheim, portrait of Amschel Rothschild, *c.* 1836. Oil on canvas. Private collection. Photo: akg-images

p. 518. (*top left*) Moritz Daniel Oppenheim (attr.), portrait of Carl (Kalman) Rothschild, nineteenth century. Oil on canvas. Photo: akg-images

p. 518. (*top right*) Anon., portrait of James (Jakob) Rothschild, *c.* 1824. Oil on canvas. Photo: akg-images

p. 518. (*bottom left*) Moritz Daniel Oppenheim (attr.), portrait of Nathan Rothschild, 1830. N. M. Rothschild & Sons Ltd, London. Photo: akg-images

p. 518. (*bottom right*) Moritz Daniel Oppenheim (attr.), portrait of Salomon Rothschild, 1850. Oil on canvas. Photo: akg-images

p. 520. The synagogue, Offenbach, 1930. Photo: akg-images

p. 521. Sally Israel and three friends in Bavarian costumes at Bad Reichenall, Bavaria, *c.* 1920. Postcard. Photo copyright © Jewish Museum Berlin. Donation by Monica Peiser (2005/153/5)

p. 522. Hermann Zwi Guttmann, model of the first synagogue built in Offenbach/Hessen, *c.* 1955. Cardboard, wood, paint. Photo copyright © Deutsches Historisches Museum (LD 2002/60)

p. 526. Entrance to the extended Synagogue, Offenbach. Original building, 1956, by Hermann Zvi Guttmann. Extension, 1998, by Prof. Alfred Jacoby. Photo: Werner Huthmacher Photography

p. 528. Ernst Barlach, *Hovering Angel*, Güstrow Cathedral. Bronze. Copyright © Archiv Ernst Barlach Stiftung Güstrow. Photo: Uwe Seemann

p. 530. Exterior view of Güstrow Cathedral. Photo: Bildarchiv Monheim/ akg-images

p. 532. Ernst Barlach, *Schmerzensmutter* (*The Mother of Sorrows*), 1921. Bronze relief. Nikolaikirche, Kiel, destroyed 1944. Copyright © Archiv Ernst Barlach Stiftung Güstrow

p. 533. Ernst Barlach in his studio, 1937. Photo copyright © Scala, Florence/ BPK, Berlin, 2014

p. 534. (*left*) Käthe Kollwitz, *Self-Portrait*, 1923. Woodcut. Copyright © DACS, 2014. Private collection. Photo: Christie's Images/Bridgeman Images

p. 534. (*right*) Ernst Barlach, head of *Hovering Angel*, *c.* 1980. Bronze. Copyright © Archiv Ernst Barlach Stiftung Güstrow. Photo: Uwe Seemann

p. 535. Ernst Barlach, *Hovering Angel*, after 1927, hanging in Güstrow Cathedral. Photo: SLUB Dresden/Deutsche Fotothek/Berthold Kegebein

p. 537. Georg Kolbe, *Warrior Memorial*, Stralsund, 1934–35. Bronze. Copyright © DACS, 2014. Photo: Margrit Schwartzkopff/Georg Kolbe Museum, Berlin

p. 539. Ernst Barlach, *Hovering Angel*, Antonienkirche, Cologne. Photo: Bildarchiv Monheim/akg-images

p. 541. Erich Honecker and Helmut Schmidt meeting at Güstrow Cathedral, 13 December 1981. Photo: Bundesregierung/Engelbert Reineke/Bundesarchiv, Koblenz (B 145 Bild-00005047)

pp. 544–5. The Reichstag, Berlin. Photo copyright © Reinhard Schmid/4Corners

p. 548. The Reichstag on fire, 1933 (hand-coloured photograph). Photo: akg-images

p. 549. Russian soldiers flying the Soviet flag over the ruins of the Reichstag, 1945. Photo: Yevgeny Khaldei/akg-images

p. 550. Russian graffiti inside the Reichstag. Photo: STR News/Reuters/Corbis

p. 552. The Reichstag building, wrapped by Christo and his wife, Jeanne-Claude, June 1995. Photo: Wolfgang Kumm/AFP/Getty Images

p. 554. The glass cupola of the Reichstag, designed by Norman Foster. Photo: Fabrizio Bensch/Reuters/Corbis

p. 555. Aerial view of Museum Island, Berlin, 2013. Photo: akg-images/euroluftbild.de/Robert Grahn

pp. 556–7. The "Forum Friedricianum" (Bebelplatz), Berlin. Photo: QuidProQuo

p. 559. Construction of the Stadtschloss at Humboldtforum, Berlin, 2013. Photo: Fabrizio Bensch/Reuters/Corbis

p. 560. Paul Klee, *Angelus Novus*, 1920. Ink, chalk and wash on paper. The Israel Museum, Jerusalem. Photo: Bridgeman Images

p. 563. Gerhard Richter, *Betty*, 1991. Offset print on lightweight cardboard, with a layer of nitrocellulose varnish, mounted on plastic, framed behind glass. Copyright © Gerhard Richter

Picture research: Cecilia Mackay

A NOTE ABOUT THE AUTHOR

Neil MacGregor has been director of the British Museum since 2002. He was previously director of the National Gallery in London from 1987 to 2002. His celebrated books include *A History of the World in 100 Objects*, now translated into more than a dozen languages, and *Shakespeare's Restless World*.

A NOTE ON THE TYPE

The text of this book was set in Sabon, a typeface designed by Jan Tschichold (1902–1974), the well-known German typographer. Based loosely on the original designs by Claude Garamond (c. 1480–1561), Sabon is unique in that it was explicitly designed for hotmetal composition on both the Monotype and Linotype machines as well as for filmsetting. Designed in 1966 in Frankfurt, Sabon was named for the famous Lyons punch cutter Jacques Sabon, who is thought to have brought some of Garamond's matrices to Frankfurt.

Composed by North Market Street Graphics

Printed and bound by Mohn Media,
Gütersloh, Germany

Designed by Cassandra J. Pappas